MW00986692

How to Save a Constitutional Democracy

How to Save a
Constitutional
Democracy

TOM GINSBURG AND AZIZ Z. HUQ

June 2019

To Cathy,
I hope this seems
like a work of an
alarmist in a few years!

Tom
Ginsburg

The University of Chicago Press
Chicago and London

The University of Chicago Press, Chicago 60637
The University of Chicago Press, Ltd., London
© 2018 by The University of Chicago
All rights reserved. No part of this book may be used or reproduced in any manner
whatsoever without written permission, except in the case of brief quotations in
critical articles and reviews. For more information, contact the University of Chicago
Press, 1427 E. 60th St., Chicago, IL 60637.
Published 2018
Printed in the United States of America

27 26 25 24 23 22 21 20 19 18   1 2 3 4 5

ISBN-13: 978-0-226-56438-8 (cloth)
ISBN-13: 978-0-226-56441-8 (e-book)
DOI: https://doi.org/10.7208/chicago/9780226564418.001.0001

Library of Congress Cataloging-in-Publication Data

Names: Ginsburg, Tom, author. | Huq, Aziz Z., author.
Title: How to save a constitutional democracy / Tom Ginsburg and Aziz Z. Huq.
Description: Chicago ; London : The University of Chicago Press, 2018. |
   Includes bibliographical references and index.
Identifiers: LCCN 2018016685 | ISBN 9780226564388 (cloth : alk. paper) |
   ISBN 9780226564418 (e-book)
Subjects: LCSH: Democracy. | Democracy—United States. | Constitutional law.
Classification: LCC JC423 .G488 2019 | DDC 321.8—dc23
LC record available at https://lccn.loc.gov/2018016685

♾ This paper meets the requirements of ANSI/NISO z39.48-1992 (Permanence of Paper).

AZH: To Margaret
TG: To Mom and Dad

Contents

Acknowledgments

As with all such intellectual projects, we owe a good deal to friends and colleagues who read, argued, and advised us, including Judith Albeitz, Brett Bellmore, Bojan Bugaric, Tom Daly, Brian Feinstein, David Fontana, Cesar Rodriguez Garavito, Brandon Garrett, Sam Ginsburg, Jason Gluck, Richard Helmholz, Todd Henderson, William Hubbard, Sam Issacharoff, Abby Klionsky, Hélène Landemore, Brian Leiter, Peter Lindseth, Anup Malani, Richard McAdams, Jon Michaels, Jennifer Nou, Eric Posner, Eric Rasmusen, Daniel Rodriguez, Gerald Rosenberg, Kim Lane Scheppele, Mike Seidman, Mark Tushnet, and Rivka Weill. We benefited from workshops at the University of Chicago Law School, Northwestern Law School, Princeton University, Yale University, the University of North Carolina, Universidad Externado and the Constitutional Court of Colombia in Bogotá, and Univerisitad Torcuato di Tella in Buenos Aires. We are also grateful to Dean Thomas Miles of the University of Chicago Law School, as well as the law school's Russell Baker Scholars and Frank Cicero Jr. Funds for institutional and financial support. Ginsburg also thanks the American Bar Foundation. For research assistance, we thank Leila Blatt, Ilayda Gunes, Trevor Kehrer, Emily Vernon, and Sophia Weaver.

We have developed some of the ideas that appear in this book in a number of different forums, albeit in different forms and to different argumentative ends. These include Huq and Ginsburg, "How to Lose a Constitutional Democracy," *UCLA Law Review* 65 (2018); Ginsburg and Huq, "How We Lost Constitutional Democracy," in *Can It Happen Here? Authoritarianism in America*, ed. Cass Sunstein (HarperCollins, 2018); Ginsburg and Huq, "Defining and Tracking the Trajectory of Liberal Constitutional Democracy," in *Constitutional Democracy in Crisis*, ed. Mark Graber et al. (Oxford University Press, 2018); Huq, "The People against the Constitution," *Michigan Law Review* 116 (2018); Huq, "Terrorism and the Democratic Recessional," *University of Chicago Law Review* 85 (2018); Ginsburg and Huq, "How to Lose a Constitutional Democracy," *Vox*, February 21, 2017; and Huq, "When Government Defames," *New York Times*, August 10, 2017. We are grateful to our editors at those forums—including Clay Risen, Jamie Ryerson, Christopher Shea, Quemars Ahmed, and Kathryn Brown—for comments and edits. We also thank Chuck Myers of the University of Chicago Press for his vision and guidance.

It cannot go without saying that we owe our families the largest debts. Without them, this book would not exist and would, besides, be pointless.

Introduction

How would you know your democracy is in peril? The question wracked many Americans—including us—both before and after the November 2016 presidential election. The campaign and assumption of presidential office by Donald J. Trump, a New York real-estate magnate new to political office, marked a significant rejection of both principal political parties and their elites, which he tarred as corrupt and out of touch. Among liberals, the question was not whether the Trump campaign was exceptional, but *when* he had breached the norms of democratic governance in a way that disqualified him as a democratic leader: Was it when he attacked a federal judge on the basis of his ethnicity? When he threatened to "lock up" his election opponent? When he declined to say whether he would recognize the result of a loss at the national polls? For some conservatives, the question was why liberals would even ask such questions at all. Even as they demurred to his more openly sexist, racist, and cruel remarks, many conservatives queried how exceptional Trump really was in a country where heated political debate, spilling over sometimes into ad hominem attacks and lies, has been a repeated feature of our history from the late 1790s onward.

The same debates replayed after the election. What, liberals were asking themselves, was the decisive turning point? What kind of democratically elected president falsely brags about his inauguration crowd size and then falsely alleges massive voter fraud to explain his (equally false) claim to have won the popular vote? What kind of president calls the news media the "enemy of the American people," or calls his political opponents "enemies" because they fail to clap vigorously enough at his State of the Union speech? What kind of president fires the head of the Federal Bureau of Investigation, explains on national television that he did this to end an investigation into his own campaign and family, and then repeatedly impugns the integrity of his own Justice Department? What kind of president discerns a moral equivalence between violent neo-Nazi protesters in paramilitary formation wielding torches, assault rifles and clubs, and residents of a college town defending the racial and ethnic diversity of their homes? In response, some conservatives wondered when the liberal media and elites would allow the president to catch a break? Weren't liberals the real threat, with their efforts to suppress conservative speakers on campuses, their tolerance of social disorder, and their reckless embrace of unchecked immigration?

This is a book provoked by the election of Donald Trump, but it is not a book about Trump in any direct way. We share the grave concern held by many about some of President Trump's words and deeds, but we also think it is important, and even necessary, to step back from the current moment to consider more structural forces at work casting shadows on the persistence of liberal constitutional democracy. Perceptions of impending crisis are hardly new. Using words that could be transposed forward some two hundred years with only minor alterations, the British politician and novelist Benjamin Disraeli once worried about the "disintegration of society into 'two nations; between whom there is no intercourse and no sympathy. . . .' An irresponsible, self-aggrandizing aristocracy confronted by an exploited people led by agitators with 'wild ambitions and sinister and selfish ends.'"[1] A wider lens is needed to place today's concerns in proper perspective.

As students of law and political institutions, we think it is especially important to think carefully about how laws, regulations, and especially constitutional rules in place now can either facilitate democracy's derogation or, instead, prevent it, under different socioeconomic and electoral conditions. Because we are trained and work as scholars of constitutional law from both a domestic (US) and comparative perspective, we think it is especially important to ask questions about how our basic legal institutions—the ones manifested in a nation's constitution and associated traditions—will respond to a rising risk of democratic decline.

The question of how legal and constitutional design can facilitate (or debilitate) democracy is hardly parochial in scope. Rather, many of the institutional and political dynamics apparent in the United States today can also be traced in the recent history of other liberal democracies in Europe, South America, and Asia. The interaction of political strategy and legal frameworks may vary with local circumstances, but patterns can also be observed across countries and continents. The forces at work in the United States are not so much idiosyncratic local storms or tempests as they are durable weather systems that determine the possibilities for political action. They are the climatic conditions of our political future. As such, they cry out for more general investigation.

By looking across the globe today, as well as at twentieth-century history, this book pursues that more general investigation. We ask whether there is indeed a threat to constitutional democracies broadly committed to liberal ideals today. Further, we consider whether law, and in particular the constitutional law that structures the basic institutions of government, can mitigate such risks—or whether it might even embolden the enemies of democratic survival. Our answers to these questions will be encouraging for some and disheartening for others. In brief, we argue that liberal democracies are indeed at some risk today—although the character of the risk is rather different from how it is commonly imagined. We also show that law can and should (although often does not) play a role in parrying that risk. And we imagine how constitutional design might respond better. That does not mean, however, either that law will play a facilitative role in democracy's defense, or that law alone will be enough. In particular, when a political coalition bent on eroding democratic institutions and practices takes power, it is generally too late to tinker with institutional design. Then, it is only the determined mobilization of citizens, political party elites, and officials committed to the rule of law that can preserve those institutions and practices.

Our account begins by setting out some basic terms in chapter 1. Our central construct is something we call "liberal constitutional democracy." We use this term because it highlights the role of law in constructing and underpinning democratic competition. Our approach is fairly minimalist, but not entirely so. Some scholars have tried to reduce democracy to the mere fact of elections. While this approach is useful for some purposes, we think that the quality of elections depends on elements of the legal framework. Elections are not the be-all and end-all of democracy, and countries can still experience meaningful democratic decline even if they continue to hold them. In chapter 2, we distinguish two distinct pathways away from liberal constitutional democracy. These are, to put it simply, a fast road and a slow one. We call them democratic collapse and democratic erosion. Much of our political and constitutional imagination is focused on the speedy and complete collapse of democratic institutions. But recent history shows that the greater risk in our moment is of the slow route: the gradual degradation of democracy. While this path *can* sometimes lead to total democratic collapse, the more likely endpoint is a hybrid regime, in which democratic institutions are compromised to some degree and political competition restricted. For us, this is a disturbing enough prospect to motivate more tailored thinking about remedies and preventative steps.

Chapters 3 and 4, respectively, trace the mechanisms at work in the fast and slow paths, deploying examples from both the twentieth century and from our own contemporary moment. By looking at how democracy can collapse or erode, respectively, we start to assess the probabilities associated with different sorts of risks to constitutional liberal democracies.

We then turn to the heart of our analysis. Chapter 5 asks the key question for the United States: If forces arise that wish to take the United States down one or the other of these paths, could our Constitution save us? It is conventional wisdom that the checks and balances of the federal government, a robust civil society and media, as well as individual rights, such as those included within the First Amendment, will work as bulwarks against democratic backsliding. This book takes on this claim and finds it seriously wanting. To a greater extent than commonly realized, the Constitution's text and the Supreme Court's jurisprudence makes democratic erosion more, not less, likely.

Chapters 6 and 7 zoom out to ask how we—and the rest of the world—might do better. We ask, for the United States and for other countries, how laws and constitutional design play a more positive role in managing the risk of democratic decline. Drawing on political science and comparative law expertise, we explore the practical steps that can be taken to minimize its prospects. Our focus here is on law and constitutional design—by which we mean how the basic institutions and rights of a polity are specified in a constitution or similar norms. We caution that technocratic fixes are no panacea: to the contrary, in many instances, the only way to defend liberal democracy is to fight in elections against those who seek to erode it—and to win. In concluding, we confront the question of how we can "save" constitutional democracy, by which we mean minimizing the possibility that it decays beyond recognition within our lifetimes, leaving a set of governing arrangements for the next generation that is morally bankrupt. It is a question that can and should be answered both by immediate political tactics and also by institutional reform and legal change. Our topic here is this longer term reformist agenda.

By applying the same framework both to the United States and other countries, our approach necessarily rejects claims of American exceptionalism. Ever since the Puritan governor John Winthrop declared in 1630 that the new nation would be "a city upon a hill" that would serve as a light to the world, Americans have liked to think that they have a special position in global affairs. There is an implicit but powerful belief that America is immune from challenges and moral failings that beset other countries. Hence, the phrase "American exceptionalism" emerged in American Communist circles in the 1930s to explain the apparent immunity of the United States to proletarian revolution.[2] To those who endorse this exceptionalist perspective, American democracy, celebrated around the world at least since Alexis de Tocqueville, should be uniquely robust.

Of course, it is a truism that each country is unique in some way. But many challenges do not distinguish among nations. Pandemics, wars, and macroeconomic shocks often simultaneously affect multiple countries, sometimes even the entire globe. Since the invention of the electric telegraph in 1846, political ideas, idioms, and tactics have spread almost instantaneously across borders. Starting with the revolutions of 1848 two years later, ours has been in some sense a single (if not singular) and enmeshed ideological universe. So in the study of democracy's rise and fall, it is a mistake to think that trends observed in the United States lack a parallel in other democracies. It is also a mistake to think that America is exceptional in the sense of standing aside from the current riptide of democratic backsliding.

Nevertheless, there is at least one way in which the United States *is* indeed exceptional. Our Constitution has been in continuous force since 1787. This is a remarkable achievement, with no parallel anywhere in the world. The roughly contemporaneous French and Polish constitutions died quickly. Although the adoption of our founding document in 1787 launched a global era of national constitution-making, and although it is venerated by many Americans as the key to our success as a nation, its very longevity poses a problem. Being old, and lacking an easy amendment mechanism, the US Constitution does not necessarily reflect the learning of subsequent years and decades. It instead calcifies the mistaken assumptions and prejudices of a long-dead generation. Although there is a natural inclination to hope that the US Constitution, which has underpinned two centuries of material growth and yielded global hegemony (for now), will insulate us from the global forces that are currently buffeting democracies elsewhere, this may have things backward: It is the dearth of new learning in the Constitution's text that makes that threat all the more potent and all the more urgent to address.

1

Liberal Constitutional Democracy
and Its Alternatives

We are made to ask what it is that political democracy gives us. The system is utilitarian. But is it a fit object of faith and hope?

WILLIAM F. BUCKLEY

It is a cold Tuesday morning in November 2016, and across a massive, continent-spanning nation, the polls are opening. Millions are flocking to cast their ballots and to have their voices heard. In the nation's capital, an elderly couple arrives to stand behind three nurses, who are deep in conversation as they wait in an orderly line to vote. Officials at the polls urge them all to "treasure democratic rights" and "cast your solemn and sacred ballots." Under the relevant election law, a candidate need only obtain support from three fellow constituents in order to run. By the end of the electoral process, up to 900 million people will have registered their preferences, and some 2.5 million new individuals will have been elected to office.

This snapshot of the Chinese elections to local "people's congresses," to be sure, omits a fair bit. Across town from our elderly voters, for example, a woman named Liu Huizhen is trying to leave her house to vote. Liu obtained the signatures necessary to stand as a candidate in these elections; as a result, she has been under constant surveillance. At her door, she finds a cohort of plainclothes policemen who block her way, stopping her from leaving the house. Candidates for these elections—the largest in the world if one looks solely at votes cast—are typically chosen in secret by the Chinese Communist Party. A brief opening in 2003, during which more than one hundred independent candidates registered, has been slowly closing since. By 2016, few were willing to declare themselves candidates as Liu did. In Qianjiang City, activists campaigning for independent candidates were followed by police and blocked from speaking with voters. In Shanghai, activists leafleting for an independent candidate were detained. Village-level elections, which emerged in China in the late 1980s, are no more competitive, since local party and township officials dominate the nomination process completely.[1]

Of course, another high-profile national election occurred in November 2016. And if the Chinese election should not be taken at face value, what of the roughly contemporaneous American contest? Consider the case of Wisconsin, where almost three million people cast ballots on a bright, crisp day about a week before the Chinese elections. But again, not everything is as it first seems. A voter identification law enacted by a Republican-controlled state legislature in 2015 requires that a person present one of several state-issued documents to vote. On one estimate, some three hundred thousand residents of the state (equivalent to 10% of the ultimate vote count) lacked such identification, often because of the expense entailed in getting it, and hence were disabled from voting. Even if you entered a polling station and cast a ballot in November 2016, the meaningfulness and efficacy of your action can reasonably be questioned. According to Nicholas Stephanopoulos and Eric McGhee, the map of legislative district lines in Wisconsin embodies one of the most extreme partisan gerrymanders in American history. Although the two parties evenly split the presidential vote in 2016, Republicans won 64% of the seats in the State Assembly. As the plaintiff in a 2016 lawsuit challenging that districting explained, that gerrymander "effectively guarantees Republican control of both houses of the Wisconsin legislature for a decade, no matter what happens in Wisconsin elections."[2]

"Elections" happened in both Madison and in Beijing in November 2016. But were they part of a *democratic* process? Conventional wisdom holds that the People's Congress elections run by the Chinese government do not qualify, but that American elections for national office do. But does this dichotomy flow simply from our unstated assumptions and parochial prejudice? In both jurisdictions, voters and potential voters could make quite powerful arguments for why the electoral process should not be taken at face value, and why those elections should not be understood as part of a democracy. How, if at all, can we tell them apart?

Any effort to understand democratic decline must start with a threshold question that is more difficult than first appears: What, precisely, do we mean by democracy? And where and when do we observe it in practice? Without a clear sense of what counts as a democracy, we are missing a necessary stepping-stone for thinking about democratic decline. It would not be possible to determine which cases to include in the study or to operationalize the notion of "decline." As the China and Wisconsin examples suggest, conventional wisdom about what properly counts as a democracy is hazy. It often fails to identify the relevant institutions or relevant, system-wide qualities that suffice for the label to fairly attach. These examples also suggest that looking to the subjective understanding of participants in an electoral process will not provide a satisfying approach. It is not just that participants in a process that should not count as democratic may be misled into believing that their participation is more consequential, and hence more substantive, than it really is. It is also that others may have an unreasonably demanding and stringent standard for what really counts as a democracy, such that it is hard to imagine any realistic system of collective choice meeting the standard.

How then should democracy be understood if we are interested in the signs and pathways of democratic decline and decay? We begin by setting out a definition of one particular species of democracy—we call it *liberal constitutional democracy*—that will provide a touchstone for our analysis throughout this book. Unlike some political theorists and philosophers, we define liberal constitutional democracy in terms of its core *institutions*—the laws, stable structures, forms of governance, and official practices that provide a supporting framework for democratic functioning.[3] By focusing on a trio of crucial institutions, our definition orients our analysis to the question of how institutional design, or institutional change, can either aid or abet democratic backsliding. We will also use the terms *liberal constitutional democracy* and *democracy* interchangeably in what follows. We do not mean to slight either the liberal or constitutional elements of our definition in doing so. Rather, it is just sometimes more convenient (and less long-winded) to talk of "democracy," once we have elaborated on that term with the more complex definition offered in this chapter.

So what do we mean by liberal constitutional democracy? Democracy has many definitions. It exemplifies what philosophers have called "an essentially contested concept."[4] Among economists and political scientists, though, the idea of democracy has been closely associated with the simple fact of elections. Most famously, Joseph Schumpeter described democracy as an "institutional arrangement for arriving at political decisions in which individuals acquire the power to decide by means of a competitive struggle for the people's vote."[5] In contrast, classicists have noted that in its original Athenian usage, *democracy* did not entail majority-rule elections, but simply referred to the capacity of the masses as a whole to govern.[6] Yet other scholars have defined democracy in terms of an abstract idea of "accountability" to the public.[7] This range and variance in definitional approaches to the term *democracy* reflect foundational disagreements about the role of collective-choice mechanisms in a democracy. It also suggests that a definition of democracy will in part reflect the needs and interests of the scholar offering it. The utility of an essentially contested term such as *democracy* arises from its ability to provide a starting point for many different lines of inquiry, whether institutional, social psychological, or normative in nature.

We resist the idea that democracy can be boiled down to a simple requirement of competitive elections. For genuine electoral competition to be sustained, something more than a bare minimum of legal and institutional arrangements is necessary. We identify three such "floor" requirements for a working democracy. These start with free and fair elections to be sure, but extend to the liberal rights of speech and association that are necessary for the democratic process; and the stability, predictability, and publicity of a legal regime usually captured in the term *rule of law*—a quality of special importance when it comes to the machinery of elections. These core institutions, we argue, are necessarily associated with the democratic ideal that seemed to attain hegemonic status after the end of the Cold War. When present, these institutions enable a distinctive form of self-government that warrants its own label.

So defined, liberal constitutional democracy obviously does not exhaust the field of contemporary forms of governance—even for systems with repeated elections. An increasing number of systems around the world have some of the outward forms of democracy without effective or genuine political competition, often because they lack full associational rights or the rule of law. We think it helpful in this opening chapter to examine briefly these alternatives to democracy as well, since they often serve as end points to the processes of decay and backsliding that are our principal interest. Finally, we defend our conception of liberal constitutional democracy against a range of potential criticisms, including what might be called the Wisconsin problem of how to take account of deficiencies in a democratic system without imposing an impossibly demanding standard.

Liberal Constitutional Democracy

In the last decade of the twentieth century, liberal democracy seemed to have triumphed everywhere. Yet today there is increasing concern that the form of democracy provides a façade for undemocratic behavior. According to the Freedom House, an American human rights organization, the number of democracies around the world has been declining since 2006, as has the quality of democratic governance within individual countries.[8] To understand how this happened, it is useful to start with a conception of democracy that incorporates the liberal and constitutional elements celebrated at the end of the Cold War (and at the American founding two centuries earlier). Further, because we are especially interested in the institutional pathways of democratic decline—and, in particular, the ways that laws and constitutions can abet such processes—it is also useful to take an institutional focus, rather than looking at sociocultural or economic prerequisites.

Our definition aims to be as minimalist as possible without simply equating democracy with elections alone. It has three conceptually separate but functionally intertwined elements. Only when they are all present together does a country warrant the label of *liberal constitutional democracy*. These are, first, a democratic electoral system—most importantly, periodic free and fair elections in which the modal adult can vote—after which, the losing side concedes power to the winning side. The second prong of our definition comprises the particular liberal rights to speech and association that are closely linked to democracy in practice. Finally, our definition looks for a level of integrity of law and legal institutions—that is, the rule of law—sufficient to allow democratic engagement without fear or coercion. We use the term *liberal constitutional democracy* because each word in that term corresponds to one of the three elements needed for a system of self-government to get off the ground.

Each of these three institutional predicates of democracy is, in our view, necessary *in practice* for the maintenance of a reasonable level of democratic responsiveness and unbiased elections. It is not enough that free and fair elections exist on paper or that liberal rights of speech and association appear in the text of a constitution. They must also be practiced realities. In the absence of the actual realization of all three institutional predicates, we anticipate that a democratic system would run off the tracks. But it may be the case that a minor deficit in just one or another element would not prevent a system from continuing to operate in a democratic fashion. In short, liberal constitutional democracy requires some modicum of all three components; it might also survive if some elements are not at full capacity.

Because this definition provides a foundation for the analysis that follows, it is worth unpacking and explaining each of these three elements of democracy in more detail. Let's begin with the idea of a free and fair election characterized by the potential transfer of power. On the first element, we follow Schumpeter's dictum that meaningful elections with a genuine possibility of alteration in actual political power are necessary to democracy. We also build in Robert Dahl's concern that elections focus on offices that in fact are seats of authoritative state power. In China, local people's congresses are of limited importance, because actual and effective authority lies within the Chinese Communist Party, an institution insulated from democratic control, notwithstanding the Party's putative commitment to the Leninist principle of democratic centralism. In Wisconsin, even accepting the most extreme assertions of partisan gerrymandering, it remains the case that there are numerous elections at multiple levels of government that can lead to some measure of democratic rotation of power. Among these are primary elections, which can be competitive even if a general election is not, as well as municipal and statewide ballots.

The second element of our definition of democracy focuses on a core of "first generation" rights of speech, assembly, and association. These "liberal" rights facilitate political competition. One cannot have meaningful political competition without the relatively free ability to organize and offer policy proposals, criticize leaders, and demonstrate in public without official intimidation. In this sense, electoral democracy is deeply intertwined with the enumeration in a constitution of certain negative rights, that is, rights against the state. In its core manifestations, moreover, liberal democracy typically rests on a delicate interplay between diverse state and civil-society institutions. These in turn depend on the enforcement of liberal rights.

Political parties are the most important kind of civil-society formation. At least since the advent of mass politics in the nineteenth century, stable democratic politics has seemed to require political parties to serve as fulcrums of coalition-formation. In the absence of parties, disparate groups and interests across diverse constituencies are likely to remain fragmented, without a common political agenda that orders and prioritizes distinct issues.[9] In contrast, as we shall see, where parties are replaced by more personalistic forms of politics, wherein regimes are legitimated by the charismatic power of individual leaders, the kind of arguing and bargaining that yields compromise among different groups is unlikely to arise. Multiparty competition, moreover, is essential to a stable democracy—which is why the Wisconsin example is so troubling to many. As we will see, when a stable party system collapses because of a loss in confidence in established parties, or where one party is captured by a charismatic outsider with a weak commitment to democracy, the persistence of democratic competition is likely to be called into question.

Liberal rights to speech and association matter to democracy in another, less direct, fashion. Democracy implies the possibility of one coalition or party turning power over to another. The exiting party, however, is unlikely to be willing to relinquish control if its members believe that state power will be used against them thereafter. Instead, orderly exit rests upon the belief that one will have voice in the new arrangements and hence can live to fight another day. Liberal rights to speech and association are a necessary prophylaxis against anticompetitive behavior on the part of prospective holders of government power. By ensuring that losers can speak, they lower the stakes of winning, and thus make political competition possible.[10]

To be clear, rights to speech, assembly, and association might not exhaust the list of rights necessary to the democratic process. Rather, they provide an essential core set of entitlements necessary for meaningful democratic competition.

Many other rights can be redescribed in derivative terms. Consider just two examples. Parliamentary immunity to speak and debate on the floor of the legislature, first of all, has a long history of being used to shield political discourse from overzealous prosecutions in medieval England.[11] In this regard, it is quite plausibly understood as merely a particular instance of a more general freedom of speech. The right to form political parties could similarly be described as part of the right of association.

The same analysis might also support a claim for some rights as being necessary for democracy, even though they neither look nor feel like the core speech and associational entitlements. In the American context, for example, the Fourth Amendment to the Constitution protects against "unreasonable" searches and seizures, and is now invoked most commonly against overreaching police officers. Originally, however, the amendment was inspired by concerns about the Crown's use of state power to target and harass dissenting parliamentarians such as John Entick and John Wilkes. That political function has been lost today, and the amendment instead is understood in practice as the basis of the federal law of policing.[12] But the lost history of search and seizure law is still illuminating. It is a reminder that, to the extent that democracy requires freedom from state coercion of opposition candidates and parties, such freedom can be described as an element of the freedoms of association and speech. These rights are not exhausted by the absence of prior restraints, but necessarily include ex post immunities from subsequent punishment or harassment by state actors (for example through invasive home searches or monitoring of private communications). Coercive treatment or intrusive surveillance of antiregime politicians, on this view, would be problematic not because "unreasonable" searches are per se wrong, but because the coercive power of the state should not be used to stifle political speech and association.

In short, liberal rights to speech and association matter to democracy's definition because meaningful electoral contestation is hard to imagine when individual citizens are prohibited from expressing views challenging the policies and claims of those in power, or from cooperating to form political and civic associations.

Finally, for our third element of democracy's definition, we draw from a conception of the rule of law by the legal scholar Lon Fuller, who focuses on a set of procedural requirements without including substantive concepts like rights or morality. We also follow the philosopher Joseph Raz's caution that the rule of law is not the same as "the rule of the good law," and has no necessary relation to equality or justice.[13] In more concrete terms, political scientists Juan Linz and Alfred Stepan have argued that meaningful elections require a bureaucratic machinery that is capable of applying rules in a neutral and consistent fashion over a nation's extended territory. In their apt words, "Democratic government and the state apparatus . . . must be held accountable to, and become habituated to, the rule of law."[14]

The rule of law is perhaps best understood by looking at its absence. What follows from this absence was nicely captured by the Brazilian autocrat Getulio Dornelles Vargas, "For my friend, everything; for my enemies, the law."[15] If the law can be wielded as a partisan tool in this way, electoral choice is distorted. In contrast, for elections to play their proper function, a number of neutral administrative functions are required that are intimately entangled in the rule of law.[16] Among other things, election rules must be clearly announced in advance to the public. Voters must be able to register in a neutral way, and censuses must reflect the actual distribution of the population. There must be officials to organize and staff poll booths, certify ballot structure, and establish counting facilities. There must be adjudicative institutions to resolve disputes, both large and small, about the conduct of the election. Some margin of error is surely permissible, but the Wisconsin example is a stark reminder that at some point the partisan manipulation of election rules conflicts with the rule-of-law ambitions of even-handedness and apolitical administration.

Beyond the parts of the state directly linked to elections, the coercive elements of the state must also be characterized by the rule of law. Sound election administration, after all, would be of little value if those competing for office feared either police harassment or the discriminatory administration of regulatory and tax regimes. All of these functions require a measure of institutionalization and legalized routines that are hallmarks of a good bureaucracy operating in accord with the rule of law. In the absence of such measures, the electoral process would be unreliable and even lopsided in ways that preclude meaningful electoral competition. By focusing on these very concrete institutional details, we hope to deploy the term *administrative rule of law* in a specific way that avoids the conceptual briar patches that similar terms have engendered in the hands of legal philosophers.[17]

These three elements—elections, speech and association rights, and a bureaucracy governed by the rule of law—are conceptually separate. They do not always run together. There are historical and contemporary instances of countries that have robust electoral democracies, even while the rule of law is weak and liberal rights lack social support. Indonesia is an example of an inclusive democracy that has a very weak rule of law.[18] Other countries have the elements of a "thin" rule of law and civil liberties without genuine political competition. Singapore is perhaps the leading instance here.[19] Finally, constitutionalism is feasible in the absence of either liberal entitlements or

democratic rotation.[20] Indeed, as we shall see momentarily, there is no necessary nexus at all between liberal democracy on the one hand and constitutionalism on the other.

Despite the possibility of only loose coupling among our three definitional
elements, the effective operation of democracy is most likely to be characterized by their entangled and mutually supportive operation. Working well,
each of these three institutional elements sustains and reinforces the other,
producing a latticework of practices, institutions, and attitudes that together
provide the necessary framework for democracy. Liberal constitutional democracy emerges as a *system-level* effect of these institutional building blocks.

The three institutional elements of free elections, rights to speech and association, and a bureaucratic rule of law are also enmeshed in mutually reinforcing ways that produce a stable democratic equilibrium in many cases.
As we have already noted, some elements of the rule of law are surely necessary to sustain even the thin Schumpeterian concept of democracy. The rule
of law is also, in some sense, a product of democratic rotation, because the
prospect of alternation of political power via free and fair elections incentivizes investment in constitutional rules and enforcement.[21] When officeholders have no expectation of such rotation, conversely, their incentive to respect
and foster rights of speech and association wanes. Finally, the protections of
the rule of law provide an assurance to electoral losers that their defeat will
not lead to permanent exclusion from power.

These patterned interactions suggest at least the possibility of a robust
democratic equilibrium in which a set of behaviors and dispositions becomes
self-sustaining. In this vein, we can think of *democracy* as denoting a system-
level effect that emerges when all three institutional predicates are operating
tolerably well.[22] As we have noted, this system-level effect will not emerge
if any one of its three institutional predicates fails completely. Assessment
becomes difficult, requiring discerning judgment and a careful evaluation of
facts on the ground, when there is only a partial failure of one or more of
these institutional prerequisites.

As a system-level characteristic resting on three somewhat abstract and
general institutional traits, our definition of democracy is not amenable to
precise quantification. It is thus vulnerable to criticism for its imprecision
and lack of empirical tractability. To be sure, there are existing measures of
"democracy," such as the Polity and the Freedom House scores that capture
elements of what we mean, and we shall refer to these measures from time
to time precisely because they are convenient and widely consulted.[23] But we
readily concede that it is hard to quantify the confluence of three system-level
properties. Nor is it obvious how to measure with precision concepts such as

the bureaucratic rule of law. Part of the difficulty of quantification flows from the fact that none of the three institutional predicates that we describe are ever likely to be perfectly achieved. All democracies, however well-functioning, are likely to fall short in some ways in respect to one or more of the three institutional building blocks we have described. Democracy, as we have defined it, is an ideal type. But even if it is never perfectly achieved in practice, it remains useful for orienting evaluation. Perfection may be unattainable, but that doesn't mean we can't distinguish the better from the worse.[24]

As a result, our three institutional criteria do not provide slide rules for estimating the robust growth or decay of democracy. They instead act as lenses, directing our attention to the necessary elements that sustain it as a going concern. How much decay a given democracy can take in any one of these elements is a question of judgment. The point at which the fibers of institutional practice have become sufficiently knotted together to sustain democracy is also a matter of judgment. We offer our evaluations of particular cases, though we hasten to add that we do not think that our assessments are beyond dispute. One class of cases in which those judgments will be especially contestable concerns what has been called "democratic careening," in which a polity alternates between populist and oligarchic forms of democracy, both degraded in different ways, without quite collapsing. Thailand in the early 2000s was an example of a polity initially characterized by gross inequalities that then experienced a bout of authoritarian populism (followed, as we shall see, by an outright collapse of democratic institutions). How one characterizes Thailand's trajectory depends on how one evaluates each step in its erratic stagger, and we duly recognize the difficulty of such contextual assessments.[25]

The United States as a Liberal Constitutional Democracy

Asking how democracy works under the US Constitution is one way to think through how this kind of judgment would work. The exercise suggests that a certain skepticism about the health of democracy in the American context is warranted. But we also think that (with important qualifications and ratifications) the United States is properly ranked as a liberal constitutional democracy. A threshold complication is that, at the very inception of the Constitution's creation and ratification in late 1780s, there was considerable elite resistance to the idea of a "democratic" system of government. The framers described their system as a republic, rather than a democracy. The most democratic element of their system, federal elections to national institutions, were not designed to directly transmit popular preferences, but instead to strain them through an elaborate filtration mechanism that comprised the

House, Senate, and presidency.[26] Given that elitist conception, it would be surprising indeed if a democratic ideal had been quickly and perfectly realized in the United States.

Of course, the history of democracy in the United States was to be anything but straightforward. Take the first of our three institutional predicates— the fact of free and fair elections. Racial minorities and women, most notoriously, were excluded from the franchise, as well as from much else, for most of American history. Long periods of American history have been characterized by franchise restrictions, malapportionment, and suppression of constitutional rights, along with the existence of subnational authoritarianism in parts of the country.[27] It was only in the 1940s that the US Supreme Court began to dismantle the entrenched social and political structures of racialized authoritarianism in the south, and it was not until the 1970s that those efforts could be said to have borne meaningful fruit in political and social outcomes.[28] Even today, state-level electoral practice is characterized by numerous exclusionary and suppressive practices. These include, but are not limited to, the use of gerrymandering in states like Wisconsin and North Carolina to entrench one political party beyond electoral rotation. They include the interaction of racialized mass incarceration and the pervasive disenfranchisement by states of people with felony convictions—more than six million people (or one out of forty members of the voting-age population) in the last presidential election. The use of voter-identification laws to suppress some elements of the electorate also falls harder on racial minorities.[29] Of course, politicians' efforts to entrench themselves are endemic in any system.[30] But some tactics are so gratuitous, repressive, or ugly—and so wanting in other redeeming qualities—that they must count strongly against any evaluation of democratic quality.

The United States is hardly a paragon when measured against our other criteria of democracy, either. Rights-based liberalism, for example, is compromised by the systematic under-enforcement of many individual rights. The resulting large gaps that remain between the law on the ground and the law on the books are another cause for deep embarrassment.[31] And the United States also performs quite poorly with regard to the bureaucratic rule-of-law prong of our definition, at least in the electoral realm. Electoral administration in the United States is fragmented and institutionally weak because of "path-dependent state primacy over electoral regulation, the lack of existing federal infrastructure to monitor elections nationally, as well as the weak political will to establish robust federal electoral institutions."[32] In the vacuum created by the absence of federal authority, we have a mix of state-level regimes of very different quality, with some states—think Florida in 2000 or

Ohio in 2004—raising serious questions as to their integrity and reliability. System-level vulnerability to foreign infiltration is only one consequence of this fragile, jerry-rigged system.

But perfection is not to be expected from actual, existing democracies. These weaknesses do not completely undermine the American claim to democratic credentials. They *do* demonstrate the potential for wide variance in the quality of democracy's three institutional predicates, even within a single country, between different regions and communities. Yet for all these challenges, it remains the case in the United States that the average adult citizen selected on the street at random could, if she so wished, both vote and also run for political office. Without denying that financial resources and social networks play massively important roles in candidate viability, the freedoms to vote and run for office are widely distributed, if only because of the legal and institutional underpinnings of elections. Without denying the persistence of both individual animus and structural forms of exclusion, it is the case that racial minorities and women can and do run successfully for office. This means that, while far from ideal, American democracy is still not in so great a state of disrepair as to be disqualified from the very label.

It is worth underscoring that our definition of liberal constitutional democracy is also consistent with a wide variety of institutional arrangements and policy preferences. It encompasses both the robust administrative state of the post–New Deal federal government and the looser arrangement of "parties and courts" that preceded it.[33] It can abide in a centralized or federalized system; work through parliamentary or executive-led administrations; and coexist with a variety of other institutional arrangements. We hence reject the view among some that the gradual concentration of power in the executive presidency in the United States *ipso facto* contributes to democratic derogation. The United States has maintained a large regulatory apparatus, governed by the rule of law, at least since the New Deal. In that period, it has held an uninterrupted series of national elections to the presidency and Congress in which questions about the direction and intensity of federal regulation often have been front and center. In the 2008, 2012, and 2016 election cycles, for example, the role of federal regulations in the health-care field was a central point of electoral contestation, and the attempted fulfillment of related election promises has preoccupied many federal elected officials of late. In this light, the claim that the United States is not a democracy because it has too large a regulatory apparatus seems to us to reflect not a judgment about democracy, per se, but a preference about the scope and nature of regulation. It is a question that is properly addressed through the democratic process. It is not evidence of incompatibility with that process itself.

Our approach is also consistent with a wide range of solutions for democracy's so-called "boundary problem." This problem arises because every democracy relies upon some definition of the relevant group of citizens entitled to participate in elections. One might think this should include everyone affected by a particular policy, but all democracies restrict the franchise to those above a certain age, and some limit the vote to those possessing full mental capacity. Furthermore, given that almost any national government's actions have spillover effects on many other persons outside the polity, using an "effects" test to define who can vote yields no practicable or defensible limit.[34] Simply put, the United States (or France, or Sweden) is not about to enfranchise the citizens of Aleppo or Waziristan because its foreign policy decisions influence whether they live or die. All democracies fall short of the ideal of enfranchising all those whose interests are affected by decision-making.[35] And the practice of democracy has always involved limitations on the franchise. We thus use as a rough rule of thumb whether or not the modal adult actually residing in the country can vote and run for high office: this means that the United States today would be included, though Hong Kong (where the franchise is restricted and candidates are carefully screened) would not be. Since the modal adult is usually female, countries in which women are not enfranchised would certainly not count. Hence, on our definition, the United States cannot be called democratic until 1919 at the very earliest.

Finally, our definition is "liberal" in the sense of demanding recognition of certain negative rights of speech and association. This is related, although not identical, to liberal political practice as defined by Edmund Fawcett in his recent account of liberalism: "a search for an ethically acceptable order of human progress among civic equals without recourse to undue power."[36] Liberalism, in this view, is not restricted to laissez-faire endorsement of free markets (as Europeans use the term *liberal*), commitment to the New Deal and civil rights (as Americans mean), or political liberalism as it has come to be understood by philosophers in the wake of John Rawls. We think that, in general, most liberal constitutional democracies will be "liberal" in Fawcett's capacious sense. As a result, it is worth emphasizing, our concept of a liberal constitutional democracy does not require "liberal" policy choices in the American sense, the European sense, or even in Fawcett's sense. To the contrary, it is consistent with illiberal policies, such as violations of racial, religious, and sexual-orientation freedoms, grave economic inequality or deprivation, or lack of social services provision. We assume a baseline that is *democratic*; but this is no guarantee of *good* or *decent* governance in any robust, normative sense. Our concept, in other words, is not as normatively loaded as it could be because it recognizes and accommodates the mutability of democratic choice and its capacity for grave moral error. But by including some elements of liberal rights and the rule of law, we seek to recognize that even this minimalist conception needs some institutional context. We also do not pack any requirement of democratic responsiveness into our definition. There is still a good deal of sharp-elbowed debate about the appropriate measure of democratic responsiveness among political scientists. Rather than introduce that complexity into our definition, we maintain a focus on democracy's institutional predicates, rather than its outcomes.[37]

It is worth stressing that liberalism and democracy have not always been in accord; we do not mean to suggest that their reconciliation is an easy one. Nevertheless, we have attempted to pick out a distinct set of systemic features shared by many political systems in the post–World War II period. We think this set of practices borrows from liberal, constitutional, and democratic traditions and ideas, and hence we use a compound term. This is not to say it fully reconciles the tensions between those distinct values. Actual political practice always fails to resolve all theoretical questions. Creative democratic politics instead trades in constructive ambiguity and makes a virtue of muddling through. Nevertheless, we view liberal constitutional democracy as a political *modus vivendi* that is distinctive and recognizable as a feature of the contemporary world.

Alternatives to Liberal Constitutional Democracy

No one form of government serves as the antonym of liberal constitutional democracy. Polities can be defective with regard to any one of the three elements—liberalism, constitutionalism, or democracy—or be missing all three. Wisconsin's elections can be criticized along the third of these criteria, China's along all three. The result is a series of "blurred and imperfect" boundaries between democracy and its alternatives, in addition to myriad pathways away from democratic ordering toward one of a range of alternatives.[38] A complete taxonomy of these nondemocratic possibilities would take us far afield, but it is worth quickly mapping a few alternatives that are particularly salient today.

Even in the immediate blush of post–Cold War triumphalism, the idea that democracy would work as a universal aspiration drew sharp rebuke. In an interview with the journalist Fareed Zakaria, Singaporean Prime Minister Lee Kuan Yew criticized the "liberal, intellectual tradition" upon which European and American democracy rested. Three years later, Zakaria articulated a broad notion of "illiberal democracy," in which democracy flourished, but both constitutionalism and liberal rights were de-emphasized, as a worryingly prevalent alternative to liberal democracy.[39] Importantly, what came to be known as "illiberal democracy" or, in one part of the world, "Asian democracy" emphasized the collective harmony over individual expression. Duties, not rights, were at the core of a well-ordered society; liberty had to be balanced with security, and participation with effectiveness.[40]

Singapore is a polity in which there are generally free and fair elections, an absence of overt, violent repression, and a stable and reliable bureaucratic rule of law. Lee's People's Action Party, however, has dominated post-independence electoral politics, in large part because opposition politicians have been harassed with libel suits and threatened with prosecution under a sweeping Internal Security Act, while newspapers, the internet, and public spaces are all closely regulated to minimize opportunities for political mobilization.[41] At the same time, elections are not without practical impact. The ruling party uses them to identify important policy goals and problems to respond to, and sometimes to identify promising political talent. It also occasionally loses individual seats even if there is no real uncertainty over who will win overall in national elections.

The Singapore model is hardly the only alternative to liberal constitutional democracy on offer today. Steven Levitsky and Lucan Way use the general term *competitive authoritarianism* to describe regimes in which formal democratic institutions continue to operate, but where incumbents either violate formal legal rules or use those same rules as instruments for greatly diminishing or eliminating effective competition.[42] In Singapore, libel law and press regulation can be directly applied as instruments of political repression. In other regimes, in contrast, incumbents deploy blunter instruments to suppress the substance of democratic competition while keeping its external accoutrements in place. In the UN-administered 1993 elections in Cambodia, for example, the Cambodian government was responsible for more than seventy documented killings and more than one hundred nonlethal assaults on opposition political figures.[43] Reliance on illegal force does not preclude the abuse of legal powers. In 2017, the prime minister elected in 1993 and still in office successfully sued in the country's Supreme Court to dissolve the main opposition party.[44] Whether the instruments of entrenchment are lawful or not, their result need not be the complete elimination of democratic contestation. They can instead produce a severe tilting of the playing field so as to constrain the opportunities for electoral rotation in the ordinary course of politics. "Competitive authoritarianism" is a label that highlights the absence of democracy proper, as opposed to some weaker sense of competition. One might say that competitive authoritarianism is an illiberal democracy in which party rotation in power is no longer a genuine possibility at all.

Importantly, the deterioration in democratic institutions may not be as complete as in Singapore or Cambodia. The term *illiberal democracy* captures a broad set of ambiguous cases. Today, many illiberal democracies arise through the victory of candidates or parties that pursue authoritarian policies, try to extinguish the political space for dissent and competition, and aim to capture the machinery of state that provides for fair elections and administration. Such politicians and parties pursuing an illiberal democratic agenda have a paradoxical quality. On the one hand, they can claim a democratic mandate. On the other hand, they strive to dismantle democracy from the inside out. We shall encounter many examples of such elected anti-democrats in the course of this book—including leaders and parties in Venezuela, Hungary, Poland, and Turkey—and also document their attempts in more established democracies, such as Israel and Japan.

Often, these antiliberal movements are called *populist* in character, although that term is ambiguous and itself requires definition. One of our tasks, therefore, in setting the groundwork for an analysis of the institutional pathways of democratic decline is to understand precisely what the label *populist* entails.

As an example of the sorts of complexities that arise in defining the boundary between democracy and its antitheses, consider the case of Iran after the 1979 Islamic Revolution. In May 2017, 41 million Iranians cast ballots in a presidential election that reelected the relatively reformist and pragmatic Hassan Rouhani over his opponent Ebrahim Raisi, by a margin of 18.5%. This large margin of electoral victory is especially striking because Raisi was supported by, and closely aligned with, a clerical establishment led by supreme leader Ayatollah Ali Khamenei. Under the December 1979 Constitution, Khamenei, as unelected supreme leader, exercises significant authority over the courts, the military, and the media. He is closely aligned with the unelected Council of Guardians (which vets all candidates for elected office), and the Expediency Counsel (which has constrained reformist legislatures by, for instance, barring investigations into agencies controlled by the supreme leader). When reformist candidates like Rouhani and Mohammad Khatami win, it is against the wishes and interests of this clerical establishment. This entrenched power center, moreover, actively resists popular exercise of the franchise through its control of courts, its regulatory powers, and its instruments of direct coercion, such as the Revolutionary Guards. All of these tools can be used to narrow the scope of pre-polling competition and tighten the range of policy choices an elected reformer can pursue.[45] Given these sharp, repressive limitations, it would be misleading to characterize post-revolutionary Iran as either a full-bore democracy or a pure instance of competitive authoritarianism. Rather, it is an illustration of the many variations that lie between those poles—and the possibility that a single constitutional regime might veer within the range of competitive authoritarianism closer or further away from a democratic pole.

Iran is an instance in which the constraints imposed on democratic choice are justified by the invocation of religion. In Singapore, democracy is managed in the name of "cultural" values, communal harmony and economic stability. In other contexts, the constraint upon democracy arises from the de facto dominance of one political party over all others. Mexico, Malaysia, and Taiwan have in the recent past been examples of multi-decade, one-party dominance coupled with some external trappings of democracy.[46] In yet other contexts, it can be personalist politics, mixed with corruption or ethnic favoritism, that undermines genuine democracy.

In sum, the space of competitive authoritarianism is bounded on one side by liberal constitutional democracy, and on the other by authoritarianism. On neither side is the border crisply delimited, so debate is inevitable about when a democracy has become or is becoming an authoritarian regime. Drawing that boundary is especially challenging because democracy can be geographically uneven within a polity, especially if it delegates authority down to subnational states or regions with their own elections. The authoritarian enclaves of the Jim Crow southern United States are one historical example; the Indian state of Bihar, which is characterized by pervasive government corruption, election-related murder, intimidation, and kidnapping, is a contemporary instance of how subnational democracy can be degraded in ways that are independent of the quality of national-level politics. In contrast, in American states, such as Wisconsin, that are characterized by intensive partisan gerrymandering, the authoritarian label plainly lacks force, however stacked the electoral deck may be.

The pure authoritarian model that lies on the other side of the competitive authoritarian model is characterized by the complete absence of effective political competition. An authoritarian regime is one that lacks any meaningful political pluralism, where there is little political mobilization, and where a leader or a small group exercises power within formally ill-defined limits.[47] It is frequently the case that legal and extralegal means are used to quash completely political opposition in an authoritarian regime. But this is not necessarily so. It is possible for an authoritarian regime to secure high levels of cooperation and endorsement from its public by appealing to economic success (as in China) or by invoking nationalist tropes (as in Russia).[48] Moreover, as Chinese elections illustrate, authoritarianism is not incompatible with the holding of elections that elicit substantial and enthusiastic public involvement. As much as democracy, authoritarianism can be a popular form of political practice.

Nevertheless, authoritarian regimes do not lose power in elections, even if they hold them. Instead, roughly three-quarters of intra-regime transitions in authoritarian contexts involve power moving from one family member to another, such as the transition between the Castro brothers in Cuba.[49] In other cases, a party may have an orderly succession process that functions irrespective of elections: the Chinese Communist Party, for example, has an internal mechanism for determining who succeeds to the top (a mechanism recently transformed by Xi Jinping's move to abolish the presidential term limits found in the Chinese constitution.) Power may be transferred within an authoritarian regime, but it is only through revolutions, coups, foreign interventions, or negotiated, "pacted" transitions that such regimes themselves die.

Nor do authoritarian regimes lack written constitutions, courts, or other rule-of-law accoutrements. Rather, authoritarian regimes deploy the trappings of written constitutionalism to their own ends. Constitutions then operate as devices of "hegemonic preservation," by which preexisting elites craft mechanisms and institutions that preserve their grip on power.[50] Constitutions hence extend the power of certain groups or institutions by coordinating disparate elements of an authoritarian regime and by enabling control of subordinate officials within a government. In particular, the leader of an authoritarian regime may be uncertain about the continuing commitment of allies. Constitutional devices such as legislatures and advisory councils provide a means to monitor and sustain those allegiances.[51]

Authoritarian regimes come in many flavors. One is headed by the military. Turkey, for example, lapsed from a period of uneasy civil-military coalition through the 1970s into outright military rule in 1982 in a violent coup d'état. In that year, the military's general command dissolved the national assembly and political parties, detained many civilian politicians, and installed a new Constitution, which technically remains in force thirty-five years later. The 1982 Constitution fashioned new institutions of military control, such as a National Security Council that acted as a *de facto*, agenda-setting cabinet in charge of setting the government's agenda and directing sensitive policy matters, as well as a system of State Security Courts that ran parallel to the ordinary civilian courts. Even as it deepened military control of ordinary politics, the constitution insulated the military's budget from civilian influence and entrenched a generous array of state subsidies for soldiers and their families.[52]

Another form of authoritarian regime is oriented around a single person or party. In the post-1933 National Socialist regime in Germany, for example, a charismatic leader, Adolph Hitler, and his Nazi Party allies exercised sweeping and largely unconstrained authority as they led the country into expansionist war and the moral catastrophe of the Holocaust. The Nazi regime cemented its power by the repression of Socialist politicians and parties, and through violent internal purges, such as the infamous Night of the Long Knives. Those authoritarian powers, importantly, did not stem from a formal Nazi constitution. Indeed, the Nazi government never abrogated the liberal August 1919 Weimar Constitution. Instead, it operated under an emergency Enabling Act, which was periodically renewed through the 1930s and early 1940s, that dispensed with a legislature and vested the Nazi leadership with extraordinary power to rule by decree. What made Nazi Germany authoritarian, therefore, was *not* the specific constitutional form preserved throughout the 1930s and early 1940s, but rather the unfettered and near-exclusive scope of on-the-ground power exercised by the regime.[53]

Absolute monarchy, of course, is the ultimate form of authoritarian regime, but it is a category that has gradually shrunk over the last two centuries. Countries such as Saudi Arabia, Brunei, Oman, and Qatar are still ruled by leaders whose authority is absolute. But there are no new monarchies being set up today, and most of the world's monarchs coexist with constitutional democracy.

Is Liberal Constitutional Democracy Worth Defending?

We believe that liberal constitutional democracy is morally superior to the alternatives we have mapped out. This superiority flows, we think, most obviously from democracy's commitment—at least in theory—to a principle of political equality in which each citizen's voice counts to the same extent. It is sometimes assumed (although not universally believed) that political equality means that democracy is more likely than other systems to adopt public policies that account for all citizens' interests, whereas its alternatives are more likely to yield policies that account for only some of those interests. Consistent with these virtues, democracy rests on a principle of "simple respect" for the capacity of ordinary men and women to engage in reasoned deliberation on public affairs, and a corresponding skepticism about our ability to identify *ex ante* an elite that is better able to govern.[54] None of this is to say that democracies consistently adopt wise, humane, or moral policies. They don't. Nor do they always prevent elites from capturing and hoarding political power.[55] They don't. But all else being equal, we think they are more likely to further these ends in more cases than their competitors.

Of course, there are legitimate critiques of democracy in theory and as observed in practice. One focuses on performance. Any political system can be evaluated on both legitimacy and effectiveness, which are separate, if mutually reinforcing, dimensions. It is not hard to identify authoritarian regimes that outperform democracies in many ways, particularly economic growth. Consider the astounding contrast between authoritarian China and democratic India in recent decades, and ask, as if one could choose, whether it would be better to be born an average citizen in one or another country during the past generation. Setting aside political dissidents and ethnic minorities, it is apparent that the median citizen of China has seen her life transformed, while the median Indian remains impoverished. Of course, this example does not prove the general superiority of authoritarianism. While some dictatorships may do well, their variance is much higher: for every Lee Kuan Yew or Bismarck, there is a Pol Pot or Idi Amin. Setting aside the comparison of India and China, the predictable middling performance of democracies seems preferable, at least if one has any sense of risk aversion.

Another critique of democracy focuses on the tight nexus observed between it and capitalism. An eloquent proponent of this argument is the German sociologist Wolfgang Streeck, who has published a sequence of closely argued articles and books in the wake of the 2008–9 financial crisis contending that global financial capitalism in its current form generates inequitable and destabilizing results that ultimately undermine democracy. Streeck points to the plight of Greece within the European Union as an example of a democratic polity where the effective policy-setting authority of democratic institutions has been sapped entirely by the dynamics of global capital flows.[56] Streeck surely has a point. But our incorporation of liberal ideas into the definition of democracy is a thin one, including only the individual liberal rights to speech and association, and so is not inherently tied to any particular economic program. It is compatible with but does not require redistributive policies of the kind that Streeck and others advocate, which we think can be established and successfully implemented within a democratic framework.[57]

Properly conceptualized and measured with an appropriate skepticism, we think that liberal constitutional democracy is superior to the alternatives on display today. We also do not think that democracy collapses under the weight of its internal logical contradictions or its concessions to global capitalism. We recognize that there are many valid criticisms of democracy as it is actually institutionalized in particular countries, and we take up some of them in later chapters. But while democracy may not always yield wise or decent policies, it does better than the next best option. No other system of government is built on the principles of equal dignity and simple respect. No other form of government makes the airing of its own flaws so central a part of its intrinsic appeal. It is for these reasons that it is worth asking whether, as a form of government, it is at risk or on the decline.

Is Liberal Constitutional Democracy Receding?

COUNTRY-LEVEL TRENDS

Is democracy in decline around the world today? Much depends on what is meant by democratic decline. What political scientists call "the Third Wave" of democracy emerged in 1975, with the end of dictatorships in southern Europe. Since then, there have consistently been more countries classified as democracies than as dictatorships or as belonging to the intermediate category of hybrid regimes. The number of democracies continued to expand throughout the 1980s, and increased after the end of the Cold War. But in the first decade of the twenty-first century, the number of countries classified as democracies began to decline. While their number still exceeds the number of nondemocratic regimes in most indicators, the trend seems to be in the wrong direction.

Instead of counting heads, we might look at the quality of democracy. Within-country variation is as important as cross-national variation. Using a variety of empirical measures of democracy, including those from Freedom House, Polity, and the Economist Intelligence Unit, one can track movement upward or downward in the assessed level of democracy. While some countries have deepened their democracy, others have regressed in the past decade, suggesting that some kind of democratic decay is at work in some countries, but not all. In 2017, Freedom House found declines in the quality of democracy in seventy-one countries, labeling the trend a crisis.[58] And in its 2016 democratization index, the Economist Intelligence Unit downgraded the United States from a "full democracy"—one characterized by basic political freedoms and civil liberties, and a political culture conducive to the flourishing of democracy—to a "flawed democracy," in which generally free and fair elections are marred by infringements, governance problems, and low levels of political participation.[59]

Countries are growing farther apart in their levels of democratic performance, and new democracies have failed to emerge. In part, these data reflect the failure of a hoped-for "Fourth Wave" of democracy, which might have crested with the Arab Spring had events gone differently. In only one country in the region, Tunisia, can we see a significant democratic advance. High levels of social mobilization elsewhere in the region did not produce reform, and this matters in any assessment of democracy's status today.[60] It demonstrates the resilience of the authoritarian form of government, manifested in local security forces' willingness to repress and international actors' unwillingness to withdraw support for repressive regimes. Similarly, in the late 1990s in China, the process of economic liberalization seemed to be generating a measure of political reform, such that newly appointed Prime Minister Zhu Rongji could pronounce in 1998 that "of course I am in favor of democratic elections." Twenty years later, any optimism for democracy seems far-fetched in light of Xi Jinping's aggressive crackdowns on lawyers and intellectuals, his elimination of constitutional term limits, the country's close scrutiny of social media, and its increasingly heavy-handed approach to protests, dissent, and the severe management of even limited elections in Hong Kong.[61] This stalling of democratic progress and the entrenchment of violent authoritarian rule for another generation or two—as has happened across the Middle East, with the exception of Tunisia—must count as a *defeat* for democracy, not merely a matter of indifference.

What of developments in so-called "swing states"? These are critical states that may have an immediate impact in their regions, producing demonstration effects and spillovers in other democracies. Scholars have documented such diffusion of policy effects in many areas, from international trade policies to social welfare policies and formal constitutional design.[62] Like other policy choices, democracy spreads around the world in waves. As a theoretical matter, there is no reason to think that antidemocratic movements, policies, and strategies do not also spread across borders in like fashion. Indeed, far-right parties in Europe with antisystem views first emerged in France and then appeared across Europe in a process of "cross-national diffusion."[63]

Consider the recent experiences of three regional flag bearers for democracy: Turkey (for the Middle East), India (for South Asia), and the Philippines (for Southeast Asia). In each case, there is evidence of a decline in the quality of democracy. Even if this is a return to a historical standard of competitive authoritarianism—as is arguably the case for Turkey—these developments may have spillover effects because of the influence and exemplary effect of those nations.

Turkey has experienced intermittent military rule since the mid-twentieth century. Both its 1961 liberal democratic constitution and its 1982 constitution were chosen by bodies selected by the military, which saw its veto power entrenched over many important domains of national policy. Starting in 1987, Turkey nevertheless experienced free and fair elections alongside persisting military constraints on civilian rule. In 2002, the Justice and Development Party (AKP) came to office, and initially pursued a reformist and liberalizing agenda consistent with the goal of eventual accession to the European Union. Starting in 2010 or 2011, commentators observed an increasing reliance on authoritarian practices by the AKP and reduced democratic space for its opponents. This included increasing restrictions on liberal rights of speech on the part of the media and on rights of association on the part of political opponents of the AKP or the Turkish state. Critics were targeted for arrest or harassment. The bureaucratic rule of law—another leg of democracy's institutional tripod—has since 2014 come under strain, with accumulating evidence of electoral abuses and manipulation.[64] The AKP's authoritarian shift reached new heights in 2016–17. Following an attempted coup, the Erdoğan government deepened its purge of both the state and civil society. Homes were raided. Blacklists of suspected traitors circulated. To lose one's job or one's freedom, it was enough to bank with Bank Asya, which had been founded by the allegedly disloyal Gulenist movement, or to work at a Gulenist-affiliated hospital or university, or to have children attend a Gulenist-run school.[65] This erosion of Turkish democracy is especially important because, until just a few years ago, the country had provided a powerful counterpoint to the repressive and authoritarian regimes that have long characterized most of the Arab Middle East. In that region, autocratic regimes have beaten back democracy and retained the "president for life" model.[66]

The vector of democratic quality in India has changed in a different, more subtle way. Although it has held generally free and fair elections since independence in 1947, India cannot claim to have been persistently democratic, either across space or time. Only some Indian states have been able to supply the rule of law and liberal rights necessary for effective democracy.[67] Furthermore, national-level democracy has suffered tragic lapses. The 1950 Constitution gave the prime minister broad decree authority "for the purpose of removing any difficulties." When, in 1975, Prime Minister Indira Gandhi faced a serious judicial challenge to the bona fides of her election, she declared a state of emergency. In the following two years of emergency rule, 110,000 people were detained, generally without the ability to challenge the detention's legality in court.[68] Although Indian democracy recovered from emergency rule, its imposition remains good evidence of that democracy's fragility.

The most recent retreat from democratic norms is not as stark as Mrs. Gandhi's recession. It arises against the context of high electoral participation rates and sharp contestation, particularly in subnational elections, that make India more democratic now than it was in 1947.[69] The downswing is associated with the rise of the political foe of Gandhi's Congress Party, the Bharatiya Janata Party (BJP), which has held the prime minister's office since 2014. Under the BJP, press freedoms have narrowed as a result of censorship, attacks on journalists, and prosecutions of sedition.[70] Of equal import, the core of BJP support is supplied by a family of "extremist cultural and social organizations" that are seen by many as having an "anti-system" orientation, in that they deny the legitimacy of secular and Muslim claims to participation within the Indian polity. This electoral base has caused some commentators to worry that the BJP may be "running with the hares and hunting with the hounds, inclined to go along with electoral democracy as long as it brings votes and power."[71] This concern was stoked by Prime Minister Narenda Modi's early decision (since reversed) to mandate the use of Hindi for all official documents—a bold and exclusionary move in multilingual India—and his seeming tolerance of communal violence related to Hindu opposition to the cultivation and slaughter of cows. These concerns were amplified by a June 2017 decision to target for police scrutiny India's main investigative news entity, in what is understood in India to be retaliation for adverse coverage of Modi.[72] If India does not present the full array of democratic backsliding manifested by Turkey, there are nonetheless enough worrying parallels between the early moves of the AKP and the current approach of the BJP to provoke concern that Modi is following the path taken by Erdoğan.

A marked decline in the quality of Indian democracy, like recent events in Turkey, would likely have a large demonstration effect beyond its borders. India's immediate neighbors, Pakistan, Bangladesh, Nepal, and Sri Lanka, have all struggled to either install or maintain liberal constitutional democracy, with varying degrees of success. To the extent that advocates for democracy in those countries draw inspiration from India, an abrupt shift in the regional giant would erode the strength of these neighboring democracies.

The Philippines, too, was an early leader in a part of the world known for limited democracy. Elections were held regularly from independence in 1946 through to Ferdinand Marcos's declaration of martial law in 1972. Though he was elected, Marcos presided over a period of repression characterized by electoral fraud, corruption, and political violence, including the murder of his political opponent, Benigno Aquino Jr., in 1983. In 1986, however, the People Power Revolution swept Marcos from office and led to the restoration of democracy under the leadership of Aquino's wife, Corazon. Since then, democratic institutions have held in the country, despite numerous failed coup attempts, an impeachment crisis that required the armed forces to withdraw their support from President Joseph Estrada in 2001, and a failed proposal by President Gloria Macapagal Arroyo to extend her term in office. In short, democracy in the Philippines has held on despite difficult circumstances.

Yet all is not well. The recent challenge comes not from threats of military rule but from a populist president, Rodrigo Duterte, who has endorsed and allegedly participated in extrajudicial killings. The number of extrajudicial deaths that have occurred under Duterte as of mid-2017 already exceeds by a good margin the number killed during the entire period of military rule in Chile. The extension of the practice from reputed drug dealers to political enemies may have already begun. In 2017, the president issued veiled threats to stop enforcing judicial orders and overt threats to abolish the human rights commission.[73] He jailed a political opponent, Senator Leila de Lima, on drug charges. In late 2017, the country continued to be plagued by election violence and the killing of journalists, for whom it has been declared to be one of the deadliest countries in the world. A 2009 massacre in Mindanao that has been called the single deadliest event for journalists in history remains uninvestigated; courts have done little to apportion guilt or prevent new killings.[74]

During the Cold War, the Philippines was held out as one of the few electoral democracies in Asia, and its 1986 revolution was a central event in the Third Wave. Yet the quality of its democracy has now been surpassed by neighbors such as South Korea and Taiwan. While constitutional institutions have resisted frontal challenges in the form of coups and incumbent takeovers by elected leaders, the stagnation and decline of Philippine democracy is apparent.

ATTITUDES TOWARD DEMOCRACY

Data concerning national-level trends is not the only potentially relevant evidence of a democratic decline. One of the editors of the *Journal of Democracy*, Marc Plattner, recently flagged "democracy's dwindling prestige."[75] Others have observed that democracy has lost some of its luster among the publics of nondemocratic regimes because of the challenges to American and European democracies flowing from the 2008 financial crisis and recession, as well as perceived political dysfunction and gridlock in the United States.[76] We think the faltering of faith in democracy as a worthwhile system of government is relevant in that public support is necessary for democracy's three institutional foundations.[77]

Survey evidence from around the globe concerning attitudes to democracy—in particular, data from Europe and the United States—supports the view that democracy is under corroding pressure. Even citizens of consolidated democracies, such as the United States and the European Union states, are becoming more cynical about democracy's virtues, more skeptical that they are meaningfully able to participate in and influence national politics, and more open to authoritarian forms of government. Perhaps the best global data derives from the World Values Survey (WVS), a consortium of social scientists in one hundred countries that has conducted rigorous, population-wide opinion surveys since 1981.

Let's start with the United States. Over the past three decades, the proportion of US citizens who believe it would be a "good" or a "very good" thing for the "army to rule" has soared from one in sixteen to one in six. Among the cohort of rich young Americans, moreover, the proportion of those who look favorably on military rule is more than one in four. The WVS instrument also asks about a strong leader who does not bother with elections. In the 2011 survey, 35% of Americans thought this was a very good or fairly good idea (and nearly half of Americans also think that it would be fairly good or very good for technocrats to make decisions). This contrasts with the 1995–1997 wave, when just over one-fifth of Americans approved of a strong leader. The same pattern of increasing tolerance of, and even approval of, autocratic forms of government can be identified in the same period in countries ranging from Taiwan, South Korea, and South Africa to Russia, Turkey, and the Ukraine.

The WVS data suggests a difference between age cohorts. In the 2011 survey, almost four-fifths of Americans thought democratic governance was fairly good or very good for the country. That figure drops to 72%, however, for those under thirty. In addition, Americans are less intense in their attachment to democracy in the abstract than citizens of other countries: only 37.8% (26.8% for those aged thirty and under) rated democratic governance as "very good." This was a drop from findings of 43.2% in 2006 and 50.5% in 1999. By way of comparison, the comparable figure in Germany was 64.8%. In response to the question of how important it is to live in a democratic country, 46.5% of Americans now assert that it is "absolutely" so—but that number drops to 29.2% for those under thirty. Finally, Americans' belief in the legitimacy of democratic outputs, measured in terms of both satisfaction and perceptions of corruption, have eroded dramatically over the past decade.

Not all scholars are convinced that these data points provide cause for concern. Pippa Norris finds the decay in democratic affinities to be limited to a class of Anglophonic countries, but absent in Spain, Norway, the Netherlands, Chile, Germany, Hungary, and France. She further observes that the cohort effect identified in the 2010-2014 WVS survey data also appears in the 1991 and 1995 data. The young, that is, have consistently become more skeptical (or perhaps more demanding) of democracy. In a similar vein, Eric Voeten finds no evidence that democracy is declining in popularity in comparison to autocratic or hybrid regimes. Both Norris and Voeten also exploit voting and survey data from the United States beyond the WVS to suggest that, in practice, older rather than younger citizens are more cynical about democratic institutions, as an "age-cycle" theory of democratic attitudes might suggest.[78]

The evidence of diminishing psychological affinity for democracy, in sum, must be understood in context. Such evidence may be more important in countries like Turkey (where the threat to democracy emerges from elected incumbents) than in countries like Egypt (where the threat materializes from nonelected actors, such as the military). It is hence not a measure of the whole bundle of current pressures on democratic practice. Perhaps the best way to summarize the evidence is to say that, in certain national contexts, the stability of the democratic system rests on an increasingly fragile basis of popular support. Depending on the measure of democracy one uses, this fragility can seem minor or severe.

IS DEMOCRATIC DECLINE NEW?

Having assembled this evidence, we think another approach to the evidence is worth considering, one that expands the time-frame of analysis: How did democracy fare over the whole of the twentieth century? Is democratic decline new, or have we always been living in the democratic end days?

Worries about democracy are hardly new; they seem cyclical. Indeed, the twentieth century was characterized by a series of pendulum swings from exuberant optimism to melancholy skepticism about democracy's prospects. At different times, the might of Kaiser Wilhelm's army in Germany, the economic success of Joseph Stalin's five-year plan set against the Great Depression's catastrophes, and the seemingly unstoppable economic rise of East Asian "tigers" have provoked waves of doubt about democracy.[79] At other times, such as at the end of the Cold War, democracy has been described as having triumphed over all other alternatives.

Some have argued that these cycles in public confidence are hard-wired. After successfully adapting to new challenges, democratic publics develop confidence in their long-term resilience.[80] But this confidence induces complacency, allowing problems to fester. When those problems eventually come to a crisis, the democratic polity usually does adapt, but only just enough to survive. Confidence returns, and the cycle starts anew. Perhaps not by coincidence, the same cycle of despair and exuberance is said to afflict advocates of liberalism.[81] Democracy and liberalism alike enable human self-realization. They allow us to pursue our noblest aspirations and also indulge our most embarrassing and wretched vices. The absence of each can be sorely felt, and their presence decried precisely because of the embarrassments that liberty entails. Under liberalism and democracy alike, that is, we have no one to blame but ourselves and nothing to distract from the ugly pageantry of human choice freely exercised. Little wonder that both should be characterized by fitful optimism punctuated by stark pessimism.

But of course, anti-liberals are not immune from failure. The Kaiser conceded defeat. Stalin's agricultural collectivization proved a bust from Ukraine to the Urals. East Asian capitalism has not proved an enduring model in either declining Japan or the *chaebol* economy of South Korea; nor has it proved an exportable economic model. Democratic capitalism has not collapsed under the weight of its own contradictions; despite repeated obituaries, its grave-digger has yet to be christened. Even the financial crisis of 2008 did not im-mediately send us into a global depression, provoke a new world war, or lead to the breakup of the international order. This suggests that citizens are not well positioned to judge whether their democracies are in crisis and that they are prone to misdiagnose whatever they perceive to be bad public policy as a systemic threat to democratic stability. In short, the system of liberal constitu-tional democracy often gets blamed for particular policy outcomes rather than its systemic deficits, even as people ignore its remarkable ability to maintain a roughly tolerable modus vivendi among citizens of widely different opinions.

At the same time, the historical record contains at least one other instance in which democratic hopes were high, only to be dashed by a global catas-trophe. In the wake of World War I, seventeen new democracies were estab-lished around the world, leading British historian James Bryce to conclude that democracy was "a natural trend, due to a general law of social progress." By 1933, however, democracy was receding around the world, with Estonia, Latvia, Lithuania, Italy, Portugal, Poland, Brazil, Argentina, Uruguay, Japan, and Germany all moving from democracy of a sort to one of the various forms of authoritarianism.[82] This first democratic recession only deepened in the 1930s. The democratic Spanish Republic lasted just a few years before Gen-eral Franco came to power in 1939, crushed opposition on both the left and right, and installed an authoritarian regime that lasted until the mid-1970s.[83]

The swift rise and fall of democracies in the 1920s and 1930s cannot be understood outside the macroeconomic context of the day. Japan provides a snapshot of how a strong global economy could enable democracy at one mo-ment, while global turbulence could sink it the next. Democracy in Taishō-era Japan emerged after World War I, and by 1926, all adult males were able to vote, and parliamentary parties formed governing coalitions through 1932. But in the wake of the Great Depression and the Japanese military's 1931 deci-sion to invade Manchuria, a series of governments dominated by military lead-ers took control in 1932, leading ultimately to the overtly totalitarian "New Order" regime of the war years.[84] Another example is Germany, whose ini-tial postwar democratic success is often forgotten. In January 1919, 83% of Germany's electorate cast their votes for a Constituent Assembly. This body would go on to draft a constitution that embodied both liberal freedoms and a broad commitment to social democracy. Some 28.5 million men and women voted for the first Reichstag in June 1920. Democracy would last little over a decade, however, because of the severe economic strains created by the

Depression, the ongoing burden of war-related reparations, and, finally, the centrifugal forces of violent challenges from both the extreme right and left to the 1919 constitutional order.[85]

But despite its pockets of success, the more general failure of post–World War I democratization, coupled with the collapse of the overarching liberal project of international reordering under the League of Nations, rapidly led to the horrors of the World War II. Some of the gravest moral catastrophes of the twentieth century, then, are to be found coursing dark and bloody from the ruins of failed democracy. Surveying their legacy, any worry about crying "wolf" itself seems overblown.

*

Our mapping of the democratic recession around the world raises difficult questions of causation: Why has the democratic recession happened, and why has it happened now? To paraphrase Zhou Enlai's apocryphal quip about the French Revolution, it may be too soon to tell.[86] The necessary evidence for discerning answers will manifest only slowly. And the democratic recession of the early twenty-first century takes many forms in widely disparate economic, social, and political circumstances. It is far too early to say with confidence that there is any one cause. Indeed, it would be quite striking if the same underlying force explained the collapse of the Muslim Brotherhood in Egypt in 2013, the rise of elected officials with authoritarian tendencies in Turkey in 2002, the intervention of the Thai military to end elections in 2014, and the general shift in European vote share toward parties or candidates with a loose or even adversarial relationship to democracy in 2016–17. While we will from time to time weigh in on debates about the deep, structural causes of democratic decline, our focus throughout this book is not on "root" causes but on the more mundane, more tractable, questions of how institutions and laws designed to support democracy can work quite differently as the facilitators of democratic decline and even demise.

2

Two Pathways from Liberal Constitutional Democracy

Everyone at one time was a Social Democrat.

ADOLPH HITLER

Sometimes, the day and the hour on which democracy dies can be marked with precision. It was around 9:00 p.m. on the subzero evening of February 27, 1933, when a Berlin fire station received word of a fire in the main hall of the German parliament building, the Reichstag. The new chancellor of the Republic, Adolph Hitler, arrived at the Reichstag building around 10:20 p.m. with his vice chancellor, Franz von Papen, and his Nazi Party colleagues Hermann Göring and Joseph Goebbels. It is said that Göring immediately declared the fire the work of a Communist conspiracy, while Hitler turned to Von Papen and exclaimed, "This is a God-given signal, Herr Vice-Chancellor! If this fire, as I believe, is the work of Communists, then we must crush out these pests with a murderous fist."[1]

As he spoke, the Reichstag police had already found and arrested a young Dutch construction worker, Marinus van der Lubbe, as he rushed through other parts of the Reichstag trying to set yet more fires. Rudolf Diels, the head of the Prussian political police and one of the non-Nazi officials at the scene, later recalled arriving that evening to find van der Lubbe "naked, sweating, and smeared with dirt" but with a "wild look of triumph" on his "pale, emaciated young face." Diels interrogated van der Lubbe, and examined the Communist pamphlets stuffed into his pockets, which were "of the kind that were publically distributed," and concluded that the "little fire-raiser" needed no helpers and had indeed acted alone. But when Diels told Hitler, the chancellor was incredulous. "It's a really ingenious, long-prepared thing," he told Diels, "These criminals have it all worked out nicely, but they've miscalculated, haven't they, my Party Comrades! These people don't suspect at all how much the people is on our side."[2]

With the Reichstag's ashes still smoldering, Göring instructed police to deploy lists of Communists that had been prepared months and years earlier, and to arrest and shoot those on the list. Diels and others ignored the second part of the order, but carried out the arrests. At the same time, Göring's advisor, Ludwig Grauert, drew up an emergency decree suspending several provisions of the Weimar Constitution, including the freedoms of speech, press, and association, the right to privacy of "postal, telegraphic and telephonic communications, and warrants for home arrests." Presenting what was to become the Reichstag Fire Decree to his cabinet, Hitler declared that "The psychologically correct moment for the confrontation has now arrived," claiming that the struggle against Communists "must not be made to depend on judicial considerations." The emergency decree was presented to President Paul von Hindenburg the next day. Hindenburg signed it. On March 3, 1933, in an election during which storm-troopers patrolled the streets, and campaigning on behalf of Social Democrats and Communists was effectively banned under the emergency decree, the Nazis won a bare majority (51.9%) of the German vote. The Reichstag Fire Decree itself was not repealed during Nazi rule.

On March 24, 1933, the new Reichstag passed by two-thirds vote a "Law to Relieve the Distress of the People and the Reich," also known as the Enabling Act, which empowered the Reich chancellor to rule for four years without president or parliament. Under the Enabling Act, all parties—including the Catholic Zentrum party that had provided the Nazis with crucial votes—were dissolved. On his own authority, Hitler was to renew the Enabling Act in 1937 and again in 1942. Free elections were not held again in Germany until 1949.[3]

The burning of the Reichstag marked a turning point in the collapse of interwar German democracy, even if the social and institutional seeds of that collapse had been festering for many years. Popular anger had already built over economic deprivation, war reparations, and the seeming dysfunction of repeated ruling coalitions formed under the Weimar Constitution. The Nazis had already gained 37% of the vote in the July 1932 elections,[4] and German civil society was already deeply polarized by 1933. The Nazi Party had exploited Weimar's "associational mania," by recruiting activists within existing organizations and leveraging them to expand the party's appeal.[5] And conservatives such as von Papen and Hindenburg had long beforehand decided that alliance with the Nazi Party was a wise tactic to keep Socialists and Communists from power.[6] The Reichstag fire nevertheless provided the springboard for the Nazi assumption of power. In so doing, it has provided a template for how emergency powers, allegedly to be deployed against violent terrorists, can be instead turned against the democratic state itself. The striking fact that van de Lubbe seemed to have acted alone, moreover, demonstrates the irrelevance of the actual organized terrorist threat to the Nazis' seizure of power. Sincerely or not, Hitler and his cabinet acted as if the specific facts of the Reichstag fire were less relevant than their own underlying belief in the need for a violent cleansing of the political sphere.

But there are times when the dating of democracy's demise presents a greater challenge. Consider now the fates of Senators Hiram Revels and Blanche Bruce of Mississippi, and Representatives Robert Delarge of South Carolina and Jefferson Long of Georgia. These men were among the sixteen African-Americans elected to the forty-first and forty-second US Congresses during the 1870s in the aftermath of the Civil War and the Reconstruction Amendments to the US Constitution.[7] All were elected because of the large number of votes African-Americans could cast in the American South as a result of the Fifteenth Amendment, which had been ratified in 1870. This declared that the "right of citizens of the United States to vote shall not be denied or abridged by the United States or by any state on account of race, color, or previous condition of servitude." Of course, Southern whites did not accept this development without resistance. Having lost the ability to keep African-Americans from the ballot box, Democrats in the Senate challenged Revels's right to be seated. They argued that he had not been a citizen for the requisite number of years, relying on the Supreme Court's prewar decision in *Dred Scott v. Sandford* that African-Americans were not citizens. Yet after a vigorous debate, Revels was seated.[8] A new African-American presence in American politics seemed assured both as a theoretical matter of constitutional law, and as a practical matter.

Yet it was not to be. The ability of African-Americans to participate in American politics in 1870, and to elect Revels, Bruce, and others, was not to last, even if it did not end overnight. A key moment was the 1876 presidential election between Democrat Samuel Tilden and Republican Rutherford B. Hayes. The campaign in the lead-up to that vote was marred by racial violence, including a July 4 massacre in Hamburg, South Carolina. After ballots were cast, election boards in Florida, South Carolina, and Louisiana invalidated enough results to give Hayes victory, provoking a Democratic challenge to the certified election results and a prolonged period of electoral and constitutional uncertainty. In the complex bargaining process that ensued, Hayes emerged victorious—but at the cost of abandoning the policy of Southern Reconstruction that the Republicans had pursued since the Civil War. As *The Nation* explained presciently, "The negro will disappear from the field of national politics."[9]

The end of nineteenth-century democracy for African-Americans did not come abruptly. In the deep South, the policy of "home rule" was enforced through an accumulating wave of electoral fraud and the threat of violence in the immediate wake of 1875, and the Republican Party's regional presence had crumbled by 1877. Elsewhere, racial disenfranchisement worked through the slow processes of party realignment and step-by-step legal transformation. In the face of a surging new political force called the Populist Party, Democrats successfully deployed racist themes as a "strategy for the reconciliation of alienated white men" through "a closing of the white man's ranks." It worked. By 1900, southern Populists had largely accepted that their aims could be achieved only by giving up alliances with black voters.[10]

At the same time, across the upper South, some African-Americans continued to vote, and even to hold office in city councils and some county seats through the 1880s and into the 1890s. On the one hand, their ability to provide constituent services waned as Democratic-controlled state governments took increasingly hard lines. On the other, a range of both formal and informal measures kept African-Americans from casting ballots. In some places, complex registration requirements gave local registrars vast discretion, which they used to keep black voters disenfranchised. Residency requirements, felon-disenfranchisement rules, de facto and de jure literacy tests—all these were ways to keep the vote white. Grandfather clauses allowed registrars to exempt voters whose ancestors had cast votes before 1867, a test that by definition excluded African-Americans. Poll taxes fell disproportionately on African-Americans. A system of "white primaries" allowed the only election that counted, the Democratic primary, to be run by and for whites alone. In 1873, there were sixty-four blacks in the Mississippi legislature; in 1895, there were none. South Carolina had had a black majority in its lower house in the 1870s; by 1896, only a single black representative remained. By 1900, every southern state except for North Carolina had enacted a direct restriction on the franchise with the purpose and effect of disenfranchising African-Americans. It would be sixty-five years before the Voting Rights Act would start to dislodge those barriers, and another seven years before a black representative was sent to Congress from the South.[11] In the interim, the South of the United States operated in a fashion that was functionally indistinguishable from a one-party authoritarian state, with not only law but also extralegal violence, such as lynchings, enforcing a strict cultural and political hegemony.[12]

*

We start with these two stories of democracy's demise because they illustrate two speeds—fast and slow—at which laws, constitutions, and institutions can be repositioned or decommissioned in order to downgrade democracy. On the one hand, the German example shows how democracy can end in a single, identifiable moment, as state institutions are abruptly redeployed from broad, democratic aims to the narrow, antidemocratic end of undermining the rule of law, electoral competition, and the possibility of liberal rights. On the other hand, the gradual changes to laws, institutions, and practices observed at the end of the nineteenth century in the American South were occasionally direct but more often indirect articulations of racism that diffused through politics, law, and a set of extralegal political practices that included outright violence.

Since the first decades of the twentieth century, in short, it has been clear that the *speed* of democratic decline can vary quite dramatically. Yet this point is often forgotten, and its consequences not elaborated. This chapter flags the speed of democratic decline as a centrally important variable. The threats to liberal constitutional democracies in the twenty-first century can be sorted into two distinct types—each with its own mechanisms and pathways—depending on their speed. We call these types *authoritarian collapse* (i.e., the risk of a rapid, wholesale turn away from democracy) and *democratic erosion* (i.e., the risk of slow, but ultimately substantial unraveling along the margins of rule-of-law, democratic, and liberal rights). These are obviously "ideal types," with the actual observed examples of democratic breakdown sometimes exhibiting traits from both kinds of democratic failure.

Speed matters because, as we move from fast to slow, the kinds of *legal and institutional tools* used to unroll democracy seem to change. Whereas emergency powers and military coups are important to fast democratic breakdowns, a different and rather more complicated set of levers turns out to be critical when the democratic decline is slow. The two processes also usually have different endpoints. Typically, a fast collapse will yield a clearly authoritarian form of government. In contrast, a slow erosion is far more likely to end up with some kind of competitive authoritarian structure with more than merely skin-deep accoutrements of democracy. Subsequent chapters will explore these different toolkits in detail. But to understand when and how different tools can be deployed, it is useful to start by having in hand the simple taxonomy of the fast authoritarian collapse and the slow democratic erosion.

The Fast Road: Authoritarian Collapse

The collapse of Weimar Germany in the space of a month and its supersession by a regime that was not only authoritarian, but also fascist in character, demonstrates that a democracy can collapse *completely and rapidly*. It is certainly true that such a collapse, as in the German case, will have long-term causes. As in Weimar, the antecedent constitutional system may already show strains or lack popular legitimacy. Likely, a constellation of already powerful elites—the Hindenburgs and von Papens of the German story—are already maneuvering to protect their own agendas. Indeed, in a powerful recent history, Benjamin Carter Hett has argued that Marinus van der Lubbe could not have been responsible for setting the fire, and that the Nazi machinery itself set in motion the terrorist incident that allowed it to consolidate its power.[13]

Nevertheless, as in Weimar Germany, the critical changes in laws, institutions, or constitutional foundations in such cases tend to occur very rapidly. The Reichstag Fire Decree "put an abrupt end to constitutional rights and the rule of law in Germany."[14] The event used to justify that extraordinary action is plainly a turning point of great importance to understanding the legal and institutional mechanisms by which democracy is sapped. This change to the democratic order need not be formal and legalistic in character. Indeed, it is worth emphasizing once more that in the German case, the Weimar Constitution was never abrogated; instead, Hitler exercised emergency powers pursuant to the Enabling Act through to the end of the war. Still, to insist on the formal continuity in legal texts is surely to miss the point. Even if the Weimar Constitution was "'good law'" in some sense in March 1933, there is no question that the de facto constitutional system in operation in Germany had abruptly changed. The end product of that rapid shock in Germany was a government that was thoroughly and violently authoritarian, and ultimately committed to morally abhorrent policies.[15]

We call this phenomenon "authoritarian collapse." It is a collapse, in some respects, to a historical norm. For democracy, as a historical matter, is the exception rather than the rule. Apart from a "very local Greek" phenomenon some 2,500 years ago, democracy in some shape or form had "faded away almost everywhere" until roughly the end of the nineteenth century.[16] Moreover, that very local Greek form of government was radically different in scale and operation from most twentieth-century democracies (although it is hard not to be struck by the parallel exclusions of women and other classes from both ancient Greek and pre-twentieth-century democratic polities). The use of lotteries to fill public office, the extent of public involvement in both the assembly and the council, and the complex use of juries in fourth-century BCE Athens all distinguish democracy's initial manifestation as quite different in form and effect from modern iterations.[17] Apart from this peculiar interlude, however, the dominant form of government in both the West and the rest of the world for the past 2,500 years has been some variant on the absolute state.[18] In anything but the most myopic perspectives, that is, democracy is a deviant bloom, not the norm.

Although the 1980s and the 1990s are most often characterized as a heyday of democracy, they were not without their authoritarian regressions. Indeed, the two main mechanisms of autocratic regression—the military coup, and takeover by a political incumbent—were already visible at this time. We have noted the Indian Emergency of 1975, which suspended democratic rule in India until the 1977 elections. Some form of elective authoritarianism might well have persisted under Indira Gandhi's Congress Party after 1977, had not the Janata Party unexpectedly seized victory at the ballot box. Prior to the elections, indeed, it had been imagined that the vote would legitimate the use of emergency powers and entrench Congress Party rule, much as the German elections of March 1933 had done.[19]

In 1980, the Turkish Armed Forces under General Kenan Evren executed a military coup in the context of coalitional instability, street violence, daily political assassinations, and economic turmoil. Evren dissolved the parliament, arrested trade union and party leaders, and began a period of direct military rule that lasted three years. Some analysts view Evren's decision as a sincere articulation of the military's belief in its historical role as the guardian of the republican order established by Atatürk.[20] Noble sentiments, however, did not translate into a quick shift back to civilian rule, despite the decline in political violence after the coup. Rather, a new constitution was adopted in 1982—one still in force today, albeit with extensive amendments—that eliminated the Senate, thinned the lower house, and expanded presidential authority. Its Provisional Articles announced that Evren would be president for seven years, ruling with a non-elected National Security Council. In 1983, new statutory frameworks for political parties and elections were promulgated, expanding bureaucratic control over party recognition and democratic contestation.[21]

Finally, Peru in April 1992 suffered an autocratic collapse when the populist president Alberto Fujimori executed a presidential coup (*autogolpe*) in which he closed the Congress, suspended the constitution, and fired much of the judiciary. With a handful of cabinet officials, he declared a new "emergency government of national reconstruction." Troops arrested much of Peru's fragmented opposition leadership and held government buildings. As in the German case, these actions had broad public support, in part because of Fujimori's success in demonizing established elites and political opposition, in part because of popular anger at "neoliberal" economic reforms, and in part because of the ongoing violent insurgency led by the Shining Path. He was thus able the following year to secure a new constitution via referendum, and then two years later to win a presidential election.

Despite the adoption of these formal trappings of democracy, Fujimori, with the aid of his intelligence advisor Vladimir Montesinos, exercised an unprecedented level of power through the systemic corruption and suborning of state institutions and a mix of bribery and blackmail. Fujimori's regime collapsed only in 2000, when a videotape documenting Montesinos's corrupt actions was leaked to the press.[22]

In all of these cases, an authoritarian collapse was followed by a sustained period of autocratic rule. But autocracy need not be permanent: India, Turkey, and Peru all reverted to civilian rule after a time. Another example of a (slow) return to democracy occurred under Chile's junta, which operated in an environment in which legalism was powerful. In 1988, General Pinochet held and lost a referendum that would have extended his rule for eight years, allowing a gradual return to democracy.[23]

While it would be easy to assume that a military coup or the declaration of a state of emergency necessarily leads to democracy's permanent suspension, matters are not quite so simple for two distinct reasons. First, as we have explained, the modal authoritarian today does not wholly dispense with the accoutrements of democratic rule, such as notional opposition parties and elections. Elections, parties, and parliaments can be useful to authoritarian rulers. They may try to use elections as showcases of their prestige and popularity—think of the Kazakh President Nursultan Nazarbayev's 2015 victory by a margin of "97.5%." Elections can also operate as a mechanism for splitting and bribing the opposition, thus heading off challengers. Or else they can be mechanisms of credible self-constraint intended to encourage private, revenue-generating economic activity without a fear of state appropriation. Elections can also provide autocrats with useful information about what policies the public is concerned with and about which politicians have talent. But elections also pose the risk of dramatically changing the perception of an autocrat's vulnerability. This in turn can set off an unraveling crisis of confidence, not only among the autocrat's supporters in the police and military, but also among the general public. For example, during the 1990s, Serbian President Slobodan Milošević maintained a system of competitive authoritarianism. This system, however, foundered in 2000 when the aptly named Democratic Opposition of Serbia showed surprising success at the ballot box.[24] A year later, Milošević was arrested for corruption and ultimately extradited to stand trial in the Hague for war crimes.

Second, as Ozan Varol has argued, there are instances in which a coup d'etat can have a "democratic" character inasmuch as the military's intervention is intended and in fact does lead proximately to a period of democratic rule.[25] Varol cites the 1960 military coup in Turkey, the 1974 Portuguese coup, and the Egyptian coup of 2011. But the Egyptian military's support for democracy as a system has proven rather fragile.[26] And we think the 1960 Turkish case is more ambiguous than Varol makes it seem. The Demokrat Party ousted by the coup may have used legally dubious means, but it still represented a "group of middle-class entrepreneurs and businessmen" who resented the power of secular bureaucratic and military elites, much as the AKP represents a distinct social formation today.[27] It may, therefore, be more accurate to view Portugal's Carnation Revolution of 1974, which overthrew the "New State" regime, as a highly unusual species of military intervention—one that had the intent and effect of promoting, rather than retarding, democracy.

The Slow Road: Democratic Erosion

A liberal constitutional democracy can also degrade incrementally without collapsing. Although not fully appreciated today, this is the tale of the South from roughly the 1880s to the late 1960s, discussed earlier in this chapter. We selected a subnational case to illustrate the possibility of slow decay without full collapse because it is familiar, as well as being too quickly sidelined in more celebratory discussions of American democracy in long historical perspective. But this kind of slow decay is remarkably common at the national level too. Indeed, it is the most common species of democratic recession in the contemporary context. Hence, it merits close attention so that we understand the institutional and legal pathways by which it occurs.

DEFINING EROSION

We label the slow form of democratic decay a *democratic erosion*. Because this concept is less familiar than the absolute collapse to autocracy, it is useful to begin by offering a formal definition. We define such erosion as *a process of incremental, but ultimately still substantial, decay in the three basic predicates of democracy—competitive elections, liberal rights to speech and association, and the rule of law.* It captures changes to the quality of a democracy that are, on their own, incremental in character and perhaps innocuous; that happen roughly in lockstep or as part of a common program; and that involve some deterioration of our trio of necessary institutional characteristics—the quality of elections, speech and association rights, and the rule of law. Importantly, erosion occurs only when a substantial negative change occurs along *all three margins* of liberal constitutional democracy. This is because it is only when substantial change occurs across all three necessary institutional predicates of democracy that the system-level quality is likely to be imperiled.

Erosion is a more complex and nuanced phenomenon than collapse, and it is helpful to offer a number of immediate clarifications up front. These are worthwhile in part because, for reasons we explore further in subsequent chapters, democratic erosion is now the more common form of decline.

First, it is no accident that we characterize one of the two important forms of democratic failure in terms of the three institutional elements of our initial definition of democracy: The decline of democracy should be understood in terms of its constitutive elements. This does not mean, however, that substantial decay can never occur in (say) the rule of law and electoral competition without liberal rights to speech and association being affected. Nevertheless, we think this is unlikely to happen. Because the three institutional predicates of democracy described in chapter 1 are closely intertwined in practice, we think it will be the rare case in which two of the three decline together, even as the third is left unaffected. In part because there will inevitably be close cases, moreover, we do not define democratic erosion in terms of its endstate. Such a definition would have the added disadvantage of being impossible to apply because it would never be possible to say for certain that a polity was in its "end-state."

Second, erosion requires the identification of a moment in time in which there was a democracy that could deteriorate. The case of the post-Reconstruction American South discussed above thus counts because there was a period in the 1870s and 1880s in which effective electoral competition, including competition for the votes of African-Americans, occurred. But things get trickier if there is disagreement on whether democracy existed in the first instance. Some commentators, for example, have argued that the Russian political system that emerged from the collapse of the Soviet Union was always "incapable" of acting as a "conduit for autonomous popular interests."[28] If that characterization is correct, Russia is not a case of erosion, because its baseline status quo in the 1990s cannot be ranked as democratic.[29] We recognize that Russia may be a marginal case of "erosion"; nevertheless, the Russian context provides so rich a catalogue of erosion's forms and instrumentalities that it is hard to ignore entirely if we are interested in how democracy declines.

Third, erosion does not *typically* result in full-blown authoritarianism. Instead, its outcome is some form of competitive authoritarianism, in which elections of a sort occur, where liberal rights to speech and association are not wholly stifled, and where there is some semblance of the rule of law. As we noted in chapter 1, it will often be difficult to discern the boundaries between democracy *simpliciter* and competitive authoritarianism, just as it can be difficult to separate the latter from polities that are simply authoritarian. Even purely authoritarian regimes sometimes engage in the hypocritical semblance of competitive elections for reasons we have already flagged.[30] Where that practice collapses into pure charade—and thus moves from competitive to simple authoritarianism—is surely a matter of judgment.

Fourth, an important quality of democratic erosion, one that might pro-voke objections, should start to come into focus: Because erosion occurs piecemeal, it necessarily involves many incremental changes to legal regimes and institutions. Each of these changes may be innocuous or defensible in isolation. It is only by their cumulative effect that erosion occurs. A sufficient *quantity* of even incremental derogations from the democratic baseline, in our view, can precipitate a *qualitative* change that merits a shift in classifica-tion.[31] Hence, evaluations of erosion demand a system-wide perspective. For just as democracy, liberalism, and the constitutional rule of law are properties of political systems as a whole, so too their degradation cannot be captured except from a systemic perspective. As a result, there will be cases where dis-putes arise as to whether a sufficient aggregate amount of backsliding has occurred, or whether a particular institutional change even counts. The exis-tence of contentious borderline cases as a result of necessary vagueness, how-ever, does not undermine the utility of the concept. Many vague concepts turn out to be perfectly serviceable in ordinary language. (Do you count hairs on a person's head before declaring him bald? Or tally grains of salt before finding that there is a heap on the table?). So long as a concept's vagueness in application is recognized, we see no reason to reject the concept.[32]

IDENTIFYING EROSION

Democratic erosion can be observed in its starkest form in the Latin Ameri-can context. Venezuela, for example, was beset in the 1990s by an economic crisis due to the decades-long decline in its oil industry, coupled with a col-lapse in its party system. Between 1994 and 1999, President Rafael Caldera confronted these pressures by fashioning a parliamentary pact with the op-position Democratic Action Party, and by resisting calls to follow the Peru-vian example of the self-coup, or *autogolpe*, as it has come to be known. His successor, Hugo Chávez, however, ran on a populist platform of opposition to corrupt and collusive elites, and a vow to sweep established parties "from the face of the earth."[33] Lacking a legislative majority, Chávez successfully called for a referendum on a new constituent assembly, in which his allies won an overwhelming majority. That assembly closed the Congress, purged the ju-diciary, and appointed new election authorities. The new constitution elimi-nated the Senate, banned public funding for political parties, and boosted the power of the president.

The ensuing national legislature then passed a steady stream of laws that chipped away at the three institutional predicates of democratic practice. In 2000, for example, the Organic Law of Telecommunications allowed the government to suspend or revoke broadcast concessions if "the interests of the nation, or if public order and security demand it." A 2005 law expanded the criminal prohibition on *desacato*, or "insult," making it illegal to be "disrespectful of government officials." And in 2010, the Law for the Defense of Political Sovereignty and National Self-Determination prohibited nongovernmental organizations that "defend political rights" or "monitor the performance of public bodies" in Venezuela from receiving public funds. In the course of this steady and corrosive drip of restrictive laws, elections continued to be held. Chávez's opponents boycotted the 2005 legislative elections; he handily won a 2006 presidential election and then took off the gloves. Several opposition leaders were prosecuted or forced into exile. Journalists critical of Chávez were hit with defamation charges, and Radio Caracas Television, a major television station, was forced off the air. In 2006 and again in 2010, the government fired hundreds of judges in lower courts, and left a threat of removal and criminal prosecution hanging over those who remained.

After Chávez died in 2013, his successor, Nicholas Maduro, continued to sap liberal constitutional democracy using a wide range of tactics. Independent media channels came under greater regulatory attention, while the government established an increasing array of public news sources, including new newspapers in Valencia, Maracay, Cojedes Guárica, and Petare. In the April 2014 election, which Maduro won by a bare 235,000 votes, the opposition alleged that the government harassed voters, paid citizens to bring people to the polls, and committed outright fraud. In March 2017, the Maduro-aligned Supreme Court attempted to shut down the opposition-controlled National Legislature, in what appeared to be an effort to eliminate the last institutional foothold of opposition resistance. After that bid for absolute control failed, Maduro announced in May 2017 his intention of holding a new constituent assembly, which would have the power not only to draft a new organic document but also to dissolve public bodies and convene new elections. That summer, he engineered a popular vote that provided a legal basis for moving forward with this second assembly, a move that, in our view, essentially ended Venezuelan democracy.[34] When democratic support falters, leaders like Maduro seek to return to the power of a carefully curated "people," in this case to exercise constituent power. And when his own attorney general protested the end of checks and balances, Maduro had her bank accounts frozen and barred her from leaving the country, ending any plausible semblance of the rule of law.

The eastern European states of Poland and Hungary also provide examples of democratic erosion, to which we will return in greater detail in later chapters. It suffices here to observe that both have been characterized by the same piecemeal accretion of measures that impinge on free and fair elections, liberal rights of speech and association, or the administrative rule of law. At least to date, the process of erosion has not proceeded as far in either Poland or Hungary as in Venezuela, although the relevant political coalitions in those countries have been in power for shorter periods and so may yet get to the same level of democratic decay.

In addition to these clear cases of erosion, there are instances in which the extent of erosion in the institutional predicates of democracy is more difficult to classify. Debates will inevitably arise as to whether certain cases fall under our label, and judgment must be exercised as to whether the backward motion observed is sufficient to be worrisome.

Hybrid Cases

The distinction between collapses to autocracy and democratic erosion turns on the *speed* of legal and institutional change. We have thus contrasted the dramatic and quick transformation of the Weimar state in 1933 with the more protracted decay of democratic practice in the post-Redemption American South, as well as with the downward progress of Venezuela under Chávez and Maduro. We have further suggested that, as a general matter, quick collapses end in full-on autocracy, whereas slow erosion yields some species of competitive authoritarianism. But there is one nuance to that account that we must flag before turning to the specific institutional and legal mechanisms at work in democratic decline: Because erosion is a process of incremental downward change, there is no reason to think it must stop at any particular point. To the contrary, it is quite plausible that a process of erosion might continue until the point that a polity had passed into unmodified authoritarianism. We think it is still appropriate to call these cases of erosion, because the slow and incremental nature of the change means that a particular set of institutional and legal tools are likely to be observed. But the distinction in end-state is obviously significant.

Perhaps the most plausible examples of this phenomenon are Turkey and Venezuela. In chapter 1, we described the incremental process by which the Erdoğan government consolidated its legal authority, silencing dissenting voices in the media, bureaucracy, and political spheres. This process of erosion, however, markedly accelerated after an attempted coup in July 2016, which was followed by an "unprecedented" wave of arrests and ousters from public office.[35] The question in the wake of this coup is whether electoral competition, accompanied by open debate and fair administration, is even possible in Turkey. Some commentators perceive an "end" to democracy in

Turkey, whereas others offer more nuanced assessments, which underscore the continuing popularity of President Erdoğan and the AKP party.[36] We suspect that this question will only be resolved if and when the AKP faces a serious electoral threat, which would happen if it sustained a grave loss of popular support. Only under those circumstances could we see whether the AKP party was willing to move from competitive authoritarianism to unmodified authoritarianism.

In this chapter, we have similarly framed Venezuela under Hugo Chávez as a paradigmatic case of democratic erosion. But many have perceived his successor Nicholas Maduro's effort to elicit a new constitution as a "lurch to dictatorship." This process was perfected with the 2017 Constituent Assembly, which essentially eliminated the opposition-held National Assembly in the context of ongoing violent protests against the government. There does not appear to be any prospect that Maduro would ever be willing to allow the democratic rotation of power, though one might imagine someone within his coalition replacing him (and whether this would entail a return to democracy is far from clear).[37] As with Turkey, the classification of Venezuela as either a competitive authoritarian or a properly authoritarian regime might depend on the precise month in which the question is being asked, and the time frame of interest to the questioner. Nevertheless, we have no doubt that the nearly two-decade process of institutional and legal change that led the nation to its present state is properly called erosion, leading in incremental steps to the end of democracy.

*

Unhappy democracies, like unhappy families, fail in different ways. We have offered a rough binary between fast and slow types of failure. A large reason to slice up the global democratic recession in this way is to facilitate a close look at the precise institutional, legal, and constitutional mechanisms through which decline occurs. It is to that task that the following two chapters turn, investigating first democracy's fast collapses and then its slow erosions.

3

When Democracies Collapse

Do you think bad politicians should be given a chance of political comeback; and if there is conflict again, who will solve it and by what means?

THAILAND'S PRIME MINISTER PRAYUTH
CHAN-OCHA, *May 2017*

It was, when it happened, a bloodless death. At three o'clock on a Tuesday morning in May 2014, army chief general Prayuth Chan-ocha announced a state of emergency across all of Thailand. By dawn that morning, troops and tanks were poised at key intersections of the ordinarily tumultuous and traffic-clogged streets of Bangkok, Thailand's capital. Yet, unlike coups in some other countries, there was no human tide swelling into the streets to challenge the tanks, no plumes of tear gas or mass arrests—only a few shots fired into the air in a western suburb of Bangkok as police dispersed a crowd of red-shirted demonstrators. Across the rest of the capital, an eerie calm prevailed. Some residents and tourists seized the chance to get a selfie with a tank. Although national television stations suspended broadcasting that Tuesday, and a night-time curfew was announced, debate about what was happening raged unabated on social media and the internet. The BBC's man in Bangkok ruminated that the supporters of the Pheu Thai Party—then, the party elected to national office—would be "extremely annoyed and frustrated." But not roused to a vigorous defense of democracy itself? Seemingly not. Eventually, somewhat later that day, General Chan-ocha appeared on national television and told the Thai people, "This is not a coup. The public do not need to panic and can continue with normal life." In accordance with this non-pronouncement, Prime Minister Niwatthamrong Boonsongpaisan explained that his government was still in place, and would both push through ongoing economic reforms and hold new elections in August.[1]

Of course, it was not to be. While the coup itself was relatively bloodless, civilian control was not restored. The public mobilization by ousted political parties to resist a new constitution was thwarted by arrests, by the aggressive use of a law that prohibits criticism of Thailand's monarchy, and by the periodic ad hoc detention of opposition politicians for "attitude adjustment."[2] A little less than three years after the coup, Thailand's new king, Maha Vaji-ralongkorn, signed into force Thailand's twentieth constitution. This new organic document envisaged new elections late in 2018. It circumscribed civilian power dramatically. In particular, the military-controlled Senate would have the authority to appoint the prime minister, with the consent of just a quarter of the elected House. As a result, under the new system, no one party—and especially not the Pheu Thai Party that had been deposed in May 2014—would be likely to dominate in the legislature. In addition, military officials, including rank-and-file soldiers charged with domestic policing duties, would have absolute immunity under the new constitution from criminal charges, including homicide.[3] It seems unlikely that there will be any return to democracy for Thailand in the near term.

The subdued tenor of the Thai democratic crisis of May 2014 is perhaps easy to grasp when situated in its broader historical sweep. Coups in modern Thailand are neither new nor particularly surprising. Since 1932, the country's history has been punctuated by a series of rapid and sometimes violent swings to and from participatory forms of government, including more than a dozen military coups.

The period since the 1970s, when democracy started to take meaningful root, has been especially turbulent. Even a brief summary of events conveys some of the complexity of what Dan Slater usefully labels "democratic careening."[4] A student uprising in 1973 catalyzed the drafting of a new, more liberal and inclusive constitution. In October 1976, only a year after that constitution came into force, however, the military seized power in a violent coup in which two hundred-odd died and thousands fled the country. The ensuing technocratic, but military-led government of General Prem Tinsulanonda tried to legitimate its power under a new, albeit only weakly democratic, constitution adopted in 1978. Prem presided over an eight-year period of technocratic rule in which unelected bureaucrats implemented painful fiscal and economic reforms aimed at kick-starting the economy. The next two decades witnessed periods of democratic rule punctuated with coups, followed by technocratic governance. A liberal and democratic constitution was adopted by a somewhat representative Constitutional Drafting Assembly in 1997.[5] Following yet another military coup in 2006, the constitution was superseded in 2007 by yet another organic document. This one was written by the military and then put to the Thai people in a referendum (although the Thai military reserved the right to impose any earlier constitution if their proposal failed).[6] All this turmoil goes to illustrate some of the basic empirical insights of work on coups: a country that has a coup once is much more likely to have a coup again—and again, and again[7]—and a country in which there is only a weak attachment to democracy will ironically find that the costs of sudden authoritarian reversals can be quite low. Life goes on, as General Prayuth said, democracy or dictatorship notwithstanding.

The Thai situation also illustrates another odd feature of some antidemocratic coups: These are often launched, at least notionally, to save democracy from its own (often populist) worst self. Lurking in the background of the May 2014 coup was a fear of a populist threat to the democratic order from the Pheu Thai Party. The latter was a lineal successor to the Thai Rak Thai ("Thais love Thais"), or TRT Party founded by telecommunications billionaire Thaksin Shinawatra. Rather than cultivate the support of the army or the monarchy, Thaksin's TRT Party appealed to voters disaffected by Thailand's turn to economic neoliberalism by invoking nationalist themes and promising large cash handouts to struggling rural areas. Once in power in June 2001, Thaksin tried to establish direct control over the military. He also paid only perfunctory homage to the Thai monarchy, which has long had a close alliance with the military and a correspondingly large place in Thai political life.[8] He shifted toward a distinctly antiliberal form of populism, intimating that the rule of law, freedom of criticism, human rights, and checks and balances should all be swept away.[9] The army ousted Thaksin in a September 2006 coup, perhaps forestalling a slide away from democracy under the TRT. But the TRT continued to win subsequent elections. After Thaksin's sister Yingluck took over as prime minister, she too was deposed by a judicial order just before the May 2014 coup.[10] This dynamic, in which democracy is abrogated allegedly to "protect" democracy, can be seen in recent years also in the military removals of Honduran President Manuel Zelaya in 2009 after he proposed abolishing presidential term limits, and of Niger's President Mamadou Tandja in 2010, when he in fact succeeded in eliminating those limits.[11]

The Thai military apparently so despises and distrusts the Shinawatras that they have crafted the 2017 Constitution's electoral and legislative structure as an elaborate mechanism designed to keep the TRT and its successors out of power. The constitution includes a long period of "national reform" before elections, a process that will include moral education and screening of political parties. From one perspective, these actions can be construed as a military intervention to save democracy from itself. But from another perspective, the army's intervention enacts an elitist impulse on the part of an entrenched military and allied bureaucracy to preserve control over the state against the advent of democracy—precisely the same motives that, one might argue, once impelled the Turkish military to intercede repeatedly in that country's politics. The new constitution, therefore, can either be understood as a permanent entrenchment of nondemocratic power into a competitive authoritarian regime or, alternatively, as a way to prevent a powerful and disruptive populist force from coming into power and acting in ways that undermine the smooth operation of democracy.

Coups like Thailand's are not unique. Just a year after the Thai collapse to autocracy, the Egyptian military ousted the then-elected president, Mohamed Morsi, and installed a general, Abdel Fattah el-Sisi, in his stead. Similar coups have happened in recent years in Bangladesh (2007), Mauritania (2008), Guinea (2008), Guinea-Bissau (2012), and (somewhat anomalously) Zimbabwe (2017). Nor are they the only way in which a democracy can collapse suddenly. While Hitler had attempted a coup against the Bavarian government in November 1923, an event later known as the Beer Hall Putsch, we have already seen that this is not how he ultimately seized power.[12] The legal instruments through which the Nazi Party was able to assemble a near-absolute monopoly on political power were first the Reichstag Fire Decree and second, the use of emergency powers under the Enabling Act. More recently, there are the cases of Indira Gandhi's 1977 emergency and President Ferdinand Marcos's 1972 decision to use emergency powers to abrogate ordinary democratic rule and impose a new constitution.[13] Latin America, rather than Europe or Asia, provides perhaps the most dense thicket of historical examples of both coups and misused emergency powers.[14] So severe is the problem that one scholar, reviewing Latin America's experience with emergency powers, has concluded that "[n]o elections, no delicately orchestrated set of presidentialist musical chairs, and no transitions from authoritarian to elected governments will succeed in consolidating constitutional democracy without drastic reform of these constitutional foundations of tyranny."[15]

Emergencies can lead to the *misuse* of legal rules, whereas coups typically involve the *circumvention* of legal rules.[16] Emergency powers, that is, are often (although not always) sketched out in a constitutional or statutory text, although, as we will see later, the US Constitution is an exception in this regard. Autocratic collapse results from the failure of designers to think through the ways in which formally designated emergency powers can be misused. For instance, in the German example, both the Reichstag Fire Decree and the Enabling Act formally remained within the bounds set out by the Weimar Constitution—but the latter's design failed to check the deployment of its emergency powers to abrogate political competition. Hence, the design question in the emergency powers context relates to how precisely the latter are crafted in the first instance. Even if good drafting cannot preclude the possibility of extralegal action, can the threat be hedged? Military coups, by contrast, tend to be extralegal. The army sergeant who arrests the president and declares martial law is typically not appealing to a specific legal text, even if he claims to be defending nation or constitution. As a result, the art of "coup-proofing" is not a matter of writing a rule against coups into the constitution. Rather, it is more a matter of designing a civil-military relationship in which coups do not arise in the first place.

The civil-military relationship is at the heart of another inquiry that arises in the context of understanding the global democratic recession. We have included in our account of the recession instances in which long-nurtured hopes for popular self-rule fail at the starting gate: The Arab Spring looms large in this regard. Close attention to the events that separated democratic success (as in Tunisia and, at least initially, Egypt) from democratic failure (as in Egypt later, as well as in Yemen, Syria, and Libya) suggests that the organization of the military plays an important part in determining whether the democratic wave crests or continues. Hence, we also examine the manner in which military organization can impede or enable democracy's long-delayed launch.

Understanding when and how authoritarian collapse happens requires first a sense of the global frequency of military coups and emergency invocations that abrogate democracy. It also means examining the specific institutional conditions which lead to military coups and abuses of emergency powers. We thus start by sketching what is known about the socioeconomic conditions in which authoritarian collapses occur. Then we drill down to look at how constitutional and institutional design can either raise or lower the chances of such events.

The Global Toll of Autocratic Collapse

How common is the quick collapse of a democracy? Drawing on the Polity IV database, we tried to identify recent cases of authoritarian collapse. We narrowed our search by defining as a democracy any country that scored six or more on the Polity2 scale in the relevant year. We then searched for countries in which that Polity score then fell below that threshold, dropping by at least three points in a single year. This excludes not only cases in which democracy remained stable, but also instances of erosion—that is, instances in which a gradual and partial decline in the quality of a democracy occurs over multiple years, without a complete collapse. Table 3.1 below presents data on a number of such authoritarian reversals, including the duration of the antecedent period of democracy that was interrupted, and the reasons for democratic collapse. We also include data on the wealth of the country (measured in per capita Gross Domestic Product) at the time of a collapse: the literature on

TABLE 3.1. Post–Cold War collapses

Country	Drop in Polity2 score	Years of prior democracy	GDP per capita	Cause of collapse
Armenia 1995	−3	5	$1915	Electoral irregularities
Belarus 1995	−7	4	$4228	Incumbent takeover
Gambia 1994	−15	29	$1220	Coup d'etat
Haiti 1991	−14	1	$1326	Coup d'etat
Haiti 1999	−5	5	$1308	Postponed election
Lesotho 1998	−8	5	$1021	Electoral violence/ external intervention
Madagascar 2009	−7	17	$700	Military intervention to transfer power
Mali 2012	−7	21	$777	Attempt at incumbent takeover
Niger 1996	−14	5	$510	Coup d'etat
Pakistan 1999	−13	12	$1760	Coup d'etat
Peru 1992	−11	12	$3742	Incumbent takeover
Solomon Islands 2000	−8	23	$1401	Ethnic violence
Thailand 2006	−14	14	$7280	Coup d'etat
Thailand 2014	−10	3	$8450	Coup d'etat
Turkey 2014	−6	30	$12127	Incumbent takeover

democracy identifies wealth and democratic continuity as primary deterrents of authoritarian reversal.

This brief survey suggests that authoritarian reversals are quite rare. This conclusion is confirmed by Gero Erdmann's 2011 study of thirty years' experience of democratic backsliding. Using different data, Erdmann looked for instances of democratic backsliding in the late twentieth century. He found fifty-three cases, but only five of these involved a full transition from democracy to an authoritarian regime.[17] In another study, Adam Przeworski looked at a different time period and, using different methods, identified roughly seventy-five authoritarian collapses.[18] Moreover, these studies all suggest that the rate of such collapses has been declining over time, a trend-line that occurs against a more general fall in the number of coups in both democratic and nondemocratic settings over the last few decades.[19] The Polity database also records coups and coup attempts in both democratic and nondemocratic contexts. From 1960–1989 there were 145 successful coups, whereas there have been only 36 successful coups thereafter.[20] Perhaps because full-scale collapse, whether by coup or other means, is relatively rare, political scientists have developed the countervailing concept of democratic consolidation: the idea that after some time, democracy becomes "the only game in town" in a given national context, such that a collapse into pure authoritarianism becomes much less likely.[21]

The comparative infrequency of authoritarian reversals creates an inference problem. Without a sufficient number of cases, it is hard to draw strong conclusions about what factors produce democratic breakdowns. Still, some tentative generalizations can be drawn from the limited pool of cases that we can observe, with regard to the background social, economic, or political conditions that make these events likely. These ambient conditions are distinct from the institutional and legal design decisions that make coups and the abuse of emergency powers more likely. It is thus appropriate to break out three background conditions of nations—wealth, democratic age, and social homogeneity—before turning to the question of how institutional and constitutional design can handle the risks associated with emergency powers and coups.

To begin with, it is striking that so few cases of collapse to autocracy, whether in our data or in Erdmann's, occur in a high-income country.[22] Indeed, one of the most renowned predictions in the political science of democracy is the claim, associated with Adam Przeworski, that a democracy became "impregnable" when it attained a per capita income of $6,000 (about $9,100 in today's dollars).[23] (In contrast, there is a live disagreement about whether ongoing redistribution tends to cause elites to seek shelter through an intervening military).[24] The wealth/democracy correlation may arise because a certain level of wealth, sufficiently widely distributed, provides a buffer against democratic collapse in some way. Edward Luttwak assumed as much when he argued that a "running dialogue between rulers and the ruled . . . if there is a section of society that is sufficiently literate, well fed, and secure enough to talk back" makes the rapid and complete abrogation of political power impossible or difficult to sustain for more than a brief period. In Luttwak's (informal and nonquantitative, but still piercing) account, what matters are the democratic expectations that inevitably arise in a population sufficiently comfortable in economic terms for some to take a strong interest in politics.[25]

Alternatively, some recent evidence suggests that the causal arrow may run in the other direction. That is, it may be that democracies may be better at fostering economic growth than authoritarian regimes, whereas those autocratic rulers that do foster economic growth either push through democratizing reform, or alternatively lose power. As a result, autocracies would tend to be associated with low growth.[26] Whatever the direction of causality, the conventional wisdom that high-income democracies are not vulnerable to decline seems to be an artifact of the absence of full-scale *collapses* in such national contexts.[27] Yet even this observation must be somewhat qualified, given cases like the May 2014 Thai coup. The nominal per capita GDP of Thailand in 2014 was $8450. Although slightly below the (inflation-adjusted) floor set by Przeworski and colleagues, this is still hardly a dismal standard of economic development.

In addition to economic robustness, the probability of authoritarian collapse declines with regime age. According to political scientist Milan Svolik's careful study, "Any country that has been democratic for 52 or more years as of 2001 is estimated to be consolidated with at least 90% probability."[28] As insulation from military coups, consolidation happens even more quickly, and Svolik suggests that the probability of a military coup falls to almost zero if a democracy survives two decades.[29] Hence, many of the quintessential instances of democratic collapse are found in young democracies. The Weimar Constitution, for example, was drafted in 1919, some 14 years before the Reichstag fire. Japan also had a new and only weakly institutionalized democracy in the 1920s, before it too reverted to authoritarian nationalism. And the Spanish Republic lasted just five years before Franco came to power in 1938. The relative youth of a democracy may matter, because young democracies tend not to have developed the institutional and social supports upon which older democracies can rely. Indeed, an important study by Ethan Kapstein and Nathan Converse suggests that young democracies are in particularly acute need of strong institutional checks on political power in order to prevent democratic unraveling of varying kinds, a finding that we elaborate and supplement in later chapters on democratic erosion.[30]

Finally, the presence of deep social cleavages along religious and ethnic lines may also make democratic decision making more costly and hence more difficult. One reason for this may be that the presence of densely networked ethnic or religious groups may facilitate the sort of surreptitious coordination that is necessary to a coup. Consistent with these intuitions, one study demonstrates that the presence of large, relatively homogenous ethnic groupings that are economically distinct from each other is associated with a higher incidence of authoritarian reversal.[31] That study did not consider the possibility, however, that constitutional and legal design might mitigate intergroup tensions. For instance, a constitutional designer can use either geographic segmentation to create zones of autonomy for different groups, or set forth minority rights in relation to language, the law of personal relations, or the availability of governmental benefits. Or a designer might encourage cross-group cooperation in politics through other means. Where these are successes—and there are many reasons why legal accommodations of this type can either fail or have unanticipated effects—it may be that social cleavages are less likely to undermine democracy.

Wealth, age, and social homogeneity, in short, help insulate a country from authoritarian collapse. Yet it is important to underscore that the protection supplied by these system-level characteristics is probabilistic, rather than certain. None are guarantees. We thus turn to the question whether there are institutional design choices that render democratic polities more vulnerable to either the misuse of emergency powers or to a military coup d'état.

Emergencies and Institutional Design

Constitutional designers have long included provisions that permitted exceptional forms of state action in response to unexpected and hazardous circumstances, above and beyond the ordinary powers delegated to a government. The Roman Republic, for example, contained a system whereby the Senate, which operated much like a contemporary executive through its decree power, could instruct the Consuls to appoint a dictator for a period of up to (but no more than) six months. Upon this declaration, the Senate suspended its own function, and the dictator could not only make arrests and suspend rights, but also use military might as he saw fit. At the end of the six months, however, all his powers and legal decrees reverted to their ordinary institutional homes.[32] This model of emergency powers has historically proved influential in part because it was rediscovered and celebrated by the Florentine political theorist Machiavelli.[33]

This Roman model contains what might roughly be described as the two main species of emergency powers. First, the Roman Constitution allowed for a shift in the form of the political regime. Emergency powers had the effect of changing the actors charged with day-to-day governing authority. Indeed, the Roman model involved the temporary creation of a new actor, the dictator, who would assume most political power. Second, the constitution allowed for retail derogations from existing laws and rights. That is, the dictator could dispense with the ordinary forms of legal process and use even military power with the Senate's approval. This distinction—between changing the institutional forms of political action and amplifying the discrete powers of an existing set of institutional players—is an imprecise one at the edges. If an existing institutional actor is given sufficient discrete, new emergency authorities, at some point the aggregate effect of such delegation is to transform the governing regime by creating an effectively new kind of state entity.

Still, the distinction is useful in thinking about how emergency powers can be employed to undermine democracy.

In the modern era, constitutions have drawn on both types of emergency power. Indeed, some 90% of constitutions in force today have some provisions on emergency powers.[34] Between 1985 and 2014, some 137 countries invoked a state of emergency at least once.[35] Moreover, the specific kinds of emergency authorities have multiplied. For example, many legal regimes permit derogations of individual rights in response to violent crises, such as war or terrorism. Others envisage extraordinary powers to respond to financial crises or foreign policy shocks. Sometimes emergency powers are described in a nation's constitution. In other instances, they are set out by statute. And sometimes, emergency powers are used so extensively and pervasively that their very label starts to sound like a misnomer.[36]

Beyond the different substantive areas in which emergency powers can be exercised, there are also two different ways in which particular powers can be calibrated in relation to the background body of existing law. One possibility is that emergency power might take the form of ex ante licenses, which allow a state actor such as the Roman dictator to act without legal restraint in emergencies. Alternatively, there is what Oren Gross calls the "extra-legal measures" model, in which officials are expected to take actions in violation of the law when responding to an emergency, but must seek some after-the-fact democratic blessing of these actions. The canonical example of the latter is President Abraham Lincoln's decision to authorize military detention at the beginning of the Civil War, and his subsequent submission to Congress of a request for indemnification for any civil judgments that resulted from it.[37] Finally, emergency powers might be differentiated in line with the demands of international human rights law. A bill of rights, for example, might permit derogation from some rights but not others in a period of crisis.[38]

The sheer range of emergency authorities makes it important to be precise about how such powers can be used to undermine a democracy's ongoing operation. An emergency power that changes the political regime, in our view, presents a qualitatively different risk from a power that simply permits certain actions that would be otherwise unlawful. Emergency regimes present grave risks to democracy, whereas a narrower set of emergency powers may present greater short-term risks of rights violations, though not always the complete end of democracy.

The collapse of Weimar is the canonical example of an emergency operating as a direct gateway from democracy to an autocratic regime. The Reichstag Fire Decree and the Enabling Act changed the identity of the key decision-makers and veto-gates in government, but did not change the specific substantive powers of the government. To be sure, the emergency powers of arrest and detention wielded by the Nazis after March 1933 played an important role, but it seems likely that such authorities would still have been exercised in different, more restrained ways had the Nazis not already consolidated power. After all, even fully democratic states use deadly force and detention, often without criminal trial, to deal with certain social problems. Such regimes differ from the Nazis not so much in *what* powers they use, but in *how* and *why* such powers are used.

Democratic collapse can also happen largely through a shift in the locus of power rather than the use of brute force. Only a few years after the Reichstag Fire Decree, in 1935, the Brazilian autocrat Getúlio Dornelles Vargas invoked emergency powers to overthrow his own government and, with the backing of the military, install an *"Estado Novo."*[39] In Colombia, the 1886 Constitution allowed the president to declare a "state of siege," and thereby to substitute himself for the Congress through the use of *"decretos legislativos,"* or executive orders, with the force of law. In some moments in Colombian history, the "state of siege" has overtaken the ordinary constitutional status quo as the default form of government. Between 1949 and 1991, for example, there was a state of siege in thirty out of forty-two years. Most important changes to national policy were accomplished by *decretos legislativos* rather than ordinary laws.[40]

The use of retail emergency powers of coercion and detention to achieve the same end is, to be sure, possible. For example, the decision of President Ferdinand Marcos on September 22, 1972, to declare martial law marked the end of democratic contestation: opposition politicians either aligned themselves with Marcos, or found themselves facing confiscatory orders targeting their businesses and economic resources.[41] But the use of such retail, coercive emergency powers as a lever to pry apart democracy seems less common than the use of regime-shifting emergency authorities to the same end. The "who" of emergency powers, once again, seems to matter more than the "how."

It is worth noting that all of these examples involve the explicit and overt use of emergency powers to abrogate quickly an ongoing democratic system. We are thus not concerned here with a more subtle point about emergency powers, first developed by the German jurist Carl Schmitt. According to Schmitt, emergencies are unpredictable and open-ended, such that the power to recognize an emergency is no less than the power to suspend the rule of law. Although some contemporary legal scholars have been much taken by Schmitt's logic and have decided, in effect, that discretionary powers to act in emergencies can never be checked, this problem is of greater theoretical than practical interest.[42] In practice, areas of opaque discretionary authority, such as those permitted by emergency powers, do coexist with domains in which the legal rules are fairly crisp and certain. And officials within government do not often infer from the fact that they can declare an emergency for a limited purpose the more general proposition that they can also unravel the rule-of-law in its totality. The existence of occasional grey areas—and even black holes—in the law, in other words, is perfectly compatible with a predictable and orderly exercise of state power. Even law students, in our experience, understand that areas of legal uncertainty can happily coexist with crisp rules. In practice, widely held norms of legality and a positive orientation toward the regular operation of a liberal constitutional democracy together seem to insulate countries against the nihilistic unraveling of legality that Schmitt embraced.[43]

Two basic design principles have been proposed to limit the misuse of regime-shifting emergency powers in particular. First, the final authority to decide on whether there is an emergency should not rest with the dictator herself. Second, the duration of the emergency should be fixed. The Roman model, in which the Senate decided on the existence of the six-month emergency, embodied both these conditions.[44] Consistent with this, many modern constitutions tend to anticipate the onset of an emergency and to provide temporally limited powers to address it. Four out of five of these also stipulate that declarations of emergency require the concurrence of at least two institutional actors identified in the constitution, as a safeguard against unilateral abuse.[45]

Many of these modern constitutions have been designed in the wake of the death of the 1919 Weimar Constitution, which did not contain a temporal limit on the use of emergency powers. Commentators typically focus on its Article 48, which allowed the president to "take the measures necessary for the restoration of the public safety and order, and, . . . if necessary, intervene with the armed forces," but required that he consult the Reichstag, which had the power to revoke emergency measures. Article 48 assumed the ongoing operation of the Reichstag as a checking institution, notwithstanding the president's power to dissolve that body.

But was Article 48 really the cause of the Weimar Republic's collapse? After all, Article 48 powers had been employed throughout the turbulent 1920s without fatally compromising democracy. And it was not the Reichstag Fire Decree itself that marked the end of democratic contestation, even if it did signal the beginning of the end of the democratic left in Germany at the time. Rather, it was the Enabling Act that concentrated authority in Chancellor Hitler's hands by eliminating the legislative branch. (The courts had never imposed much constraint on the Nazi program; to the contrary, they were often eager accomplices in the corrosive use of state violence against leftist and Catholic opposition to the Nazis). And the Enabling Act, which paralleled a 1923 legislative delegation, was not the work of the chancellor alone, but the Reichstag, and contained within it a time-limit. The Reichstag, not the president, dissolved itself and created an emergency regime with no effective check on government power in a way that was not plainly contemplated by Article 48. The experience of Weimar, in short, suggests that any emergency regime power must be formally and textually limited, not only by requiring an acoustic separation between authorizing and authorized bodies, but also through a firm time limit. In addition, a constitution can usefully prohibit the use of emergency powers to prolong states of emergency or to create new institutions that are independent of political safeguards. One way of doing so is by textually mandating the continued operation of effective checking institutions.[46] It also suggests the limits of textual safeguards of democracy where the parties and movements that comprise the nation's key political actors are not committed to democracy. In Weimar Germany, as in the recent history of Thailand, there is only so much that sound institutional design can do without underlying commitments from political actors to maintain democracy as a going concern.

No legal specification of emergency powers, of course, can provide perfect insulation against the misuse of such powers against democracy. But the imperfection of legal safeguards should not be confused with Schmitt's broader claim that the law is ineffective in the face of unexpected crisis. Perhaps the greatest temptation to that confusion is fueled by the argument, common among American legal scholars, that the executive branch tasked with using emergency powers is more efficient and more knowledgeable than either the courts or the legislature. From this point about comparative institutional advantage, it is possible to slide quickly into a conceptually distinct Schmittian skepticism about legal restraints more generally.[47] But even this first argument about comparative institutional advantage is far weaker than it seems. Whatever their institutional advantages, executives vary in quality and in susceptibility to the distorting pressures of ideology and populist pandering. Some chief executives are wise and will rely on the internal epistemic resources of the executive branch. Some do not. More generally, the expertise necessary for and the utility of wise unitary action by the executive are often vastly overstated. The argument for executive supremacy is often based on an "apples to oranges" comparison of an idealized presidency and an actual legislature: It is easy, that is, to bemoan the divisive and slow process of democratic debate, and to be dazzled by the allure of speedy executive action, without noticing how deeply flawed executive responses often can be. A system of judicial and legislative checks, moreover, does not preclude the leveraging of executive branch expertise. It simply ensures that the expertise, rather than bureaucratic ambition or naked prejudice against a discrete and vulnerable minority, is in fact the basis for a policy intervention.[48] There is no cause, in short, for blanket skepticism about the capacity of good institutional design to reduce, if not eliminate, the risk of autocratic collapse through emergency power.

The Military Coup as Democracy's Pallbearer

Considered as an instrument of democratic destruction, the military coup is quite unlike an emergency. Most importantly, it does not need to rest on a claim of legal authority within the existing constitutional order. Coups are by definition illegal, whereas the use of emergency powers at least purports to remain within the law. That does not mean, however, that constitutional and institutional design cannot be used to address the risk of a coup. Rather, a constitutional designer must consider how to integrate the military into the larger framework of government in such a way that coups become less, rather than more, likely.

The archetypal model of the military coup occurs when the army deposes an incumbent democratic leader by force. The Thai coup of May 2014 exemplifies this possibility. Such interventions are more likely when, as in the Thai case, the incumbent leader has antagonized other political elites, who either encourage or tolerate military intervention. Similarly, the military coup of 2013 that ousted Egyptian President Mohammed Morsi was facilitated by the fierce popular opposition that the Muslim Brotherhood's time in office had generated. The military also sharply perceived Morsi's diplomatic postures, particularly in respect to Syria, as the bungling of "ignorant amateurs."[49] More generally, it might be expected that coups would be more frequent when the military could find support from elites fearful of the party in power.[50] Coups are also catalyzed by civilian governments' efforts to exert control over the military. A 2008 coup in Mauritania, for example, was precipitated when President Sidi Ould Cheikh Abdallahi attempted to fire four senior military officers.[51] In Thailand, some have asserted, Prime Minister Thaksin's relationship with the Thai military soured—with results we have already seen—when he attempted to interfere with the autonomy of the appointment process for commanders. With this possibility in mind, the failure of Thailand's military coup to segue into democracy anew is rather less puzzling.

But the threat of a coup is not limited to cases in which the armed forces escape from civilian control. Sitting, democratically elected figures can seek to deploy the military to entrench their power. Successful or not, such efforts can end in coups. For example, the regime of the former army officer Hugo Chávez that came to power in Venezuela in 1998 treated the military as a partner, not an adversary, to be folded into governmental programs for delivering social services and alleviating poverty. While many military officers were placed in key positions in government ministries, Chávez tightened the control exercised by the president over promotions within the military. Civilian control of the military thus became a device for weakening democracy, rather than a way of strengthening it. In a variation on the Venezuelan trajectory, civilian politicians' efforts to suborn the military can go off the tracks and lead to a coup against the putative authoritarian leader. Starting in 2008, for example, Honduras's president Manuel Zelaya pressed for a referendum on a new constituent assembly that would abolish the constitution's term-limit provision, allowing him to potentially run for reelection. When Congress and the Supreme Court rejected this proposal, Zelaya turned to the military, seeking its aid in conducting something like a referendum on whether a new constitution was needed. The commander of the armed forces refused. Zelaya fired him, triggering the resignation of his civilian minister of armed forces and the entire military high command. When Zelaya then tried to force a poll, the Supreme Court ordered him deposed. The military arrested him, and exiled him to Costa Rica.[52]

The unusual case of Taishō and early Shōwa Japan offers a variant on this theme. This brief period in the early twentieth century witnessed unprecedented democratization in Japan. Crucial reforms of the period included the emergence of real party politics and passage of the General Election Law of 1925, which liberalized election rules and granted universal male suffrage. The Meiji Constitution, however, was centered around a divine emperor, to whom the military claimed direct allegiance. Beginning with a calculated attempt to invade North China without authorization in 1931, and accelerating throughout the 1930s, military officers acted in an increasingly independent manner. Despite multiple coup attempts, civilian rule nevertheless remained formally intact throughout World War II, even as party politics were terminated in 1940. The military's rise to power was neither unconstitutional nor reliant on "emergency" powers. It simply required artful interpretation of vague constitutional rules in a manner that left the traditional monarch as the formal authority. "Civilian" control remained intact, but often with military men in the prime minister's seat.[53]

Most studies of civil-military relations focus on the obvious risk—that of a military that acts on its own—rather than the subtle risk, in which civilians use or allow the military to end democratic competition. Even as to this risk, close students of the behavior of militaries are skeptical that there are simple legal or constitutional fixes to the problem. In his leading study on civil-military relations, Samuel Huntington advocated "objective civilian control" of the military, which entailed "militarizing the military, making them the tool of the state." Huntington explains that this means that civilians must set policy ends, even as the military must supply "instrumental means" to achieve those ends. In effect, Huntington suggests, the military obtains professional autonomy over the management of its own operations in exchange for allowing civilian leaders to decide on what the military's objectives should be.[54]

The creation of such "objective civilian control," however, can occur either through legal design or as a consequence of traditions and conventions. One approach would be to use one of the raft of "coup-proofing" measures often observed in nondemocratic contexts. These include stacking the military with ethnic or familial cohorts; using political commissioners, as the Chinese Communist Party does, to limit officers' discretion and to embed political control down to the platoon level; or dividing the military into rival services or units which can be played off against each other.[55] There is little evidence, however, that these measures are in fact associated with lower coup risk.[56]

More modestly, an impressive empirical analysis by Milan Svolik suggests that the adoption of a presidential system in an otherwise fragile democracy that is at risk of authoritarian reversal means that democracy is less likely to become consolidated and will thus remain more susceptible to other forces that lead to a breakdown.[57] Hence, it would appear that, whereas fine-grained institutional design of the specific powers and structure of the military does not have a major impact on the risk of a military coup, the larger choice of political structures—presidential, parliamentary, or otherwise—has some role in calibrating coup risk, albeit in an indirect fashion.

Alternatively, formal rules may be ineffective at building culture. Looking at the United States, Huntington did not think that the provisions of the 1787 US Constitution ensured civilian control. Rather, he diagnosed the latter's origin as "extraconstitutional, a part of our political tradition but not of our constitutional tradition."[58] In a similar vein, other scholars have advocated a "cult of professional control" or an ethics of obedience.[59] This socialization, however, must be more nuanced than some of these authors have suggested.[60] It is not enough that a military culture reflect a deep commitment to civilian control. It is also necessary for that culture to rest on respect for constitutional civilian rule, such that there will be little appetite for pleas by presidents or prime ministers to abrogate the democratic order. In countries with stark social or ethnic cleavages, this sort of culture can be undermined when an elected leader and the majority of the military share a group identification. For example, in Cameroon, Paul Biya has maintained power since 1982 partly by stocking the military with members of his Beti ethnic group. Even when Biya permitted multiparty elections in 1992, he was able to leverage his control over a coethnic military to eke out wins at the polls.[61]

The Fledging Democracy and the Military Coup

The military does not merely play a role when an existing democracy comes to an impasse. It also matters as to whether democracy gets off the ground in the first instance. Consider the divergent paths of countries in the Arab Spring. In Tunisia, General Rachid Ammar, the army chief of staff, refused to follow President Zine al-Abidine Ben Ali's order to support his Presidential Guard in suppressing street protests that had erupted in December 2010. In Egypt, the military initially hedged its bets, with senior leaders continuing to work with President Hosni Mubarak and with some units engaged in the arrest and abuse of protesters. It was only in February 2011, when Mubarak's forces intensified their use of violence, and his public support correspondingly cratered, that the armed forces turned against the regime. On February 10, eight days after the new wave of violence started, the Supreme Council of the Armed Forces under Field Marshall Mohamed Hussein Tantawi pushed Mubarak out of office and into internal exile. By contrast, when popular uprisings broke out in Bahrain in February 2011, and then in Syria in March 2011, the military in both those countries responded unhesitatingly to orders to use force to suppress popular protest. In Libya and Yemen, yet another story unfolded, with the military fracturing into distinct elements that arrayed along different sides of emerging civil wars. The result in both countries was a bloody bout of fratricidal violence.[62]

The failure of a potential "Fourth Wave" of democratization in the 2010s, in short, is in large measure the result of the military's strategic decision making. Popular movements such as those in the Arab Spring succeed when they are able to detach the military from an autocratic regime.[63] While the strength and tactical savvy of the nonviolent movement for democratic change will influence the army's calculations, the array of responses in early 2011 that could be observed across the Arab world suggests that the prior structure and orientation of the military will also be important factors in determining whether democracy will advance. A key variable seems to be the incumbent regime's previous success in meeting socioeconomic demands, including those of the armed forces, before protests start. Beyond that, it seems that where the armed forces are internally divided (as in Yemen and Libya) or aligned by ethnicity with an autocratic leader (as in Bahrain and Syria), they are less likely to defect in the face of popular resistance.[64] Another important factor is the institutional interests of the military, including its need to maintain internal cohesion and discipline, its desire to protect its image and legitimacy, and its more crude economic interests in terms of maintaining financial support or preserving enterprises run by the military.[65]

By necessity, there is usually no single constitutional design decision by which a democracy-minded founder can ensure that an armed force will make the right decision when faced with one of these choices. Moreover, all the militaries of countries that experienced the Arab Spring were formed under conditions of authoritarianism. Their initial design was not crafted with the preservation of democracy in mind. Nevertheless, the different ways in which internal structure can shape responses to pro-democracy movements helps explain the failure of the early twenty-first-century hopes for a new wave of democratization. And more speculatively, these experiences point to the value of building professional, socially heterogeneous, and independent-minded armed forces, where possible, in the context of new democracies.

The Future of Authoritarian Reversal Revised

This chapter has surveyed the extent and the underlying mechanisms of authoritarian collapse. We have paid little attention to one mechanism that captured the political imagination during the twentieth century: violent revolution. We spend little time on the topic because we believe it is largely defunct in general and has never been much of a threat to an established liberal democracy. The 1979 Iranian Revolution marks the last major non-democratic revolution, and it led to a replacement of a military strongman by a theocracy. Notwithstanding its survival as an epithet wielded by some on the political right and as a utopian imaging in some left-wing offerings on college campuses, state Marxism is dead as a political force. Organized political violence in established democracies is far less frequent than it was in the 1960s and 1970s. However else democracy ends, it is unlikely to be in a violent revolution.

In this regard, it is worth restating and underscoring one of the key findings from large-n empirical work on democratic collapses: The rate of such collapses is declining. The use of emergency powers to change the fundamental nature of a democratic regime is no longer common, and the frequency of military coups has been shrinking over time. This hardly means that the problem of authoritarian collapse can be treated as purely historical. Even coupled with the picture of a global democratic recession we have offered in chapter 1, it does have a suggestive implication: The coup and the emergency regime change are yesterday's instruments against democracy—with the exception of polities such as Thailand, which have fallen into a habit and expectation of coups. The Thai example with which we began, therefore, is an exceptional one. It is unlikely to prove contagious in contexts where there is no tradition of military seizures of power. Similarly, revolution has never been successful in established democracies. Technological and institutional developments that have increased the raw power and reach of the state only make revolution less likely than it was in, say, 1848 or even 1979.

But to the extent that a political actor wishes to derogate from democracy today, there is more than one pathway open to her. The fact that one has lower transaction costs will make the other trajectory comparatively less attractive. An easier path, that is, makes the hard road less desirable. A dynamic of this sort may well be at work in the declining frequency of authoritarian collapse. And if so, this is all the more reason for focus on and concern about the low-cost alternative to authoritarian collapse that we detail in the next chapter—democratic erosion.

4

When Democracies Decay

Democracy is like a streetcar: You ride it until you arrive at your destination, then you step off.

RECEP TAYYIP ERDOĞAN, 1996

It was a day freighted with symbolism. Thirty-one years after Hungary's Communist government hanged Imre Nagy, who had led the 1956 uprising against Soviet rule, Nagy's body was reburied with pomp in Budapest's largest square. It was, so it seemed, the closing of a dark chapter in the nation's history and the opening of a bright new one. Among the speakers was an eloquent spokesman for the Federation of Young Democrats, one Viktor Orbán. In an eloquent speech that is well remembered in Hungary to this day, Orbán condemned Hungary's old guard and decried "the dictatorship of a single party."[1] At the time, Orbán was the shaggy-haired leader in a student movement called Fidesz. Within a few months, the Cold War was over, and fresh optimism about democracy's prospects, particularly in long-suffering Eastern Europe, seemed not just plausible but obviously justified. By the early 1990s, Fidesz had became a political party with Orbán at its head, wielding "the language and the vocabulary of the Liberals."[2] Its early motto was "Don't trust anyone over thirty-five." Quite remarkably, it retained this age limit on membership until 1993. This did not translate into electoral success. Running on an agenda that emphasized the protection of private property, the role of the market, and a minimal role for the state, Fidesz obtained a vote share in the single digits. Over time, however, Fidesz's language and policies moved toward the populist right. From 1998 to 2002, the party was one of three in a ruling coalition; with the exception of a few "alarmingly rightist" statements, however, it did little to suggest that it would be taking the nation on a radically different path.[3]

In 2010, however, Fidesz swept back to power by trouncing the beleaguered and weakened Socialist Party in the first election to follow the global financial crisis. Although Fidesz won only 53% of the vote, it secured 68% of the available legislative seats, thanks to an electoral system designed to prevent legislative fragmentation and divided governments. In the 386-seat parliament, Fidesz took 263 seats, while the Socialists managed only 56. The winning party had campaigned on a right-of-center agenda streamlining government bureaucracy, granting citizenship to ethnic Hungarians living abroad, and halving the number of parliamentary deputies. Once in power, however, Fidesz quickly exploited its two-thirds majority to draft a wholly new constitution. Hungary had never had a post–Cold War constitution, but had massively amended its Communist-era document. Passed on April 25, 2011, by strict party-line vote, and without a popular referendum, this new constitution dramatically altered the form and substance of Hungarian politics.

Consider here its effect on institutions responsible for protecting liberal rights of speech and association, and otherwise enforcing the administrative rule of law. The new constitution enlarged the Constitutional Court, immediately giving Fidesz a raft of new appointments. Whereas under the prior constitution's so-called *actio popularis* jurisdiction, almost anyone could challenge a law's constitutionality, the new constitution sharply limited access to the Court. In 2013, the constitution was amended to retroactively void all of the Constitutional Court's decisions prior to the enactment of the new constitution, including a set of decisions that had been hailed abroad as models of progressive judicial activism in the 1990s.

The constitution also created a new National Judicial Office, controlled immediately by Fidesz, that wielded broad powers not only over case selection but also over the assignment of cases across the judiciary. The electoral system was altered in ways that, as observers quickly noted, would deepen the asymmetrical legislative seat advantage already enjoyed by Fidesz. Further, independent entities within the executive branch that are essential to the administrative rule of law—including the Electoral Commission, the Budget Commission, and the Media Board—were reformulated and restocked with Fidesz loyalists, all with twelve-year terms of office.[4]

These are not the only important changes that Fidesz under Orbán made once it came into power in 2010. Indeed, in the course of this chapter we shall have cause not only to return to these changes, but to explore several others. They are but a taste of the party's strategy, one which has clearly worked. By 2014, the changing electoral landscape was manifest even in the course of a brisk walk across Budapest. Dozens of fifteen-foot-tall advertising kiosks proclaimed "Only Fidesz!," while Orbán's face, lips curled into a half-smile, dominated billboards across the city. In contrast, opposition flyers were to be found solely on cheap plywood, nailed to trees or utility poles. The difference in exposure was not the result of heightened popularity. Rather, soon after Fidesz's election in 2010, the parliament had enacted a new law regulating billboards that drove the country's second largest manufacturer of billboards out of business, leaving a Fidesz-linked company as the dominant market player. On the radio or the television, meanwhile, one would be exceedingly unlikely to hear any criticism of Fidesz or Orbán. Under a 2010 media law, the government had gained broad authority to direct content and to impose sanctions when media outlets fail to comply. One former journalist for the respected state broadcasting channel Magyar Televízió summarized the change there by saying that before 2010 "it might have been a pro-government channel, but it was with soft distortions, putting things in a certain frame and doing it with light criticism. But after 2010, it was direct manipulation and lies. We were not journalists anymore, and we were deceiving the public continually."[5]

Notwithstanding this media blitz, and notwithstanding an opaque electoral system that tilted the playing field even further toward Fidesz, the party only captured 44.5% of the vote in April parliamentary elections, giving it 66.8% of the seats. Still, Fidesz remained the largest party, and even picked up about a hundred and thirty thousand new voters. Notably, Fidesz's solicitude for the "Hungarians abroad," which included legislation granting them the right to vote, paid off: Some 95.5% of them voted for Fidesz.[6] Two months after the election, Orbán gave a speech at the Bálványos Free Summer University and Youth Camp, in which he explained the direction he had in mind for the nation:

> [The] Hungarian nation is not a simple sum of individuals, but a community
> that needs to be organized, strengthened and developed, and in this sense, the
> new state that we are building is an illiberal state, a non-liberal state. It does
> not deny foundational values of liberalism, as freedom, etc. But it does not
> make this ideology a central element of state organization, but applies a spe-
> cific, national, particular approach in its stead.[7]

Notwithstanding the equivocation of "freedom, etc.," the repudiation of liberal constitutional democracy as an ideal could not be clearer.

The trajectory of Hungary is far from unique. It has been recapitulated, with some national variations, in Venezuela, Turkey, Bolivia, Poland, and Russia, among other countries. One can also see traces of the same dynamic at work in putatively consolidated and mature democracies, such as those of India, Israel, the United States, and many European countries. These various experiences demonstrate that not every wolf bares its teeth and claws or stands outside the door baying for blood. Some threats to liberal constitutional democracies do not announce themselves as such. And they are all the more dangerous for it. In many of these cases, voters and commentators initially embraced parties and leaders that would eventually be responsible for the slow but serious process of democratic erosion.

Consider here again the Turkish case. After the attacks of September 11, 2001, talk of a clash of civilizations was very much in the air. Ignoring the experience of countries like Indonesia and Bangladesh, many commentators have asserted that democracy was not compatible with majority Muslim societies, and a diverse, plural, global religious tradition was treated as a simple, single bloc by many in positions in geostrategic authority. Into this milieu strode the confident Recep Tayyib Erdoğan, fresh from a stint as reformist mayor of Istanbul, Initially, Erdoğan seemed to offer a new, moderate Islamist political party, the Justice and Development Party (AKP), that seamlessly melded deep faith and a commitment to democracy. This combination was welcomed in many quarters inside and outside Turkey, hungry for a more complex vision of compatibility between faith and democracy. Erdoğan's cynical instrumentalism about democratic institutions, evident in the 1996 quotation used as an epigraph for this chapter, was ignored. Perhaps observers were hoping that his sentiments were either ancillary or transitional, some kind of phase he would go through, like an unruly and feckless teenager, on the way to mature, global citizenship. Indeed, after the AKP won a landslide election victory in November 2002, earning nearly two-thirds of the seats in parliament, one of Turkey's leading journalists explained, "The public breathed a sigh of relief." A tumultuous cycle of coups, elections, and the disbanding of popular Islamist parties that had lasted decades seemed likely to be at an end.[8]

Yet, as we have already glimpsed in passing, some fifteen years later, Turkey's democracy and its rule of law have suffered grievous blows, and not from the Kemalist military that was responsible for the history of previous coups. The technology of antidemocracy has changed. Today, many of the journalists who hailed Erdoğan's early victories are either in jail or unemployed. Tens of thousands of state employees have been purged. The president has gained unprecedented control over judges and prosecutors thanks to his party's legislative reforms. And in a popular referendum held in April 2017, Erdoğan secured a slate of constitutional changes that transformed Turkey's parliamentary system, concentrating power in a rejiggered presidency. In effect, this legitimated Erdoğan as a new kind of sultan, dominating the country as no one had since Ataturk and the Ottoman emperors before him.[9]

This chapter is about what happened in Budapest, Ankara, Caracas, and beyond. We have labeled this process democratic erosion. We have defined it as the slow but substantial decay of all three of the institutional prerequisites of liberal constitutional democracy. These are free and fair elections, liberal rights of speech and association, and the administrative rule of law, particularly as it pertains to the possibility of fair elections. Democratic erosion does not take one form, and it does not have only one end point.[10] The process has moved at different rates, faced different obstacles, and triggered different counter-reactions across diverse countries. In setting out its progress, we will necessarily postpone discussion of the countervailing responses it elicits. But these exist, and, as we explore in chapter 6 and the conclusion, they have the potential to shape political developments. This is important to keep in mind, even here. In Turkey, for example, the constitutional referendum's consolidation of de facto political power in a single party generated a massive public protest march from Istanbul to Ankara.[11] In Hungary, the proposed closure of the Central European University generated the most acute public protests to date.[12] In Venezuela, meanwhile, demonstrations against Maduro intensified in 2017 and 2018 into rolling waves of street violence, with roving bands of men and women armed with plywood shields and makeshift weapons confronting armed riot police backed with armored personnel vehicles and tear gas launchers.[13] The trajectory of each of these conflicts over liberal constitutional democracy depends, in short, on many local contingencies. The result of democratic erosion should not be presumed to be irreversible or final.

We focus in this chapter, though, on the playbook of officials, elected and otherwise, for eroding the three institutional predicates of liberal democratic order. To begin with, we show that democratic regression has become the most common form of democratic backsliding. It is for this reason vital to understand the tactics involved. To that end, it is useful to start by exploring the *styles* of democratic politics that conduce to policies and practices antithetical to the substance of liberal constitutional democracy. This means taking seriously the idea of "populism" as a distinctive political style and also focusing on ways in which the system of political parties upon which national democracy typically depends can go off the rails. The heart of this chapter—and in some ways, the core of our book—is the subsequent exploration of the specific tools and instruments that can be seen being used across different cases of democratic erosion. Not all these tools are used in every case we examine—but there is a remarkable similarity among the legal and institutional instruments of democratic erosion—an underlying coherence of mechanisms that lends credence to our decision to treat these cases as a single phenomenon.

We map five specific mechanisms by which democratic erosion unfolds. By analyzing all of these mechanisms side by side, we arrive at a clear understanding of the specific elements of constitutional design that either exacerbate or mitigate the risk of such democratic erosion. The five measures are

- the use of constitutional amendments to alter basic governance arrangements;
- the elimination of checks that operate between different branches;

- the centralization and politicization of executive power as exercised through the bureaucracy;
- the contraction or distortion of a shared public sphere in which liberal rights of speech and association can be exercised; and
- the elimination or suppression of effective partisan political competition and the related prospect of rotation out of elected office.

In setting out these tools, we draw mainly on the clearest cases of erosion—Hungary, Poland, Venezuela, and Turkey—since these are the instances in which the decay in democratic quality is most difficult to dispute. But where necessary, we also look further afield. There is, alas, an increasingly diverse pool of cases to draw on, and in due course we will drink deeply from it.

The Global Diffusion of Democratic Erosion

We live in an era of easy and rapid legal borrowing and transplantation across jurisdictions. Innovations in fashion, music, and business spread across borders, and law is no exception. Smoking bans, for example, started in some municipalities in the United States, spread to states, and then diffused to many other countries around the world. The right to a free public education was articulated first in the French Declaration of the Rights of Man of 1789, and spread from there to Haiti, Norway, and other countries early in the nineteenth century. The rapid rise of information technology and the twenty-four-hour news cycle has only lowered the cost of borrowing laws and governance technology.[14] Policy diffusion across international borders is usually understood as a positive development, as good ideas can spread quickly, and learning can be aggregated across jurisdictions. But diffusion is a normatively neutral phenomenon. Bad ideas can spread as quickly as good ones through many of the same mechanisms. Democratic erosion is one example of this.

Erosion is the main form of democratic political decline across Latin America, Eastern Europe, Russia, and Asia. In sheer numbers, a larger number of countries have suffered declines in democratic quality than have undergone some form of democratic collapse. Scholars of comparative politics have been observing incremental regression in a wide range of countries, including Russia, Hungary, Poland, Thailand, Turkey, Ukraine, Venezuela, and many others.[15]

The trend may be accelerating. In chapter 3, we noted that Gero Erdmann's study of democratic trends between 1974 and 2008, identified only five full collapses out of fifty-three instances in which a democracy shifted either to a "hybrid" or an "authoritarian" regime.[16] Here, we focus on the forty-eight cases in which the shift away from democracy was not absolute but incremental and subtle; it has happened "in many different ways and for many different reasons."[17] Moreover, the conditions that characterize authoritarian collapse, in particular its association with younger and lower-income democracies, do not hold in respect to democratic erosion. Older democracies (such as India and Venezuela) and high-income countries have experienced substantial losses in democratic quality, even though they do not experience authoritarian collapses. A half dozen of Erdmann's cases were high-income countries that backslid into hybrid regimes. Moreover, as a historical matter, the United States has not proved immune from such backsliding, even if it has not yet and probably will not soon collapse into authoritarianism. For instance, by the commonly used Polity IV measure, the United States suffered a first decline in its democratic performance from 1850 through 1870, as debates over slavery and secession bubbled up into violent insurrection in Kansas and then throughout the Union.

It is hard to rigorously quantify the frequency of democratic erosion. Nevertheless, we pursue some suggestive analyses to determine whether the empirical determinants of erosion are consistent with those produced about the better-studied question of collapse. While we have no perfect measure of liberal constitutional democracy, we can use crude proxies drawn from the general literature on democratization. Specifically, we look at three different measures of democracy: the Freedom House index, which codes countries as Free, partly Free, and Unfree for every year since 1972; the Polity Index, which rates countries on a twenty-one-point scale in terms of democratic quality since 1800; and the recently released Liberal Democracy Index from the Varieties of Democracy Project (V-DEM), a sophisticated measurement exercise that tries to capture latent qualities of democratic governance. The Liberal Democracy Index captures "the state of electoral democracy, equality before the law, individual liberty, judicial constraints on the executive, and legislative constraints on the executive," and so is a fairly good proxy for our purposes.

For each of the three indicators, we constructed two new dummy variables, Erosion and Collapse. For Freedom House, Erosion marks any year in which there was a shift from Free to Partly Free ($n = 56$), and Collapse marks any drop from Free to Unfree.[18] For Polity, we consider that Erosion has occurred in any year in which there was any decline, so long as the country had a baseline score of six or higher in the prior year, unless the drop fell to the level of zero or below, in which case it is called a Collapse. For the V-DEM Liberal Democracy Index, any decline of 20%–50% in the rating is considered as an Erosion, so long as the baseline is higher than the mean score for the

TABLE 4.1. Frequency of collapses and erosions

Indicator	Coverage	Collapses	Erosions
Freedom House	1972–2016	7	56
Polity	1800–2015	39	90
V-DEM Liberal Democracy	1900–	15	79

world in that year. Any decline of greater than 50% is a Collapse, so long as the prior year was at least at the global mean. In other words, we are not looking at moves within pure autocracies.

As Table 4.1 indicates, democratic decline is not rare, but erosions dominate collapses in absolute numbers.

Using the Polity metric, which has the longest coverage, some fifty-five countries have experienced an episode of democratic erosion at some point in their history. This suggests that roughly one out of three countries will, in its lifespan, experience a meaningful decline in the quality of its democracy. Even though many of these polities remain democratic, they have undergone a process of what we call democratic erosion.

Figure 4.1 captures this trend across time. It shows that since the 1980s, and especially in the midst of the wave of democratization at the end of the Cold War, softer erosions far outnumber outright collapses. In part this is a result of the larger denominator: with more democracies in place, there is more room for backsliding. But it also indicates that the era of coups is on the decline. Interestingly, the figure also shows a recent sharp drop in the probability of erosion. This is in part an artifact of the data, which ends in 2014, before several of the more troubling cases discussed in this chapter. But the drop is also a function of the smaller denominator.

All this suggests that the technologies of democratic recession have changed over time. Whereas earlier authoritarian waves in Africa and Latin America took the form of military coups or revolutionary Socialist regimes, the current wave of authoritarianism is strategic and sophisticated in its use of the democratic form. The resulting polities are notionally governed under a democratic constitution and according to the dictates of law. But rulers manipulate the law to reflect their interests, undermining the substance of constitutional democracy, albeit without losing its form.

Why has this happened? In an online appendix we provide an exploratory empirical analysis that suggests that the determinants of erosion and collapse are fairly similar.[19] In both cases, the most important insulating factors are wealth and length of democratic experience. Erosion is best understood as a

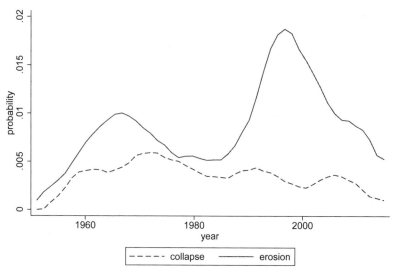

FIGURE 4.1. Frequencies over time of democratic erosion and collapse.

partial substitute for authoritarian collapse. The incremental erosion of liberal democracy's institutional and social premises typically yields forms of concentrated state power immune from democratic oversight. The degree of concentration or immunity from democratic control, though, may be less than would be achieved through a coup or an emergency declaration. But in expectation, democratic erosion seems to be a more attractive path away from democracy because it attracts less resistance. Simply put, it is easier to observe and evaluate a single rupture from democratic practice than it is to observe and evaluate the aggregate effect of many incremental cuts into democratic, liberal, and constitutional norms. Because no democratic system is perfect, there will always be some number of such violations. The precise point, however, at which the volume of democratic and constitutional backsliding amounts to democratic erosion will be unclear—both ex ante and as a contemporaneous matter.

At the same time, backsliding may involve a slippage of liberal democratic institutions into "fluid and ill-defined" arrangements, a condition in which uncertainty over both diagnosis and remedies is inevitable.[20] Under such circumstances, there will be no singular act or decision that marks a decisive break in the democratic order and signal a shift toward some form of competitive authoritarianism. Political scientists such as Barry Weingast and Thomas Schelling, as well as legal scholars such as Richard McAdams, have underscored the importance of such highly salient "focal points" in facilitating collective action in defense of legal and democratic norms. A focal point in the form of a clear constitutional text, for example, matters when diffuse social and political actors otherwise find it costly and difficult to determine whether and when a democratic system is in peril. As Weingast has explained, a menu of clear and crisp rules that serve as focal points can operate as switches. Their violation works as a coordinating signal that democracy is under threat. By contrast, the absence of a focal point will make it more difficult to organize popular resistance to the antidemocratic consolidation of political power. So it is precisely because it does not come dressed as a wolf that the threat of democratic erosion is so grave. Like the proverbial boiling frog, a democratic society in the midst of erosion may not realize its predicament until matters are already beyond redress.[21]

Given these dynamics, it is unsurprising that democratic erosion has come to dominate authoritarian collapse as the instrument of choice for unraveling democratic institutions. And, for scholars and analysts, "focusing on the military and on classic coup politics as privileged objects of research may be morally, politically, and empirically questionable."[22]

Democracy Against Itself: The Paradox of Democratic Erosion

Here, though, we face a truism that ought to be a puzzle: Cases of democratic erosion begin as liberal constitutional democracies. Unlike coups and emergencies, the force that unravels ongoing democratic contestation is often, if not necessarily, internal to the democratic system. Indeed, it is typically a political figure, party, or coalition that has just won a democratic majority for some office. This is true for Fidesz, which won a close but clear popular majority in the 2010 parliamentary election that brought it to power the second time. Moreover, in many cases, the figure or party driving the move away from democracy has not just won one election, but retains the support of a majority of the people through several election cycles, or at least more support than any other plausible ruling coalition. Hence, even if Fidesz slipped below a threshold of majority popular support in 2014, it nonetheless had far more popular support than its closest opponent, the Socialist Party. In Turkey, similarly, the AKP has won election after election. To be sure, the April 2017 referendum in Turkey was far closer than had been expected, with the constitutional changes sought by Erdoğan being approved by a bare 51.3% of the vote (and that in a campaign marred by violence against opposition politicians and serious allegations of fraud).[23] But it seems unlikely that the AKP will lose a national poll any time soon. Where a leader or a party has the support of a majority of the electorate, or at least a decisive plurality, what incentive do they have to resort to antidemocratic measures as a means of maintaining power? Why, that is, should democracy consume itself from within?

The answer, we think, lies in the ideological dynamics of the democratic system. Under certain conditions, the ordinary operation of democratic competition can produce ideologies and dynamics that corrode the foundations of democracy. Rather than a machine that persists on its own, democracy is rather an unsteady equilibrium, constantly at some risk of generating from within the forces of its own demise, even if, in most cases, it muddles through.[24] We identify two such dysfunctional styles, which we call *charismatic populism* and *partisan degradation*. While both may result in the systemic dysfunctions that result in erosion, the two routes are distinct. One emphasizes an individual leader, while the other hinges on a partisan or ideological position that emerges as a matter of party-level competition. Neither seeks to explicitly end democracy in the sense of ceasing to hold regular elections with some superficial veneer of competition. This distinguishes them from cases of authoritarian collapse. At the same time, however, neither style is loyal to the inherited rules of democratic contestation. Both, instead, dismantle those rules for political gain.

CHARISMATIC POPULISM

Populism is best viewed as democracy's dysfunctional cousin. It exhibits many of the same morphological characteristics but lacks the moral appeal and long-term stability of a healthy democratic regime. Among the many definitions of populism available in the political science literature, we adapt one offered by Jan-Werner Müller.[25] As we interpret his account, populism is less a matter of policy preferences and more a matter of the guiding assumptions about how democracy can and should work, and how leaders can and should relate to the people.

There are two key characteristics to Müller's account of populism. *First*, populists assert a "moralized antipluralism" based on a belief that "they, and they alone, represent the people," whereas any other electoral option or policy choice is illegitimate and perhaps futile. *Second*, the populist has a "noninstitutionalized notion of 'the people'" This means that the populist asserts or assumes that there is a singular and morally privileged understanding or will that has not been manifested through the formal structures of democratic choice. Müller quotes Perón's assertion that "the political leader does what the people want" as an instance of such a claim of immanent and noninstitutionalized popular will.[26] Whereas, on the ordinary understanding of democracy, the actions of a specific coalition or leader are always amenable to critique as unrepresentative, on a populist's understanding, it is not possible to challenge or doubt the decisions of a populist leader, who has a direct knowledge of the people's will. In practical terms, this means that populists tend to organize their election campaigns by targeting political and cultural elites. The latter are tarred as traitors or leeches that stand in the true people's way and prevent them from realizing their full potential.

The AKP of Turkey provides a useful example of populism at work. Prior to the party's victory in 2002, it was standard fare for bureaucrats and army officers to refer to the very substantial tranche of religious Turks as "reactionary or retarded," a contempt manifested in the policy of excluding those with beards or head coverings from public service. With some reason, therefore, the devout ranks of the Turkish lower and middle classes could perceive in Erdoğan and his party a vindication of their status as Turkish citizens against the previously hegemonic secular norm. It is the continued support of those segments of the public that has sustained the AKP party for more than a decade and a half without major changes to the electoral system or major election fraud.[27] After about 2010, the AKP in general, and Erdoğan in particular, have made an increasingly overt nationalist and populist claim to legitimacy. He has made a habit of referring to "my people," and of asking his critics, "We are the people. Who are you?"[28] This political logic is facilitated by the AKP party's organization around a hierarchical "cult of Erdoğan,"[29] which reinforces and confirms his claim to a distinctive and unique mandate on behalf of people and nation. It is this populist logic that animates and informs the violent suppression of demonstrations in Gezi Park, the attacks on independent news agencies such as Zaman and Cihan, and the dismantling of independent elements of the state that might have checked the AKP party's policies on legality or corruption grounds. The challenge to democracy posed by the populist stance and tactics of the AKP Party can be generalized—and indeed, we shall see it recapitulated, and even extended, in Venezuela, Bolivia, Hungary, and Poland (among other places). It is also implicit in the political styles of Berlusconi's Forza Italia, Modi's BJP, and Trump's Republican Party. So understood, populism is having something of a global renaissance these days.

A useful feature of Müller's definition is that it has been detached from the ordinary left-right axis of European and American political contestation. Although much attention has been focused on right-wing nationalist populism in recent years, charismatic populism is not confined to the political right. Hugo Chávez in Venezuela, Evo Morales in Bolivia, and even Rafael Correa in Ecuador can be ranked as populists. Even within the latter group, though, there are differences. Correa's form of populism, for example, was far milder than Chavismo, and has not proved as inimical to continued democratic contestation.[30] Indeed, we think that Müller's definition might even stretch to include American presidential candidate Bernie Sanders's call for a political revolution against Wall Street, to the extent that it entailed a kind of demonization of enemies inimical to "the people." (Other features of Sanders's campaign, we hasten to add, do not fit the same bill). Indeed, anti-elite mobilization of various sorts is a recurring and proper feature of democratic politics. It arises as a demand for accountability and thus plays a useful role in ensuring that the government does not deviate too far from popular preferences or systematically neglect the interests of a meaningful tranche of the population. Populism can emerge either in the form of a new party or through a populist candidate's capture of an established party; the plausibility of each of these pathways depends on the details of a nation's electoral system and its legal arrangements for selecting established party candidates. Even if it seems that candidates and parties employing this rhetoric are antisystem, they typically accept the overall architecture of democracy, including a nominally free media, courts, free and fair elections, and a bureaucratic apparatus that is distinct from partisan formations.

In its paradoxical appeal to and simultaneous attack upon democratic practice, populism exploits and amplifies basic dilemmas of liberal constitutional democracy. Where the latter supplies no criteria for the identification of its own demographic and political boundaries, populism stipulates those boundaries by the brute force of will. Where democracy requires elaborate procedures to solve cycling problems, refine the quality of deliberation, and protect minority interests, populism offers strident appeals to parsimony and simplicity: Vote for me, and the real voice of the people will be realized. Populism, in short, takes advantage of the deep theoretical difficulties hard-wired into modern democratic procedures as a means to dismantle the legitimacy of political competition, the rule of law, and liberal rights. Hence, while the contemporary populist may initially seek to work within democratic institutions, democracy. as Erdoğan explained, is merely the publicly supplied mode of transportation to another goal.

With these distinctions in place, we are well situated to see how populism poses a distinct threat to liberal constitutional democracy. The contemporary form of populism that centrally concerns us here is a charismatic one. It involves a single leader whose beliefs license her to speak directly for the people, to demonize as alien and illicit all political foes, and to insulate herself from both legal and electoral accountability. Because the populist leader alone channels and manifests the will of the people, there is no need for intermediate institutions of traditional representative democracy. Indeed, by implication, institutions such as courts, legislatures, and ombudsmen that resist the populist program are instruments of a corrupt and illicit elite. If the leader has a unique ability to intuit the people's desires, then there is no need for any other institution to help articulate or represent the people, or to stand in the way.

It follows from this logic that populists will adopt tactics that place pressure upon the election framework and undermine its free and fair character. Populists will commonly point to the complexity of the electoral and governance system, with its tendency to generate gridlock or compromise, as a justification for their criticisms. This is known as the "Bagehot problem," after the great British journalist and constitutional theorist Walter Bagehot. He pointed out that complex institutional arrangements for representation that seek to account for a plurality of interests rarely appear clear or fair to the average citizen. While Bagehot himself invoked this as a justification for monarchy, the opacity of a modern representative democracy can be used to justify other alternatives to collective self-determination through elections.[31] The popularity of populists will rest on their asserted ability to slice the Gordian knot of representative democratic institutions and to replace that overly complex machinery with a single demagogic gesture—a gesture that both reflects and realizes the people.

A populist party is also likely to assemble a political party or movement that is "antisystem" in the sense that it is simply incompatible with the necessary institutional predicates of democracy depicted in chapter 1.[32] Populist rhetoric disparages the legitimacy of competitive elections, the circulation of parties in and out of power, and even the possibility of criticism of populist leaders when they are in power. When in power, therefore, populists have a ready ideological justification for dismantling the administrative rule of law that works as condition precedent to public confidence in electoral systems and ordinary government. They also are ideologically predisposed to target political enemies, especially former elites, with public attacks or even criminal punishment. Although they may flirt with violence, often by relying on assaults and brutality from supporters within and outside the government, the populist will not overtly embrace the extermination of political foes. This reticence distinguishes today's populism from prior waves of revolutionary populism, such as those associated with China's Mao Zedong or the Khmer Rouge movement in Cambodia, whose end goal was not merely taking and holding power but permanently consolidating it through violent revolution.

In addition, populists can mobilize support, and possibly win office, by violating informal or legal norms. By demonstrating that they are in some sense above the ordinary law (which, by stipulation, is corrupt and contemptible), populists manifest a charismatic power to transcend the system they seek to discredit. In all these ways, the populist's style of political claim-making and governing poses a threat to liberal constitutional democracy. The animating intuition of populism is articulated with surprising clarity by its figureheads and their acolytes. As the primary drafter of Venezuela's 1998 Constitution put it in describing Hugo Chávez's early days in power, "We really thought of Chávez himself as the government."[33] In the end, the populist also seeks to scale the commanding heights of political power as a means to restricting those institutions and ultimately monopolizing them. The populist's belief in his or her (and it is quite possible to have a "her," as in the case of Argentina's Cristina Fernández de Kirchner) unique relationship to a univocal people is translated into institutional form.

The charismatic basis of populists' claim to legitimate rule also has implications for the manner in which they govern. Populism is a "thin" ideology in the sense that it is consistent with many combinations of policies, only some of which are logically related to the representational claim on which populism is founded.[34] Some, like Perón or Thaksin Shinawatra, follow through on redistributive promises. Others, in contrast, pursue regressive policies. The Fidesz Party, but not the Polish populist Justice and Development Party, has pursued aggressive cuts to welfare programs, although in other respects its policies are better described as statist than neoliberal.[35] The immateriality of results as a metric of democratic legitimacy also invites corruption, which is often endemic under populist regimes. Even in still-competitive democratic contexts, such as Austria's and Italy's, the venality of the Freedom Party and the Lega Nord have done little to dent their standing with the voting publics.[36] In Turkey, accusations of corruption leveled at Erdoğan and his son have also not compromised his popularity.[37] Indeed, it is possible that there is even an affirmative political benefit to populists from breaking the rules. When a populist leader says, "See, I violated these rotten laws," she not only slights the importance of legality and of respect for the democratic system overall, but also shows a quasi-magical ability to defy it. The violation of established norms, whether by inciting violence, failing to make routine disclosures, or engaging in nepotism, reflects the populist's claim of being aligned against rather than with the political system in ways that may well redound to their ultimate electoral benefit.

Populists' seeming insensitivity to the outcomes of their policy choices has implications for their electoral strategies. For if populists tend to be more corrupt and less outcome-focused than other candidates or elected officials, they have good reason to frame their campaigns *not* around substantive policy issues, but around the emotional questions of belonging and exclusion, of loyalty and betrayal, and of insiders and outsiders that define their political identity. This has a tendency, over time, to drive elections—the motor of democratic accountability—away from a focus on meaningful, practical metrics of success toward the inchoate and emotionally volatile terrain of belonging, or even blood. Hence the intimate connection between populism and various strains of ugly, sometimes violent, ethnic or religious nationalism. In so doing, the populist excavates and deepens yet another deep fissure in democracy's necessary foundations—the assumption of a shared citizenship despite differences in ethnicity, religion, or language.

While a democratically elected populist leader can dismantle the democratic predicates that made their rise to power possible in the first place, the populist leader may not only represent the views and harness the passions of either a substantial plurality or a majority of the country; he may also plausibly claim to speak for a group that had previously been excluded or marginalized from national politics in the past. Populism arises out of demands for accountability and in situations where traditional party systems are fragile or under strain. In this sense, populism has a double-edged character: It can at once work as a vindication of voices squeezed out or ignored in a democracy and, at the extreme, can leverage the support of those same excluded voices to eliminate the pluralistic character of the public sphere and even end democratic contestation.

PARTISAN DEGRADATION

A second mechanism of erosion that arises through the operation of democratic choice is *partisan degradation*: By this we mean the deterioration of a competitive party system into a species of political competition that undermines the institutional foundations of democracy. There are two ways in which partisan degradation can occur. One pathway relates to charismatic populism and can be addressed relatively briefly. The second, however, is distinct and benefits from more extended discussion. This is especially so as it supplies an opportunity for thinking about where democratic erosion starts and what to make of national cases in which erosion has not set in along all three of the institutional prerequisites that we have identified.

The first way in which partisan degradation can occur is through the decline of an established and competitive system of political parties so as to leave open a political gap for a new populist leader to seize power. Venezuela is a straightforward example of this dynamic. Between 1958 and 1998, national politics in Venezuela were dominated by the *"punto fijo"* regime, a "pacted" arrangement involving an agreement between two powerful political parties, the center-left Acción Democrática and the center-right Social Christian Party (COPEI), to engage in the periodic alternation of power. In the 1980s, the collapse of global oil prices and a foreign debt crisis placed great strain on this arrangement. An early sign of difficulties to come came in 1993, when COPEI's founder, Rafael Caldera, broke from the party and ran for the presidency as an independent. While Caldera won, his accession was immediately followed by a severe banking crisis. By 1998, the two established parties' vote shares in legislative elections had fallen to below 50%. The stage was set for the ascent to power of Hugo Chávez, who had led a failed coup attempt some years before. A collapse in a long-standing structure of partisan oppositions, in short, directly opened the political opportunity for a populist with authoritarian leanings to seize power.[38]

Not every collapse in an established party system, however, will lead to an opening for a populist candidate. Party systems can realign. Instability in the overall party system is in fact quite common, even in seemingly entrenched European democracies.[39] Realignment also does not necessarily entail an opening for populists. In the 2017 French presidential elections, for instance, both the established right (Republican) and left (Socialist) candidates failed to get to the second round of voting. Both were beaten by the populist National Front candidate Marine Le Pen. But then Le Pen was beaten by the centrist Emmanuel Macron's new En Marche Party (even though she secured almost twice as large a vote share as her father had in a second-round presidential run-off election in 2002). En Marche and allied parties went on to win 350 of 577 seats in France's National Assembly immediately thereafter, while the National Front won only 9 seats. Similarly, in the United Kingdom, the 2015 election and the Brexit referendum seemed like harbingers of a party realignment in which the left-leaning Labour Party would collapse. But a 2017 snap election called by Conservative leader Theresa May led to a surprising rebound in Labour support, especially among younger voters.[40]

The second way in which change in the structure of the party system can lead to democratic erosion does not require a collapse of that system or a spike of populist fervor. It just requires one side to win really convincingly. In this scenario, however, the relevant actor is a party rather than a personality. Of course these two categories may blend into each other. We present them as distinct for analytic clarity.

In normal times, liberal constitutional democracy involves a rough kind of equilibrium between parties, in which competition occurs within a set of fixed rules. When in power, parties accept the rules of the game—including the rules and norms sustaining the three institutional supports of democracy—

because they reasonably anticipate the possibility of rotation out of power and the possibility of being in opposition.[41] In this fashion, the rules of the democratic game tend to become, as Barry Weingast argues, "self-enforcing," even absent any assumption about political culture. Reciprocity means that everyone has skin in the game.[42]

But this steady, competitive state might fail if one party becomes functionally invulnerable to rotation, such that it lacks an incentive to consider the consequences of disregarding the rules of the democratic game. Under these conditions, a party acting to maximize self-interest—and lacking any intrinsic populist motivations—might seek a political advantage from changing the fundamental rules of the game itself. For example, a party might seek to restrict associational life to its own partisan advantage, using restrictions on particular kinds of organizing or demonstrating. It might try to exert control over the media, using techniques such as licensing newspapers or websites. Or it might resort to outright censorship through criminal prosecutions or simple violence. These actions would degrade the public sphere in derogation of our second prerequisite of liberal constitutional democracy. Alternatively, the hegemonic party might politicize the selection of judicial, bureaucratic, and prosecutorial offices that are supposed to be insulated from partisan conflict. It might do so with an eye to using these elements of the state to entrench itself even further against political competition, as well as more simply to further favored policy ends. For example, in the vast majority of democracies, appointments to the judiciary involve some insulation from direct control of the executive branch. Indeed by some definitions, an independent judiciary must be appointed in a nonpartisan way, with multiple actors involved.[43] But these formal, arms-length structures can themselves be manipulated, and a party that seeks to extend its control over all branches of government will be motivated to do so.

We have already seen one extreme example of partisan degradation at work in Venezuela—a nation that has travelled, by any measure, a long way down the path of democratic erosion. But it is possible to discern partisan degradation at work in other, seemingly well-established democracies. Here, we briefly examine Japan and Israel. These are countries in which democratic regression has not (yet) occurred, but which have witnessed some deterioration in one of the three necessary elements of liberal constitutional democracy. Such cases usefully illuminate the border between a fully functional democracy and one that has started to regress. These case studies hence shed light on what the first buds of erosion look like, even if those buds do not eventually bloom into an autocratic spring.

Consider first the Japanese case. Since 1955, political power at the national level has been more or less monopolized by the Liberal Democratic Party (or

LDP), with brief opposition interludes in 1993 to 1994, and 2009 to 2012. Prior to 1993, the LDP was decentralized and fragmented, saddled with weak prime ministerial leadership, and checked by a strong, elitist national bureaucracy. The result was a focus on economic issues. There was relatively little effort by the LDP to undermine the democratic rules of the game, although it did rely on clientalist patronage politics and a redistricting system that heavily favored rural votes, in order to keep its majority status.[44]

In contrast, the current LDP prime minister, Shinzō Abe—who is, like many present and former LDP ministers, a member of the controversial nationalist organization Nippon Kaigi—has taken a different tack, adopting policies that suggest a measure of impending partisan degradation.[45] First, Abe has proposed an amendment to Japan's Constitution to emphasize that freedoms and rights are accompanied by duties and obligations, and must be exercised in ways that do not violate the public interest and public order. This amendment would specifically append Article 21's simple and unqualified guarantee of "freedom of speech, press and all other forms of expression" with a significant limitation clause: "Notwithstanding the foregoing, engaging in activities with the purpose of damaging the public interest or public order, or associating with others for such purposes, shall not be recognized."[46] While limitations clauses attached to constitutional rights are not unusual in other constitutions, critics have noted the vagueness of phrases like "public order," whose invocation tends to receive extreme deference from Japanese courts. In a Japanese context, public order may be expansive indeed: even without such a qualification, the courts have never struck down a national law for violating the freedom of expression.

Second, and relatedly, the Abe government has enacted a series of acts in recent years that seem to inhibit public discourse. In 2014, a sweeping new Specially Designated Secrets Act took effect, punishing leakers of government secrets, including journalists who "instigate" leaks.[47] This further centralized control of information that might undermine the governing party's claims, and hence saps the force of democratic competition.

Third, the Japanese Diet (or parliament) in June 2017 passed a controversial "anticonspiracy" bill. Its nominal justification is a concern about terrorism around the 2019 Rugby World Cup and the 2020 Olympic Games. But the law criminalizes planning and conspiracy to commit some 277 criminal offenses. These include stealing forest products, exporting cultural property without permission, and copyright violations—matters with no colorable connection to sporting events. Critics fear the measure will further stifle press freedoms.[48] Meanwhile, the Supreme Court has approved police surveillance of Japanese Muslims based solely on religious affiliation, without evidence of wrongdoing.[49]

Finally, Abe has been widely criticized for organizing a crackdown on media critics, including the firing of reporters who have engaged in aggressive investigative reporting, and a government threat to revoke the licenses of broadcasters deemed hostile to the administration. A conservative businessman was appointed to the head of the public Japan Broadcasting Corporation (*Nippon Hōsō Kyōkai* or NHK) in 2014, and said that the organization should "not deviate from the government's position in its broadcasting." Recent scandals suggest close collusion among government and the organized media. In 2016, a government minister warned that broadcasters could have their licenses revoked if they were not politically "impartial." In 2017, the organization Reporters without Borders dropped Japan to 72nd out of 180 nations in terms of press freedom, explaining that state attacks on the media "are endangering the underpinnings of democracy in Japan."[50] That these changes in the media environment have been accompanied by a proposal to reduce the amount of question time allocated for the opposition in parliament suggests a desire to push partisan advantage in the core of democratic institutions.[51] All this does not necessarily constitute erosion as we have defined it, since it concerns only a partial backsliding of one of our three elements of liberal constitutional democracy. Elections are still regularly held and competitive, and the courts remain autonomous if quiescent. Instead, it is evidence of the potential for partisan degradation to set in during prolonged one-party rule, a process that might, given time, imperil the other elements of liberal constitutional democracy.[52]

A somewhat similar dynamic can be discerned in the case of Israel. It seems fair to say that Israeli democracy reflects the internal tensions implicit in the founding commitment to being both a Jewish and democratic state. In terms of its status as a liberal constitutional democracy, by our definition, Israel clears the bar. It has free and vigorous public elections. No groups are fully excluded from participation, even the otherwise highly marginalized Arab minority within Israel. It maintains a rule of law centered around a Supreme Court that remains well respected both domestically and abroad. And it has a set of core civil liberties for freedom of association and expression that facilitate political organization and protest, even for outsiders. To be sure, both its domestic electoral structure and its respect for human rights in the occupied territories have been subject to vigorous and extensive criticism. Its electoral system, which is the more pertinent object of criticism here, uses proportional representation with a low threshold and so rewards smaller parties. In practice, coalitions have tended to overweight the voice of ultra-orthodox groups; an informal agreement among the largest parties in the Knesset furthermore excludes the Arab members of parliament from joining government coalitions. Most of the criticism of the election system and Israel's record on human rights, however, is by and large orthogonal to our institutional definition of liberal constitutional democracy.[53]

In our context, a different set of policies triggers concern. Specifically, recent legislative moves by a right-of-center coalition headed by Benjamin Netanyahu are a potentially troubling departure from democratic norms. Although as we write he is currently under investigation in relation to a corruption scandal, with the threat of prosecution very much in the air, Netanyahu has been prime minister for much of the last two decades, thanks to his ability to cobble together different coalitions as befits the needs of the moment. We can thus focus on him as a potential agent of partisan degradation. With this in mind, consider recent legislation passed by the Knesset that has aimed at the free operation of the domestic political sphere. One somewhat ambiguous example that has garnered a good deal of criticism at home is the country's adoption of an "NGO transparency bill." Adopted in July 2017, the bill imposes a suite of disclosure requirements on not-for-profit groups that receive funding from foreign governmental sources. These groups, in practice, are mainly critical of settlements in the occupied territories, even as the settlements themselves are supported largely by nongovernmental donations from outside Israel that need not lawfully be disclosed. It is no small irony for a country that was dependent on foreign donors for its initial decades of existence, and which continues to receive massive military aid from the United States, to use the fact of foreign funding as a political cudgel. We note that the example is ambiguous because transparency in funding is not on its own incompatible with democracy, but in this case the foreign support is not seeking to undermine democracy either. It simply intervenes on one side of a vigorous domestic dispute.

Beyond the NGO bill, the Netanyahu government has sought to limit criticism in the public sphere. It has created a civil action against those who call for a boycott against the country. It has proposed criminalizing any commemoration of the Day of Independence as the Nakba, the term used by Palestinians to denote it as a disaster, though the final version of the law did not include criminal penalties. Minister of Culture Miri Regev introduced a "loyalty in culture" bill to penalize artists who express ideas judged to manifest disloyalty to the state and has sought to defund artists whose work she disapproves of on ideological grounds.[54] Exclusionary forms of politics have also arisen in the religious and educational domain. The Chief Rabbinate, which has an affinity with several right-wing parliamentary parties, has taken a severely exclusionary turn, issuing blacklists of orthodox rabbis whose conversions will not be recognized by the state and, through the Ministry of Interior, conducting forms of "extreme vetting" before allowing Jews to immigrate under the Law of Return. The Ministry of Education has sought to introduce a "code of conduct" to prevent academics from expressing views in the classroom on public issues.[55] Even parliamentary speech, which lies at the heart of the democratic process, is being constrained. In 2016, the Knesset passed a law allowing members to be expelled for what the majority deems to be incitement, racism, or advocacy of struggle against the state. This tool seems most likely to be wielded against the Arab minority members. In a move that seemed to target the democratic rule of law, Netanyahu's Knesset allies in 2017 introduced a bill calling for a ban on corruption investigations of sitting prime ministers. All these incremental, illiberal shifts add up. In a telling sign, the Economist Intelligence Unit ranks Israel as a "flawed democracy" chiefly on the basis of its poor score on civil liberties. In 2016, Israel ranked eighty-fifth for civil liberties, clustered around lower-ranked "flawed democracies," such as Sri Lanka and Malaysia, as well as higher-ranked "hybrid regimes," such as Mali and Honduras.[56]

Neither Japan nor Israel can yet be ranked as a case of democratic erosion. Support for democratic institutions among the public remains strong in both places. In our judgment, the damage to the three institutional predicates of democracy is not sufficiently extensive to justify the erosion label (although we recognize that matters might look different to those on the sharp end of exclusionary tactics). Rather, both usefully illustrate how a state of one-party hegemony, in which partisan competition is degraded, and the dominant party can reasonably expect to remain in power for the medium term, can induce the first moves toward such erosion. In such a context, the dominant party lacks a sufficient expectation of being out of power to refrain from institutional changes that undermine the possibility of fair competition. In this way, near-term hegemony creates incentives to fashion conditions for long-term hegemony. Because a robust and competitive party system is a sine qua non of any going democratic concern, its failure can produce policies that damage the viability of that system.[57] In both Israel and Japan, liberal rights of speech and association are being circumscribed in ways that seem likely to influence the dynamics and content of political debate. These harbingers of potential erosion illustrate a party-based mechanism, in addition to charismatic populism, whereby the decay of democratic institutions can be animated by forces emerging from within the polity.

Partisan degradation can lead to a range of end-states. On the one hand, it is by no means certain that either Japan or Israel will tip into full-scale erosion. This depends on whether their hegemonic coalitions attempt to undermine other institutional predicates of democracy, such as free and fair elections or the administrative rule of law. Whether a coalition pursues such a path is highly contingent on its internal makeup, the personalities wielding power, and the responses of the electorate. On the other hand, party dynamics can conduce to an absolute collapse in democratic processes. The sudden collapse of the Weimar democracy was preceded, for example, by the increasing unwillingness of the Social Democratic Party in the late 1920s to form political coalitions, and by its willingness to block the formation of coalitions by others. These actions yielded a polarized and unstable structure of parties circulating through elected office. Similarly, Argentina's early twentieth-century experience with democracy before the military coup of September 1930 was also undermined, perhaps fatally, by intense conflict between a dominant political party and excluded political factions.[58]

The reasons why partisan degradation slips into democratic backsliding on some but not other occasions are only beginning to be understood. As the examples of both Japan and Israel show, one-party rule can persist for many years without slipping into democratic erosion. To date, local explanations rather than general theories dominate the scholarly literature. One study of South Africa, Hungary, and Turkey, for example, suggests that hegemonic party rule becomes dysfunctionally autocratic when there is a sharp social cleavage, and the opposing party draws support from the other side of that divide. Another analysis of Evo Morales's rise to power in Bolivia, by contrast, emphasizes the role of party elites in exacerbating social cleavages.[59] When each side of a bilaterally divided nation perceives the other side as extreme and as imperiling its very existence, politics can assume a zero-sum character. Something of the dynamic is apparent too in the run-up to the American Civil War of the 1860s—and perhaps also in the increasingly unbridgeable partisan divide in the United States of today.[60]

Common to these accounts is a coincidence of partisan degradation with a more general perception that the party system reflects a deep and intractable social or cultural cleavage. Of course, the perception of an irreconcilable social divide might emerge from partisan conflict, rather than driving partisan conflict in the first instance, so it is important to be cautious about attributing causality. What does seem evident, though, is the clear and present danger to democracy of a hegemonic party operating in the context of perceived or actual deep social divides.

The Legal and Institutional Mechanisms of Democratic Erosion

Democratic erosion is typically an aggregative process made up of many smaller increments. But those measures are rarely frontal assaults on one of the three institutional predicates of liberal constitutional democracy, of the kind that might be associated with an overtly totalitarian or fascist regime. To the contrary, many of those incremental measures are "conceal[ed] under the mask of law."[61] The patina of legality is misleading. Even though most or even all of the individual steps are taken within constitutional limits, in sum they lead to qualitative changes in the legal and political systems. The key to understanding democratic erosion is to see how discrete measures, which either in isolation or in the abstract might be justified as consistent with democratic norms, can nevertheless be deployed as mechanisms to unravel liberal constitutional democracy.

The Hungarian and Venezuelan scenarios with which we began this chapter, along with similar cases, reveal five particular legal and institutional mechanisms through which erosion occurs. The five mechanisms we identify are deployed, on the one hand, to directly attack the administrative rule of law, liberal rights of speech and association, or free and fair elections. Alternatively, they undermine the supervisory and remedial mechanisms that make free speech or free democratic choice feasible. An analytic thread—between the threefold definition of liberal constitutional democracy, the corresponding definition of erosion, and the array of mechanisms through which the latter plays out—ties together the various parts of our account. Despite the linkages between the mechanisms described below and the project of democratic erosion, it is still worthwhile to look closely at specific cases, because the tools of erosion are often quite subtle. Indeed, one of the most important aspects of our analysis is that it identifies tools that operate within the bounds of law and often appears on first examination not only as perfectly normal, but even as defensible on one or another policy ground.

Our aim in what follows is to isolate these five mechanisms as distinctive backsliding strategies. To be clear at the start, however, these mechanisms overlap in practice. A formal constitutional amendment might be (and indeed has been) used to eliminate interbranch checks, as we shall see shortly. The elimination of a competitive media environment and the extinguishing of partisan competition are intimately related in practice. Nevertheless, the nuances separating these different tactics are sufficiently important to warrant separate treatment.

FORMAL CONSTITUTIONAL AMENDMENT

The first and perhaps most obviously available pathway to democratic erosion uses formal constitutional amendment as a tool to disadvantage or marginalize political opposition and deliberative pluralism. As we have already

seen in Hungary, the Fidesz Party seized on the happenstance of a supermajority share of legislative seats in 2010 first to amend and then to replace the
nation's constitution. Constitutional change then enabled Fidesz to tilt the
electoral playing field in its favor, as well as allowing it to capture the judiciary
and independent elements of government, such as the Electoral Commission,
Budget Commission, and Media Board.

But the changes aimed at entrenching Fidesz and eliminating the possibility of democratic rotation do not exhaust the species of problematic constitutional amendment. To use David Landau's suggestive phrasing, "abusive" constitutional change can also come in more subtle forms. According
to Landau's cross-national study, antidemocratic constitutional amendments
typically concern either electoral regulation or the extent to which the rights
of individuals and minority groups are protected.[62] Consistent with Landau's
insights, the 2010–11 changes to the Hungarian Constitution provide two examples of ways by which constitutional change can undermine democracy.

First, the Orbán government's ability to achieve these changes depended
upon quite careful manipulation of parliamentary rules, changes that could
easily be viewed as technocratic and neutral so far as the maintenance of democracy is concerned. For instance, in 1995, the constitution had been changed
to require a four-fifths vote of parliament to recalibrate the rules for changing the constitution. This 1995 amendment, however, was not itself protected
from amendment by less than four-fifths of parliament. Fidesz thus used its
two-thirds supermajority to eviscerate the four-fifths threshold in the 1995
provision, thus dissolving what might previously have seemed a fairly secure
barrier against constitutional changes. Similarly, the old constitution had required a majority of the political parties in the legislature to agree to candidates
for the Supreme Court before they could be elected upon a two-thirds vote.
Once more, Fidesz deployed its potentially transient supermajority as a means
to eliminating the multiparty check on new judicial appointments, leaving the
power to staff an expanding Supreme Court in the hands of the increasingly
hegemonic party. Its justification for these centralizing constitutional changes
at this time, offered with no apparent irony, was that Hungary remained under
the thumb of its Communist heritage, the one-party dictatorship that Orbán
had so eloquently decried as a young radical in 1989.[63]

Second, the effect of a constitutional design may not be obvious until its
operation over time. Analysis in a longer time frame must also account for
partisan effects. For example, among the new additions to the constitutional
architecture made by Fidesz was a new budget council with three members
selected by the (Fidesz-controlled) parliament for terms ranging from six to
twelve years. This new budget council could veto any budget that added to

the national debt and hence was touted as a commitment to fiscal rectitude. But the council has quite a different effect on electoral dynamics—one that is potentially inconsistent with its fiscal role: The constitution also gives the parliament an annual deadline of March 31 to pass a budget, and it allows the president of the republic to dissolve the parliament if it fails to meet that deadline. To see the pernicious effect of this institutional innovation, imagine that the opposition to Fidesz wins a legislative majority in the coming years. They will still have to pass a budget, but the (Fidesz-controlled) budget council can always veto that budget up to the point when the (Fidesz-controlled) presidency can dissolve the parliament for . . . failing to pass a budget. In practical effect, therefore, the budget council is an instrument of one-party hegemony beyond the loss of a parliamentary majority—one that, if Fidesz is sufficiently disciplined, is unlikely to have any effect on budgeting in the ordinary (Fidesz-controlled) run of things.[64]

Constitutional amendment is not an inevitable part of democratic erosion. For example, in Poland, where another populist administration has sought to entrench a hegemonic position by emulating Fidesz, a higher threshold for constitutional amendment closed off that route.[65] In contrast, constitutional transformation has become a common element in the toolkit of populists, particularly in Latin America, seeking to degrade democracy. In 1998, for example, when Hugo Chávez became president, he faced an ideologically hostile Congress and Supreme Court. Rather than seeking a legislative pact with the opposition, as the previous president had done, Chávez called for a referendum to hold a new constituent assembly. He made this appeal notwithstanding the fact that the constitution of 1961 then in effect, contained no provision for a constituent assembly, and instead vested the authority to amend in the legislation. As in Hungary, however, a procedural innovation had profound effect: Chávez's Fifth Republic Movement won the ultimately held referendum by a massive 85% and went on to sweep the July 1999 polls for election to the assembly itself.

As we have seen already, this first Chávista constituent assembly declared itself "legally omnipresent." Targeting the president's political foes, it closed Congress, purged the judiciary, and gutted the electoral bureaucracy. In this fashion, the constitutional amendment *process*—in the form of a constituent assembly—rather than the substance of constitutional amendments themselves can become a vehicle for erosion. Constituent assemblies of this ilk are likely to be particularly attractive to populists such as Chávez, who claim to be exercising the sovereign power of the people directly and personally against a corrupt political elite. In the span of a few months, though, the assembly also fashioned a new constitution that radically reshaped the electoral

landscape of Venezuela. Its substance was quite relevant to the trajectory of
Venezuelan democracy. Perhaps most importantly, it dramatically increased
the power of the presidency. Among other measures, a single four-year term
limit was replaced with a limit of two six-year terms. It also added a suite
of new powers to the executive branch. While plausibly labeled democratic
if viewed in isolation, the 1999 constitutional text is instead better compre-
hended in tandem with the institutional purges conducted by the assembly.
In that context its antidemocratic effects are readily apparent. Further, where
Chávez has resorted to putatively democratic means to entrench himself and
been rebuffed, he has responded in ways that show his shallow fidelity to
actual democracy. Hence, when voters rejected a slate of changes had had
put before them in a 2007 referendum aimed at concentrating his power, his
response was unequivocal. "Enjoy your shitty victory," he is reported to have
said, even as he committed to achieving the same changes through executive
orders—a commitment he fulfilled in short order.[66]

Both Rafael Correa in Ecuador and Evo Morales in Bolivia also relied on
extensive constitutional amendment as an opening gambit in a process of
democratic erosion. Correa achieved his desired amendment after engineering the removal of more than half the members of Congress.[67] In Bolivia,
Morales's Movement toward Socialism (MAS) also convened elections for a
new constituent assembly but then failed to obtain the two-thirds majority
necessary to exercise the degree of control Chávez had in Venezuela. MAS
nevertheless achieved many of the constitutional changes it sought, in part
by manipulating the assembly's procedures, and in part through violently
preventing opposition legislators from casting key votes. The final text of
the new constitution, indeed, was approved while the assembly was sitting
in Oruro, a city near La Paz, in a building surrounded by protesting crowds
that prevented opposition politicians from even entering. To some observers,
both the process and the result moved Morales squarely into the position of
"competitive authoritarian," whereas other commentators have stressed the
ways in which MAS modulated its positions and found compromises with
the opposition.[68]

The 2009 Bolivian Constitution imposes a two-term limit on presidents.
Nevertheless, in 2014, Morales ran for and won a third term of office after obtaining a Supreme Court ruling to the effect that his first term, which began
prior to the constitution coming into force, did not "count."[69] Having failed
to obtain the ability to secure a fourth term by popular referendum, Morales
and his allies turned to the courts, securing an implausible and audacious
ruling that term limits violated his human rights.[70] As we write, he is prepar-
ing to run once again. In many other cases, term limits designed to prevent

an individual leader's entrenchment in a position of supreme authority have been weakened or eliminated by constitutional amendment. For example, in 2015 Rafael Correa secured an amendment to the Ecuadoran Constitution lifting term limits from 2021, although he subsequently gave up his office, and his successor reversed the constitutional amendment. In Russia, President Vladimir Putin, when confronted with a term limit that would have displaced him from office, simply arranged for a constitutional amendment that would strengthen the powers of the prime minister, an office he duly occupied for a term. Putin then returned to the presidency in 2012. Sri Lanka's President Mahindra Rajapaksa engineered a constitutional amendment in 2010 to allow him the chance to run again in 2016, despite term limits. Similar dissolutions of constitutional term limits have been observed from Azerbaijan to Uganda. The proposal to abolish presidential term limits in the Chinese constitution in February 2018 presents a more complicated case, because it does not arise against a background of ongoing democratic contestation—but nevertheless shows nicely how important time limits are as mechanisms for diffusing and sharing political power. Indeed, the importance of term limits as constraints on democratic erosion is perversely demonstrated by the manner in which they are now attacked. Whereas in an earlier era, simply ignoring the constitutional constraints on a president's term was quite common, in the period since 1989 more than three quarters of attempts at term-limit extension have proceeded via constitutional amendment. And the vast majority of these attempts have been successful.[71]

THE ELIMINATION OF INSTITUTIONAL CHECKS

The daily practice of liberal constitutional democracy relies upon a measure of institutional differentiation within government. There is a long tradition, dating back at least to drafters of the American Constitution, such as James Madison, and to the great French liberal François Guiznot of taking "the radical illegitimacy of absolute power" as a touchstone for liberal politics.[72] Or, as Hannah Arendt put it, by temperament and institutional practice, "liberals are not totalitarians."[73] The practical implication of this insight—which might seem banal, but which has been mightily resisted by some recent American scholars of constitutional law—is that a necessary part of a liberal constitutional government is a measure of "articulation" of distinct and different elements within government. These elements operate in tension with each other, allowing a plurality of voices, interests, and concerns to be expressed, thereby providing a constant check on the temptation for those in power to believe themselves infallible.[74] Similarly, there is a tradition of institutional design in postwar Europe of assigning authority to constitutional courts, or other unelected entities, as a form of insurance against the destructive power of popular sovereignty. That tradition, for apparent historical reasons, is a response to the horrific second quarter of the twentieth century, in which Europe drove its way headlong "into hell."[75] In contrast, the concentration of authority within the state makes it easier to misuse power and undermine the democratic process.

Institutional differentiation within government can be supplied in many different ways. An obvious approach is to carve up government into distinct branches—legislative, executive, and judicial. This is, to be sure, no panacea. In a democratic system characterized by partisan competition, it has long been known that when the same party captures both the executive and the legislature, those branches will not be adverse to each other.[76] But this kind of skepticism—which has been developed most acutely in the American context—is easily overstated. There is ample evidence that even the much-maligned American Congress is capable of asserting institutional interests, especially in historical moments of increasing executive-branch strength.[77] We focus first on the division of government into branches, particularly courts and legislatures, both of which might check an overbearing executive.

Courts

Comparative constitutional law scholarship has emphasized the role of constitutional courts in institutional differentiation within government. In the Ukraine, for example, the Supreme Court prevented Viktor Yanukovych from fraudulently stealing an election in 2006. In Bulgaria, the high court has invalidated presidential efforts to interfere with the judicial budget and staved off efforts to stack the wider judiciary with former Communist Party members. In Mongolia, a newly created Constitutional Court repeatedly rebuffed efforts by the parliament to appoint its own members to the cabinet, although the court was eventually defeated. This patchwork record suggests that constitutional courts are no panacea. Of particular importance here, in contexts of hegemonic one-party rule, is that courts themselves can be targets of institutional capture.[78] In Turkey, up to the period of AKP rule, the courts were very active in protecting the interests of civil servants, the universities, and the judiciary itself, but relatively quiescent on matters of civil liberties—a pattern that reflected the social bases of support for judicial interventions.[79] Under hegemonic AKP rule, however, they have over time lost their distinct vantage point and institutional standing.

The role of courts should not be overemphasized. It may be that judicial intervention is more important to the prevention of partisan degradation ex ante than to undoing its effects once it has materialized. Merely because courts have the institutional capacity to check a process of democratic erosion does not mean they will do so, absent the necessary orientation and motivation. For example, Weimar judges never exercised an effective restraint on pre-1933 presidential aggrandizement of power in Germany. And despite being well-established and legalistic in orientation, they failed to supply any meaningful resistance to the manifold horrors accompanying Nazi rule. To the contrary, the Nazi Party was able to leverage existing judicial institutions to marginalize or destroy competing political organizations.[80] Courts, that is, might be more important in the early stages of democratic erosion than in its final stages, and then only if judges are already animated by a commitment to liberal values, constitutional rule, and democracy. When a judicial appointment system selects for partisan loyalty, say, over these systemic values, judicial resistance to democratic erosion is unlikely to emerge.

Legislatures

The importance of a robust legislature as a forum for many distinct voices within the polity is perhaps self-evident. Legislatures are arenas in which political disagreement can be channeled and resolved, often through partial, ideologically uneasy, and temporary compromises. As well as embodying the daily operation of such democratic processes, they also reflect a liberal understanding that conflict is inevitable within any polity, but must be contained rather than allowed to spill out into overt violence.[81] The centrality of disagreement to the function and work of a legislative body is embodied in the formal recognition of an "opposition" with an "institutional responsibility" to "oppose, to scrutinize the government, to hold them accountable for their decisions." In many instances, this institutional responsibility is formalized in the text of a constitution in terms of specific procedural rights for the legislative opposition within the context of parliamentary debate. But the formal recognition of legislative opposition rights, while useful, is not necessary to the creation of an effective legislative body capable of providing a platform for diverse perspectives and values.[82] We see how important legislative bodies are by looking at, for example, the "antiparliamentary" turn of the Weimar chancellorship after the 1932 fall of Heinrich Brüning presaged and catalyzed the collapse of constitutional democracy in the wake of effective legislative constraint of the presidency.[83] More generally, it is hard to see how a successful democracy can persist for long if its legislative houses have been dismantled or rendered ineffective as forums for the continued airing of policy disputes.

Undermining Judicial and Legislative Checks

Recent cases of democratic erosion supply a number of instances in which interbranch checks have been systematically and deliberately dismantled. Although it is not unique, Eastern Europe provides particularly vivid examples. As we explained at the beginning of this chapter, Fidesz's central reason for seeking constitutional amendments after its election in 2010 was to weaken the Constitutional Court. That body had previously played a vigorous role in the immediate post–Cold War era. Between 1989 and 1995, that tribunal invalidated one-third of all national legislation passed, including "lustration" measures to keep former Communist officials from office and proposals to amend the constitution by popular referendum in order to establish a directly elected head of state. It is not without irony that the legislative monopoly over constitutional amendment that the court had once defended would ultimately prove its unraveling as an independent check in the constitutional order.[84]

A yet more protracted battle over judicial independence occurred in Poland. The Law and Justice Party (PiS) is one of a number of parties formed in the wake of the transition from Communism to represent those marginalized by the swift transition to a market economy. The PiS, however, styled itself in opposition to the former Communist regime and claimed to speak for a genuinely "Polish," and specifically Catholic, set of values. In this regard, it is not a novel kind of social movement. Since the nineteenth century, Poland has had a strain of conservative, anti-Semitic, and anti-Ukrainian Catholicism that first took the institutional form of the *Endecja*, or National Democracy, movement. While the PiS had previously come to power in 2005, it had failed to build a coalition with other nationalist or populist parties, and had therefore to rule as a minority party. In 2015, however, not only was that constraint removed, but the PiS benefited from the example of Fidesz as a model for a populist attack on liberal constitutional democracy. Despite a narrow popular base, the PiS won both the presidential election and an absolute majority in the parliamentary (Sejm) elections in 2015. Democratic Poland had until that point had only coalition governments. But, as in the Hungarian case, the PiS was able to achieve electoral dominance through a quirk of the post–Cold War election system designed to promote responsible government: Vote thresholds for both the party and party coalitions in parliament led to an unusually high number of wasted votes (16%), and thus to a PiS victory.[85]

Unlike the trailblazing Fidesz, the PiS lacked a sufficient parliamentary majority to amend the constitution. Nevertheless, it was able to use both legislation and the appointments power to assail the independence of the Constitutional Tribunal. To begin with, it was lucky to be able to profit from a strategic blunder by the opposition Civic Platform Party, which had previously held national power. In the June prior to the 2015 election, the Civic Platform Party had tried to accelerate the filling of five then-impending vacancies on the Constitutional Tribunal, and selected five candidate judges. But the new, PiS-affiliated President Andrzej Duda simply refused to administer the oath of office to them, while the newly installed PiS government moved to annul their nominations by amending the tribunal's organic statute.

What followed was a prolonged, head-on confrontation between the new PiS government and the tribunal. The government refused to acknowledge last-minute appointments of the previous government, appointed new judges, and passed a law increasing the quorum to make a decision. The law also required the court to hear cases in the sequence in which they arrived at the court, preventing an immediate review of the law itself. Again, as with the changes to the Hungarian Constitution, the full implications of these rules became evident only when one looked at their interactions. The new two-thirds rule, for example, interacted with the new PiS appointments to negate de facto the existing tribunal's power to nullify PiS legislation, even if a quorum was present.[86]

The tribunal then faced a crisis of personnel and procedure: Should it accept amendments that would leave it unable to hear a challenge to the very law disabling it, or should it resist these seemingly technical changes to jurisdiction and adjudication? Its response was unequivocal. In March 2016, the Constitutional Tribunal invalidated the bill containing many of these measures. But the PiS answer was equally unyielding. The PiS government simply announced that it would ignore this decision, and duly refused to publish it in the tribunal's official gazette. As the honorary speaker of parliament said, in a concise summary of populist logic, "It is the will of the people, not the law that matters, and the will of the people always tramples the law.[87] And in the end, the "people" did indeed have the last laugh. By the end of 2016, a sufficient number of judges' terms had expired to give the PiS a majority—effectively ending this interbranch skirmish on the PiS's terms.[88] But the skirmish was not the end of the war, By 2016, street protests had started, with judicial independence as a central point of contestation, and PiS efforts to subdue the courts would continue.

The near-complete demolition of an independent Constitutional Tribunal in Poland in the space of less than two years provides a number of lessons on how institutional differentiation can be undermined. To begin with, the PiS relied on a series of changes to the size and practical operation of the Tribunal. It did not, with a couple of exceptions, frontally attack the court's independence. Rather, the party found ways to suborn the court as an institutional actor so that it would pursue or, at least, not stand in the way of the PiS agenda. Second, the procedural sophistication of the PiS shows how, even operating within normal constitutional rules, a determined actor can paralyze and undermine safeguards of legality. An outside observer looking for overt violations of law would have found few red flags in respect to the Polish situation. Indeed, although Europe's institutions eventually expressed concern about the erosion of the rule of law, the PiS's observance of formal legality during this first skirmish with the judiciary allowed it to remain within the broad framework of European governance.[89] Criticisms and intervention from supranational entities were further impeded by the fact that the political effect of the PiS's procedural tinkering would have been quite hard to predict. With both the Fidesz constitutional amendments and the PiS reforms to the Constitutional Tribunal, it was difficult to appreciate the effect of a seemingly neutral procedural change without playing through its interactions with both existing and future rules. And even when an antidemocratic action was relatively clear, it was still difficult to come up with a metric or benchmark for evaluating that action.[90]

We have focused here on efforts to undermine the judiciary as a check on the hegemonic political program of a party that wishes to turn a theoretically transient electoral victory into something more stable and permanent. Assaults on legislatures, while not unknown, are less common—in part, because there are other ways to undermine the quality of democratic competition indirectly. Consider two examples.

In March 2013, the Czech Republic's first directly elected president, Miloš Zeman, sought to transform the country's parliamentary system into a semipresidential one. The government is supposed to be responsible to the lower house, and until 2013, the head of state was elected by joint vote of the two legislative houses. A charismatic former prime minister and former chair of the Czech Social Democratic Party, Zeman ignored the parliamentary element of the Czech constitution and directly appointed his own government under Jiří Rusnok. Zeman thus used the prestige and legitimacy of the new presidential election to arrogate to himself the key power of government formation that had previously belonged to the parliament, disarming it by assuming what is perhaps its most important checking power. Zeman went on to rule in a populist tenor, raging against refugees and inveighing against Islam. In January 2018, he won a second presidential term.[91]

In a similar vein, in Venezuela in April 2017, a Supreme Court dominated by judges appointed by Presidents Hugo Chávez and Nicholas Maduro dissolved the National Assembly, which was dominated by the opposition, and assumed the legislature's powers. The intended effect of the order was simply to do away with the legislature as a check on presidential power. In the face of intense criticism both internally and from overseas, however, Maduro allegedly instructed the court to reverse its order. While the court did so, it exempted from the reversal legislative powers to authorize joint business ventures and oil projects with foreign partners. The restoration, in short, was partial, and the exceptions advanced Maduro's efforts to maintain control over key sectors of the economy.[92]

In short, indirect efforts to bypass the legislature are more common strategies than are outright attacks on legislators. In part, this results from simple political calculation. Whether erosion is driven by charismatic populism or partisan degradation, its leader will often have allies in the legislative branch. As a result, capture rather than destruction of that body is likely to be of greater long-term value. More broadly, it is striking that across this range of examples concerning the judiciary and the legislature, there are few acts of clear-cut illegality. Violation of the law, whether statutory, constitutional, or international, is hardly necessary, given the subtle ways in which appointments, procedures, and timing measures can be used to undermine the checking force of other governmental branches.

CENTRALIZING AND POLITICIZING EXECUTIVE POWER

In the cases of Hungary, Poland, the Czech Republic, and Venezuela that we have so far examined here, the antidemocratic drive came from the executive: Prime Minister Orbán in Hungary, and Presidents Chávez, Maduro, and Zeman in Venezuela and the Czech Republic have been driving forces. In Poland, a "radical and divisive" leader of the PiS, Jarosław Kaczyński, had served as prime minister from 2006 to 2007, but withdrew from the 2015 campaign frontline in favor of more moderate voices. He nonetheless continued to have a decisive influence on the party's decisions once it had secured a lock on office.[93] Whether the pressure on democracy emerges from charismatic populism or from partisan degradation, the executive branch is typically the driving force in the unraveling of democracy's three institutional predicates. We have already flagged the possibility of resistance to executive-driven democratic backsliding at the branch level and the mechanisms that can be used to disable it. But there is no reason why checking mechanisms cannot also be constructed within the executive branch. Indeed, the third mechanism of democratic erosion hinges on the anti-democrat's effort to dismantle the internal executive safeguards of democratic rule.

To see why it is necessary to think about checks on government above and beyond those supplied by rival branches, consider the United Kingdom. Until the creation of the Supreme Court of the United Kingdom in 2009, the unwritten British constitution vested all governmental powers in Parliament, which exercised not only the legislative power, but also the executive power (through the prime minister and the Cabinet) and supreme judicial power (through the Judicial Committee of the House of Lords). The absence of a formal separation of powers in the British system did not mean that the pre-2009 British government was totalitarian in character. Rather, internal divisions by party, by institutional temperament and habit, and, in the case of the civil service, by professional orientation, generated a set of restraints that would be missed by a casual glance at the formal governmental organizational chart.

Even when a constitution does contain a formal separation of powers, moreover, it is unwise to assume that its branches operate as unitary blocks. The sheer complexity and range of tasks that a modern democratic government is tasked with accomplishing—from the provision of social welfare, to policing, to the cultivation of an educated and healthy population, to the national defense—all but ensures a high degree of institutional differentiation within the executive. A central feature of effective governance is autonomous bureaucratic capacity, insulated from political control at the day-to-day level. Indeed, bureaucracies that operate "according to written rules and created stable expectations" have been an essential component of the powerful centralized state since the Chinese Qin dynasty.[94] Hence, it is all but certain that the executive branch of a modern democracy, even within a separation-of-powers system, will be characterized by diverse and heterogeneous arrays of agencies, departments, taskforces, lobby groups, "quangos," and other colorful institutional types.[95]

When a leader or movement bent on corroding democratic quality comes to power through fair elections—as has happened in Hungary, Poland, the Czech Republic, and Venezuela—they are not only confronted with other branches of government that may remain in the hands of ideological hostile forces. They likely also inherit a bureaucratic machinery staffed by individuals who are either aligned with another party or, even if not so aligned, are committed to rule-of-law values or institutional norms that hinder the practical program of consolidating political power. These internal elements of government can stand in the way of erosion, and their dismantling is another site of potential movement away from democracy.

At first blush, this may seem odd and counterintuitive. Bureaucracy is not commonly thought to be a natural ally of democracy. To some, it has seemed "plain" that the policymaking capacity of a developed bureaucracy is in tension with the ambition of democratic control.[96] On this view, the expertise supplied by a bureaucracy operates as an alternative source of knowledge and authority to make policy judgments that can crowd out popular views. We are skeptical of this strong claim, and our definition of democracy does not rule out reliance by democratic actors on the expertise of others to achieve their chosen policy ends. Indeed, it is more plausible to think that stable bureaucratic repositories of expertise are a necessary predicate to democratic rotation without destabilizing policy choices or disorienting jolts to state practice.[97] A second way in which democracy and bureaucracy might be thought to clash relates to staffing. The stable and rule-bound operation of a bureaucracy requires a certain measure of insulation from redistributive politics in their pathological form. Where bureaucratic positions and favors are allocated on the basis of political connections, there is no particular reason to expect effective government. In the late nineteenth century, for example, the US federal government was characterized by a high-degree of "party-managed clientalism," constantly teetering on edge of outright corruption."[98] When democracy is reduced to a matter of doling out goodies to clients and family, it may be "at odds" with bureaucracy. So it is a good thing when democracy cannot be equated with merely the most effective forms of client patronage.[99] There ought to be a gap between the operation of democracy and the crass, naked fact of redistribution to political allies.

But it is not just that bureaucratic autonomy is compatible with democratic impulses. There are in fact five distinct ways by which bureaucracy can *facilitate* and *preserve* democracy. First, early bureaucracies, from those of imperial China through nineteenth-century Prussia and beyond, have evolved formal rules that restricted state power by clearly establishing "the boundary between private and public resources."[100] Even the early Chinese emperors, typically depicted in the stereotypical argot of unbridled "oriental despotism," were to some extent constrained by the system of rules in which the state operated.[101] Bureaucracies are thus pivotal barriers to the misuse of state power either for the private gain of officials or for the electoral gain of a ruling faction. It is this basic insight that underwrites the growing literature on the "internal separation of powers" in American administrative law. In this literature, scholars have noted that there are a range of professionals, "lawyers, scientists, civil servants, politicians, and others" who are "directly and indirectly" empowered by the complex structures of regulatory law to advance or retard policy goals in ways that often cut against the immediate preferences of elected actors.[102] In our view, the normative claims that can be made about the internal separation of powers should not be overstated, and current scholarship has an excessively optimistic bent. The mere fact of institutional fragmentation does not support the further inference that disparate parts of the administration will interact in ways that produce generally beneficial results. It is also possible that diversity will generate a destructive cacophony. Nevertheless, from the point of view of heading off democratic erosion, internal tensions in the bureaucracy's design are probably more beneficial than anything else.

Second, bureaucracies tend to be conservative, incrementalist institutions. This quality both hinders rapid democratic change and makes meaningful democratic decision making feasible by preserving decisions beyond the life of the enacting coalition. The bias toward the status quo is symmetric: Just as bureaucratization may make progressive reform difficult to achieve, it also slows down rapid shifts away from liberal, constitutional, and democratic norms in the face of political movements that seek to challenge them.

Third, bureaucracies produce neutral information that is necessary to the operation of modern democracies. From the population census to macroeconomic data and measurement of the extent and effects of climate change, technocratic experts generate unbiased information upon which policymakers can and should rely to make decisions. Putative efforts to erode democracy often involve attempts to manipulate the truth and thereby to shape public perceptions of policy priorities (in particular, threats to the polity) for narrow partisan gain by sabotaging the production of unbiased empirical data. These attempts can involve selective leaks, allegations of fake news, or simply politically motivated falsehoods. Given the current environment, in which contests over what count as basic facts often characterize popular politics, unbiased information produced by a trusted bureaucracy can hinder democratic erosion.

Fourth, in the absence of an effective bureaucracy, a potential anti-democrat can use a patronage-based state structure to buy support from political elites and citizens in ways that undermine the efficacy of electoral mechanisms.[103] As Francis Fukuyama has explained, an unhealthy clientalism often involves the "larger-scale exchange of favors between patrons and clients [via] a hierarchy of intermediaries."[104] Such clientalism is different from a measure of democratic responsiveness in the form of pork-barreling and mundane interest-group politics that characterize the normal operation of any democracy. As with many other questions of sound democratic design, we can be more confident of the need to draw a line between healthy responsiveness and stultifying bribes than of its precise location. Indeed, one person's healthy pork-barreling is another's catastrophic clientalism. But the existence of close or contested cases does not mean that the line itself does not exist. Here, we need not try to draw that line with precision. Rather, it is enough to say there are certainly cases in which the distribution of state resources has the practical effect of throwing up insurmountable barriers to electoral rotation. In those cases, clientalism achieved at the expense of bureaucratic autonomy becomes an instrument of democratic erosion. In contrast, it has long been noted that a meritocratically selected bureaucracy can work in practice as a vehicle for mobility and political representation of groups that might otherwise be shut out of politics. There is little doubt, for example, that the US federal bureaucracy is more socially inclusive and more representative of the average American in terms of class and race than, say, the elected Congress.[105]

Fifth, and finally, it is rarely the case that either a leader or the leadership of a political party will personally violate rights to speech, association, or due process so as to consolidate their monopoly on political power. (The president of the Philippines, Rodrigo Duterte, is a self-confessed exception here). Instead, it is generally some element of the bureaucracy that is tasked with carrying out policies on the ground. We have already seen in chapter 3 that the willingness of the military to turn against a popular uprising can be a key factor in determining the trajectory of a democratic uprising. But the same dynamic generalizes to the context of established democracies. The efficacy of an antidemocratic project will often turn on the willingness of a bureaucracy to capitulate. But where there are already rules that prohibit official violations of speech, associational, or due process rights, however, bureaucrats will find it easier to resist. Even if not perfectly enforced, those rules work as focal points helping to coordinate administrators' expectations about other activities. If each official, that is, knows that others know of a rule and hence anticipates that they will follow it, then she has less incentive to violate the rule. This coordinating effect will be reinforced if bureaucrats believe they are likely to be punished in the future (perhaps after a change in regime) for violating the rules. In this fashion, constitutional constraints on elected leaders that are in practice necessary for democratic rule can emerge from the normal operation of a bureaucracy.[106]

In practice, therefore, attacks on bureaucratic autonomy are an important part of democratic erosion. In many instances, this takes the form of targeted attacks on distinct elements of the bureaucracy that were designed with a checking, rule-of-law function in mind. In Hungary, for example, we have seen that Fidesz reorganized the Media Council, the Budget Counsel, the National Bank, the Elections Commission, and the Ombudsman Office, often with the simple expedient of removing incumbent officials. In addition to these formal efforts to scale back checks on the executive, Fidesz also annulled a law that required the offer of some justification for the firing of a government employee. With an array of offices to hand out and no limits on how many more offices could be made available, Fidesz was able to take an existing strain of patronage within the Hungarian system and turn it into an organizing principle of government. From 2010 onward, only those business entities with ties to the government were able to win government contracts (ironically, including those funded by the European Union). State-owned entities severed ties with institutions, and in particular media outlets, that had ties to the opposition. Artists seeking state support were expected to join an organization that had a long-standing campaign in favor of Fidesz and against the left. The bureaucracy, in short, moved from being an arm of the state to being an arm of the party.[107]

In Turkey, the AKP party has similarly turned the state into an instrument of party control, albeit in a slower process that responded to threats to the AKP's electoral might. At a local and municipal level, the government bureaucracy uses social services, health services, and public housing services as "tools of political patronage," transforming what had in the past been the material presence of the state into the material presence of the party.[108] So too at the higher echelons of government, where patronage is more rule than exception. Even before the attempted 2016 coup, constitutional amendments in 2010 had changed the structure of the Constitutional Court and the High Council of Judges and Public Prosecutors (or HSYK)—bodies that had previously served as secularist checks on the AKP—to make them more pluralist. These changes were initially welcomed by Turkish liberals and the European Union as means of weakening the military's hold on politics in general and the courts in particular. But another sharp change occurred three years later, when a corruption scandal implicating dozens of AKP members arose. After forty-seven arrests—including several of high-level ministerial and local officials—Erdoğan and his allies broke with the judiciary and responded to the perceived threat to their political authority by tarring the prosecutors as "agents" and "guilty." But rhetoric did not exhaust their repertoire. The government followed up with regulation that dramatically changed the responsibilities of judicial police, who are responsible for aiding public prosecutors. About a hundred judges and prosecutors were transferred away from corruption cases, and in March 2014 the government enacted further reforms to the HSYK, transferring more power over prosecutors to political appointees.[109] The politicization of the bureaucracy only accelerated after the July 2016 coup, as police forces, the army, the judiciary, and the education sector all experienced dramatic purges of those not affiliated with the AKP.

Finally, the deployment of a captured bureaucracy against political foes is also a potent tool for erosion. In Russia, for example, the Putin administration has used the selective enforcement of tax laws to control the media and political opponents. For instance, the media tycoon Vladimir Gusinsky was prosecuted for fraudulently withholding $10 million from the government in connection with a privatization deal after Gusinsky's television channel criticized Putin over the Chechen war.[110] We will see other, even more creative weaponization of the ordinary forms of government in what follows.

SHRINKING THE PUBLIC SPHERE

The practical operation of liberal democracy requires a shared basis of knowledge and beliefs, and a shared space in which deliberation on the basis of that epistemic foundation can take place. The term *public sphere* was usefully deployed by Jürgen Habermas to refer to an institutionalized arena of discursive interactions in which citizens deliberate about common affairs.[111] Democratic erosion can involve a conscious deterioration of either the first, epistemic element of the public sphere, or its second, deliberative element.

To see the role of both these epistemic and deliberative elements, consider the full democratic process. At the beginning, elections bring coalitions to power. The winning coalition then enacts policies with consequences for the citizenry. Subsequent elections at which those coalitions seek renewed democratic authority would be a mere formality in the absence of information about the consequences of enacted measures. Even charismatic populists who run on the platform of representing the true voice of the people rarely highlight the fact that the people are materially worse off (or, if they do, they blame it on the nefarious influence of elites or some unfortunate and disfavored minority group). When they are working properly then, elections make "the elected an object of control and scrutiny."[112]

By contrast, elections become corrupted and dysfunctional when they cease to have a meaningful relationship to the actual behavior of officials in office. In many cases, elections turn on voters' emotional affiliation with a particular politician rather than any judgment about the politician's expected efficacy. Such elections are hardly the democratic ideal. For elections to serve their proper function, there is a need for a continuous flow of reasonably accurate information about the interaction between government policies and external conditions. To be sure, this epistemic foundation need not be perfect.[113] But at some point, information failures can become so extensive and asymmetrically tilted in favor of one coalition or candidate that they render the exercise of democratic choice futile.

To make this point more concrete, imagine a government that purports to produce public security by the extensive use of detention powers targeting discrete minority populations. The government fails to disclose that the minority in question does not actually include a large percentage of individuals who pose a security threat. Moreover, it employs a divisive language of identity-based differences to vindicate this policy and to bolster political support among nonminority voters. The absence of accurate information about the government's policy not only facilitates grave violations of individuals' human or constitutional rights, it also allows the government to exploit those grave violations as a means of amplifying public support. Incomplete information thus not only leads voters to erroneous judgments but allows government to promote exclusionary ideals and also to eliminate dissenting minorities from the electorate. All this alone might not amount to democratic erosion. Indeed, the example is modeled by the internment of Japanese-Americans during World War II. This was a horrific and gross violation of human and constitutional rights, but it was not necessarily a failure of democracy per se (and, indeed, is not generally understood in canonical histories as an inflection point of American democracy).[114] Nevertheless, it is easy to see how a charismatic populist or a hegemonic political party might exploit epistemic shortcomings of this kind as a way of limiting accountability and of channeling public discourse into charged forms of crude identity politics.

The recent retrenchment of democracy around the world provides examples of the ways in which the shared epistemic foundation of democracy can be corroded. Our opening example of Hungary illustrated how regulation of the state media and private media—be it the airwaves, billboards, or the internet—can serve to shore up one party's grip on political power without formally abrogating the electoral trappings of liberal constitutional democracy. But this dynamic is hardly confined to Hungary. In 2000, the Chávez government in Venezuela, for example, enacted a media law that gave the government free rein to suspend or revoke broadcasting licenses, as "convenient." Four years later, another statute barred the electronic transmission of material that could "foment anxiety in the public or disturb public order." Using those laws, Presidents Chávez and Maduro have narrowed the reach of independent media and expanded the role of government media. For example, in 2007, the government revoked the broadcasting license of the main private television station, RCTV, because of its programming choices during a 2002 coup attempt. It has also established local and municipal "communitarian channels," allegedly for local voices. But because funding for these new channels comes from the state, they have little effective autonomy from the government. The government's control over its own advertising contracts and its ability to alter rules for the importation of materials and foreign currency have also been used to pressure independent media. In 2013, it pushed out the owners of a major broadcaster, Globovísion, and of two major print news sources, El Universal and the Grupo Capriles, in favor of more pro-government management.[115]

In Turkey, the attack on the epistemic and discursive foundations of democracy has used both indirect measures of control and brutally direct instruments. Major newspapers, such as *Taraf* and *Zaman*, have not only been shuttered, but their archives have been removed from the internet. In effect, they have been deleted from the historical record. State patronage, in contrast, flows to pro-government news outlets owned by business figures close to the AKP. These outlets then give sustained coverage to the AKP and to President Erdoğan. Notwithstanding legal mandates of neutrality, the state-run Anadolu Agency and the Turkish Broadcasting Authority allocate most of their resources to favorable coverage of the ruling party. If those measures fail, there is always the jackboot and the jail cell. As of early 2017, some 148 journalists had been imprisoned in relation to their professional activities in Turkey, making the country the world's leading jailor of journalists. By 2017, Turkey had become one of the most repressive environments for journalists globally.[116] In addition, leading public voices, such as the author Ash Erdoğan, the linguist Necmiye Alpay, and the economist Mehmet Altan, have been arrested on the basis of alleged connections with terrorism or sedition.[117]

These rounds of suppression, studded with outright repression, can be seen across the entire set of eroding democracies. In Poland, the PiS enacted a media law in December 2015 that required all broadcasters to have a board controlled by the government. It then "sidelined" a constitutional body charged with ensuring media independence. It further "appointed a PiS spin doctor as president of public television" and "purg[ed] journalists and media workers suspected of lacking enthusiasm for the government's political agenda."[118] Similarly, in Sri Lanka, the government of Mahinda Rajapaksa, another nationalist politician with authoritarian leanings, suppressed and intimidated journalists using the broad restrictions of the Official Secrets Act and the 1979 Prevention of Terrorism Act.[119] In Russia, the Putin government has squeezed out independent media, enacted a wide range of measures tightly controlling election-related activities, prohibited the replication of "extremist" materials in the press, and created an "Internet Blacklist" of verboten web sites. It has also supplemented repression with a subtle form of exploitation, deploying the media as a means of getting "insight into the fears and needs of particular groups," and of creating an image of democratic back-and-forth via live call-in sessions chaired by President Vladimir Putin himself. The result is a media environment in which only government-approved messages are effectively circulating in the public sphere and where the media help the government acquire information about its citizens rather than vice versa.[120]

Another element of the Russian experience bears emphasis: We have focused here on state mechanisms for restricting or dominating the public sphere. A powerful alternative, however, is simply to pollute it so much that it becomes ill-suited for democratic ends. As Tim Wu has argued, an entity bent on distorting the information environment can now achieve its goals more easily by exploiting the limited capacity of most citizens to absorb information than by active censorship. He explains that with the advent of the internet, and the corresponding expansion in the sheer volume of available speech, it has become easier to drown out politically damaging speech than to ban it. For the Russian government, as Peter Pomerantsev has explained, information is thus understood "in weaponized terms, as a tool to confuse, blackmail, demoralize, subvert and paralyze." It is arguable that this has become part not only of Russia's domestic politics but also of its geopolitical strategy, through state sponsorship of the RT news channel and the alleged promotion of various false or misleading news stories in the international press, and on Facebook and Twitter.[121] Such news penetrates American media with increasing frequency and effect.[122] Given the tendency of successful antidemocratic strategies to spread, it seems likely that this measure, in its infancy now, will be an increasing part of the arsenal of erosion—and a tool of geopolitical influence with particularly acute effects on democratic nations.

Here the role of social media is particularly important. Only a few years ago, during the Arab Spring, Google and Twitter were celebrated, even by their own leaders, for the possibilities of bottom-up organization and mobilization. But states have responded with a set of tools to censor, repress, and poison the social media for their own ends. Crucially, these ends are not limited to maintaining power: Russian social media interference with the United States election suggests that the tactics can be used in efforts to undermine democracy abroad. Indeed, a survey taken after the 2016 American presidential election found that almost a third of Americans had encountered one or another fraudulent news story, and between 80% and 90% could not tell whether the story was true or not.[123] Because these technologies have not been around for long, established democracies have only started to struggle with how to maintain their public-regarding quality—for example, by imposing legal duties on platform managers or penalties on users who engage in false or misleading speech. Since these efforts are in their infancy, it is too soon to be confident about which work well (or even whether regulating social media is feasible). But it would be a mistake to write off such efforts on free speech grounds without considering their effects. Elections already exist in highly structured and regulated environments by necessity. Given the extensive government involvement in the management of elections, the libertarian claim that the state has no role in regulating relevant speech can only be maintained by ignoring reality. Instead, it is better to think about how, if at all, to mitigate the use of social media to undermine other countries' polls within the larger institutional architecture of election regulation.

The public sphere, of course, contains more than the social media, newspapers, and television stations. It also contains a wide array of private associations—clubs, not-for-profit organizations, religious institutions, and the like—that play an important role in democratic mobilization, deliberation, and accountability. Civil society, as it is sometimes called, is not an unalloyed good. In the early 1930s, the Nazi Party used the Weimar era's dense civil society as a means to mobilize the mass movement that propelled it to and sustained it in power.[124] In the contemporary context, religious organizations can also play at best an ambiguous role in the context of unstable democracies. Appeals to religious identity supply a supervening identification that transcends and can even undermine appeals to a democratic constitution. We have already noted that the Polish PiS appeals to a nationalistic version of Catholicism as a core element of its populist ideology. In Russia, the Putin government has entered into a "close alliance" with the Russian Orthodox Church as an alternative source of legitimation in the absence of an untainted democratic mandate.[125] And in Iran, a religious establishment, in close association with allies in the military and bureaucracy, has been instrumental in limiting the scope of democratic rule.[126]

Where civil society does not support an authoritarian vector or status quo, an antidemocratic coalition or official can directly target the civil society elements—journalists, lawyers, NGOs, and foundations—that might mobilize to slow a movement away from liberal democracy. Recent experiences with erosion suggest that libel law and nonprofit regulation provide potent instruments to this end.

Here, the stagnation of democratic practice in Russia illustrates how registration and libel laws can be wielded for antidemocratic ends. Consider first libel law. In May 2012, the Putin government reintroduced criminal liability for libel, which had been repealed by the Medvedev administration. This 2012 measure imposed large fines and even sentences of up to 480 hours of forced labor for "the spread of false information discrediting the honor and dignity of another person or undermining his reputation." The law also envisaged the retroactive reopening of previously suspended or terminated suits. The amendment catalyzed a wave of libel suits against the media. Libel suits have been used, for example, by regional governments to fine and imprison journalists who published stories about waste and abuse.[127] Of course, the Putin administration is not the only one to use libel prosecutions (and the threat of libel suits) aggressively to limit the flow of information critical of the government. In Turkey too, President Erdoğan has deployed the libel law generously against both domestic and international critics.[128] And in early 2018, Indonesia's parliament adopted rules to allow suits against those who undermine the honor of parliament or its members.[129]

In addition to libel, the direct regulation of not-for-profit organizations— a tactic we have already seen proposed in Israel—provides a scalpel that can neatly target opposition segments of civil society. Again, Russia provides a crisp example. Under President Putin, a suite of NGO and "anti-extremist" laws have been enacted with "deliberately ambiguous language" and wielded in "an unprecedented campaign of reprisals against civil society."[130] As in Israel, as we have already noted, certain foreign-backed NGOs have been singled out for harsher scrutiny by legislative action based upon the positions they take in domestic political disputes. In Russia, restrictions were also placed on foreign funding. Relevant NGOs were required to register as foreign agents; to provide quarterly reports on their activity, funding, and expenditures; and to submit to surprise inspections. Many prominent NGOs, including Memorial and Transparency International, have refused to comply with the measure, which was explicitly framed by its sponsors as an effort to undermine their credibility.

Registration, though, is not the sole hurdle that foreign-funded groups face. In a step that seems related functionally to this stepped-up NGO regulation, an amendment to the treason statute enacted in 2012 treats the dissemination of state secrets to foreign or multinational organizations, and not just foreign governments, as a serious criminal offense. Such a measure directly impinges on the work of organizations such as the human-rights group Memorial and the anticorruption group Transparency International. Tellingly, the first entity to be charged with failing to register was Golos, a major election-monitoring organization—one that had revealed widespread voter fraud in 2011 by the Putin government.[131]

The technology of restrictions on NGO funding and activities is spreading globally in a striking example of antidemocratic policy diffusion of the kind we described in chapter 1. Between 2013 and 2016, the UN Special Rapporteur on freedom of expression, Maina Kiai, expressed concern about NGO regulations enacted not just in Israel but also in Egypt, China, Kenya, Kazakhstan, Mauritania, Cambodia, and Uganda, and the set of countries has only grown since then.[132] Even if not designed to apply selectively, like the

Israeli measure, it seems likely that selective enforcement of such laws will be used by states to shape the environment of public discourse. Indeed, it is a common theme of the wave of recent restrictions that they have particularly targeted human-rights NGOs that might challenge violations of free and fair elections, liberal speech and associational rights, or norms of rule-of-law and good governance. They target, in other words, precisely those elements of civil society that are best situated to, and most likely to, protect the institutional underpinnings of liberal constitutional democracy.

The public sphere, then, is a fragile ecosystem that depends not just on the absence of formal state coercion but also on the non-discriminatory and fair-minded application of law. A lesson of the current global erosion is that there are ample tools—sometimes blunt and bloody, and sometimes subtle and silent—for picking apart the public sphere. We see at work civil and criminal legislation, administrative rules requiring ex ante registration, and ex post penalties through tax and regulatory enforcement. Some steps may simply be designed to demoralize and intimidate. Some are lawful under domestic law, but violations of international law. In other instances, though, neither domestic nor international law speaks to the tactic. All, however, allow state actors either directly or indirectly to exclude or discredit news and news sources likely to report critically on incumbents' behavior and its consequences.

THE ELIMINATION OF POLITICAL COMPETITION

To work in practice, democracy demands the possibility of alternation in power. Partisan degradation is but one way in which that possibility can disappear. Where a meaningful opposition exists, there remain options for hobbling competition while maintaining apparent conformity with the law, even if outright violence remains out of bounds. The libel and sedition laws are one tool to this end, but others have been not only imagined but deployed. We can offer only a small sampling of the range of measures, legal or illegal, procedural, regulatory, or criminal, that can be used to push an election off the tracks.

We begin with Venezuela, where a wide range of tactics can be observed. Since 1998, elections have been "plagued by irregularities." These include allocating disparate airtime to each party; arbitrarily keeping polling stations open longer when it helps the government; barring candidates and observers; pressuring state employees and welfare recipients to vote for the ruling party; harassing voters at the polls; and threatening municipalities that do not support the government with the withdrawal of central funds. The Chávez government also created "Communal Counsels," which it characterized as new forms of grassroots participatory government, that have served in effect as "local partisan organizations during elections" in favor of the ruling coalition. In 2004, it naturalized and registered a large number of immigrants as a way of bolstering its turnout. In the same election, a list of antigovernment petitioners known as the "*Lista Tascón*" was circulated, leading to delays in voter registration and even dismissal from government jobs for those thought to be on the list. Although the opposition party protests these measures and sometimes gets irregularities corrected, new forms of tilting the electoral playing field quickly emerge to take their place. In 2017 gubernatorial elections, for example, the polling places for almost seven hundred thousand voters were suddenly moved on the eve of balloting. Many voters would have had to travel several hours by bus to reach those new polls. Careful statistical analysis of electronic votes cast in Venezuelan elections reveals grounds for concern that the amount of fraud present was substantial. Indeed, it is quite plausible that such irregularities have been outcome-determinative. In March 2013, for example, Nicholas Maduro won his first presidential campaign against Henrique Capriles Radonski by a mere 235,000 votes. When Capriles Radonski cried foul, his requests for a recount or a do-over, made both to the National Election Council and the Supreme Court, were turned aside. Still, in 2015, the opposition secured a legislative majority (suggesting that even fraud can fail to overcome a sufficiently robust popular headwind)—leading ultimately to the 2017 showdown with the Supreme Court.[133]

Fraud is quite common in backsliding. Beyond the Venezuelan case, for instance, in Sri Lanka, the Rajapaksa regime was regularly accused of election fraud, including colluding with its putative military foes, Tamil Tigers, to prevent voting in the north and east of the country in 2005.[134] But fraud is not necessary to make an election unfair. Backsliding from democracy in the Turkish case has not been characterized by fraud per se, but by the systematic construction of a tilted playing field. Especially in its early years in power, it is quite likely that the AKP party enjoyed a genuine electoral majority. The party's vote share in national elections, however, dropped from 50% to 41% between 2011 and 2015, leading it to lose control of the legislature in June 2015. President Erdoğan then called for new elections just five months later. In a context of spiking violence in the Kurdish east and southeast, the AKP was able to appeal to voters' fears about security and attain once again a 50% vote share in the November 2015 poll. But the ensuing campaign was also marred by irregularities, although not outright fraud. Provincial governors linked to the AKP, who are supposed to be politically neutral, distributed goods to voters on behalf of the party. Despite being constitutionally neutral too, President Erdoğan campaigned vigorously around the country, filling gaps in his prime minister's tour of the country.

The AKP further used measures designed not so much to appeal to voters but to suppress the opposition. In addition to exploiting its near-total control over the media, the AKP has used its control over municipal and state governments to impede opposition mobilization. Private businesses, for instance, are pressured to refuse services to the opposition. In the town of Riza, for example, the AKP-run municipality in 2015 invoked a lack of legal documents as a means of shuttering a wedding salon that had rented out its space to an opposition party. During the campaign over the 2017 constitutional referendum, permits for opposition rallies were yanked without explanation; the "No" campaign's staff were denied entry to towns, and their canvassers were simply detained on the street.[135] The state can also suppress opposition merely by not acting. In 2015, for instance, the pro-Kurdish Peoples' Democratic Party was subject to a campaign of terrorist attacks in which five were killed and 522 injured. But these attacks were the work of private terrorist groups, and the government was at fault only to the extent that it reacted slowly.

In other national contexts, more overt uses of state violence to stall electoral competition can be observed. In Russia under Putin, for example, opposition parties have been legally proscribed for having too few members. Individual opposition activists are arrested for minor offenses such as "crossing the road in an unauthorized place," "smoking in a public place," "infringement of road transport regulations by a pedestrian," and "drunkenness." In these cases, the coercive power of the state, selectively deployed, is turned into an instrument of partisan entrenchment. Given this extensive array of options, it is rather surprising that outright political assassination is ever needed in the Russian context. But apparently it is. In 2015, for example, leading liberal opposition figure Boris Nemtsov was assassinated a few minutes from the Kremlin, allegedly by Chechen contract killers. The identity of the persons who contracted for the killing has never been determined.[136]

Even if an opponent of democracy happens to lose an election, she still has means to avoid losing power. For example, when an opposition figure, Antonio Ledezma, won the mayoralty of Caracas in 2008, Chávez's government created a new "capital district" and transferred most of the budget and authority of the mayor's office to the new entity. This entity was, rather predictably, controlled by Chávez's party. Ledezma was arrested some years later and held without charge for a year; he is currently in exile in Spain. Similarly, when the ruling party lost 2015 elections to the National Assembly, it created a new legislature, the "National Communal Parliament" and sought to give it governing power.[137] In both cases, the result of electoral loss was not a transfer of power between parties, but a shift of power to new government entities precisely to keep it in the hands of one, hegemonic party.

ALL ERODING DEMOCRACIES ARE DIFFERENT

The use of democratic, constitutional forms to achieve antidemocratic ends is nothing new. But the anti-democrat's tool kit has become increasingly sophisticated of late. A careful review of available case studies suggests how a rough playbook for would-be illiberal democrats works in practice. First, run a populist platform, in which the majority is portrayed as victimized and the old order elitist. Such was the strategy of, for example, Orbán in Hungary and Erdoğan in Turkey. Emphasize threats to national security or the purity of the homeland. Next, find ways to undermine opponents in state institutions, such as the judiciary or military, through a combination of appointments, purges, patronage, and even intimidation. Perhaps use the courts to repress criticism via libel suits or the like. Critically, do not forget to manipulate the electoral institutions so as to ensure that future competition is limited. Then, attack civil society as foreign-funded elite carriers of globalist ideas that do not comport with national values. Ensure that the free media are intimidated, or diluted, so as not to provide an independent check: This is particularly easy to do in an era of privatization in which the press can literally be bought. Finally, undermine academic authority through underfunding or outright politicization. The effect of these measures is cumulative; even if one alone is insufficient to raise concerns about democratic erosion, when sufficiently numerous, they should be viewed with alarm.

Table 4.2 summarizes these strategies for several prominent cases of backsliding. In each case, save Sri Lanka, the program began with a populist election that brought to power hitherto weak interests. Notably, these populists relied heavily on rural support and in some cases on malapportionment schemes that favored the countryside over urban voters. In three of the cases (Venezuela, Hungary, and Sri Lanka), constitutional amendments were pursued that consolidated executive power and eliminated institutional roadblocks. In the others, legislative or executive strategies were pursued to the same ends. All cases were accompanied by backsliding on rights as well as efforts to shape public discourse through media restrictions or intimidation.

It is worth emphasizing that not all of these efforts were completely successful in entrenching their proponents forever. As we saw, Thailand's Thaksin was ousted in a coup in 2006, and has not been able to return to the country. His sister, Yingluck, established a government in 2011, but she too was overthrown after proposing an amnesty that many suspected would have led to the return of her brother. Thailand is thus a case where democratic erosion led to an authoritarian collapse. In chapter 6 we discuss other cases in which erosion was reversed.

TABLE 4.2. The mechanisms of constitutional backsliding

Country	Prehistory of leader	Undermine institutional checks	Restrict electoral competition	Limit rights and restrict public sphere
Venezuela, 1998–2017 [Chávez-Maduro]	Failed coup attempt by Chávez, 1992	*Abolish Congress and Supreme Court, and replace with 1999 Constitution *Intimidate and pack judiciary and bureaucracy *Rely on military personnel and immediate family members *Replace elected legislature with Constituent Assembly, 2017 *Arrest prosecutor on bogus charges	*Secured 119/125 seats in 1999 constituent assembly *Abolish term limits, 2009 *Detain opposition leader, 2013 *Undermine 2008 Caracas election	*Significant abuses of criminal process *Limit on NGOs *Revoke media licenses *Nationalize television *Censor the press *Criminalize "disrespect" of public officials
Thailand, 2000–2014 [Shinawatra x2]	Telecoms monopolist	*Bribe and pack watchdogs *Manipulate tax law for personal gain	*Vote-buying *Influence over election commission	*Extrajudicial killings campaign *Emergency rule in the south *Media intimidation
Turkey, 2003–present [Erdoğan]	Jailed political party leader	*Attempt to pack the Courts, 2006 *Purge government, army, academia, and courts in 2016 *Intimidate Constitutional Court	*Local electoral fraud, 2009, 2014 *Proposal to extend term limits with new constitution	*Mixed record— abolished death penalty and expanded voting rights; poor record on Kurdish issue *Arrests of opponents *Arrests and firing of journalists *Seizure of newspapers & revocation of licenses

TABLE 4.2. (*continued*)

Country	Prehistory of leader	Undermine institutional checks	Restrict electoral competition	Limit rights and restrict public sphere
Sri Lanka, 2005–2015 [Rajapaksa]	MP	*Govern through relatives *Centralize appointments, undermine civil service, and weaken independent bodies *Impeach chief justice 2013	*Collusion with LTTE to block elections in northeast *Jailed opponent in 2010 election *Abolished term limits in Constitution 2010	*War crimes and impunity *Takings of property in Northeast *Abduction and murder of journalists *Manipulation of GDP data
Hungary, 2010–present [Orbán]	MP	*Constitutional reform, 2011 *Lower retirement age for judges 2011 *In 2013, annulled all Constitutional Court rulings before 2011	*2014 election won 67% of seats with 44% of votes	*NGO restrictions *Revisionist history curriculum *Criminalize "imbalanced news coverage" and "insulting the majority"
Poland, 2015–present [Kaczyński]	Prime Minister	*Undermine Constitutional Court, 2015 *Eliminate civil service protections		*Take over state media from independent commission
India, 1971–77 [Gandhi]	Scion; war with Pakistan over Bangladesh	*Abuse emergency power and rule by decree *Manipulate courts after *Kesavananda*	*Imprison political opponents *Interfere with electoral machinery, 1975	*Mass arrests *Repression of strikes *Censorship

Shifts in the quality of liberal constitutional democracy, in short, need not be unidirectional or permanent. Nevertheless, they do prove in many cases to be remarkably resilient, leaving a stable equilibrium of some, if not too much, space for the opposition. The resulting style of governance may not be properly characterized as authoritarian, because it allows some genuine space for political competition, especially as to issues that do not go to core regime interests. Indeed, there are many reasons why charismatic populists or hegemonic factions in de facto, one-party systems do not make the final push into competitive authoritarianism or even autocracy. Real contestation, for example, may provide the regime with valuable information that may amplify its ability to govern, rather than undermine it. We know, for example, that authoritarians who adopt constitutions endure longer than those that do not.[138] Legal rules may also facilitate making credible commitments in the economic sphere and help the regime to coordinate its behavior internally. Or opposing political forces may simply prove too powerful to be wholly shut out. Or effective control of state resources might be secured without complete extinction of all institutional and partisan opposition. The autocrat, that is, may simply have won, so that what remains of political pluralism is little more than sound and fury, signifying no real possibility of change in what matters. Whatever the reasons, it is often the case that erosion does not lead to unfettered authoritarianism. The result instead is a dim and anxious twilight in which the forms of democracy coexist uneasily with the substance of authoritarian rule.

5

Will American Democracy Persist?

Anything can happen to anyone, but it usually doesn't. Except when it does.
PHILIP ROTH, *The Plot Against America*

Dateline: Washington, DC, November 2024. For the second time in three election cycles, a populist billionaire has won an Electoral College majority to become president of the United States. Drawing a cue from her recent predecessors, she had campaigned in fiery tones, demonizing liberals, threatening to shut down the ivy-clad universities that shelter them, and to lock up the ghetto thugs and radical Islamic terrorists whom tweed-jacketed liberals defend. She promises to restore American pride and power and to take back our country from radical ruination. After a feckless four years of divided government, in which crime rates drifted up, the economy stagnated, and America's place in the world seemed to falter, the country's citizens respond to the president-elect's unequivocal promise of law and order. And as she happened to own the largest media conglomerate in the country, that message found its way to many eyes, ears, and social media accounts.

Upon taking office, the new president seizes a moment of unified government to systematically consolidate her office's power with respect to the other branches and civil society. Unlike her predecessors, she does not antagonize the courts. Instead, she handpicks allies for key judicial vacancies and looses an army of Ivy League–trained lawyers to draft each executive order and to explain how her innovations are consistent with the framers' original understandings. Judges, in response, double down on existing doctrines that command deference to the executive's policy choices, enable the use of coercion, and impede scrutiny of executive motives. A cottage industry of legal scholarship, written by scholars sensitive to prevailing political winds, celebrates the "efficiency" and "optimality" of this new judicial restraint. Scholars and judges who raise objections are peremptorily labeled "the enemy" and impugned for acting in bad faith and for unpatriotic reasons. One alternative locus of institutional power—the states—gets more mixed treatment. Aligned governors are welcomed to the White House and the Justice Department to consult on how to bolster industry and eliminate voter fraud. Hostile mayors and governors find themselves struggling under a tide of new executive orders, conditions on federal spending, and changes in federal tax and spending practices that imperil their financial footing.

Yet as her party in Congress bickers, substantive legislation continues to be rare, and executive orders have become the main form of new law-making. Even when constitutionally commanded, the congressional role has withered. The appropriations and budgeting processes are largely driven by the president's agenda. On the regulation front, Congress enacts an umbrella statute known as the "Authorization of Regulatory Force and Adjustment" (affectionately known among lawyers as "ARFA") that delegates to the president the power to "take all necessary and appropriate steps he or she deems necessary" to streamline regulations "notwithstanding any prior laws passed by Congress." Citing the White House's unique democratic mandate and credentials, the Supreme Court upholds this delegation with a bipartisan majority. The president's majority in Congress, in the wake of this decision, shutters several oversight committees as "needless burdens on the public purse."

Using her newfound regulatory power, the chief executive consolidates many government functions into the White House, creating a system of policy "czars." These positions are filled by, among others, several so-called "princelings," who are close friends and family to the president herself. Congress repeals the Hatch Act, which prohibited the use of public office for political campaigning, eliminating the boundary between politicking and governing. The Holman Rule, formerly an 1876 House budget rule that allowed individual federal employees' salaries to be reduced to $1, is enacted as a statute, and aggressively deployed to purge nonloyalists from the bureaucracy. Citing now well-established theories of the "unitary executive" and "presidential administration," the president claims the same power as a matter of inherent authority, and soon federal agencies are almost exclusively populated by those personally loyal to the new commander in chief. Traditions of independence associated with the Internal Revenue Service and the Federal Reserve are set aside in the name of "efficient" government or, when that rings hollow, more "democratic" administration.

On another front, the president urges her congressional majority to change the terms of the Federal Elections Campaign Act so that members of the two major parties alternate years serving as chair of the Federal Elections Commission, so that the president's party holds the chair during even years. Coincidentally, all national elections are held in even years. Newly responsive to the White House's concerns, the Internal Revenue Service steps up audits of media entities that compete with the president's company, along with not-for-profits providing legal services to regime opponents. Senior politicians who previously held national office find themselves subject to debilitating criminal investigations based on trivial errors in their past service. Periodically, the national security agencies anonymously leak transcripts of opposition politicians' compromising communications—often containing salacious details of internal infighting, extramarital affairs, or various sexual peccadilloes.

Outside of government, the president's media empire turns on individual civil servants and the residual few federal judges not aligned with the White House. Those who resist her policies or her growing cult of personality are flagged in a nightly Twitter blast about the "Enemies of the People." The White House staff also leaks stories of malfeasance and criminality by its enemies—many of which turn out to be baseless. Stories that cast the president and her allies in a negative light gain little traction in the press, even though they continue to be published. But it is the president and her allies who are best positioned to take advantage of defamation law, which does not allow suits against government officials. A sympathetic judiciary relaxes First Amendment constraints on libel and slander awards, and takes the extra step of enabling punitive damages in such cases. Two national newspapers on the east coast are forced into bankruptcy by litigation costs and awards of damages.

Three years later, a lone terrorist commits a suicide attack at an NFL game. On the evening of the attack, the president stands in the stadium's still-smoldering entranceway flanked by the five senior military officers in her cabinet to announce a new raft of restrictions on social media and "un-American" religious associations. She further explains that she will seek a constitutional amendment repealing the Twenty-second Amendment, which limits the president to two terms in office. State-level gerrymandering has given her party a comfortable two-thirds majority in both houses of Congress. Privately, some members of the party are dismayed but are too intimidated by the president's power and media empire to say so openly. The amendment sails through the otherwise demanding ratification process. A year later the president joins Franklin Delano Roosevelt as the second of only two persons to serve more than two terms in office, sworn in on a Bible held by her princeling son-in-law and presumptive heir.

✷

We begin this chapter with an exercise in dystopian fiction, not because we think the picture we have just sketched is likely to materialize, but to understand why it might not. Just as Margaret Atwood, in writing *The Handmaid's*

Tale, sought to rely solely on repressive measures she had culled from observed human history, so our far less eloquent counter-factual exercise has relied on legal and institutional changes that can be seen in one or another national context in which some backsliding away from democratic values has already occurred. Indeed, the real reason we begin with this unhappy tale is to ask, What is it, precisely, that prevents it from unfolding in the United States?

The United States is not immune from the risk of democratic recession that other countries around the world have experienced. To begin with, we reiterate that the United States *is* a democracy and that it is possible to identify a baseline of reasonably robust democratic development. Without idealizing either the history or current operation of America's democratic institutions, it is nonetheless possible to discern broad progress over the last hundred years. From the Nineteenth Amendment's extension of the franchise to women, through the 1965 Voting Rights Act, which de facto opened the political process to African-Americans, up to present-day efforts to reform campaign finance, there is a line of impressive efforts—most, but not all, successful—to open up the political sphere from the effective control of elites already in power. The twentieth century has also been characterized by the deepening of constitutional rights required for the effective exercise of political choice. It has also seen the institutionalization of the rule-of-law in the administrative state and the expansion (some would say metastasis) of judicial power over constitutional questions. Contrary to the perceptions of some, turnout rates among eligible voters have remained roughly constant, not declining much.[1] Again, reformers have not won every battle, especially when it comes to enabling all voices to be heard in politics regardless of financial power, and many deep and objectionable forms of socioeconomic and racial exclusion remain. But even skeptical theorists of American democracy, such as Christopher Achen and Larry Bartels, tell a story in which parties in fact compete for vote share by appealing to the electorate, prompting them about their basic identities and mobilizing them to turn out at the elections. Deeply flawed as this version of democracy might be, it is at least legible as a form of democratic competition.[2]

Yet if the arc of history has trended upward of late, there is no assurance that it will continue in that direction, or even that recent progress will be sustained. To the contrary, it is quite possible that the United States has now reached an inflexion point at which movement shifts in the other direction toward an equilibrium in which even Achen and Bartels' account of a thin, identity-based democracy would not hold. This would certainly not be because the United States has exhausted all possible marginal improvements in democratic quality. It would rather be because the United States is not exceptional or exempt from the global forces of local political dynamics that have produced downward movement in the quality of other nations' democracies.

We are unexceptional in another way: American democracy is at serious risk of erosion, even though the chance of autocratic collapse is small. The risks are structural, rather than being linked to the specific presidency of Donald Trump. It is true that the Trump presidency suddenly has rendered apparent the political dynamics of erosion, hence revealing the weakness of democracy's institutional foundation. But it is a mistake to assume that his tenure encapsulates both the beginning and the end of that threat to liberal constitutional democracy. Our assessment of the risks to American democracy, therefore, takes a longer time horizon. We focus first on the immediate political pressures toward erosion, but then we drill down on the mechanisms through which it might occur. The key question we pursue is this: Given what we know about the institutional and legal pathways of erosion in other national contexts (as developed in the previous chapter), do the US Constitution, the laws of the land, or broadly shared political norms that have developed in their service generate enough constraints to protect democracy from a serious challenge?

The Politics of Antidemocracy in the United States

The two antidemocratic forces that we introduced in chapter 4—charismatic populism and partisan degradation—can emerge within a democratic system to consume its institutional foundations from within. Were the United States characterized by neither, our assessment of the odds of erosion would be lower, and democracy's supporters could rest easier. But the odds are not necessarily in our favor, and democracy's allies cannot rest content with their victories.

The power of charismatic populism in American politics has been underscored by the success of Donald Trump's 2016 presidential campaign and the manner in which he has treated the White House as a bully pulpit. The Trump campaign and his initial manner of exercising presidential authority, were characterized by both of Jan Werner Muller's concepts of "moralized antipluralism," and a "noninstitutionalized notion of 'the people.'" When Trump asserted on the campaign trail that "the only important thing is the unification of the people—because the other people don't mean anything," and when he claimed "I alone can fix it," in his acceptance speech at the Republican National Convention, he distilled the logic of charismatic populism into crystalline sound bites. Populism also animated a rampantly nationalist campaign organized around a series of dichotomies pitting the "people" on the one hand against "crooked" elites, hordes of criminals and sexual predators from south of the border, and "Muslim terrorists," all tearing at the fabric of American civilization. Lest there be doubt about the binary antagonisms animating his campaign, Trump threatened to deploy federal criminal law-enforcement against his opponent, promised "extreme vetting" (or worse) at the borders, and committed to building a wall against the Hispanic hordes. In his first year in office, he has pursued these policies in whole or in part. He elicited violence against political opponents at rallies and, on Twitter, seemed to endorse its use against the press. His supporters have aimed a barrage of violent, ugly threats at journalists who criticize their leader, and he has characterized the media as "the enemies of the American people." And as of August 2017, he has quite directly embraced the themes, messages, and defensive postures of white nationalists and neo-Nazis.[3]

Trump's style of charismatic populism successfully appealed to voters living in racially isolated communities, who have experienced worse health outcomes, lower social mobility, less social capital, and greater reliance on Social Security income without capital income.[4] Although not necessarily directly hit by economic globalizations, these communities are ones in which processes of cultural change and economic transformation plainly appear as threats. By offering (almost certainly fallacious) promises to stem those changes, Trump exploits the anxieties generated by a dynamic and internationalized market—ironically in the service of policies that will very likely exacerbate economic inequality, deepen cultural rifts, and entrench even further the extant socioeconomic elites. Of course, since populists do not campaign on the basis of achievements and often successfully blame setbacks on the people's manifold enemies, this does not mean he will founder politically: To the contrary, the fact that Trump's regressive policies on health care, taxation, and policing will reinforce the inequalities and absolute deprivations that wrack his core supporters may well only make his appeal stronger. This is a key point that Trump's opponents fail to understand—charismatic populists are not judged on their actual records, but on the harmony between their rhetoric and the deeply felt grievances of supporters. And if the populists' actions exacerbate some of those grievances, this may well add to their electoral luster.

Whatever his ultimate political fate, Trump has demonstrated the potency of a charismatic populism that demonizes the media, the bureaucracy, and racial minorities. He has demonstrated that even open racism, flirtations with rancid conspiracy theories, and the gleeful admissions of sexual predation will not necessarily dent a populist's electoral appeal (and may even burnish it). And he has demonstrated how Twitter in particular can supply national politicians with a way to speak directly to the public, much as radio once did for Franklin Roosevelt. This allows him to circumvent the media, often by using naked lies, as a means of maintaining support and attacking opponents. This path, once opened, cannot be closed. There is no reason to expect that the Twitter-based, fact-free qualities of Trump's campaigning and governing styles will recede over time. Indeed, given their apparent success, there is ample reason to think they are here to stay. The age of Trump, in other words, need not and will not end with his exit from office, whenever and however that occurs.

Compounding the problem of charismatic populism, national politics in the United States can plausibly be described as having experienced a considerable degree of partisan degradation. In the 2016 election cycle, one political party dominated both national and state politics. At the state level in 2018, Republicans controlled sixty-eight of ninety-nine state legislative chambers, and thirty-three governorships.[5] At the national level, they had in 2018 majorities in the House, the Senate, and the Supreme Court (counting by the president who appointed the justices), in addition to control of the White House. Of course, the mere fact of one-party dominance is not sufficient to motivate concern about partisan degradation, even if it does cast a skeptical light on Trump's claim to be running *against* the political elite. But there are some signs that elements within the Republican Party do not view transient control of government offices as sufficient, and indeed regard the prospect of Democratic Party control as illegitimate. Whether these sentiments will translate into a policy agenda depends on the results of local and national polls in 2018, 2020, and the following years.

Consider three kinds of evidence of partisan degradation analogous to the arguments we developed about Japan and Israel. First, Senate Republican leader Mitch McConnell made headlines before the 2010 midterm elections by saying that "making Obama a one-term president" was his party's central strategic goal, and finished out that same presidency by refusing to allow a vote on a Supreme Court appointee on the basis of a thinly veiled attack on President Obama's constitutional legitimacy. In the interim, the legislative Republican Party in 2011 and 2013 transformed periodic changes to the statutory ceiling on US borrowing into an instrument of partisan attack, triggering downgrades of US debt.[6] In all these cases, the Republican Party placed its partisan interests above the interest in the regular and stable functioning of the federal government. Depending on one's perspective, these might either be cast as dangerous signals of an "anti-system" strain within the party, or simple evidence of greater political determination—or indeed both.

Second, Republican politicians at the state level have pressed for changes to electoral regimes that would lock in their control. We note that gerrymandering has been a tool of both parties, but as our purpose is to assess the risk of erosion now, it is relevant that most extreme gerrymandering at present favors Republicans and excludes Democrats. Technology has helped refine the tools of partisan boundary-drawing for both parties, but control of most state legislatures means only one party is in a position to exploit it. Recent innovations in election regulation, such as voter identification requirements, may also have the effect of predictably suppressing the vote in Democratic-leaning areas (although the magnitude of such effects is currently debated).[7]

Finally, the Republican Party itself has moved dramatically to the right, even as the Democratic Party has shifted only slightly to the left in the past thirty years.[8] This asymmetric move has taken some elements of the GOP to the fringes, and brought back the openly paranoid style of political discourse that Richard Hofstader famously ridiculed. This style is exemplified by an influential, pseudonymous 2016 essay, "The Flight 93 Election," that painted the United States at the literal brink of catastrophic collapse due to Democratic control of a single branch of government, and in desperate need of messianic (Republican) leadership. Consistent with this, a 2016 Pew poll found that 49% of Republicans stated that the Democratic Party made them afraid, and 46% said it made them feel anger. Although the current political landscape means our focus here is on Republican hegemony, it is worth noting that Democrats were even more likely to express fear and anger at those across the aisle. The dearth of democratic commitment to the legitimacy of opposition seems to have a bilateral character—a structural feature that does not bode well for a shared future.[9]

Although these harbingers are far from conclusive, and may reverse themselves in coming electoral cycles, we believe they provide reason to think that elements in the present Republican Party are capable of catalyzing a process of partisan degradation motivated by the belief that Democratic leadership is simply unacceptable. This belief arises from the increasing movement of Republican policy preferences to the right and also from the rise of alienated voters, hostile to democratic institutions and perhaps to democracy itself, who helped carry Trump to office. Whether partisan degradation actually occurs will depend on contingent factors such as the internal discipline of the Republican Party, and the particular actions of its leading figures. But the larger point for our argument is that US politics features both the possibility of charismatic populism and partisan degradation—and hence every reason to worry about whether its constitutional and legal architecture contains safeguards against autocratic collapse or more incremental erosion.

Charismatic Populism and Partisan
Degradation in the New Deal?

But perhaps it is too late to worry about the United States. Perhaps we have already suffered such backsliding on a national level that there is no meaningful
reason for worry now. Consider in this regard the American New Deal under
Franklin Delano Roosevelt, which began in 1933. To some, the New Deal was
a constitutional coup of such depth and such a radical character that it robbed
us of the framers' legacy. Roosevelt was certainly a charismatic leader who
spoke directly to the people and drew on their support for his power, and his
critics might label his redistributive policies as populist. Further, his coalition enjoyed overwhelming majorities in Congress beginning in 1932. So has
meaningful self-government in the United States already been lost?

We think not. The Roosevelt administration responded to the Great Depression with a range of both political and institutional changes that remain
deeply divisive today. On the one hand are those who see the modern administrative state that emerged from the New Deal as a necessary and essentially
beneficial response to changes in the economic and social pressures on the
nation. The New Deal, on this view, was a constitutional revolution—but one
to be celebrated as a popular adaptation to new challenges that built on a long
tradition of national administration.[10] On the other hand, however, are those
on the American right today who perceive the New Deal as a betrayal of the
original Constitution and of the source of what President Trump calls a
"civilizational threat" of "the creep of government bureaucracy."[11]

The New Deal, however, does not meet our definition of democratic erosion. We emphasize that this view is independent of our particular views about
the policies enacted by the New Deal coalition, which had significant consequences for American law and government. Nevertheless, we think it is worth
setting out in a bit more detail both the case for and the case against treating
the New Deal as an early instance of erosion to explain why such claims do
not hold water.

The case for that position might begin by noting that the New Deal unfolded in the midst of one of the periodic crises of confidence that democracy
has suffered. In a leading historical account of the era, historian Ira Katznelson describes a "deep worry that the globe's leading democracies could not
compete successfully with the dictatorships." This ran alongside an increasing
current of sympathy for autocratic forms of government, which were seen as
technically more efficient and better able to mobilize mass sentiment. Pennsylvania Senator David Reed declared in 1932, "If this country ever needed a
Mussolini, it needs one now." Progressive journalist Walter Lippmann ques-

tioned the wisdom of majority rule and the intelligence of the public. At the far extreme, flirtation with authoritarianism tipped over into the full-scale embrace of fascism. Some twenty thousand would gather under swastikas in Madison Square Garden in February 1929 for a "Mass Demonstration for True Americanism" led by Fritz Kuhn of the pro-Nazi Amerikadeutscher Bund.[12]

It is in the context of this heated atmosphere, one might contend, that the elements of the New Deal program must be evaluated. These elements include a large expansion of the federal government's regulatory authority over the economy through statutes such as the Banking and Securities Acts of 1933, the National Labor Relations Act of 1935, and the Fair Labor Standards Act of 1938. By shifting regulatory authority from Congress to the administration, it could be argued, at the same time as enlarging the sphere of government action, the New Deal dramatically reduced the scope of effective public control over government.[13] These shifts in the form of government were accompanied by the Roosevelt administration's assault on the US Supreme Court, which had interpreted the US Constitution to impose several constraints on the reach of federal regulation. More specifically, the proposed Judicial Procedures Reform Bill of 1937 would have permitted presidential appointment of a new Supreme Court justice to replace every one who reached the age of seventy and did not retire within six months. Although the plan was defeated in Congress, it is often argued that the Court retreated to a more regulation-friendly stance in its shadow.[14] Finally, there is the fact that, by running in and winning the 1940 presidential election, Roosevelt repudiated the informal two-term limit on presidents that had been in place since George Washington's departure from office.[15]

A historical account of the New Deal as an instance of democratic erosion suffers from a number of flaws. For instance, the New Deal did not mark a complete rupture in institutional developments, but extended trends of growing national regulation that could be discerned as early as the wake of the Civil War.[16] Moreover, the new national state that resulted from the New Deal remained insufficiently robust to mitigate the Great Depression: It was only in the crucible of World War II that it secured the coercive and fiscal powers that underwrite today's administrative state.[17] Further, the development of constitutional doctrine is more complex than the conventional story suggests: many seeds of what was to become the New Deal constitutional settlement were already in place before 1937.[18] But even setting aside questions of fact and interpretation, we do not think that the New Deal satisfies our definition of erosion, because it is not characterized by substantive negative change in any of the three institutional predicates of democracy.

Consider first the existence of free and fair elections. It is true, as we outlined at the beginning of this chapter, that the 1930s were characterized by continuing erosion and localized authoritarianism in the American South—but this cannot be blamed on the New Deal. To the contrary, southern agricultural interests imposed a hard brake on many New Deal programs.[19] But the change in the scope of national government wrought by the New Deal did not undermine the possibility of free and fair elections. Our definition of democracy does not require that government be a certain size or that citizens be assured a certain degree or kind of responsiveness. Moreover, even with the (brief, as we have noted, and so far nonprecedential) abrogation of the unwritten convention against three-term presidents, there is little evidence that the scope of electoral competition shrank in the New Deal. This was not a moment at which the *federal* government blocked partisan competition or narrowed the franchise. Rather, to the extent that it had progressive redistributive effects, the New Deal may have *enabled* effective democratic governance by facilitating civic participation. To be sure, such benefits may have helped entrench a New Deal coalition in office until the 1980s.[20] But there is a meaningful difference between constitutional change that operates through the conferral of benefits and a change that either eliminates democratic competition or the liberal rights necessary for democratic competition.

Nor was the New Deal period characterized by losses of liberal speech and association rights, the second part of our three-part definition of erosion. To the contrary, Laura Weinrib's recent historical account of free speech in the early twentieth century demonstrates persuasively that the First Amendment right to speech underwent a transformation in the interwar period, one that resulted in its broader and deeper acceptance by lawyers and judges on both the left and the right.[21] Finally, even those who attack the New Deal on libertarian or conservative grounds do not assert that the apparatus of the state was employed systematically to disadvantage Roosevelt's opponents or otherwise to derail the electoral process.

This is not to say that every element of the New Deal political program was unobjectionable from the standpoint of democratic quality. In particular, the presidential effort to pack the Supreme Court represents a low point for the rule of law in the United States. In subsequent chapters, we suggest that it has furnished a template for modern-day autocrats to follow. But the effort failed, and we do not think this incident by itself manifests sufficient backsliding on the administrative rule-of-law front. The New Deal was followed in 1946 by the adoption of the Administrative Procedures Act, which created a slate of procedural and structural checks on agency action.[22]

While the New Deal's critics do make arguments about its pressure on the rule of law, they seem to use this term in a quite different sense, related to the account offered by Friedrich Hayek of a free state with minimal government intervention.[23] This libertarian account of the rule of law is a thick one, encompassing strong property rights and a vision of incrementalist legal change embodied in the common law—features that are not a part of the thinner, procedural account of the rule of law that we use.

In short, because none of the three institutional prerequisites of democracy were damaged in the New Deal, we think it does not fit our definition of erosion. This does not settle the question whether the administrative state that emerged is to be condemned on libertarian or constitutional grounds. But we do not want to confuse such substantive choices with the question of how to evaluate democratic quality.

Will American Democracy Collapse?

Given the country's wealth and long democratic history, the risk of autocratic collapse in the United States, either by military coup or through the misuse of emergency powers, is very small, if not zero. A close reading of US constitutional institutions and rules provides some ground for believing that sudden democratic reversals are unlikely, absent serious miscalculations by political leaders. However, antidemocratic forces can marshal with greater ease to produce erosion. We consider first the risk of a coup d'état, and then turn to the question of emergency powers under the American system.

A central bulwark against a coup d'état is firm civilian control over the military. Here, the Constitution speaks with clarity. The president is "Commander in Chief of the Army and Navy of the United States." Even if President Trump has appointed military figures to several prominent positions, his deference to them is a matter of political strategy rather than a structural shift in civilian-military relations. Congress has extensive authority to regulate the military, which it has historically exercised with great vigor.[24] The Constitution's text may not permit a coup, but Samuel Huntington famously criticized its division of authority between two democratic principals, the president and Congress. He warned that this created the risk that the military might seek to set one off against the other in pursuit of greater autonomy. His view was that it was the "extra-constitutional" norms and "political tradition" of professionalism within the military that provided the main bulwark against military disruption of democracy.[25] Huntington is likely correct that bilateral control of the military creates space for military leaders to appeal alternatively to their legislative or executive superiors as befits their tactical needs. But there is little to suggest that this has to date generated corroding pressure on the norm of civilian control of the military. To the contrary, the statutory framework for the military mitigates against coup risk by dividing it into discrete services.

These stand in intense competition with each other, a division that significantly increases the coordination costs that would be required to effectuate a coup d'état.[26] Further diminishing that risk, the president has by statute a generous authority to manipulate the chain of command, through promotion, reassignment, and even dismissal—as Generals from Douglas MacArthur to Stanley McChrystal have learned.

Some have worried about the growth of military involvement in many domains of civilian life or have pointed to specific instances in which senior military leaders attempted to influence discrete policy decisions in the civilian sphere.[27] Some degree of conflict between civilian and military leadership, though, is inevitable. There is a difference between military demurrals to an order to expel transgender troops, and military direction of appropriations or undertaking major military action without presidential direction. And notwithstanding the extent of the military's policy entanglements, there is little evidence to date that the same military leadership seeks to shape the trajectory of domestic politics, let alone abrogate elections. (Foreign policy presents a different question in part because of the influence of military leaders on the ground in many parts of the world).[28] In other contexts where the military has gained outsized influence on domestic policy, such as Pakistan, soldiers have assumed roles in the administration that are usually reserved for civilians. But we see little evidence that such a diffusion of military personnel into key positions of the civilian bureaucracy has occurred beyond the White House. Even there, appointments of military figures, such as National Security Advisor H. R. McMasters and Chief of Staff John Kelly, are not wholly unprecedented, and to date have not been extended to domestic, policy-focused department heads. Nor is there reason to think it is actively sought by any powerful domestic interest group presently active in American politics. The observed pattern of isolated policy interventions, typically on matters that relate to the military's operation and missions, is not consistent with the assumption of an armed force champing at the bit of civilian control or secretly working to usurp such control. Consistent with Huntington's framing, and unlike its Pakistani, Turkish, and Thai counterparts, the US military lacks a self-image as the last defense of acceptable political order. It correspondingly has no history of interventions to save democracy from itself. Rumors of an American "deep state," therefore, are largely partisan gripes without substance.[29]

A less well-recognized source of pressure on democracy is identified by John Ferejohn and Frances McCall Rosenbluth in their historical treatment of the relationship between war and democracy.[30] In many societies, including that of the United States, democracy has been *enhanced* by the need for a citizen army, with whom leaders must negotiate to ensure adequate defense of the nation. Elites need soldiers to defend them, and in some cases will share government power with the citizenry in order to secure that essential relationship. Not all war-making, of course, involves such a bargain. But when it leads to a democratic outcome, the ongoing need for a citizen army becomes a mechanism that elicits democratic stability as a beneficial side-effect. It is worth noting that in the United States, franchise expansions have typically followed international conflicts, with women earning the vote after World War I, eighteen-year-olds during the Vietnam War, and African-Americans seeing their struggle for equality gain new credence after World War II and (after much delay and much blood) ripen into the 1965 Voting Rights Act.

Yet this equilibrium is now under threat along two dimensions—from mercenaries and automation. In the first decade of this century, for the first time in American history, the ratio of contractors to soldiers exceeded one-to-one in major theatres of war, with more military contractors than soldiers in both Iraq and Afghanistan.[31] As war becomes increasingly automated, moreover, there is a risk that it can be fought without the need for citizen soldiers—much as industrial capitalism has found itself able to dispense with the battalions of workers who had gained middle-class stability through skilled craft careers. In such circumstances, the connection between war and democracy will become attenuated, with less citizen monitoring of the military and uncertain consequences for civil-military relations. It also means that there may be less accountability for leaders pursuing expansionist military adventures. It even creates the possibility of private paramilitary forces of the kind that have played a role in undermining democracy in many Latin America countries.

Despite this, a plausible concern is that an incumbent president would use her commander-in-chief authority to abrogate democracy by exploiting the repercussions of a violent, exogenous shock—the September 11 attacks provide an archetype here—or a natural disaster. Alternatively, powerful commanders might persuade a weak president to suspend presidential elections in favor of "temporary" military rule. This concern, which overlaps with the worry about emergency powers, cannot be dismissed, especially given the utter dearth of a legal framework for addressing such an eventuality.[32] As in the context of the Arab Spring, we think the crucial determinant of this risk is the extent of identification between a president and the armed forces, and the corresponding willingness of soldiers to use force against civilians or opposition politicians.[33] Perhaps the closest precedent for this worry is the May 1970 shootings at Kent State University by the Ohio National Guard. Those shootings occurred in a charged environment, with President Richard Nixon tarring antiwar protestors as "bums."[34] It is not far-fetched to think that such a rhetorical fever pitch could be reached again, enabling larger-scale violence against protesters who objected to White House policies here and overseas. But sustained military involvement would still require a clear convergence between military and presidential preferences. It seems extremely unlikely that these would include ending democracy and undermining the framework for elections followed for the past 230 years. After all, there are close relationships between both parties in Congress and the military that have developed in respect to funding for military bases and services.[35]

For different reasons, we think the probability that emergency powers will be deployed to suspend the democratic process is quite low. The US Constitution is dissimilar from 90% of the world's constitutions in that it contains no expressly articulated emergency powers. Many constitutions tend to anticipate the onset of an emergency and to provide temporally limited powers to address it. Four out of five of these will also stipulate that declarations of emergency require at least two institutional actors identified in the Constitution, as a safeguard against unilateral abuse. These constitutions reflect learning from the Roman model and from the adverse precedent of the Reichstag Fire Decree.[36]

In the US Constitution, by contrast, the term *emergency* is not to be found in the text. Rather than providing for suspending elections during emergencies, the document leaves to Congress and the several States the authority to establish a timetable for federal elections. It gives no indication of how either derailing disruptions to voting (e.g., natural disasters or terrorist attacks) or ex post evidence of election-determinative fraud would be addressed. And it says nothing about what extraordinary military or civilian powers (if any) the executive branch can wield in times of crisis. Only two provisions speak directly to emergencies—and whereas one has proved largely ineffective, the other way well increase rather than buffer the risk of disorder and instability.

The first is the Suspension Clause of Article I, which limits "suspensions" of the habeas corpus writ except by statute in times of war and emergency. Although there is considerable evidence that the clause was understood to ensure the availability of the habeas corpus judicial remedy as a check on executive detention, both its origins and its effects remain sharply disputed. On the one hand, historian Paul Halliday has masterfully demonstrated that the habeas writ originated in English law as an instrument of monarchical control, not restraint, prior to 1600. On the other hand, even where the Supreme Court has been applied to guarantee a judicial remedy against detention, federal courts have been unwilling to exercise their authority to challenge the executive branch. This was true in the 1860s, when military authorities, fearing sedition, detained Southern newspaper editors and politicians. It is true in the context of post-conviction review of state-court convictions. And it was true when the Supreme Court in 2008 mandated judicial review for extraterritorial detentions of "enemy combatants." The resulting litigation has been characterized by deference to the government and open skepticism of liberty claims, leading to very little relief for plaintiffs. Rather, the path of that litigation is potent evidence of the ability of a hostile administration to undermine even the clear command of the Supreme Court.[37]

The other emergency power in the Constitution is the Twenty-fifth Amendment. This provides for vice-presidential succession if the president is incapacitated—say, by an act of violence. It contains a cumbersome and complex voting mechanism for resolving disputes over presidential incapacity. This might well deadlock in practice, just as the Electoral College deadlocked in 1800, precipitating a political crisis. (Then, it took thirty-six ballots for the Electoral College to declare Thomas Jefferson president.) Other rules for succession are contained in federal statutes that have been criticized as unconstitutional. If an emergency succession after the incapacitation of both the president and the vice-president were to be derailed by litigation, however, the Constitution contains no provision for early elections as a democratic replacement option. Rather than promoting certainty and reducing risk therefore, the presidential succession regime as it currently stands instead creates a nontrivial risk of slippage into chaos.[38]

But even though the US Constitution itself fails to speak crisply to the problem of emergency powers, political institutions—including the courts—have evolved a legal framework that allows for expansive new assertions of coercive state power in times of emergency. This judicially wrought framework is well suited to allowing state power to expand when under pressure. It thus diffuses the political pressure that might otherwise build in favor of democratic suspensions of legislatures or courts. It does this, however, at the price of permitting high rates of civil-rights and human rights violations to occur without remedy in the heat of the emergency, violations that historically have tended to be concentrated among racial, ethnic, and ideological minorities. Whether this particular trade-off appears wise might well depend on whether you are a member of the minority at the receiving end of these violations or among the majority that benefits from overall democratic stability.

In the absence of explicit constitutional text, legislatures and courts have developed a framework for emergency measures that in practice gives the executive branch great discretion in determining how to respond to emergencies. Since the 1970s, Congress has delegated broad and discretionary grants of emergency and war power to the executive. These powers range from emergency economic powers to freeze or even seize assets to sweeping electronic surveillance powers and inchoate war-powers authorizations occasioned by a conflict in one country but drafted to permit the use of military force far afield. The residual de minimus requirements of statutory authorization turn out to be, as Madison would put it, parchment barriers. The executive, for example, has consistently asserted authority to use military force in emergencies, even absent congressional permission; to use electronic surveillance without individualized suspicion; and to take emergency economic actions without clear statutory authority. This is true for both Democratic and Republican presidencies: The growth of emergency powers, that is, has followed a secular trend.[39]

Alongside this change, federal courts have developed a jurisprudence of constitutional rights and remedies that not only carves out many *per se* exceptions for exigency and national security, but also often categorically prohibits the grant of any judicial remedy when an executive action is taken in a time of crisis. Many constitutional rights, as a result, now contain open-ended exceptions whenever the government says there are exigent circumstances. Remarkably, these exceptions apply even when the government is itself responsible for creating the emergency.[40] Hence, the Supreme Court has developed a case law concerning free speech that is generally skeptical of legal restrictions based on the content or viewpoint of speech, and has demanded exceedingly persuasive justifications for such measures. But when the federal government invokes a concern about national security as a reason for criminalizing speech based on its content, the Court has eased off the throttle and employed less searching scrutiny. One notable beneficiary of this weakened form of First Amendment scrutiny are the criminal "material support" laws, which have been upheld even though they prohibit speech acts such as teaching international law or negotiation skills in the hope that foreign insurgents come to the bargaining table rather than resort to violence.[41]

The fragility of legal constraints during emergencies has two implications. First, emergency responses to violent crisis tend to be accompanied by substantial rates of violations of individual constitutional and human rights in the form of detentions, coercive interrogations, and punishments for speech or association. Second, constitutional and legal constraints on the government's emergency action are very elastic, so that these violations do not occasion any legal response. Officials can be reasonably confident they will not face either ex ante injunctive barriers or ex post damage awards. Indeed, it is increasingly the case that they can be confident they won't be forced to the expense and embarrassment of even a trial. They can also be reasonably confident that there will be some federal statute, somewhere on the books, that can be invoked to provide a colorable legal justification for most courses of action.

As a result of these developments, it will be a rare instance in which a desired emergency response cannot be routed through existing statutory and constitutional channels to minimize legal backlash. This elasticity means that there is little need for "special" emergency measures: most emergencies can be managed within the framework of "ordinary" statutory, doctrinal, and textual frameworks. There will rarely be any need to disrupt the democratic system in order to secure additional powers that might be perceived as necessary. This makes the case for outright authoritarianism hard to sustain. In short, we think the current constitutional regime for emergencies does not create pressure toward authoritarian collapse, precisely because it is so elastic and as such does a rather miserable job of resisting violations of individual rights. Democratic stability, then, is purchased at the cost of deep and harmful violations of individual rights when the government asserts a need for emergency action.

The flexibility of this legal matrix means that presidents have generally been able to accommodate emergency responses within existing legal frameworks. Declared states of emergency have been limited to localized territories, such as Hawaii during World War II, which was governed by martial law.[42] National elections have never been canceled or delayed as a result of war or crisis—something even the United Kingdom cannot claim. The result is a history of periodic grave violations of civil liberties punctuating the unbroken operation of democratic institutions. This matters because cross-national studies suggest that histories of governmental instability are predictive of subsequent democratic collapse.[43] If crisis tends to beget crisis, then the absence of such crisis seems to portend future stability for the United States. One way to think about this is in terms of political incentives. The absence of a history of democratic suspensions creates a large measure of uncertainty over the distributive and political consequences of authoritarian collapse via emergency rule. A prospective anti-democrat in Thailand or Turkey, by contrast, has much more information on the likely reaction of various forces in society. In the United States, however, there is no subset of interest groups that can confidently predict from past experience that it, and not others, will gain from democracy's death.

There is a risk to democracy from assertions of emergency power, we think, but it is subtler than the example of the Reichstag fire would suggest. It is not that an emergency will be used as a gateway to the abrogation of democratic institutions. Rather, by inducing or leveraging a violent crisis—a war, or a grave terrorist attack—a charismatic populist can justify incursions on the three institutional predicates of democracy mapped earlier. The fear of violence can be used to curb the media and social media, eliminate mechanisms of intrabranch accountability that superintend the federal government's action, and hasten the process of partisan degradation. Crisis then is catalyst, not a direct cause, of democratic erosion or failure.

Will American Democracy Erode?

A very different analysis applies when we turn to the rise of democratic erosion. We have already observed that the socioeconomic and political factors that drive erosion are not absent from the United States. What *is* surprisingly absent, however, are general safeguards against the specific pathways of erosion observed in other parts of the global democratic recession. Although the United States is not exposed to all forms of observed erosion—indeed, we begin by describing one way in which it is in fact better positioned than many other countries—along several other margins, the country is surprisingly vulnerable.

Our analysis here examines the US Constitution, the Supreme Court's case law interpreting that document, and other legal institutions as they currently exist. We proceed using the framework developed in the last chapter, setting out the several possible mechanisms of democratic erosion and asking whether the US Constitution can prevent them. Our emphasis throughout is on structure. It is useful, in our view, to set forth crisply the interaction between our existing constitutional rules and the threat of democratic erosion, without introducing potentially more contentious inquiries into particular political figures. We flag ways in which the text and the existing doctrine impede erosion, but also ways in which they might facilitate it by preventing the adoption of mitigating measures. In many cases, however, it is possible to imagine the Constitution's text being interpreted in a quite different way from standard positions that would be familiar to well-trained lawyers. Indeed, the range of possible alternate specifications of constitutional rules is almost unlimited, given the majestic vagueness of much of the document's text and the plasticity of the historical sources. We bracket that inquiry for now, however, in favor of looking at the law as it exists now in relation to the risk of erosion. It is only in the next chapter that we will grapple with the question whether better versions of constitutional rules could be imagined that mitigate some of the problems flagged here.

FORMAL CONSTITUTIONAL AMENDMENT

Amendments to the Constitution are made through a two-stage process that is described in Article V of the document. First, an amendment is proposed by supermajorities of Congress or of the several states' legislatures. Second, ratification requires larger supermajorities of the states acting in either legislatures or conventions. As a matter of historical practice, only Congress has proposed amendments, and, with one exception, only state legislatures have done the ratifying. The de facto threshold for constitutional amendment, therefore, is two-thirds supermajorities in Congress plus successful votes in seventy-five discrete state houses (assuming one is Nebraska's unicameral chamber).[44] While its actual rank depends on how one makes the assessment, most observers agree that the United States Constitution is one of the most rigid in the world in terms of being difficult to amend.[45] This is all the more remarkable since ease of amendment is generally a "strong" predictor of constitutional longevity.[46]

Article V receives a good deal of criticism from liberal legal scholars. They complain that it makes the Constitution antiquated, undemocratic, and in sore need of revision to account for both social and technological change.[47] Further, it is not possible to fix ambiguities in the current text. For example, when President Trump suggested in July 2017, based on an aggressive, albeit not wholly implausible, reading of Article II of the Constitution, that a president has power to pardon himself, it was not feasible to clarify the text to eliminate the possibility of a self-pardon.[48] Although these criticisms have considerable force, the stickiness of the Constitution's text has an advantage— even if an unanticipated one. It insulates us from a common strategy of erosion—the use of amendments to eliminate accountability mechanisms or entrench a charismatic populist or single party into permanent power. Whatever the costs of constitutional rigidity, this surely counts as a significant plus in any assessment of Article V.

However, Article V is not a panacea for two reasons. First, imagine that a political party gains disciplined majorities in both houses of Congress and in thirty-eight states—a level of success that the Republican party has approached in recent years. It could then utilize Article V with few limitations. The content of ensuing reforms to the American Constitution is not hard to imagine. Following patterns in other illiberal democracies, and as anticipated in our opening hypothetical, a first target might be the Twenty-second Amendment, which constitutionalized term limits in the wake of Franklin Roosevelt's presidency. Or the aim of amendment might be the entrenchment of rules that skew election results in favor of the party—for example, banning independent redistricting commissions in favor of legislative redistricting; requiring the use of the eligible electorate rather than the whole population to craft district lines; constitutionalizing a requirement of photo identification at the polls; and permanently disenfranchising those with a criminal conviction.

Several of these ideas, not incidentally, have been the topics of recent constitutional claims lodged in court by the political right.[49] Alternatively, if these seem too indirect, one might simply consider the various liberty-restricting constitutional amendments that have been proposed in Congress in recent years, mainly to overturn Supreme Court decisions related to constitutional rules on free speech and religious establishment.[50]

There is nothing *structural* in Article V that prevents such a disciplined majority with sufficient public support from using constitutional amendments to entrench its power though changes to the electoral framework or by restricting liberal rights to speech and association. Unlike the courts of many other democracies, US courts have never developed a formal doctrine of "unconstitutional constitutional amendments," as the Indian Supreme Court, the Colombian Supreme Court, and (fleetingly, in 2010) the Hungarian Supreme Court did.[51] Hence, Article V's high threshold creates the potential for two states of the world: One in which formal constitutional amendment never happens, and (echoing the Hungarian case) another in which a transient supermajority exploits an unexpected chance to turn itself into a permanent party of government. To the extent that there are traces of an unconstitutional conditions doctrine in American constitutional law, moreover, they are hardly promising. The Supreme Court in the late nineteenth century and again in the late twentieth century has often treated the post–Civil War Thirteenth, Fourteenth, and Fifteenth Amendments as subsidiary to unwritten elements of the original eighteenth-century constitutional design. The effect of these decisions has been to narrow the scope of congressional power to redress civil rights violations in comparison to the legislature's power to address economic problems.[52] In practice, that is, the Constitution has been read in ways that weaken the formal amendments intended to eliminate social stratification. The slaveholding framers of 1787 at every point have been prioritized over the enfranchising abolitionists of the Reconstruction period.

Second, it is true that the text of the Constitution has not changed much in the last century or so, and that those textual changes that have occurred have been relatively minor. For instance, the most recent amendment bars immediately effective congressional pay raises. But if we consider the range of foundational institutions that are effectively entrenched against easy political change and that are essential to the operation of the overall system of national government, it is quite obvious that *a lot* has changed. The New Deal, the Civil Rights revolution, the Great Society, the Reagan Revolution—all these historical movements left permanent alterations to the basic institutional structure of national government in the form of major statutes in the last century.[53] The Supreme Court too has assumed a large role in de facto constitutional change, even if it has labeled what it is doing as "interpretation" rather than "amendment." Recent years have seen the Court manufacture, almost out of thin air, a host of new rules and rights. These include a new individual right to bear arms, a new individual right to same-sex marriage, a prohibition on the congressional regulation of private individuals' decision not to engage in market transactions (i.e., not purchase health insurance), and a constitutional immunity for independent campaign expenditures by corporate entities.[54] These legal innovations, as this list makes clear, are not solely the preserve of liberals or conservatives. Nor are they always associated with a break from some imagined "original understanding" of the Constitution. To the contrary, the text of the Constitution is so open-textured, and the available historical material is so extensive, diverse, and contradictory, that the much-touted interpretive method of "originalism" simply serves as a mode of judicial creativity that in practice is at best partial and at worse deceitful.

There are, in short, ample ways to change the practice of the Constitution, by legislation, by judiciary, and—in the case of interracial association and same-sex marriage—largely by the sheer courage and force of will of the citizenry. A movement set on democratic erosion will therefore squeeze each of these modalities of foundational change for all that they are worth. And as we explore in the coming pages, they are worth rather a lot.

THE ELIMINATION OF INSTITUTIONAL CHECKS

The elimination of institutional checks involves the undermining of courts and legislatures in favor of a charismatic, often populist, chief executive. In the United States, the most formidable motor of erosion would be the presidency, which over time has acquired a plethora of institutional, political, and rhetorical powers above and beyond the meager list set out in Article II of the Constitution. It is difficult to imagine the sort of wholesale purges of the judiciary that have occurred in Hungary and Poland, or the deliberate circumvention of the legislative branch witnessed in Venezuela. To be sure, there is precedent from the Jefferson presidency in the form of an 1802 statute that abolished several federal courts and stripped numerous judges of their Article III commission, a statute upheld by the Supreme Court in a little-known opinion called *Stuart v. Laird*.[55] But such overt and aggressive acts of retrogressive constitutional reengineering may well not be necessary in the contemporary American context. Notwithstanding the ardent hopes of those who drafted the 1787 Constitution, it may well be that neither the federal legislative branch nor the federal courts can impose much friction on regressive executive action that unravels democracy. Those framers also looked to the states, embedded in a federalist system, as additional constraint on excessive centralization of authority. But the actual effect of federalism is at best ambiguous. The problem in the United States, in short, is not the risk that interbranch checks will be dismantled. The problem is that they were never as effective as was hoped in the first place.

In thinking about the institutional checks imposed by Congress and the court on executive action, it is helpful to draw a distinction between the capacities and the motivations of each branch. To resist the centralizing efforts of a charismatic populist, after all, requires both the ability and the willingness to do so. Without one, the other is useless. To judge just on the basis of the text of the Constitution, one might think that Congress plainly could constrain a populist presidency. Article I of the Constitution, which describes and creates Congress, gives it primacy in law-making and the fiscal powers of taxation and spending. Not a penny can leave the federal purse without legislative say-so. Legislators have power to veto appointments and to determine whether the United States will enter into international agreements and international hostilities. Beyond the text, Congress has long been understood to have a sweeping power to investigate, including to subpoena witnesses and to imprison for contempt those who do not appear. In contrast, Article II's depiction of the presidency is skeletal and subordinate to the legislative power. It contains few affirmative powers and, to the contrary, underscores the president's obligation to "take care" that legislation be "faithfully executed." Taking the text of the Constitution seriously, one sees plainly a juxtaposition between a robustly empowered Congress and a head-of-state whose role teeters on the ceremonial. It is no small irony that modern-day originalists have managed to invert this facially self-evident institutional hierarchy.[56]

Of course, the textual allocation of constitutional powers bears no relation to the actual distribution of effective institutional authorities. This is an embarrassment for constitutional purists, one that has generated the cottage industry in originalist justifications of robust executive power. But for our purposes, it is instructive in a different way: It shows that assigning *capabilities* to an institution will be fruitless unless it is also endowed with the motivations to use them. This point did not escape the drafters of the Constitution. Writing in Federalist No. 51, James Madison explained that each branch would act as a constraint on the others because "ambition must be made to counteract ambition," and "the interest of the man, must be connected with the constitutional rights of the place." The Constitution, however, contains no mechanism to align the interests of individual officeholders and their home institution. Rather, to the extent that such institutional loyalties do develop, they are spread unevenly across the three branches of government. As a general matter, they are least likely to gain traction in Congress. By design, a legislature is supposed to be a forum for ongoing political disagreement and deliberation. In consequence, at any given instant, it will house a variety of voices representing different partisan and ideological interests. In this, it is quite unlike the executive, where partisan contestation occurs *across* time through the rotation of power across a series of chief executives, and where a permanent civil service can keep its eye on branch-level interests through different administrations. By its very function, then, a legislature is much more likely to be shaped by partisan and ideological conflict than the executive, and less likely to be motivated to protect its institutional prerogatives in the manner Madison expected.[57]

One response to this asymmetry found in other constitutions, which we discuss in more detail in the next chapter, involves the creation of constitutional platforms for opposition parties within the legislature to challenge executive action. We mention it here briefly to underscore a feature that the US Constitution lacks. In the German Bundestag, for example, sufficiently large minority parties receive a certain number of committee chairs. In the British Parliament, there is an informal norm of granting losing political coalitions committee chair positions, and a more general convention that the "Loyal Opposition" has "constitutional responsibilities" to serve as a responsible check on the party in power.[58] The United States, in contrast, contains no such minority provisions. While some intracameral rules, such as that of the filibuster, give minorities some voice, these are not stable fixtures of congressional life. Moreover, the investigative powers of Congress are tied to majority status—meaning that they are least likely to be used when the risk of erosion is greatest. This is by definition in periods of unified government.[59] In short, the Constitution fails to supply the legislative branch with the necessary internal structures to ensure that it acts as an effective check on the executive in the fashion that Madison assumed.

If legislative institutional power to check the executive is larger on paper than in practice, it is worth pointing out that executive power has the reverse configuration. The Constitution is not effusive in listing the powers of the executive. Among Article II's limited textual allocations of power, the most important include the status of commander in chief, the obligation to faithfully execute the laws, and the power to make nominations and recess appointments. In practice, however, recent decades have seen a massive expansion of both legal and practical executive power and the use of instruments with a limited textual or statutory basis. These powers are often employed through executive orders of some shape or form; various decision-making bodies or councils that centralize policy control in the White House; and the use of radio, television, and now social media as a presidential bully pulpit. Many other constitutions elaborate a constitutional decree power that is assigned to the executive, which in turn constrains and limits the authority. The silence of the US model on how and when such instruments can be used to further the president's ends has given chief executives broad latitude to experiment with a range of tools to pursue policies, with no clear limits on their discretion. Congress is hence strong on paper but weak in practice, whereas presidents are weak on paper but powerful in practice. Paradoxically, this contrast flows in part from the constitutional text's verbosity when it comes to Congress, and its terseness when it comes to the presidency.

The problems created by these gaps are accentuated by a different asymmetry—this time, one that is the result of judicial action. The Supreme Court has taken a different view of delegations to the executive and of congressional efforts to retain some sort of supervisory authority over the use of delegated power. On the one hand, the Court has long allowed broad delegations of regulatory authority, in seeming recognition of the functional arguments in favor of bureaucratic administration. On the other hand, it has not allowed Congress to claw back a measure of supervisory power in individual cases. In 1983, the Court instead retreated to a rigid formalism to invalidate the legislative veto, a congressional tool deployed from the 1930s to the 1980s to exercise a measure of supervision over delegated authority. The net result of this oscillation between judicial pragmatism and judicial formalism is that there is now a set of broad delegations to the executive, but Congress has been categorically denied the ability to maintain perhaps its most direct and effective oversight instrument.[60] Rather than enabling meaningful interbranch interaction, the Court has thus hobbled one side while inviting the other's aggressive action.

Madisonian conflict between the executive and Congress will likely arise, in short, only in periods of divided government. In this regard, the American system is not very different from other presidential and semi-presidential systems in other parts of the world. In Latin America, for example, the recent wave of charismatic populists, such as Hugo Chávez in Venezuela and Rafael Correa in Ecuador, distinguished themselves by bypassing hostile legislative branches and resorting to extraordinary tools, such as a constituent assembly.[61] Were that to occur in the American context, the question would then be whether Congress could use its extensive powers to respond effectively to the sort of system-changing initiatives that have been observed in other instances of charismatic populism. Any response would not depend on the availability of that branch's formal legal capabilities, though, but on the decisions of the "pivotal" member of Congress for the purpose of (say) launching an investigation, seeking judicial enforcement of a subpoena, or overcoming a veto. To flag a theme to which we return in our conclusion, this means that immediate resistance to erosion is contingent—more a function of political dynamics than legal institutional design. At the same time, the Constitution has implications for *who* will be this pivotal member. Where a conflict turns on Congress's ability to overcome a veto—for instance, if Congress attempts to restrain the president by a new law, which is vetoed—this means that the member necessary to achieve a two-thirds supermajority will be important. Even in periods of divided government, this member is very likely to be a member of the president's own party. Hence, as far as enacting new laws against the president's will, the legislative scheme established in Article I, section 7, conduces to stasis and inaction—especially, perhaps, when the legislative proposal seeks to constrain presidential action in some fashion. This is not a promising backdrop for legislative resistance to executive-led erosion.

In Poland, Hungary, Venezuela, and elsewhere, however, it has been courts rather than legislatures that have been targeted in the early stages of democratic erosion. In many emerging democracies constitutional courts initially played important roles in policing key political transitions. While this occurred in both Poland and Hungary, perhaps the canonical example is the South African Constitutional Court's important role in the transition from apartheid.[62] For a court to play a major role, its members must once again have the necessary motivations. A court that is either closely aligned with a partisan regime or lacks the professional orientation to confront the wayward uses of state power will not be of much concern to a charismatic populist or a would-be, hegemonic political party. Here again, the Weimar courts' inaction in the early 1920s, despite their prestige and long-standing professionalism, should provide an important caution.[63]

If we are focused on their potential as checks against democratic backsliding, the US federal courts today have more in common with the inert Weimar courts than the activist constitutional court of South Africa, for three reasons. Most importantly, the Constitution's system of presidential nomination and Senate confirmation for selecting federal judges, and those of the Supreme Court in particular, runs through the elected branches. It also lacks any substantive screening criteria that might select for judges with fidelity to the rule of law or to constitutional values. Judges are instead selected on the basis of partisan and ideological commitments held by the president and the Senate. The principal reason why federal courts do not act simply and mechanically as instruments of the governing regime is that judges are appointed at different times, by different political coalitions, and then serve for life. By moving at different speeds, the usually short life of each elected regime and the longer expected tenure of each of their judges on the benches interact to produce a variegated federal bench—one composed of judges appointed at different times by distinct and ideologically varied political coalitions.[64] At this writing, there are more sitting federal judges appointed by Democrats than Republican presidents.[65] But this ideological heterogeneity is fragile. Over the medium term, a party with sustained control over the other two branches can reshape the judiciary in its image.

In the absence of ideological variation, the federal courts are likely to act as mere adjuncts to an aligned political regime, even if the latter is engaged in democratic erosion. The best example of this comes from the beginning of the Republic, when the Federalist Party under John Adams had not only appointed all federal judges, but had armed them with a powerful instrument of partisan control in the 1798 Alien and Sedition Acts. These allowed the punishment of anyone who did "write, print, utter, or publish . . . any false, scandalous and malicious writing" against the government. Justified by a theory of democratic representation that disallowed much opposition, Federalist judges used the Sedition Act to punish the Federalists' Jeffersonian opponents, at least until Thomas Jefferson won the presidency and pardoned those convicted under the Act. This early American experience shows that there is no structural reason why federal courts, when sufficiently ideologically pure, cannot act as agents of a party seeking political hegemony rather than as a check on democratic erosion.[66] Certainly, nothing in the *Constitution* dictates the latter rather than the former course of conduct.

Second, even when the federal courts are insulated from partisan pressures, it is far from clear that they have the necessary motivation to be robust shields against democratic erosion. To play that role, a court must either be willing to protect the liberal speech and association rights of regime opponents, or else be able to stand firm against efforts to dismantle either intrabranch or interbranch constraints on government power. But the institutional incentives of the federal courts have never been conducive to this role, and their jurisprudence to date is inconsistent with a robust judicial defense of democracy. To see this, it is helpful to step back and consider the longer arc of the federal judiciary's historical development.

Over the course of the late nineteenth century and early twentieth century, federal judges and justices have successfully lobbied Congress to create a judicial civil service (the Administrative Office of the United States Courts), to add a new layer of courts of appeals, and to move the Supreme Court from a system of largely mandatory to largely discretionary jurisdiction. While lobbying has built an administrative and jurisdictional structure that allows the federal courts to function independently of the other branches in many ways—managing their own budgets, lobbying Congress, and deciding on which cases to hear in the case of the apex tribunal—the federal courts have acquired legitimacy among the public in part through their association with historical causes such as the civil rights movement. Conservatives and liberals alike genuflect before the altar of *Brown v. Board of Education*, the 1954 decision invalidating separate but equal public education. Whether this esteem is warranted is a difficult question; American schools, after all, are as racially segregated now as they were in the early 1950s. But there is little question that the federal courts enjoy a measure of public support, which makes them formidable public actors.[67] Indeed, at this writing they have the highest public confidence of any of the three branches, even if that confidence is declining.

Yet the way in which the Supreme Court deploys its political capital suggests that it does not understand its institutional interests in ways that are necessarily inconsistent with the pursuit of democratic erosion. Hence, the Court has developed, largely along bipartisan lines, a body of doctrine that makes it extremely difficult to vindicate constitutional rights. In the first century of the Republic, federal courts relied on state-law equitable procedures and tort actions to vindicate constitutional rights. In one renowned case still read by many law students, for example, the widow of General Robert E. Lee, Mary Anne, used a state-law proceeding, called an "action of ejectment," to challenge the federal government's seizure of family property in Arlington, Virginia.[68] But in the twentieth century, as the courts have expanded the range and detail of constitutional rules, they have also found ways to minimize the volume of suits alleging retail constitutional violations. They have done so by fashioning a range of doctrinal barriers that limit relief, deny discovery, and discourage trials. None of these doctrines has a foundation in statute. They are cut from the whole cloth of judicial imagination. All have the effect of reducing the likelihood of success for individuals challenging constitutional violations and hence tamping down the expected volume of such cases.

These doctrinal barriers include onerous standing requirements for those who seek an injunction for fear of future unconstitutional action. They also include strict limits on when unlawful detention can be terminated by a federal court, even if a constitutional error is evident in the record. A robust doctrine of "qualified immunity" in constitutional tort cases limits not just recovery but even trial, unless a plaintiff can show that the defendant violated a rule that was "clearly established" and obvious to all. This qualified immunity regime means "all but the plainly incompetent or those who knowingly violate the law" never face trial, let alone any penalty.[69] When national security is involved, moreover, the Supreme Court has erected an additional defensive fortification by categorically barring most damages actions against federal officials, even in cases of gross human rights violations such as torture, extrajudicial detention, and discriminatory brutality due to race or religion. In the aggregate, these doctrines mean that officials can often violate individual constitutional rights with impunity, especially if they can lay claim to some sort of national security justification, however implausible.[70] These doctrines formally cover all local, state, and national officials. But as a practical matter their operation also accrues most to the benefit of federal officials—in particular, senior departmental heads and the president. For it is this latter class of apex officials who are most able to invoke national security, state secrets, or another of the broader justifications for barring judicial remedies.

This set of doctrines limiting constitutional remediation mean that the Court can shirk any response to serial constitutional violations if doing so would be divisive or damaging to the Court's reputation or workload. For as empirical studies have convincingly demonstrated, the Court is systematically less likely to intervene when political opposition is likely.[71] Applied to a hypothetical context of democratic erosion, this framework makes effective protection of democratic practice difficult, although not impossible. But more importantly, it suggests that the federal courts—notwithstanding their appetite for high-profile, pious-sounding interventions—have little appetite for such high-stakes confrontation. Capacity may be available, but motive is not.

Unlike the constitutional courts celebrated by comparative scholars, therefore, the well-established federal judiciary may lack the institutional will to impede the erosion of constitutional, democratic norms. In the face of a concerted program of democratic erosion, it may at best fire a few warning shots across the bow. Ultimately, however, the judicial arsenal is a limited one. It seems more likely that partisan alignment and judicial self-protection will converge to a quietism that preserves the courts qua institution at the cost of the Constitution, individual rights, or the orderly functioning of democratic competition.

FEDERALISM: AN ASIDE

A distinctive feature of the American constitutional system is the central role accorded the constituent sovereign states, which might be thought to operate as a third species of institutional check in addition to Congress and the courts. The resulting system of "our federalism" has been the locus of ideological and material controversy since 1787, when slave-owners and abolitionists, industrialists and plantation owners, all grappled over the protection of states' rights. But a constant thread in these conflicts has been the idea that federalism would work as an "alternative to tyranny" because it ensures the existence of multiple sovereigns through which diverse publics could articulate their preferences.[72]

The existence of subnational entities wielding substantial regulatory authority and possessing considerable regulatory capacity means that states and certain localities will almost certainly play an active role should there be a push toward democratic erosion. But it is uncertain ex ante whether federalism (or localism) will influence the trajectory of erosion in a positive or a negative direction. On the one hand, it is possible that states and localities would provide platforms for alternative, anti-authoritarian politicians and coalitions. In some instances, states and cities have the power to slow the implementation of, and even nullify, federal law. Immigration law is a potent contemporary example, as is marijuana policy.[73] On the other hand, the existence of federalism permits democratization to develop in uneven, punctuated ways. Many federated democracies—including the United States, Argentina, Mexico, and Brazil—thus have experienced what political scientists call "authoritarian enclaves" in some states or regions, enclaves that have endured for years or even decades.[74] The existence of subnational authoritarianism can have wider repercussions at the national level. For instance, a series of state electoral results and policy actions might entrench an antidemocratic coalition and render it nationally unassailable. Patterns of diffusion, whereby policies and institutions adopted in one state can spread to others, need not differentiate between pro- and antidemocratic content. One can imagine, for example, institutional innovations, such as restrictions on the ballot or hard-wired partisan gerrymanders, spreading around the country, creating a series of one-party states. Interest groups wielding model statutory language already play a central role in such diffusion.[75] Close alignment between existing networks of interest groups and a charismatic populist or an authoritarian partisan formation could generate exceedingly fast diffusion of antidemocratic tools. If a sufficient number of states embraced those instruments, both national and state-level electoral competition would become severely limited, deepening rather than alleviating democracy's plight.

A real risk at the moment is excessive sorting by population. As state legislatures become more sophisticated at line-drawing to weaken partisan competition, states may become more firmly blue or red, adopting policies that reflect a deeper ideological commitment. Coupled with other socioeconomic dynamics, this in turn may help drive members of the other party to seek refuge in states more politically attractive to them. While that might be good in terms of aligning preferences with policies, this kind of population sorting is undesirable from the point of view of democratic turnover and competition. It could, at the extreme, lead to fifty single-party states, none of which had much serious interparty competition. Obviously, this extreme hypothetical would have serious consequences for political freedoms and for the bureaucratic rule of law. But even less grave versions of the sorting dynamic might have undesirable, competition-dampening effects.

Federalism, in short, is far from irrelevant. But this does not mean its effects are predictable. To the contrary, it is difficult to know before the fact whether devolution will accelerate or retard the advent of an authoritarian or quasi-authoritarian regime at the national level in a given case. Federalism, in a worst-case scenario, creates laboratories for despotism and an alluring network of channels for retrogressive contagion. At a minimum, though, it cannot supply a reliable safeguard against erosion, and it is a deep mistake to celebrate or condemn it in an unthinking or categorical fashion.

CENTRALIZING AND POLITICIZING EXECUTIVE POWER

Democratic erosion often entails an assault on intrabranch institutions of "horizontal accountability"—the "network of relatively autonomous powers (i.e., other institutions) that can call into question, and eventually punish, improper ways of discharging the responsibilities of a given official."[76] Independent bodies for deciding when to prosecute, investigating fraud and human-rights violations, and regulating both private media and state broadcasters all fall into this category. In a well-functioning democracy, a thick ecosystem of such institutional actors works as a hedge against democratic erosion. In consequence, as can be seen in Hungary, Venezuela, Turkey, and elsewhere, it is one of the early targets of those who wish to dismantle democracy's necessary administrative rule of law.

The US Constitution lacks formal, textual protection of bureaucratic autonomy, with the limited exception of the Bill of Attainder Clause of Article I, a clause that has been read to supply some protection from targeted legislative firings.[77] By contrast, many other constitutions provide for public service or civil service commissions to govern public employment and the operation of the bureaucracy, precisely because of the risk of partisan patronage. Some 85 out of a historical sample of 822 constitutions have such commissions. And of constitutions drafted after 1989, 23 out of 215 have such commissions.[78] But our eighteenth-century document, drafted before the emergence of the modern administrative state in the late nineteenth century, could not have contemplated the need for constitutional regulation to protect the bureaucracy. Prior to the 1887 creation of the Interstate Commerce Commission, American government was largely a matter of "courts and parties," rather than regularized bureaucracies operating under stable rules and oriented toward legality and predictability.[79] Administrative institutions did exist—the Post Office, the Customs Service, a (first) Bank of the United States, and a system of seamen's hospitals all date from the first decades of the Republic—but their scope was too small to catalyze demand for constitutional protection of the bureaucracy's regularized and lawful operation.[80]

In lieu of constitutional protections, institutions of horizontal accountability in the United States have been protected by statute and by political convention. Initially, federal officials ranging from judges to tax inspectors and diplomats were compensated either through "bounties" or "facilitative payments," sums given over in exchange for services rendered. At its acme in the Jacksonian "spoils system," presidents had a pivotal role in distributing government jobs as political favors. This system, which resembles nothing so much as a massive extortion scheme, was gradually superseded by regular salaries and prohibitions on payment for services. These were precursors to the professional civil service that began to take shape in the Progressive Era.[81] Starting with the Pendleton Act of 1883, Congress fashioned by increments a civil-service system designed to promote meritocratic government and professional governance. The Pendleton Act was initially of limited effect, insofar as it vested civil servants with no protection from termination and did not mandate merit-based exams. Civil-service protections were strengthened piecemeal by statute from the 1880s through to the 1930s.[82]

Later, in 1978, the Civil Service Reform Act promoted the use of merit-based evaluations within federal administrative agencies. It also created an independent agency, the Merit Systems Protection Board, to hear appeals of personnel actions. Since then, the Court has also grafted a measure of First Amendment protection into the public employment context by prohibiting certain adverse employment decisions on the basis of party affiliation.[83] Nevertheless, the strength and coverage of these legal protections and the success of the related professionalization project should not be overstated. Even in highly salient domains, such as monetary policy, political insulation from presidential control remains today a function of political "conventions" rather than of written law. A convention is simply a regularized practice that is viewed as having strong normative justification. No legal remedy is available for its violation.[84]

A particularly important set of conventions concerns legal authority within the federal government. Formally speaking, the Department of Justice is just another executive agency, whose head is nominated by and serves at the pleasure of the president. Yet by convention, neither the president nor the attorney general interferes with or directs individual prosecution decisions or investigations. Until President Trump fired James Comey in May 2017, no FBI director had ever been terminated in the absence of serious allegations of misconduct.[85] No precedent exists, moreover, for the public pressure Trump has placed on his attorney general to begin investigations into his former political opponent, and to drop investigations into Russian interference in the 2016 election. Another important legal power is that of interpretation. The Office of Legal Counsel within the department issues authoritative legal advice to the executive branch, insulated from the president and the attorney general. Conventions insulating legal decisions from politics are critical for underpinning the bureaucratic rule of law and ensuring that prosecutorial power is not misused for narrow political ends. But the key norms, in the end, are simply conventions based on precedents and occasionally memorialized in the form of nonbinding internal documents.

We do not mean to imply that this network of laws, regulations, constitutional precedent, and norms is always ineffective. To the contrary, in ordinary political circumstances, it can work reasonably well as a check on improper self-dealing. For instance, when President George W. Bush's administration sought to hire career staff on the basis of political affiliation, the Office of the Inspector General released a damning report. The inspector general reported to the US Attorney's Office that an administration official had not only violated the relevant rules but had given false testimony to the Judiciary Committee of the Senate. In the early months of the Trump administration, laws and political conventions supplied the Office of Government Ethics with a measure of insulation to critique ethical conflicts.[86]

But political conventions are not ironclad, and the law also provides significant tools for elected leaders seeking to defang institutions of horizontal accountability. At the most basic level, presidential appointment of a head of agency openly opposed to its mission can undermine staff that wish to actively advance that mission. Staff cannot promulgate rules, conduct enforcement actions, or take any of the other routine steps of government without at least the acquiescence of the head of the agency. Those who wish to advance an agenda or have been working on solutions to regulatory problems for some time, may find themselves unable to take affirmative steps in the absence of a cooperative head. In this way, an agency head opposed to the agency's mission can preserve the status quo by resisting staff initiatives and derailing novel regulatory efforts. And as subordinate officials resign, perhaps out of demoralization, they can be replaced by less-experienced personnel who are unable to provide a robust bureaucratic check on erosion. Given enough time, therefore, the conventional and statutory checks on institutional capture are likely to fail.

The US Constitution is not just silent when it comes to the intrabranch institutions of horizontal accountability. In some tension with the Madisonian account of mutually checking branches, Article II of the document has been interpreted to constrain the operation of sensible horizontal-accountability mechanisms between the elected branches. An impressive array of both liberal and conservative jurists have argued for robust presidential control over both appointments and removals of officials from the federal bureaucracy. The argument takes many forms, and ranges over diverse levers of potential mechanisms whereby elected and partisan actors could exercise control over bureaucratic ones. In the aggregate, such controls would do much to limit the autonomy of horizontal-accountability institutions. On the appointments side, a liberal coalition of justices has recently vested the president with authority to make recess appointments, even when the vacancy does not occur within a recess, and when the recess falls in the midst of a congressional session. In respect to the president's removal power, a group of conservative justices have in the last few years reinvigorated a previously repudiated reading of Article II of the Constitution pursuant to which the president must have exclusive authority to remove certain federal officials. The marginal effect on the location of political control from either of these decisions is difficult to estimate with precision. Still, they exemplify a bipartisan drift toward greater presidential control over the bureaucracy that is at odds with the functional autonomy necessary to resist democratic erosion.[87]

In addition to these doctrinal moves, an array of influential scholars on both left and right (often with prior executive branch experience in pocket) have urged the president to experiment with new instruments of political control. As a law professor, for example, now-Justice Elena Kagan wrote an influential *Harvard Law Review* article espousing greater presidential control of regulatory decisions, in part on the basis of her experience in the Clinton administration.[88] Now-federal Judge David Barron argued in the *Columbia Law Review* that presidents should have the power to waive requirements of federal law, building on experience with the No Child Left Behind law.[89] Other scholars on the left have argued for the executive power to forbear from applying the law, or have argued that historical experiences justify sweeping executive power to calibrate enforcement regimes—for instance, in the immigration context.[90] These arguments are fairly read as animated by frustration when liberal presidents find their policy agendas stymied by divided government or litigation challenges. On the right, scholars have argued on either originalist or functional grounds for sweeping executive discretion when it comes to firing officials, directing regulation, and determining policy in domains of putative presidential expertise, such as national security.[91] Their work reflects a commitment to a robust executive as socially desirable, and a concomitant downplaying of the costs of that design choice. Scholarship, of course, is not practice. But it is telling that so much bipartisan, elite opinion downplays the value of robust horizontal-accountability institutions. Implicitly, one might say, these scholars view the risk of erosion as too low to incorporate into their normative calculus. Members of a technocratic elite, legal scholars are all too eager to assign more power to their own technocratic, elite institutions.

Advocates of a forceful executive have started to respond to the novelty of the Trump administration. One of the leading functionalist exponents of executive power, Eric Posner, has argued that because populist presidents rely on their expert agencies to achieve desired policy ends, they tend to disappoint their followers and transition to more conventional styles of government that pose no risk of antidemocratic movement.[92] There are a number of reasons to question, however, Posner's optimism about the persistence of bureaucratic autonomy in the teeth of democratic erosion. First, populists in Eastern Europe and Latin America have gained and maintained power while dismantling horizontal-accountability institutions. There is no reason to think they cannot do so in the United States, especially given the weakness of the relevant legal infrastructure surveyed above. Second, as we have noted, populists do not necessarily campaign on the basis of their achievements: they campaign on the basis of emotional appeals to a sense of shared national identity and victimization. There is ample evidence that this sort of identity-based politics explains US electoral dynamics better than Posner's assumption that voters share a welfarist orientation.[93] Finally, comparative experience from Weimar to the Arab Spring suggests that elements of the state, especially the ones that specialize in coercion, are perfectly able to support a move to plenary authoritarianism and yet remain effective. Once again, there are no grounds for confidence that the American case should be any different.

In short, there is little reason to think that the Constitution will play much of a restraining role if there is an effort to politicize and centralize executive power in the United States. Rather than operating as a bulwark of democratic practice, indeed, the design of Article II and its accompanying jurisprudence are in tension with the commitments to democracy contained elsewhere in the document. As with the choice of constitutional amendment rules, there is a tension between designing a constitution with the risk of erosion in mind, and in pursuing other ends—such as policy responsiveness and flexibility.

SHRINKING THE PUBLIC SPHERE

We have emphasized that democracy requires a shared epistemic foundation. Where the state exercises either direct or indirect veto power over the voices aired in the public sphere or the factual material therein available, antidemocratic actors and coalitions face lower barriers to the consolidation of authority. Analyzing the Constitution's ability to impede the democratic deconsolidation along this margin therefore requires an inquiry into several distinct mechanisms whereby the public sphere can be corroded. Can the government use formal means, such as libel and registration laws, to punish critics? If not, are informal substitutes available? Alternatively, can the government selectively titrate information in ways that systematically undermine public understanding of the consequences of electoral choices? And where allies of the eroding regime pollute the informational marketplace with false information with the aim of discrediting political opponents, are effective responses available under existing law? Whereas the US Constitution falls short when it comes to interbranch and intrabranch accountability devices, it fares somewhat better in respect to the legal protections of the public sphere. Interpretations of the Constitution can change, but as judicial precedents go, we think that the relevant ones in this domain are deeply embedded in American law and consequently hard to detach. Where the United States does worse, however, is in respect to assuring the *quality* of material within the public sphere, whether in terms of selecting for true over fake information or resisting selective governmental disclosure.

Consider first the use of law as a means of coercing or harassing democratic opponents. There are only a few instances in the wake of the Sedition Act of the law being used as a blunt instrument against elected officials or candidates (as opposed to immigrants, trade unionists, Communists, civil rights protestors, or various other social movements).[94] Although the Supreme Court never had the opportunity to rule on the Sedition Act's validity under the Constitution, it has discussed the Act in passing as a case study in what offends the First Amendment.[95] Absent a reorientation in the allegiance of the federal judiciary, we think it is clear that any such new measure would be declared unconstitutional (although the inevitable delay of litigation might create a period in which the executive benefits from its chilling effect). Similarly, under current law, libel cannot be used as a weapon to silence political dissent in the fashion observed in other nations. Current Supreme Court doctrine provides that a public figure (a category certainly including national political leaders) cannot collect damages unless the defendant knows its statements are false, or acts in "reckless disregard" of their truth or falsity. Special rules for the appeal of libel damage awards add another layer of protection.[96] Of course, these rulings could be overturned, or exceptions might be carved in unexpected ways. But we are skeptical that this would be easy, even for a bench aligned closely with a retrogressive regime. It now seems beyond doubt that speech that "deals with matters of public concern . . . relating to any matter of political, social, or other concern to the community," including speech critical of the government, lies at the heart of the First Amendment's Speech Clause, and that the First Amendment itself is a central principle of American constitutionalism.[97] Tearing the First Amendment doctrine of libel in particular from its doctrinal moorings would require a massive and costly intellectual reorientation.

This does not mean, however, that the modern First Amendment is a panacea. The rules created by courts to enforce that constitutional provision instead leave open several of the mechanisms by which the public sphere was been eviscerated in other cases of erosion. It is far from clear, for example, that the sort of registration laws or other regulatory tools used to attack civil society in Russia and Egypt would trigger close First Amendment scrutiny. After all, the tax code already imposes a complex set of rules and requirements for not-for-profit organizations, and these could be manipulated for partisan ends. In 2013, the Internal Revenue Service revealed that it had singled out for extra scrutiny organizations that used the "Tea Party" label, along with various other political terms. The resulting administrative delays, which raised congressional ire, were but the tip of the iceberg in terms of what an agency could do. New regulations, even if they had disparate effects on certain entities, might be difficult to distinguish from existing law, and other administrative practices might largely fly below the radar.

During the civil rights era, the Court did strike down southern states' efforts to use associational regulation as a means of suppression. In those cases, however, the Court was likely all too cognizant of the pretextual nature of the asserted basis of state action, as well as of the national support for its stand against racial segregation. In contrast, in more recent cases where the federal government has regulated an association, and where the government has pointed to some sort of national security interest, the Court has allowed not just civil penalties but also criminal imprisonment on the basis of an active affiliation with a proscribed organization.[98] With careful drafting, registration and tax requirements could be utilized by a backsliding government to indirectly regulate the public sphere to great effect.

As to less formal means of shrinking the public sphere, the First Amendment maintains a dignified and unhelpful silence. Nothing in the Constitution (or, indeed, federal law) otherwise prevents high officials from launching personalized attacks on the honesty and integrity of otherwise respected news outlets as a means of prophylactically disabling sources of future discrediting information. Or consider the possibility that either a sitting regime or its allies (whether domestic or international) strategically propagate false news stories about political opponents that are effective in defaming or discrediting them. Increasingly, automated scripts can work through social media to propagate malicious or ideological distortions, whether centrally produced or more exotically sourced. More mundanely, would-be autocrats and their allies can dilute the power of information by directly casting doubt on the quality or integrity of mainstream media sources that do follow norms of epistemic competence and integrity.[99] Because the public is not well situated to evaluate compliance with those professional norms, such attacks are quite potent.

Other countries have tried, so far with mixed results, to regulate the use of false news stories to influence elections. To date, the efficacy of such intervention remains uncertain.[100] For instance, the indictments of Russian persons and organizations who violated federal campaign laws during the 2014–16 period is an important step forward, even if it is quite unlikely that any of those indicted will ever see the inside of a federal courtroom. But even if a federal or state government wanted to respond to perceived declines in the integrity and quality of news by attacking the problem of fake news, it is far from clear that the First Amendment would allow it. In 2012, the Supreme Court invalidated a conviction secured under the federal Stolen Valor Act of a defendant who had falsely claimed military honors. Although the Court was divided and hence unable to craft a majority, a plurality of the justices wrote with evident disfavor about the criminal law's use in response even to deliberate falsehood. Rather, they emphasized that "[t]he remedy for speech that is false is speech that is true," and that, as a general matter, "suppression of speech by the government can make exposure of falsity more difficult, not less so." Such arguments, we think, are too formulaic to be of much force in practice. Various forms of regulation of media environments obviously and powerfully alter the content of the public sphere. It is naive to assume, moreover, that there is a single solution (more speech) to all of democracy's epistemic pathologies, especially in an environment where public attention is scarce, the news cycle brief, and the range of potential misinformation strategies vast. The Court may be on firmer ground if it is understood as saying that judges cannot reliably distinguish between desirable and undesirable speech suppression. But, again, that claim remains untested, and is necessarily contingent on the quality of the bench itself. Nevertheless, after that 2012 decision, broad laws to regulate false speech in the election environment, where false speech will

be especially socially costly, will likely meet strong and often decisive constitutional objections in court.[101]

Erosion also can involve positive efforts by the state to control the epistemic environment by choosing what information to withhold and what to
release. In contrast to its protection of private speech, the Constitution has
relatively little to say on what information the government *must* produce about
its activities. The Constitution in Article I mandates a census, to be sure, but
leaves it to Congress to determine how it will be funded and executed. Courts
have considered challenges to the use of different sampling techniques, but
have never confronted the possibility that the census would be underfunded
or otherwise undermined for partisan ends.[102] The possibility that the census
process would be recalibrated to partisan ends, however, cannot be lightly
dismissed. In addition, the Speech and Debate Clause of Article I gives members of Congress plenary immunity to disclose fraud or abuse in legislative
debates, and has historically provided a measure of protection for controversial disclosures, such as the Pentagon Papers. Its relevance, however, is muted
by the possibility that legislators' incentives to gather information and to disclose it to the public are quite weak in the first instance.[103]

Other, newer constitutions, whose authors were more finely attuned to the
epistemic demands of liberal democracy, have done better on these matters.
Some 40% of national constitutions in force currently mandate access to government information. In other countries, moreover, courts have created a
constitutional "right to know" that provides a robust tool for policing information disclosure regimes.[104] Lest it be thought that there is something pecu-
liarly American about resistance to rights to information, it is worth pointing
out that three state constitutions—Montana's, New Hampshire's, and Florida's—already contain rights to information from the government.[105] A clever
originalist, attendant to pieces of the Constitution that do speak to disclosure—
the First Amendment, the Speech and Debate Clause, the Journal Clause of
Article I, and the duty of both ministers and presidents to make periodic
reports under Article II—could no doubt weave an argument to the effect
that the Constitution should be read the same way.

Alas, we think such a piebald argument would not fare well in practice.
Indeed, rather than installing a "right to know," the First Amendment as currently glossed fails to prevent criminal prosecution of government employees
who leak information (even if the disclosure can be justified as in the public
interest), and does not even speak clearly to the right of journalists to publish
leaked information. As a result, the Obama Administration's unprecedented
acceleration of criminal prosecutions of leakers met no constitutional resistance.[106] It is far too soon to say that national security prohibitions cannot be

used, consistent with the First Amendment, to harass and silence journalists who wish to air the government's errors and self-dealing. But there is no reason to be optimistic on this score.

One key aspect of the epistemic foundation for liberal democracy in the United States dates to 1966, and is the work of a little-known Democratic member of Congress from California, John Moss. The Freedom of Information Act (FOIA), creates a procedural structure whereby information can be requested of the government and, in some instances, disclosure ordered by a court. It is not without its successes. A 2016 study found that some 40% of news stories that provoke policy reviews started with an FOIA request. At the same time, FOIA from its birth has been condemned as a "cruel joke" and "profoundly dysfunctional" in light of its many exceptions and the lethargic pace of government responses. Some argue that by placing the burden on individuals to seek disclosure, rather than on the government to make disclosures proactively, the act saps regulatory capacity, engenders an unhealthy adversarial culture over information, and results in regressive distributions of knowledge goods. In practice, FOIA is dominated by corporate entities seeking information for commercial use, including some entities that operate simply by obtaining information and selling it. The volume of these commercial requests crowds out FOIA's usages by journalists and not-for-profits.[107]

FOIA also does not preclude government from partial, misleading disclosures and leaks. Nor does it impede the manipulation of government secrecy classifications; erosions in the perceived or actual quality of government data; and outright manipulation. There has been a secular increase in classification in recent years and a growing consensus that rampant overclassification and pseudo-classification exist. Because classification schemes for government secrets are created by executive orders, rather than by legislation that is subject to open debate and deliberation, there is ample room for government manipulation of the information environment. The president, at the extreme, could simply deem by fiat much of the information produced by government to be classified. Nothing in current law or the Constitution prevents this from being done. If received by a compliant Congress, such a scheme could suddenly and dramatically reduce the availability of even routine government data. And there would be no legal recourse. Judges have proved themselves to be fairly docile in the face of invocations of the national security exemption to FOIA, and so will not provide much protection in the face of an executive seeking to erode democracy.[108]

For a polity committed to democracy, the United States thus has an awfully impoverished sense of what is necessary as a constitutional matter to sustain the meaningful debate that underpins robust electoral accountability.

The lonely First Amendment right to speak and criticize is not unimportant, but in other ways the legal landscape is barren. There remain plenty of ways in which democratic erosion could be advanced by the incremental evisceration of the public sphere.

THE ELIMINATION OF POLITICAL COMPETITION

There is little doubt that the United States remains a competitive democracy at the national level, even if some districts and states have become less competitive as a result of geographic sorting, partisan gerrymandering, and media segmentation. Nor is there any doubt that US politics, even if no longer characterized by the gross forms of exclusion and partisan lock-up seen in the Jim Crow south, is riddled with antidemocratic measures ranging from voter identification rules to proof-of-citizenship requirements and unjustified constraints on absentee and early voting. Many of these measures reflect a targeted strategy to demobilize minority voters—in particular, African-Americans—and reflect the important continuities within contemporary law with earlier eras of American voter suppression. While deeply dismaying, such practices are perhaps not especially surprising in a democracy where transient elected coalitions will inevitably be tempted to entrench themselves.[109] Certainly, they should not surprise when encountered in the United States, given the country's enduring history of racial subordination through formal and informal political exclusion. When it comes to democracy, Faulkner's dictum about the undying past has considerable force.[110]

While acknowledging the persistence of such sordid practices, it is still possible to ask whether a systematic effort to stifle political competition so as to enable democratic erosion would prevail. Paralleling our analysis of legal protections for the public sphere, we reach a mixed judgment here. Whereas American law responds effectively to overt and brute forms of suppression, more subtle manipulations are likely to go unchecked. On the one hand, the prospect of official proscriptions of either political parties or individual candidates of the kind observed in Russia and Turkey seems outlandish in the American context. Still, even here it is best not to be too optimistic. It is easy to forget that left-wing parties have been subject to registration, censure, and repression, particularly in the early twentieth-century, in ways that likely permanently skewed the American political spectrum.[111] If the overt exclusion of political parties and candidates seems implausible today, this may well be more an artifact of the success of historical suppression and the availability of softer, less crude tools of partisan lock-up than a tribute to our robust constitutional protection of political association.

As we have explained, judicial review of even garden-variety vote suppression is uneven, suggesting that constitutional rights, at least as presently interpreted, are not reliable safeguards of the democratic franchise. Federal courts occasionally balk at especially egregious forms of self-dealing through election law, especially when tainted by racial entanglements. But all too often, they blink when confronted with anticompetitive, incumbency-enhancing effects.[112] Indeed, the anticompetitive dimension of election arrangements has been embraced on occasion as a positive good. In 1997, for example, the Court endorsed the concentration of political authority in the two dominant political parties by permitting state electoral regulations expressly aimed at ousting third parties and third-party candidates from effective participation in balloting or electioneering in the public eye. This essentially allows a two-party political cartel to construct the rules of the electoral game. At other times, however, the Court has railed at the incumbency-protecting effect of election laws. So it is difficult to predict how regulations that deliberately undermined partisan competition would be taken.[113]

Moreover, the US Constitution lacks mention of an independent election agency at the national level. In contrast, the 1950 Indian Constitution creates an Electoral Commission of India tasked with "superintendence, direction, and control" of elections. The 1996 South Africa Constitution charges its Election Commission with the obligation of maintaining "free and fair" elections. And the 2010 Kenyan Constitution, drafted in the wake of sharp disputes over the partisan capture of election regulation, sets forth a detailed set of particularized rules and regulations.[114] In contrast, the Federal Election Commission in the United States was deliberately created in 1975 by Congress as a bipartisan, six-person commission that predictably deadlocks over many issues. Its formal powers were largely eviscerated on technical grounds by the Supreme Court in the *Buckley v. Valeo* case. The lion's share of election regulation, in any event, falls to the states, which have highly variable-caliber systems of election administration. There, the absence of any consistent standard of professionalism among election administrators makes the maintenance of the rule of law in respect to their functioning challenging.[115]

Even when a party loses elections, it can still undermine its opponents in the weeks-long window the Constitution and American law can allow between a poll and a turnover in power. Consider two examples. First, in late 2016, the North Carolina legislature sought to redefine the powers of the governorship after Democrat Roy Cooper won the election in a close vote. The bill as first proposed would have removed the governor's powers to appoint trustees of the state university, eliminated 80% of the governor's staff, and required cabinet appointments to be approved by the state Senate. It would also have revamped election administration and required that the supervisory body be evenly divided between Republicans and Democrats—but with Republicans holding the chair in even years, when all state-wide elections are held. The measure, however, was temporarily put on hold by a North Carolina state court in February 2018, and its injunction was largely upheld on appeal on state constitutional law grounds.[116] Like the Chavista response to an opposition win in Caracas municipal elections, the immediate legislative response to Cooper's win reflects an effort to retroactively redefine the rules of the democratic game to entrench one party in power. And there is no doctrine in American constitutional law that proscribes it.

Second, a political leader intent on derailing an election might instead seek to deploy the prosecutorial might of the US government to taint or despoil another candidate's reputation. US attorneys formally serve "at the pleasure" of the president, and a historically strong, informal convention precludes dismissal for reasons other than misconduct. In December 2006, however, seven US attorneys were dismissed without obvious good cause. Subsequent inquiries strongly suggested (without ever confirming) that the group had been picked out by the White House for declining to pursue partisan agendas in their choice of indictments. In May 2017, President Trump fired the director of the Federal Bureau of Investigation. Unlike the 2006 firings, the president this time pointed to an ongoing investigation related to his campaign as a reason for the firing, brushing aside reasons supplied by his own staff and the Justice Department. Government lawyers pointed to previous internal legal opinions asserting broad presidential authority to fire subordinates under Article II of the Constitution as a legal basis for his action, notwithstanding the sharp conflict of interest at stake.[117] The net effect of these precedents is to cement political control over prosecutorial decisions, even when partisan considerations are more than likely at work.

Their effect, moreover, cannot be gauged without accounting for other legal doctrines that dramatically constrict the ability of criminal defendants to obtain discovery of a prosecutor's motives.[118] These rules mean that even if a partisan influence upon a prosecution was legally problematic, there would typically be no way to prove it. One cannot demand or subpoena a prosecutor's documents even if one strongly believes that she acts on the basis of an improper partisan motive. If the prosecutorial appointment process becomes corrupted, the good faith that is assumed to protect against abusive use of the criminal law cannot be assured. In sum, there is little beyond the thin tissue of political convention, occasionally embodied in internal rules and regulations, to prevent the tremendous powers of the federal prosecutorial apparatus from being swung against selected political contestants on partisan grounds.

Democratic Regression: American Style

American constitutional law is exceptional in many ways. The United States has an exceedingly old and very brief Constitution. Our treatment of emergency powers, free speech, election administration, the right to know, and many other issues are out of step with recent practice. At the same time, in terms of the risk to democratic stability, the United States seems to be marching closely in step with other elective polities around the world. Not only has the United States been swayed by the same charismatic populist dynamic that can be observed unfolding in many other nations, but the risks that partisan degradation poses to its constitutional democracy look awfully similar to the risks manifested elsewhere.

Autocratic collapse by coup or mismanaged emergency power, we think, is not likely in the American future. Unlike Thailand, the United States lacks a tradition of coups; neither the military itself nor domestic interest groups are inclined toward such usurpations of democracy as a result. In contrast, we have mapped out a range of ways in which the US constitutional system's eighteenth-century design leaves it vulnerable to the twenty-first-century threat of erosion. There are elements of the Constitution—in particular Article V and the First Amendment as applied to libel and some political speech—that would provide a measure of resistance to competitive authoritarianism or its variants. But many other elements of the Constitution—Article II's account of presidential power, the separation of powers generally, the form of Article III judicial independence, and certain First Amendment doctrines—that make it quite vulnerable to antidemocratic action.

All this is not to say that the US Constitution's design is unwise, or that erosion is inevitable. Rather, constitutional design reflects a series of trade-offs, pursuing some values and responding to some risks at the cost of leaving other potential gains on the table. The elements of the constitutional design that we have criticized as courting democratic erosion were crafted with other concerns and other preoccupations in mind. But just because a constitutional provision is justified in terms of the goals of its drafters in 1787 hardly means it is likely to provide an effective response to a new kind of systemic risk that has emerged only two centuries later. Only a heedless and blinkered nostalgia would hold as much. Moreover, our analysis does not necessarily mean that erosion is likely: instead, our claim is simply that Americans would be deeply unwise to rely on the constitutional and legal infrastructure already in place to defend our democracy. In the face of a real threat of erosion through either charismatic populism or partisan degradation of the kind we postulated at this chapter's opening, more is needed.

6

Making Democratic Constitutions that Endure

> I cannot help fearing that men may reach a point where they look on every new theory
> as a danger, every innovation as a toilsome trouble, every social advance as a first step
> toward revolution, and that they may absolutely refuse to move at all.
>
> ALEXIS DE TOCQUEVILLE

In retrospect, the portents of democracy's impending collapse had been there from the day he came to power in 2005. A member of an important family of politicians from Sri Lanka's achingly beautiful south, Mahindra Rajapaksa became prime minister off the back of a populist campaign appealing to the country's Sinhala Buddhist majority. He railed against the nation's Tamil and Muslim minorities. He promised a hard line against the Tamil Tigers movement, which had run an exceptionally brutal, two-decade insurgency in the north of the country. Once ensconced in office, Rajapaksa appointed family members to key positions and invoked the same populist playbook that we have seen passed from Venezuela to Poland, to Turkey, and on to India and Israel—heaping scorn on political opponents and cultivating an ugly hatred of minorities. Opening a cancer hospital in the seaside town of Galle in 2007, for example, he memorably warned that a "virus has entered the body politic today . . . to invite foreign powers for the greed of power." Two years later, he promised that Sri Lanka would have "no more minorities."[1]

In due course, the "virus" was addressed with the full treatment familiar from other cases of democratic erosion. Rajapaksa rescinded the cease fire with the Tigers that had been in effect when he came to office and instead launched a savage war to retake the north of the island. Press censorship was justified as necessary during wartime. Beyond legal forms of censorship, journalists grappled with harassment or worse. In January 2009, a prominent local editor and Rajapaksa critic, Lasantha Wickrematunge, was shot dead as he left his home for work. Another editor, J. S. Tissainayagam, was arrested and sentenced to twenty years for his critical war coverage. Civil society more generally was not spared. In 2014, as the culmination of a long campaign against human-rights organizations in particular, the Rajapaksa administration announced that nongovernmental organizations would have to register with a new military-affiliated administrator, desist from press conferences or public statements, and refrain from training journalists.[2]

Rajapaksa leveraged his decisive 2009 military victory over the Tigers politically by undermining interbranch checks, especially from the courts. Under the Seventeenth Amendment to Sri Lanka's constitution, which had been enacted in October 2001, a depoliticized "constitutional council" was tasked with selecting judges and authorizing their elevation onto higher courts. With the support of a friendly chief justice, however, Rajapaksa refused to convene this council. Instead, he selected allies as judges, while deploying the administrative powers of the chief justice's position to punish judges who strayed from the government's agenda. On the ground, legal remedies were scarce for those detained, particularly for those of Tamil extraction. By and large, the violent behavior of both police and the military went unchecked. As internal checks on his power fell away, Rajapaksa successfully pushed for the adoption of a suite of constitutional amendments with the support of a two-thirds parliamentary supermajority. The ensuing Eighteenth Amendment abolished the constitutional council, replacing it with a mechanism that allowed direct political control over judicial staffing. It also eliminated a two-term limit on the presidency, opening the door for Rajapaksa to stay in office until his son was well positioned to take over. Finally, the Amendment defanged other institutions of horizontal accountability created by earlier constitutional amendments, including independent commissions to oversee the judiciary, the police, the public service, the electoral administration, and bribery and corruption.[3] Using these new powers, Rajapaksa jailed former allies, notably General Sarath Fonseka, who had led the military campaign against the Tamil Tigers.

The drama of democratic erosion that we have seen playing out in earlier chapters seemed to be moving into the final act, but in January 2015, the story went off script. Seeking the third term allowed by the amended constitution, Rajapaksa lost an election. The defeat was a close one—his former ally Maithripala Sirisena obtained 51.3% of the vote—but decisive, with turnout high. Sirisena had crucially won over a large share of Sinhala Buddhists as well as Tamil and Muslim votes. This was in spite of, not because of, the conditions in which the poll took place. During the election, Rajapaksa's image was "ubiquitous" on billboards around the country, and his campaign rallies filled stadiums, while Sirisena's barely filled parking lots. A few months later, when Rajapaksa attempted a comeback in parliamentary elections, Sirisena informed him in no uncertain terms that he would never be made prime minister given his "blatant racism" against Tamils and Muslims.[4]

In many ways, Sri Lanka is a quite unpromising showcase to identify the tools for undoing a slide away from democratic practice. It was led by a charismatic populist who encouraged partisan degradation by stoking ethnic tensions. The country had just endured a long and violent civil war that left its institutions fragile and its social fabric frayed. In the run-up to the 2015 election, most state institutions remained captured, and the electoral playing field was far from level. And yet, in a remarkable moment, it was not "the People"—that mythic, abstract, entity—but a more motley set of *people* who spoke up on behalf of the messy, fractured, inconclusive, and necessarily imperfect processes of democracy. An intraparty split, not a sustained opposition movement, led to Rajapaksa's fall.

Sri Lanka is not alone in staving off a slide from democracy. During the interwar collapse of European democracies, not all efforts at imposing fascist rule prevailed. The Popular Front coalition in France, which came to power in 1936, banned the sort of paramilitary groups that had aided the Nazi rise to power in Germany. French conservatives declined to ally with fascist groups such as the Croix de Feu. "The importance of the republican tradition" to the French people's sense of themselves did important work. In Denmark, the four mainstream political parties kept populist radicalization at bay by working together to mitigate the effects of the Great Depression and to deny any effective political opening for radical parties on either the left or the right. In Finland, an extreme right movement called Lapua emerged in 1929 on the heels of the Great Depression, sweeping the country and initially eliciting concessions from established politicians. But the Finnish courts imposed punishment for acts of political violence, and, as in Sri Lanka decades later, a crucial faction on the right turned against Lapua to form a "Lawfulness Front" with Social Democrats, National Progressives, and other parties.[5] The interwar period is not exceptional in the fact that it contains close cases. In the Third Wave of democracy, military regimes in Latin America and Southern Europe faded away, and thereafter a number of countries, ranging from Colombia to the Philippines and Zambia, have stepped back from the brink of democratic failure.[6]

These "close calls" differ in important ways. Some are near scrapes with authoritarianism (or short dalliances with competitive authoritarianism). Others are examples of the effective use of safeguards against erosion; and still others are characterized by proper transitions from extended periods of authoritarian rule to democracy. A theme that emerges is the importance of political support for democracy as a going concern, and the importance of political choices by potential allies of a movement or leader hostile to democracy—and this is a theme to which we return in our conclusion. Here, though, we want to stress a different point: The fact that democracies can experience close calls points toward the need to consider how legal and institutional design might better equip political actors committed to democracy to navigate systemic risks and stave off democratic failures. More specifically, since the threat to democratic quality today entails the degradation of both already established and new democracies, which are both distinct from full-on collapse into dictatorships, it seems useful to consider two closely related but distinct questions. First, how should the designer of a new constitution think about institutional design choices, given the newly crystallized threat of democratic erosion? Second, what can a country like the United States, which is constitutionally vulnerable to erosion and may be experiencing symptoms of charismatic populism or partisan degradation, do about it? That is, what can be done at the moment of constitutional design, and, separately, what can be done in the midst of a democratic decline?

Taking these two vantage points presses us toward two distinct kinds of prescriptions. One, which we take up in this chapter, is a set of steps that would be taken as a matter of optimal constitutional design for liberal, democratic polities to insulate themselves against democratic erosion. The other addresses the question of whether existing weaknesses in a constitutional system can be cured. In the US context, the currently enactable range of legal and constitutional responses to the risk of erosion is relatively small, if only because we think it is unlikely that the current Supreme Court and the current Congress, given their institutional and ideological makeups, would support significant institutional overhauls. We therefore loosen the constraints on our analysis, and ask in the next chapter not only what kinds of change are feasible now in light of actual American politics and institutions, but also what might be desirable constitutional reforms to consider once the window of institutional reform has opened a crack more. Just as in Sri Lanka, Finland, and France, remedial institutional reform requires political breathing room that only successful democratic mobilization can create.

Challenging the wisdom of the US Constitution is something of a heretical matter in the United States, but both exercises that we undertake are consistent with some of our traditions. The framers—a quasi-religious term that itself is telling—are revered on both left and right. Their canonization is something both Lin-Manuel Miranda and Bill O'Reilly can agree upon.[7] This unblinking reverence to their specific decisions is a bit paradoxical. The framers themselves had a deep empirical bent. Their constitutional design reflected not only the lessons from past constitutional experiences—James Madison famously asked Jefferson for books on the subject when the latter was in Europe—but a willingness to challenge received wisdom. Indeed, the

Constitution represented a defiant rejection of the conventional wisdom that democracy was possible only in small republics and could not survive in an expansive American empire. It was, as Alexander Hamilton said at the beginning of the first Federalist, an experiment to determine "whether societies of men [sic] are really capable or not of establishing good government from reflection and choice."[8] So we are skeptical that they would have endorsed the tendency among future generations toward a blind and unquestioning retention of old institutions without verification of their fit for current conditions. Instead, Jefferson's famous words about constitutional change better capture the progressive and empirical spirit of the founding era:

> Some men look at constitutions with sanctimonious reverence, and deem them like the ark of the covenant, too sacred to be touched. They ascribe to the men of the preceding age a wisdom more than human, and suppose what they did to be beyond amendment. . . . But I know also, that laws and institutions must go hand in hand with the progress of the human mind. As that becomes more developed, more enlightened, as new discoveries are made, new truths disclosed, and manners and opinions change with the change of circumstances, institutions must advance also, and keep pace with the times.[9]

In this sort of Jeffersonian spirit, some recent scholars and constitutional experts have challenged the continued relevance of the framers' design. Constitutional law professor Sandy Levinson calls for rewriting "Our Undemocratic Constitution." Political scientist Larry Sabato has proposed twenty-three amendments for "A More Perfect Constitution." And retired Justice John Paul Stevens has proposed six amendments to restore American democracy.[10] This spate of elite criticism suggests that the founders' imperfections are more than a theoretical possibility, and that there is some public space for considering reforms—and considering whether there are better starting points for constitutional stories in the first instance.

These questions are worth asking again now because of the new risks we have charted, and because of the new stock of knowledge available for answering them. One of the clear themes of recent scholarship on comparative constitutional design is that the choice set of institutions on offer has evolved since 1789. Early constitutions borrowed heavily from the American model, but subsequent constitutions, even within a particular country, have tended to drift away from it, as innovations are incorporated into subsequently adopted texts. The two panels of figure 6.1 provide some sense of this phenomenon. The dots show how constitutions adopted over time look in terms of their formal similarity to the US Constitution, using a metric developed by the Comparative Constitutions Project. Figure 6.1a demonstrates that countries

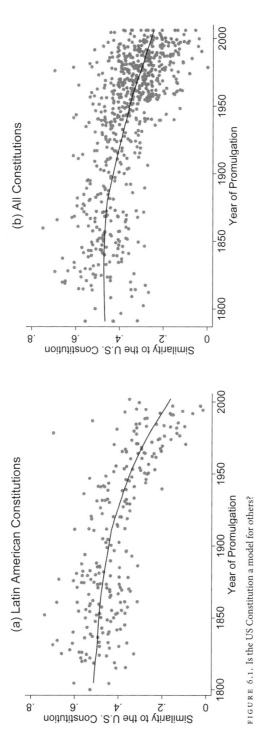

(a) Latin American Constitutions

(b) All Constitutions

FIGURE 6.1. Is the US Constitution a model for others?

Source: Tom Ginsburg, Zachary Elkins, and James Melton, "Comments on Law and Versteeg's 'The Declining Influence of the United States Constitution,'" *New York University Law Review* 87 (2012): 2088.

in Latin America, a region with a set of old nation-states and thus a rich constitutional history, have moved away from the American model over time. Figure 6.1b indicates the same for the broader set of all countries. In each case, the US model seems to have declining power. New countries are making new choices and not simply following old patterns.

Constitutional designers around the world, then, have heeded Jefferson's advice that the design of "laws and institutions must go hand in hand with the progress of the human mind. . . . We might as well require a man to wear still the coat which fitted him when a boy as civilized society to remain ever under the regimen of their barbarous ancestors."[11] Consistent with this Founding Era wisdom, our aim is to show first what a brand new nation might do if it was just emerging today and was concerned to minimize the risk of democratic erosion. In the next chapter, we ask specifically about less radical changes that the United States today might adopt to reduce the risk.

Oddly, however, the question of how constitutional design might generate a measure of insulation against democratic erosion has not been investigated deeply before. Perhaps because of the post–Cold War confidence in the inevitability of democracy's global spread, few constitutional scholars have devoted much time to thinking about how to harden new or established democracies against erosion. Tellingly, one must go back to the interwar period to find the closest precursor to the inquiry pursued in this chapter. The German political scientist Karl Loewenstein fled Germany in December 1933, and penned a pair of important articles on "militant democracy" in the *American Political Science Review*. Loewenstein pointed to the emotional and non-intellectual appeal of fascism to argue that democracies have to take repressive measures—including party bans, restrictions on free assembly and free speech, prohibitions on public office, and even citizenship-stripping— in order to safeguard democracy against its internal enemies. It was an idea with a remarkable afterlife. The German Constitutional Court drew on Loewenstein's principle of militant democracy to ban the quasi-Nazi Socialist Reich Party in 1952 and the German Communist Party in 1956. At least twenty-one other democracies have experimented with various forms of party bans, with a range of results.[12] Restrictions on hate speech of various forms are much broader and are found in many democracies today as a result of Loewenstein's influence and other factors.

Loewenstein was correct, we think, to worry about the capacity of democracies to protect themselves from the corrosive effects of internal antidemocratic forces. But, for a number of reasons, we think that his militant democracy framework, which focuses on the legal restriction of democracy's internal enemies, is inadequate and even dangerous in practice. It is inadequate, in the first instance, because it does not speak to the situation in Poland or Turkey, which are already slipping into competitive authoritarianism and have lost the opportunity to install needful frictions. Nor does it have much to say to polities such as the United States, where a charismatic populist is in charge at this writing, or perhaps even Israel and Japan, where potentially hegemonic party coalitions are parlaying electoral gains into institutional reforms to consolidate power. Even in its core applications, moreover, we think that Loewenstein's advice is too dependent on the model of the Nazi ascent to power to capture the range of ways in which more mainstream parties today turn to erosion as a means of remaining in power. The range of design decisions that can mitigate the risk of erosion is wider than Loewenstein's concept of militant democracy—or so we hope to show.

Worse, we think militant democracy is a very risky strategy for the associational rights that are at democracy's core. In Europe today, associational bans, bars on public office, and a range of other forms of coercion are used in putative defense of democracy against minorities, especially Muslims—even though Loewenstein's justifications are not present in respect to the targeted groups. In this fashion, the repression he licensed in the name of democracy has slipped its moorings in the defense of democracy. Contrary to much hyperventilating commentary, European Muslims are members of a numerical minority who have no chance at seizing political power to overturn democracy, and who will not be demographically significant in the near future. Rather than standing at the precipice of political hegemony, Muslims in Europe face considerable discrimination in job markets and social interactions, as well as an ample share of hateful treatment in public. Under European human rights law, the choice to wear Muslim garb justifies exclusion from certain public and private workplaces, even though the choice to display Christian symbols in the classroom is tolerated. Antiterrorism measures, in particular France's extensive use of emergency powers after a series of attacks in Paris, have led to the closure or close surveillance of many mosques and Islamic associations.[13]

The use of militant democracy's methods against a discrete minority that presents no plausible political risk but is already subject to high levels of social and economic discrimination showcases the danger of Loewenstein's concept: It is amenable to use against not only those who present an actual threat, but also those who are perceived as alien and therefore unworthy of inclusion in the body politic. Paradoxically, the use of militant democratic methods in Europe feeds the narrative of charismatic populists, who paint the continent as under siege, and who use migration and security issues as wedge issues to attack existing political elites.[14] In this way, the tools of militant democracy can stoke the very fires they were designed to extinguish.

Hate speech bans are another tool of militant democracy that are sometimes applied in erratic and unpredictable ways. A speaker at an academic
conference in Austria, for example, was fined for saying that the Prophet
Mohammed had a "thing for little girls."[15] A Catholic bishop in Belgium, in
contrast, was unsuccessfully sued for repeating church teaching on homosexuality in a magazine interview.[16] And the singer Bob Dylan has been charged
in France with inciting hate, for an interview in which he vaguely compared
Serb attitudes toward Croats with Jewish attitudes toward Nazis.[17] Such high-
profile cases matter because they calibrate widely shared beliefs about the
scope of permissible speech. Moreover, even if not leading to convictions,
criminal prosecutions can have a chilling effect. At the same time, however,
policing hate speech has not prevented far-right parties, some with racist
leaders, from mobilizing and winning significant public support in many European countries by deploying more subtly evocative invitations to prejudice,
and by exploiting specific policy flashpoints such as terrorist attacks and the
migration crisis. It seems implausible to think that rules against hate speech,
whatever their justifications on other grounds, can be warranted on the basis
that they effectively protect democratic norms.[18]

But if militant democracy cannot hedge against the risk of erosion, what
can do so? Are some constitutional designs more susceptible to the risk of
backsliding than others? In pursuing these questions in this chapter, and in
drilling down on the US situation in the following chapter, we need to underscore two caveats. First, we must emphasize that institutional design is always
a task of optimizing across various risks. By identifying institutions that can
slow down democratic erosion, we are privileging that risk over others, such
as gridlock, unresponsiveness, and the adoption of substantively bad policies.
Complicating matters further, these various risks are not unrelated to each
other or to the risk of erosion, in that they might in the mid-term undermine
the legitimacy of the democratic system as a whole. Here, for the sake of analytic clarity, we narrowly focus on the possibility of erosion at the hands of a
charismatic populist or a dominant political party as the immediate targets of
analysis, even as we recognize that those forces do not emerge from nowhere
and cannot be opposed without catalyzing other constitutional risks.

Second, to reiterate a point we have already hinted at, the example of Sri
Lanka with which we opened this chapter provides clues that formal institutional design will not be sufficient on its own. The success or failure of a
democratic enterprise ultimately depends on the extent to which people—
including those within the ruling alliance—are willing to reject the allure of
charismatic populism or partisan degradation through political action in the
public sphere. This is, as we shall explore in the conclusion, a matter of po-

litical strategy and sometimes of the contingent preferences of those who are in a special position to stop erosion. In this regard, we diverge most sharply from Loewenstein's account of militant democracy: We think that constitutional design and political strategy are necessary, but we do not think they are ever sufficient. Democracy demands from its participants a certain political morality. In the absence of that political morality, nothing in the toolkit of constitutional designers will save constitutional democracy. Design, in short, can go only so far without decency.

Constitutional Amendment Rules

Constitutional change is necessary for constitutional survival. No polity subsists outside geopolitical, economic, social, and technological change. And no polity can survive unless it responds to such pressures. As a result, rules to facilitate change to the text of a constitution are a core element of national constitutions. Amendments can keep a constitutional system up to date with changing times, in addition to allowing for the correction of unintended errors in the original design. From this Jeffersonian point of view, amendments ought to be relatively easy to adopt. Indeed, one of us has argued elsewhere that, from the point of view of facilitating constitutional endurance, most constitutions are too difficult to change.[19]

At the same time, an amendment rule that allows for too much change too quickly can threaten the very purpose of constitutions. These are meant to entrench certain elements of the constitutional design beyond purely self-interested manipulation by the transient government of the day. Many of the cases of democratic erosion that we have discussed, including those of Poland, Hungary, and Sri Lanka, have used constitutional amendments to help entrench a particular party or leader in power and to foreclose the possibility of democratic rotation. They have ended term limits, packed the courts, and changed the electoral system through constitutional amendment. Often these entrenchment strategies have been justified by an appeal to the people's will, a rhetorical trope that resonates with the choice of constitutional amendment as a pathway of legal change. Accounting for this history might suggest that the best strategy for a constitutional designer concerned about erosion would be to have a relatively rigid amendment rule. But this might be too quick a lesson to draw. For a constitution that it is *too* rigid invites its own replacement because it cannot cope with exogenous shocks. By producing deadlock, excessive rigidity might invite the very tragedy it seeks to forestall. A successful amendment rule, therefore, must navigate a trade-off between two kinds of erosion-related risks generated by both rigidity and flexibility.

One solution to this puzzle, offered by advocates of militant democracy, is to identify certain provisions in the constitution that are immune from change. The Indonesian Constitution, for example, states that the unitary status of the state is unamendable.[20] The German Constitution, employing a similar strategy to different ends, protects the federal character of the constitutional order with its so-called "eternity clause," which insulates the "basic principles" contained in the first twenty articles.[21] Indeed, some two-thirds of the constitutions now in force contain some such entrenching clause. Like the Indonesian and German examples, such clauses often reflect the risks that animated constitutional creation in the first instance. But even if the text of a constitution does not entrench selectively in this fashion, courts can step in to gloss the document in similar terms. Indeed, a judicially created doctrine of unconstitutional constitutional amendments has emerged in countries such as India to provide a functional equivalent to the German and Indonesian eternity clauses.[22]

While superficially attractive, this variable entrenchment strategy provides no fail-safe against erosion. Because these doctrines are not self-enforcing, much of the work in guarding against "unconstitutional" constitutional amendments must be done by the courts, whether the document is embedded in text or precedent. To be sure, judges in a remarkably wide range of contexts, including both weak and strong democracies, have stepped up to block majorities from enacting rules that violate core principles of the constitutional order. But judges provide no fail-safe. The central role played by the courts can perversely raise the stakes in political battles over who controls the courts. This is not a contest that advocates of democracy can or should be confident of winning. While, in the first instance, judges can be insulated from immediate political interference, constitutional provisions on judicial appointments, removal, and salaries are rarely immunized from constitutional amendment. Hence, it is typically fairly easy for a would-be autocrat to first gain control of the judicial apparatus before turning to amending other features of the constitution. As we have seen, this is the strategy that has been deployed in Poland by the PiS, and it has echoes in Sri Lanka, Hungary, and Venezuela (among other contexts).

But varying the level of entrenchment is only one option, and not necessarily the best option, for designing an amendment rule to hedge the risk of democratic erosion.[23] Other possibilities involve the use of higher vote thresholds, an increase in the number of discrete steps involved in the amendment process, or the addition of a larger number of institutional actors to approve an amendment. An especially promising institutional design option, used in some Scandinavian countries, is to extend the amendment process across time. Here's how it works: A legislative majority proposes an amendment, which then must be reconsidered after a new election. Then, a new majority (or two-thirds supermajority in the case of Finland) must pass the same amendment again. This may be followed by a referendum (for example in Denmark). In short, passing a constitutional amendment requires not just a designated majority, but the ability to sustain that majority over time through an intervening election, which presumably changes the composition of the relevant legislative bodies and allows the public an indirect say on the amendment. This increases the number of opportunities for a clarifying moment of democratic recommitment of the sort observed in Sri Lanka with Maithripala Sirisena's election.

This sort of multiple-stage design seems to us well-suited for preventing erosion through constitutional amendment. To begin with, it reduces the risk of a Hungary-type erosion, in which a single election with an anomalous outcome leads to the near-complete capture of political power by one party. Even if such an election occurs, a multiple-stage amendment process will require voters to have another say before the constitution can be transformed in partisan ways. Yet the Scandinavian approach also need not lead toward over-entrenchment, because the thresholds for passage are relatively low. Amendments in Scandinavia tend to be fairly technical, but on occasion they can be substantial and generate significant public debate. The big point is that monumental political changes should be subject to sustained consideration by the polity. In that vein, imagine what might have happened in 2016 if the Brexit process had been understood to require two referenda separated by six months, or at the beginning and at the end of any preliminary negotiations with the European Union. The effect of such sequential polls on the information about Brexit available to voters, and of the sustained exposure of the voting public to false narratives about the potential economic and migration-related consequences are hard to estimate—but impossible not to speculate about.

Yet another constitutional design choice that may help immunize against erosion is to involve multiple institutions with distinct constituencies. In many countries, constitutional amendments are scrutinized by courts for constitutionality *before* promulgation for consistency with basic constitutional commitments. This might serve to prevent, for example, a constitutional amendment firing all opposition judges, or otherwise undermining judicial independence. Similarly, in many countries a figurehead president or monarch has the last word on constitutional change. This step might also work to slow down backsliding, but hinges on the existence of a range of preferences across different institutions. Where a single party or movement captures, licitly or otherwise, all the bodies involved, it will make no difference.

The Choice between Parliamentary and Semi-Presidential
Forms of Government

We turn next to the possibility of designing government to reduce the risk of erosion. We consider first the decision—long a topic of contention among constitutional scholars—about how to structure executive-legislative relations. We then turn to the design of courts. If we wanted to choose a constitution solely to minimize the risk of backsliding, is there a particular system we should prefer? While there may be no version of liberal democratic constitutional design that is completely immune from backsliding risk, there are nevertheless meaningful differences among alternative variants that might affect their vulnerability. Moreover, there are ways in which the American constitutional design can be tweaked to lower the risk of erosion.

In early 2017, many analysts feared a wave of charismatic populist candidates would sweep West European elections, setting them up to undermine liberal democratic institutions in the same way that Polish and Hungarian populists have done. The Netherlands and France, it was feared, would follow Britain's Brexit vote and the United States' presidential election and veer to the populist right. From one point of view, these fears proved justified. Geert Wilders in the Netherlands did increase his seat share in parliamentary elections. Indeed, he obtained the second largest share of seats.[24] Marine Le Pen in France found her way to the run-off in the presidential election, albeit against a virtual unknown, Emmanuel Macron, running at the head of a completely new and untested party.[25] Yet neither Wilders nor Le Pen "won" in the sense of taking control of government, or even coming close to that goal. In contrast, the far-right populist candidate in the presidential election of 2016, Norbert Hofer, lost by a meager 30,863 votes, and secured a re-run of the election after improprieties were discovered; Hofer then lost a rerun decisively. In legislative elections the following year, however, the Austrian People's Party won 63 of 182 seats, giving the populist right a chance to head the government.[26] Given how close these countries came to seeing political power captured by openly antiliberal populists, it seems worth asking whether the design of their electoral systems either increased or decreased their vulnerability. Do the alternative constitutional designs of these political systems— parliamentarism in the case of the Netherlands, semi-presidentialism in the case of France—deserve any credit or blame for limiting the success of populist, "antisystem" candidates?

The range of choices for how to organize government has changed over time. When the American Founders drafted the Constitution, they invented a novel way of selecting a singular head of state with some measure of formal legal authority, a figure they labeled the president. In Europe, by contrast, kings or queens selected through hereditary means continued to head the state until well into the nineteenth and early twentieth centuries. As a result, early European constitutions devoted a fair amount of attention to the technicalities of monarchic succession. Few, of course, had anything to say about popular selection. Once the position of head of state was to be selected rather than inherited, constitutional designers had to figure out how to pick the person. The US Founders' solution was the Electoral College, which employs a complex system to intermediate between popular preferences and the choice of chief executive. This is frequently decried as undemocratic. Indeed, the Electoral College has on five occasions led to the election of a president lacking a majority of the popular vote. And as demographic disparities between small and large states increase over time, moreover, there is every reason to think that the Electoral College will, with increasing frequency, produce winning candidates who lack majority support across the country as a whole.[27]

In contrast, the United Kingdom had evolved a parliamentary system over several centuries of gradual negotiation between elite nobles and merchants with the king. Similar legislative bodies, such as France's Assemblée Nationale and the Cortes of León and Castile, emerged as forums for negotiation between monarchs and various tiers of society, only to evolve in more or less dramatic ways over time. In the nineteenth century, across Europe, politicians and parties that reflected the rising social pressure for more popular, less exclusive forms of government won election to parliaments. From that institutional berth, they battled monarchies over state power and access to fiscal resources. Eventually, in every European country, monarchical control over legislative bodies withered. When monarchs yielded through negotiation, as in Britain, they survived as neutered constitutional monarchs that exercise only a ceremonial role. In such cases, effective executive power often shifted to a prime minister directly accountable to the parliament, often through a vote-of-no-confidence mechanism. The centrality of parliament leads to the label *parliamentary* for such systems.[28] Lest one think that the parliamentary model fits only small polities, it is also used for a continent-sized federalism in Australia, which modeled many other aspects of its Constitution on that of the United States and consciously rejected the separation-of-powers model.[29]

Where monarchs resisted the advance of parliaments, as in France, in contrast, they were deposed with violence and eventually replaced with a republican mode of government. This led to the need for a formal head of state—that is, a president. In some countries, this led to another alternative constitutional design known as semi-presidentialism. This was first developed in Weimar Germany and then stabilized in Fifth Republic France.[30] In semi-presidential

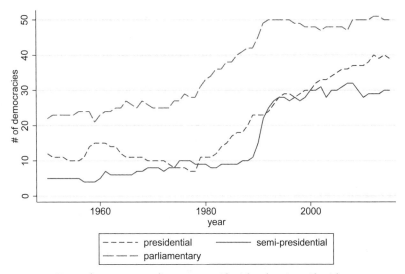

FIGURE 6.2 Forms of government: parliamentary, presidential, and semi-presidential.
Source: Authors' calculations based on data from Jennifer Gandhi, Jose Cheibub, and James Raymond
Vreeland, "Democracy and Dictatorship Revisited," *Public Choice* 143 (210): 67–101.

systems, a directly elected president serves as the head of state, sharing executive power with a prime minister who has some accountability to parliament.
This model has become increasingly popular around the world in recent years.
There are now more semi-presidential systems than pure presidential systems
in operation today (although there is also much variation within each type,
which we do not wish to suppress).[31] Figure 6.2 illustrates the trend lines in
choices of governmental form around the world.[32]

A large literature in comparative politics compares the merits of these different systems.[33] Again, it is important to emphasize that a range of different, potentially conflicting goals can be pursued through the choice of presidential versus parliamentary forms—including stability, economic growth,
military resilience, and participatory depth—and a concern with democratic
erosion is but one among many plausible ends. These ends are in some tension and must be reconciled through compromise. Nevertheless, a central
divide separates advocates of presidentialism and parliamentarism in the
existing political-science literature as to the durability of different kinds of
regimes. Opponents of presidential systems have noted their tendency to lead
to constitutional breakdowns. In contrast, they observe, no established parliamentary democracy had ever suffered a collapse into a new, authoritarian
mode of governance. They argue that presidentialism, by its nature, creates a
single office at the center of the political system in a way that raises the stakes

of electoral politics and creates a zero-sum, winner-take-all competition. It also incentivizes rewarding one's supporters once in office, while denying one's opponents political benefits. If the winner really does take "all," as seems to have happened in Venezuela and that was in progress in Rajapaksa's Sri Lanka, elections might be accompanied by political violence. They would necessarily catalyze disaffection among large portions of the population, leading to democratic breakdown as many took up alternative, perhaps violent, means for realizing their political ends. Because parliamentary systems allow for greater distributions of political benefits, it has been suggested, they generate a lower risk of system-level instability. Consistent with this argument, one recent study finds that presidential democracies are ten times more likely than other democracies to suffer an authoritarian collapse through incumbent takeover.[34]

Another line of criticism concerns the performance of government, gauged in terms of how capable the government is of generating new and responsive policies. While presidentialism can produce strong leadership, it can also lead to gridlock when the opposition party controls the parliament. As Americans have observed firsthand in recent decades, divided government can mean that little new law is passed. They can even generate destabilizing confrontations.[35] This might in turn seed disappointment with democracy as a whole, because the system cannot promptly deliver effective and responsive policies. The government itself comes to be seen as a source of unsettling risk. Parliamentary systems, in contrast, are less prone to gridlock, since the government by definition enjoys the support of the legislature. Depending on the nature of the electoral system, they may require coalitions of many different parties to govern. Coalitions can moderate positions even as they hamper strong leadership. Systemic reliance on coalitions can also create a risk of hold-ups by minority parties, which might try to act as kingmakers. It is nevertheless telling that countries picking their first constitution in recent years have avoided presidentialism.[36]

The most recent statement in the presidentialism-parliamentarism debate suggests that we should not attribute too much to the statistical associations between presidentialism and democratic breakdown. José Cheibub has demonstrated that it may not be that presidential systems lead to breakdown, but that unstable countries tend to choose presidentialism.[37] Countries emerging from military dictatorship, he suggests, might adopt a presidential system so the leading general can run for office. Conversely, civilian leaders afraid of military takeover might wish to consolidate power in a single office. For example, Turkey's recent constitutional reform, which was designed to consolidate one man's control, led to a much stronger presidency, but occurred after, and indeed responded to, the failed coup attempt of 2016.

What of the relative performance of different systems as checks on erosion, rather than more dramatic and rapid collapses? How do they compare in practice when it comes to erosion-related risks? While remaining cognizant of Cheibub's cautionary point, we think there are some reasons to think that parliamentary democracies might be less vulnerable to erosion than presidential ones, *ceteris paribus*. To see why, notice that parliamentary government allows more voices to participate in policymaking. It also furnishes a more ample toolkit of ways in which to deal with antisystem movements. Few parliamentary systems are truly two-party, and so parliamentary systems do a better job of giving voice to minority perspectives. Small ethnic groups, linguistic minorities, and political outliers will usually do better in a system of proportional representation, used in many parliamentary systems. This feature allows fringe, antisystem parties to obtain a national platform relatively quickly. But in so doing, it may also serve to keep them from ever taking power. In the 2017 Dutch election, for example, no party took more than 22% of the vote—but all political forces agreed that they would keep the charismatic populist Geert Wilders out of power. Even when an antidemocratic force captures a substantial tranche of seats and comes within sight of power, it will likely have to form a coalition with other parties more committed to a democracy. Coalition governments of this sort are unlikely to engage in democratic erosion, at least unless politicians seriously blunder. Hence, even though parliamentary systems give antisystem members voice quickly, they will not often allow that voice to corrode the quality of their institutions.

In contrast, in a presidential system such as that of the United States—where legislative competition tends to be binary because of the first-past-the-post system and is closely tied to presidential competition—charismatic populists cannot obtain any power unless they win the presidency. Usually, this means capturing the nomination of one or another major party. The candidate-selection mechanisms for presidential elections, though, are commonly in the control of the party rather than the state. Indeed, control over how a presidential candidate is selected might be viewed as an important element of party autonomy from state control. At the same time, this associational freedom comes at a cost for democracy writ large. Major parties may also be tempted to adopt selection systems that are especially open to outsiders in the wake of electoral defeats in an attempt to cultivate a wider constituency, and a more active "base." This strategic impulse creates an opportunity for the entry of antidemocratic candidates. And since major parties inevitably lose some elections in a well-functioning democracy, the risk of defeat leading to capture of the candidate-selection process by antisystemic forces may be unavoidable in a presidential system. As a result, presidential systems may be systematically vulnerable to the risk that the leaders of a political party lose elections and then miscalculate, or lose control of, a candidate-selection process, thereby allowing a candidate hostile to democratic persistence to come to power. In our view, this risk is potentially a serious one.[38]

A second reason to prefer parliamentary systems concerns their responsiveness to shifting political conditions. Because parliamentary systems do not have fixed-term executives, they can often respond with greater speed to shifts in public opinion. As a result, they can avoid some destabilizing showdowns. In a parliamentary system, moreover, leaders serve as long—or as briefly— as they retain the confidence of the parliament. A parliamentary system can thus jettison bad leaders but also retain good ones—provided they are recognized as such by the public and elected officials—in ways that make them more immediately responsive. Hence, when a charismatic populist comes to power, that leader must in fact continue to maintain majority support within the legislature. In many cases, this will require a deliberate cultivation of other parties and factions. These features of parliamentary systems might temper autocratic tendencies, even if they do not assure democratic rotation or the exit of charismatic populists from office. For example, before transforming the system to a presidential one, Turkey's Recep Tayyib Erdoğan continued to work with minority legislative parties, in part as a means of maintaining broad majority support.[39] In this manner, although parliamentarism might not prevent charismatic populism, it may be able to blunt some of its most damaging effects.

Yet another beneficial side-effect of this vulnerability of political leadership to legislative challenges is that a parliamentary system does not need to resort to term limits to ward off the possibility of a "president for life." It is hence less vulnerable to crisis when a would-be autocrat runs up against a term limit and seeks to reengineer the constitution to stay in power, a dynamic often observed in several backsliding democracies. As a global matter, violations of term limits turn out to be quite frequent. By one accounting, fully one-quarter of fixed-term executives who make it to the end of the maximum constitutional term in place when they took office will try to stay on. The batting average of these attempts is very high: roughly 80% are successful.[40]

Consider in this regard how parliamentarism would affect the tenure of leaders in the United States—setting aside the question of whether these leaders could even have been elected at all in a different constitutional system. As the country approached its fateful election of November 2016, Barack Obama continued to enjoy a strong approval rating of more than 50%. Barred by the Constitution from running again, he joined Bill Clinton and Ronald Reagan as recent presidents able to leave office on a high note. Had the United States been a parliamentary system, Obama, Clinton, and Reagan would all have been able to serve for more than eight years. On the other hand, other leaders would not have made it to a full term. Jimmy Carter took office in early 1977, but by mid-1978 his approval ratings had dipped below 50%. George W. Bush found himself in a similar position in his second term, and his ratings did not touch 50% after mid-2005. In a parliamentary system, Carter and Bush might well have been discarded mid-term, whereas both Reagan and Clinton might have stayed beyond their actual departure from office. All this suggests (counterfactually) that a direct dependence on continued popular support for survival in office might well have obviated the need for term limits. This would have aligned political leadership with popular sentiment more closely, perhaps mitigating disillusionment with democracy, and also leading to unpopular leaders being ousted before they can resort to institutional tinkering as a way of entrenching their power.

To be sure, presidential systems may sometimes appear to be more responsive to public demand than parliamentary ones in part because the position of chief executive can more easily claim to uniquely represent the people. But we think that this appearance is misleading. Instead, parliamentary government may well be more responsive to popular demands, even though it might appear less transparent and responsive to the public. In a parliamentary system, the coalition that forms the government perforce has power to enact new laws in short order. Political victory therefore leads to immediate and often visible change in the law. Meanwhile, presidential systems that separate the legislative from the executive court experience gridlock, especially when the polity is closely divided. When a parliamentary system deadlocks, by contrast, mechanisms such as the vote of no-confidence enable rapid changes in leadership that tend to dissolve barriers to action. Hence, while the parliamentary system leads to instability in *government*, the presidential system can lead to instability in the *institutional regime* as a whole.[41] An intuition along these lines motivated the great theorist of the English Constitution, Walter Bagehot, to advocate the fusion of legislative and executive power and to criticize the American presidential system.[42] In a similar vein, some decades later and on the other side of the Atlantic, Woodrow Wilson suggested that the Industrial Revolution necessitated a more centralized, parliamentarian federal government, in which an executive-driven cabinet would replace parliamentary committees as drafters of legislation.[43] More recently, distinguished political scientists Thomas Mann and Norman Ornstein, in their searing indictment of American politics, conclude that a "Westminster-style parliamentary system provides a much cleaner form of democratic accountability than the American system."[44]

There is a third reason for preferring parliamentary systems as hedges against democratic erosion: they seem to have more effective instruments for maintaining accountability and checking efforts at charismatic populism and partisan degradation. For example, the regular appearance of the government in parliament in the form of an organized "question-time" provides a form of routine accountability. By signifying the dependence of political leadership on a broad platform of legislative support, and its necessary openness to questions from all sides, institutions such as a parliamentary question time refute the claims of charismatic populists to have direct and unmediated access to the public. Of course, one can quickly see how question time might, given a weak opposition, devolve into simply another platform for a charismatic leader. But our point here is that the institution makes that sort of degradation less likely in the first instance.[45]

In addition, parliamentary systems are more open to the intuition that not only those who hold power, but those in opposition, should have formalized and entrenched entitlements of the sort that can be leveraged to protest and resist democratic erosion. We have already mentioned the fact that some parliamentary and semi-presidential systems formalize the idea of a loyal opposition. They recognize the centrality of adversarial argument to the effective operation of democracy. In Germany, for example, committee chairmanships in the two legislative houses, the Bundestag and the Bundesrat, are apportioned according to the percentage of seats each party has in each chamber.[46] Moreover, both the dominant and the opposition parties have a role in selecting members of the Federal Constitutional Court. Half of that body is selected by the Bundestag, which decides based on a two-thirds vote of its Judicial Selection Committee. Half is chosen by the Bundesrat, also acting by two-thirds vote. In practice this means that a party that loses an election still influences judicial picks (though it could also allow a dominant party to pack the courts if it wins the necessary majorities, as happened in Hungary).[47] In contrast, in a presidential system such as that of the United States, legislative oversight is done primarily by congressional committees, but this means that in periods of unified government, there may be no regularized mechanism for holding the government of the day accountable at all. As we shall see below, there is no reason that opposition powers cannot be replicated in presidential systems such as that of the United States in some form. But it seems clear that they flow more logically and immediately from the organizing logic of parliamentary systems.

We do not want, however, to be too optimistic about parliamentarism. Rapid legislative change can also lead to rash and foolish decisions.[48] Parliamentary systems can become unstable as a result of interaction between the underlying electoral system and the party structures. Interparty competition in a new democracy can lead to instability, and even open the door to military coups.[49] Finally, the Polish and Hungarian cases suggest that if an antisystem party does seize power in a parliamentary system by an absolute majority, it might immediately be able to use the legislative power to lock in its electoral hegemony (although the same would likely happen in a presidential system). Without sufficient instruments of horizontal accountability, this can lead, as in Poland and Hungary, to rapid democratic erosion. Since the same rapid degradation can also happen in presidential systems, this simply means that choosing a parliamentary over a presidential system is no panacea. Perhaps the best way to summarize the matter is as one of competing risks: if the threat to democracy is from a charismatic populist, a parliamentary system may be better; if the threat is from partisan degradation, presidentialism might be a preferable option.

There are certainly counterarguments against parliamentarism. It is likely the case that a parliamentary system such as that of the Netherlands will allow antidemocratic parties to gain an official platform quicker. We have cast the response from established parties as wise and cautious. But cool heads may not always be in command. Parties that accept the democratic system may be uncertain about how to respond and may allow antisystem forces to seize a role as kingmakers.[50] It was the breakdown of coalition government in the late 1920s and early 1930s in Weimar Germany that opened the way for the National Socialists to assume a pivotal role through an alliance with conservatives.[51] Further, there is the possibility that mainstream parties will mimic the rhetoric and policies of the antisystem populists, so that in substantive policy terms there is little difference. Mark Rutte, the prime minister of the Netherlands, was criticized by some for shifting political rhetoric in an anti-immigrant direction to contain Wilders. This can lead to morally despicable policies, but seems unlikely to conduce to democratic erosion.

Unless one takes a militant democratic position, the inclusion of antidemocratic forces within a parliament is not necessarily to be deplored—such forces, after all, do reflect the strongly held beliefs of some citizens. And even from a militant democracy perspective, a critical question in predicting the effects of such inclusion is whether or not the groups are committed to the state monopoly on violence. For example, we might ask whether antisystem parties have associated paramilitary wings of the kind seen in 1930s Germany and possibly foreshadowed in Charlottesville, Virginia, in August 2017. Private violence, when aligned with an antidemocratic candidate or slate, we think, raises questions and risks of a wholly different order.

We should also say a word about semi-presidentialism, which, as noted earlier, combines some of these features of parliamentarism with the enhanced accountability of a directly elected president. Whether for reasons of function or fashion, this model has surged in popularity through widespread adoption in Africa and Eastern Europe, and now rivals "pure" presidentialism and parliamentarism in terms of global popularity. Semi-presidentialism has the advantage of having a potentially unifying national figure who can stand above the fray of day-to-day politics yet still remain directly accountable. At the same time, semi-presidential systems can maintain a more mutable prime minister's office that responds more quickly to changes in popular preferences. On the other hand, semi-presidentialism is often criticized because of the gridlock that arises during periods of divided government, as France has experienced on occasion. Ultimately, a choice must be made based on both these costs and the potentially larger benefits.

In terms of the specific risk of erosion, we see both up and down sides to semi-presidentialism. On the negative side, semi-presidentialism creates institutional resources that can be exploited to the detriment of democratic stability. In both Turkey and Russia, for example, the notionally ceremonial president's position, or a weak prime ministership, has provided charismatic populists with a convenient waiting area when term limits kick in. Semi-presidentialism might also be good for populists: it might suit, for example, a populist president whose command of policy detail is weak in comparison to her communication skills. The prime minister, in this set-up, takes up the policymaking slack.

On the other hand, semi-presidential systems have one more protection against tyranny if the president must cooperate with an accountable prime minister to get anything done. Polish President Andrzej Duda's decision to veto proposals to entrench partisan control of the Polish judiciary in July 2017 is a useful example of how different elements of a semi-presidentialist system can work as an effective check, despite partisan alignment within government (though we do not yet know if Duda's action will be consequential for Poland's ultimate fate).[52] Moreover, many semi-presidential systems employ a two-stage presidential election system. Even though this is conceptually and empirically distinct from semi-presidentialism, and indeed began in the Third Republic in France, it is worth highlighting for its anti-erosion benefits. The two-stage system involves an initial round in which many candidates compete. If none gets a majority of the vote, a second round is held between the top two vote-getters in the first round. This allows people to vote their "true" preferences in the first round, whereas the second round forces many voters to choose their "least-bad" option. Such a system can suppress the possibility of a president coming to power after having been recognized by many, but not all, as a hazard to democratic stability.

A final note on the design of presidentialism concerns term limits. Since term-limit violations are a common mechanism for democratic erosion, they should be guarded against. To this end, there are ways to make term limits more effective. Consider in this regard the recent crisis caused by a clause in the Constitution of Honduras, noting that a president who *proposed* extending the term would lose office immediately. In 2009, President Manuel Zelaya's proposal to have a referendum on a term-limit extensions was opposed by Congress and challenged in the Supreme Court, leading to his removal from the country by the military. This act generated significant controversy and was considered by many to be a coup d'état. In our view, this characterization misses the point. The Honduran military did not seek to rule, and never held actual political power, and so its intervention may be characterized as a kind of democratic coup d'état.[53] Coups are not to be taken lightly, but critics of the Honduran military were emphasizing the (remote) fear of collapse and ignoring the more immediate danger of erosion presented by Zelaya. In any case, even without focusing on the specifics of this case, automatic triggers for the removal of presidents from office, tied to specific steps of democratic erosion, seem to us a wise policy. If a democracy chooses not to adopt term limits, it might consider a system in which the vote share required to win high national office increases in successive terms.[54] For example, if an ordinary majority is required to win a first term, a second term might require an absolute majority, and a third term a supermajority of 55% or more.

Rethinking Judicial Independence

We have seen that the judiciary is often one of the first victims in an eroding democracy, and it is easy to understand why. When properly functioning, the courts can stand in the way of autocratic attempts to curtail liberal rights of speech and association, and can prevent charismatic populists from dismantling other checks on their authority—including elections, legislatures, and internal instruments of horizontal accountability. The very attention lavished on courts by aspiring autocrats suggests that they matter in democratic erosion. Yet, as we argued in chapter 4, some successful democracies, such as that of the United States, do not have an institutional design likely to insulate the bench from partisan entanglements or to ensure that the judiciary can protect all three of the institutional predicates of democratic rule. Hence it is worth asking whether there are fixes, either in the context of a new constitution or with an eye to the current American landscape, for the problem of judicial independence.

THE ROLE OF CONSTITUTIONAL
COURTS IN NEW CONSTITUTIONS

The Third Wave of democratization, which began in the late 1970s and crested some time earlier in this century, was accompanied by a major development in democratic institutional history: the spread of specialized constitutional courts around their world and the broader expansion in the powers of courts more generally. To illustrate, in 1910, less than a quarter of constitutions in force provided for any power of judicial review. A century later the figure was roughly 80%. More than half of the countries with judicial review centralize the function in a designated constitutional court.[55]

The paradigmatic function of constitutional review is usually thought to be protection of democracy. In particular, it is understood to involve preventing legislative majorities from trampling on the rights of minorities and so entrenching themselves in power. This democracy-protecting function has indeed served to help consolidate democracy in myriad environments. It deserves celebration.[56] Less frequently observed is that this justification has also served as a catalyst for the expansion of powers granted to constitutional courts in many countries—power that can be used for many ends. Constitutional courts today are now granted an increasingly wide range of powers related to the protection of democracy, including powers to oversee and certify elections; to conduct impeachment proceedings; to regulate political parties in the name of militant democracy; and to approve declarations of states of emergency. Constitutional courts have become linchpin institutions to prevent constitutional backsliding. They are the Swiss army knives of constitutional design.[57]

An important example for our argument is found in Colombia, where the Constitutional Court has been widely celebrated for a series of decisions on individual rights.[58] After its creation in the Constitution of 1991, the court became quite a popular institution in a country with a tradition of state weakness. It faced a significant test, however, when faced with President Alvaro Uribe's attempt to avoid leaving office. A popular president who had led a successful campaign against leftist guerilla groups, such as the Revolutionary Armed Forces of Colombia (FARC) and the National Liberation Army (ELN), Uribe wished to stay in office beyond the single term contemplated in the 1991 Constitution. The entire logic of the constitutional scheme, in some sense, hinged on the single presidential term. That limit meant that each president would only be able to make a minority of appointments to key institutions like the Central Bank, Judicial Council, and Constitutional Court. In 2005, as his first term came to a close, Uribe was riding high in the polls, and, through his allies in Congress, obtained a constitutional amendment to let him run again. A case was brought before the court challenging the constitutionality of the proposed amendment. The court upheld it but suggested that there were certain procedural limits to constitutional amendments.[59]

Uribe handily won reelection. At this juncture, his rule turned darker. He had Supreme Court deliberations wiretapped and journalists surveilled. As in other instances of democratic erosion, he began to assert more control over the election machinery and judicial appointments. In 2010, a still-popular Uribe placed his weight behind yet another constitutional amendment, now one that would allow him to seek a third term in office. This time, constitutional change was slated to occur through a popular referendum. But now, the Constitutional Court held, first, that the proposed referendum was unconstitutional on procedural grounds and, second, that the amendment itself was unconstitutional on substantive grounds. Drawing on the doctrine of unconstitutional constitutional amendments, the court explained that the amendment would be an unconstitutional "substitution" of the constitution. In its judgment, the court stressed "in detail how a president with twelve consecutive years in power would have tremendous power over various institutions of state, including those institutions charged with checking him." A second extension of the presidential term, it reasoned, would in effect constitute a "substitution" of the constitution since it would allow the president to "name members of the central bank, the attorney general, the ombudsman, the chief prosecutor, and many members of the Constitutional Court."[60] The justices also expressed concern about media dominance by a three-term president. In other words, the justices took account of how the sheer duration of one person's rule would influence not just the separation of powers but also the larger ecosystem of institutions necessary for restraining executive branch behavior. Uribe accepted the court's decision and withdrew his candidacy for the 2010 presidential race.

This decision represents an example of a Constitutional Court almost single-handedly saving constitutional democracy. The challenge in the Colombian case came not from partisan degradation but from a successful leader who had performed well in terms of policy metrics, and who sought to transform a temporary popularity into more permanent political power. While Uribe's style is more popular than charismatic populist, he therefore nevertheless represented a threat of democratic erosion. The only institution able to stop him was the Constitutional Court—and in this case it proved up to the task. Strikingly, that body contained four members out of nine who had been appointed by Uribe. Yet it was able to muster a majority of six out of nine members to rule against the president's ambitions. Colombia, like Sri Lanka under Rajapakse, was a near miss for democracy.

There are other examples of constitutional courts playing democracy-enhancing functions. In South Africa, for example, the high court played an important role in constitutional creation and is starting to play a small role resisting corruption within the ruling African National Congress party. When President Zuma was found to have used public funds to refurbish his private residence, the Constitutional Court in late 2017 demanded that parliament act. Although the Court did not demand Zuma's removal, it did find in the Constitution an obligation for parliament to have a mechanism for removal in the event of improprieties. Within a few weeks, Zuma was forced from office by political pressure from both within and outside his party.

Despite these examples, it is not wise to rely exclusively on judges to be a safeguard, particularly when liberal and constitutional norms come under sustained attack. As we have seen in other contexts, the very power of constitutional courts makes them attractive targets for the forces of erosion. A leader bent on democratic erosion who is thwarted by a recalcitrant, law-abiding court will generally find another, more roundabout way to achieve the same anti-democratic goal. Hence it may be better to think of judicial safeguards of democracy as mechanisms to buy time for the popular and elite defenders of democracy to regroup for a renewed electoral challenge.

This opens up the question of how apex courts might be protected from capture by political forces bent on eroding democratic institutions. Leading comparative-law literature on the design of constitutional courts has not focused on this question. On the contrary, it has underscored the *mutual* construction of judicial independence and democratic competition. Both the formal and actual power of constitutional review tend to expand as political uncertainty increases. As a result, the creation of judicial independence in the first instance is a function of democratic competitiveness and the prospect of rotation in power.[61] When political parties foresee that they might one day be out of power, they tend to prefer a larger role for courts as protectors of political minorities. In contrast, when one party thinks it can dominate political life for at least the foreseeable future, it tends to prefer weaker or more subservient courts. This mutually reinforcing dynamic among judicial power, democracy, and the rule of law illustrates a more general, and familiar, point: Liberal constitutional democracy has a systemic quality. It is more than just the sum of particular institutions, and cannot be sliced up into discrete components without losing much of importance.

The argument that judicial power is dependent in important ways on democratic competition helps explains how judges can secure effective political power in the first place. But it also foregrounds the deep, structural risk that democratic erosion poses. It explains why courts are early targets in processes of erosion such as those observed in Sri Lanka or Hungary. It is not just that judges might impede erosion. It is also that courts, once created, can become a kind of *instrument* of erosion. Political leaders may want to imbue them with extensive formal powers once they are captured, stock them with cronies, and turn the law loose on their enemies, in line with Gertulio Vargas's dictum, "For my friend, everything; for my enemies, the law." Indeed, consistent with this dynamic, constitutional review plays a very different role in an autocratic context. Nested in an undemocratic regime, it can work to repress associational and speech rights while providing a "rule-of-law" fig leaf to hide electoral manipulation. At the same time, these functions do not mean that putative autocrats always want wholly subservient courts. Some have argued that in weak democratic environments that characterize democratic erosion—neither fully authoritarian nor democratic—independent judges can also serve to guarantee the post-tenure safety of leaders, providing a kind of bespoke insurance policy.[62] In short, democratic erosion is likely to lead to a diminishment of judicial independence. But even when a polity makes a transition to full autocracy, we are may observe a residual measure of autonomy on the part of judges.

All this is not to say that it is impossible to promote judicial independence against a backsliding tide. One institutional solution that has been quite popular in recent decades is the empowerment of a special institution, embedded within the constitution, as a means to manage the judiciary by exercising independent control over judicial appointments, promotions, removal, and budget, free of transient partisan winds. These judicial councils, as they are called, are now found in more than two-thirds of constitutions in force. They are defended as means to protect judicial independence by giving judges a role in their own management.[63] But the scholarly literature is not so sanguine. In many cases, judicial councils can quickly become instruments for political control of the judiciary, rather than means of ensuring its independence. Hence, Sri Lanka's Rajapaksa used impeachment to remove hostile judges. He also refashioned the process of judicial appointments through the Eighteenth Amendment's elimination of the constitutional council. Indeed, one of us has suggested in a recent empirical study that it is *only* a combination of constitutional protection against removal from office and appointment processes insulated from political institutions that can enhance judicial independence in practice.[64] More generally, the lesson of comparative experience is that judicial independence from political control is a tricky matter that requires a combination of insulating devices to protect courts from capture, and also that nostrums about the virtues of independent courts should not detract attention from the relative ease with which a judicial safeguard against democratic erosion can be disabled.

INTERNATIONAL COURTS AND REGIONAL ORGANIZATIONS

No matter how carefully institutions are designed in a constitution, domestic judges can still be targets of pressure and manipulation. They will be especially vulnerable if they do not have a built-up stock of public or elite reputational capital. Since new constitutional courts are unlikely to have this reservoir of popular legitimacy upon which to draw, it is important to think about a class of monitors of democratic performance who might be less vulnerable to political manipulation—namely, international courts and institutions. For parts of Africa and all of Latin America and Europe, regional trade and human rights tribunals play an important role in protecting constitutional democracy by adjudicating legal complaints against governments. For example, when Hugo Chávez sought to fire judges who were not voting as he liked, the Inter-American Court of Human Rights ordered Venezuela to reinstate them. When in 2016 the Gambian president sought to remain in office after losing an election, the Economic Community of West African States (ECOWAS) threatened to sanction the country. After a coup d'etat in Mali in 2012, the African Union suspended the country from membership, as it has done in other instances of democratic collapse. And, with regard to Sri Lanka, the European Union used the prospect of conditional trade concessions to encourage compliance with rule-of-law norms—suggesting that international pressure can achieve the same effects as a formal regional framework. These examples show that, for some countries, international and regional organizations can play a significant and important role in monitoring democracy, preventing backsliding, and promoting the structural predicates of liberal constitutional democracy.

For a country writing a new constitution to prevent backsliding, integrating regional and international law can be a wise design choice. Providing for the direct application of international human rights treaties for example, and making them enforceable by individuals in domestic courts, is a way to achieve a measure of protection for some elements of liberal constitutional democracy. Providing for the superior status of international law in the event of conflict with domestic law is another strategy. Affirming membership in regional organizations that are capable of punishing defection from norms of liberal and democratic governance is yet a third.

The strategy of internationalizing commitments, however, is not available to every country and is by no means foolproof. Regional organizations have proved themselves much more successful in supporting democracy than have international ones like the United Nations. But even in Europe, where regional institutionalization has the longest historical pedigree and the deepest roots, supranational institutions have not taken sufficiently aggressive steps to counter backsliding in Hungary and Poland in any effective manner. Furthermore, many parts of the world, notably in Asia and in the Middle East, lack access to robust regional instruments. Nor does availability translate always into use. For the United States, such a strategy *is* available. The Senate could ratify the American Convention on Human Rights, which would give citizens access to the Inter-American Court of Human Rights. Of course, ratification alone, experience suggests, does not guarantee enforcement. Several liberal democracies—including Chile and Mexico—have failed to implement decisions of the Inter-American Court when they touch what political elites perceive to be core political interests. At a minimum, though, external organizations provide a point of leverage when other forums are unavailable.

In this fashion, domestic institutions can be supplemented by regional and international ones. There is little cost from the perspective of liberal constitutional democracy to recognizing and leveraging this fact, but there is some risk in placing too much stock in such external actors. Furthermore, implementing international decisions is not costless. In some cases, implementation depends on the cooperation of the domestic judiciary itself (casting us back to the problem of weak domestic institutions). In our view, international organizations seem to have had the most influence in stopping erosion in regions like Africa, where democratic institutions are weakest, and have yet to realize their full potential elsewhere.

Horizontal Accountability in New Constitutions

A central lesson from comparative constitutional studies for those interested in checking democratic erosion is the importance of the new ecosystem of institutions promoting what Guillermo O'Donnell calls "horizontal accountability."[65] This set of institutions is tasked with the questioning, investigation, and eventual punishment, of unlawful or self-dealing uses of official responsibilities. We think it is useful to ask whether some of these institutions can also be arrayed in a new constitution as safeguards against erosion. Our proposals for constitutional and institutional reform interact with other ideas of constitutional design already laid out here. Because the functions of oversight and accountability for rule-of-law values can be separated from the primary functions of making and executing laws, we need not rely on those primary institutions—that is, courts and legislatures—to achieve accountability. Still, it is worth noting that parliamentary systems of government do not appear to suffer from greater levels of corruption, mismanagement, or propensity to backslide. Indeed, there is significant evidence that parliamentary systems are *less* prone to these risks, especially corruption.[66]

Before turning to specifics, we think it is worth flagging and rejecting two objections. Some influential scholars have argued that restraints on executive power are doomed to fail. Drawing on Carl Schmitt's theory of the exception, for example, Adrian Vermeule has advanced the claim that American administrative law is "Schmittian," insofar as it is riddled with gaps and "openly lawless" domains.[67] One can draw from this work a more general skepticism about the possibility that the laws regulating the executive's daily functions can restrain and channel official behavior in meaningful and useful ways. With his coauthor Eric Posner, Vermeule has also characterized efforts to constrain executive discretion with respect to national security matters (and more generally) as necessarily futile.[68] These and other commentators conceive of retrospective elections as the primary, and indeed only, effective constraint.[69]

There is much to be said in response to these celebrations of unbridled power, and we only sketch a conclusory reply here.[70] Neither theory nor practice, in brief, in our view supports the conclusion that a powerful executive branch will be constrained by prospective electoral pressures, or that checking institutions are exercises in futility. There is no general reason to think that executives will deploy their power solely for the public good in the absence of institutional checks and safeguards. To believe so requires heroic assumptions about elected officials—assumptions that are, as experience from Sri Lanka to Hungary, Venezuela, and even the United States shows, quite unjustified. It is, rather, unrealistic to think that retrospective voting will generate appropriate pressures to channel government power toward the social good.[71] For one thing, it requires unwarranted assumptions about what voters know and how they use that knowledge. It is striking that advocates of the Schmittian state tend to spend almost no time on questions of how voters can evaluate government performance effectively if officials have plenary control over what information about that performance they must disclose.[72] We also do not think that it is impossible to establish a bureaucratic structure characterized by legality, regularity, and due regard for the administrative rule of law. To the contrary, such systems are found in many constitutional democracies. Finally, there is no logical inconsistency between the delegation of broad administrative powers and the installation of internal and judicial mechanisms to incentivize the proper use of those powers. To the contrary, those checks supply a means of verifying that executive power, when used, is in fact based on actual expertise and motivated by some version of the public good—as opposed to founded on errant fear or prejudice, or oriented toward partisan degradation and the erosion of future democratic checks. Administrative regularity and legal constraints on executive action, in short, are complements rather than competitors of democracy properly understood.

Our positive argument, in contrast, draws on the thinking of James Madison, but also deviates from it in important respects. Madison's view was that institutions would compete for power, and so limit any one from taking over the system, as a consequence of institutional loyalties, resulting in a sort of interbranch balance. Many believe, however, that there has been a secular increase in executive power in many democracies, as a result of technological and economic change. This thwarts any effort to fashion a stable interbranch equilibrium that persists over time. It means that there is a need not so much for a counterweight as for a means of constantly recalibrating the institutions that monitor and discipline the executive in order to empower them against the growing toolkit of information-gathering, bully pulpit, and first-mover advantages wielded by the modern administrative leader. Moreover, rather than assuming that branches will be averse to one another, it is useful to design these counterweight institutions so that they are uniquely focused on a single mission of disciplining the use of state power. Consistent with this view, Bruce Ackerman has argued for innovations such as a separate "Integrity Branch" to be folded into good constitutional design.[73] But the basic insight is not new. Something similar was postulated in the form of the "Control Yuan" in the Constitution of the Republic of China. The Control Yuan was modeled by Sun Yat-sen on the ancient Chinese institution of the Censorate, rather than being borrowed from European or American constitutional experience. The point here is that design innovations, seeded through careful attention to comparative experience, may not be needed as a one-off matter but as a constant feature of modern democratic life.

Indeed, modern constitutions are replete with examples of horizontal accountability being institutionalized at the constitutional level in quite varied ways. For example Chapter IX of South Africa's Constitution provides a set of "state institutions supporting constitutional democracy" including the Public Protector (a sort of ombudsman); a Human Rights Commission to promote and protect human rights; a Commission for the Promotion and Protection of Cultural, Religious, and Linguistic Communities; a Commission for Gender Equality; an Auditor-General; and an Independent Electoral Commission. Many other constitutions have similar bodies, along with counter-corruption

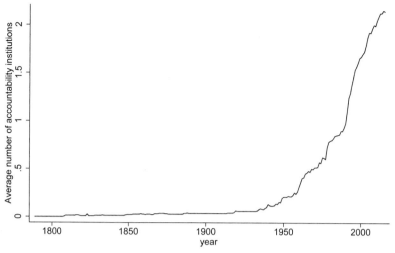

FIGURE 6.3 New accountability institutions in constitutions around the world.

commissions, judicial councils, civil service commissions, and other bodies. The typical constitution today has four such bodies, and the number is increasing, as figure 6.3 shows.

A modern-day Madison would surely adopt *some* horizontal-accountability institutions within the scheme of government. He would hardly rely on inter-branch competition, federalism, and retrospective voting as the sole mechanisms to check government, given the observed weaknesses in these mechanisms. For as we have seen, both the horizontal and the vertical separation of powers are incomplete responses to the problem of democratic erosion (let alone to the problem of misused governmental power more generally). But once she has mastered this insight, there is a wide range of horizontal-accountability mechanisms from which to select.

Rather than trying to canvas the full range of observed variation on this front, we focus here on a handful of particularly useful innovations. Consider first the constitutionalization of the ombudsman, which originated in Sweden in the early nineteenth century and thereafter spread to many other constitutional democracies.[74] While they come in a range of different institutional forms, all forms of the practice involve designating an official to monitor the conduct of public administration for legality and, in some versions, substantive fairness. The particular details and powers of the office, of course, vary across different national contexts. In some countries, the ombudsman is a plural office; in others, it is a single individual. The most powerful ombudsmen can investigate, report, and even lodge legal cases against any government agency. For example, in South Africa, the Public Protector

can investigate "any conduct in state affairs, or in the conduct of public administration in any sphere of government" that is alleged to have been "improper, or to result in any impropriety or prejudice."[75] This office was critical
in initiating the investigations into the misuse of public funds to upgrade
President Zuma's family compound. They found that the president should
pay back some of the expenses in a 2014 report. President Zuma complied
by paying back roughly half a million dollars in 2016 (raising questions, in so
doing, about how he earned that money!)

Ombudsmen are not unique. They are often supplemented by institutions devoted to identifying and punishing high-level corruption, which has
been a particular blight on many new democracies. In a related vein, civil
service commissions help to insulate meritocratically elected bureaucracy
from patronage-based appointments, which are a significant channel through
which corruption can be manifested. They do so by providing overall policies
to promote professionalism and to eliminate bias, and also supervising the
hiring, promotion, and retirement of officials based on neutral, meritocratic
criteria. More than one-fifth of national constitutions have a provision for
such an institution. Again, the basic idea is not alien to American shores.
At least seven US states also have analogous bodies in some constitutional
form.[76] The basic intuition can be translated into many other national and institutional contexts. Hence, consider the various independent election bodies
that help draw district boundaries, maintain accurate voter rolls, and ensure
fair polling and counting practices.[77] There seem to be substantial potential
benefits associated with each of the horizontal-accountability institutions, although the extent to which they materialize in any particular context varies.
We return to the utility of such election-monitoring bodies below, when we
consider how best to protect democratic competition.

In concluding, it is worth noting that there is a potential benefit from
having not just one but a *network* of checking institutions. While more institutions naturally increase the complexity of government, along with its cost
and inefficiency, such costs are offset by an important quality in the context
of erosion: A broad set of accountability institutions means that a putative
autocrat must capture more of them in order to achieve total control over
a political system. One can thus view institutional multiplicity as a kind of
insurance policy against the failure of any particular institution. Simple arith-
metic implies that multiple and overlapping accountability institutions are
more difficult for a backsliding leader or party to capture that one or two
such bodies. In thinking about these institutional add-ons, we once again
find it best to view constitutional design as a holistic exercise. It is not a matter of putting discrete pieces into place; rather, it is a problem of designing a

complex, interactive machine, in which a dynamic back-and-forth between different elements produces effects that could not be predicted from the isolated analysis of one institutional feature alone.

Protecting the Public Sphere

We have to this point been mainly concerned with the manner in which government is structured. It is time to turn to the question of how constitutions and laws organize the private sphere. This is principally a matter of how the liberal rights of speech and association are to be protected. But it also spills over into questions of how associations, and in particular political parties, are to be regulated.

Democracy, in its ideal form, is a system in which parties compete on policies, preferences, and values. The possibility of a meaningful policy debate requires to some extent a common epistemic basis for these contests. You may prefer lower taxes to more equality, and I may prefer the reverse. Unless we can agree on most of the factual questions related to these different policies, at least to some extent, our debate is likely to deadlock quickly. Of course, individuals engage in various forms of motivated reasoning and self-delusion. But without the possibility of access to truthful facts, it is hard to see how governance or progress can ever happen. Democracy as a result depends to a degree not generally appreciated on neutral institutions to produce unbiased information and then to evaluate and disseminate it. Facts are common property; it is their implications that ought to be contested. Neutrality in the production of primary data is therefore a bedrock of democracy, while pluralism in the assessment and interpretation of such data enables and informs partisan competition. When both influential private actors and public figures undermine both the value of factual accuracy and also the public's traditional sources of facts in favor of systematically misleading and erroneous sources, we think that the quality of democratic competition necessarily suffers. Similarly, when official sources of information and analysis are constrained or corrupted, the epistemic basis of democracy is threatened.

There are powerful forces working to undermine the public sphere in many countries. The economics of the news media business have pressed toward ever-greater consolidation, yielding fewer hands at the tiller determining what kind of news is available. At the same time, the practice of journalism itself has been radically decentralized in ways that enable both new forms of truth-seeking and obfuscation. In many countries, there are fewer truly authoritative sources of news than even two decades ago. And there have been systematic attacks on those that remain by backsliding leaders and parties, who know a soft target when they see one. Social media have been used by both state actors and private ones to influence elections through the dissemination of false news, even as the "fake news" charge undermines trust in any and all sources. Government officials have also stepped up libel prosecutions in some countries. Civil society, too, is under significant and sustained attack in many countries, with core freedoms of association, expression, and assembly violated in more than half the world's countries in 2015.[78] The UN Special Rapporteur on the Promotion and Protection of Human Rights and Fundamental Freedoms while Countering Terrorism has described this wave in lurid terms as an "ideological pandemic."[79] A key mechanism beyond libel is the use of legislation to hinder civil society's ability to attract funding and to disseminate information. Sri Lanka innovated, as we saw at the opening of the chapter, by specifically regulating the activities of civil society actors. The engineers of democratic erosion and outright dictators learn from each other. Each understands well that epistemic competition is the enemy of political consolidation—hence the vigorous search of late for ways to pollute the public sphere.

The associational rights central to democratic life depend, like all rights, on politics and courts to protect them. These institutional features are hard to engineer, but careful and thorough articulation of the rights in constitutions may go some way toward that goal, at least in certain contexts. While there is no foolproof way to write a bill of rights—and we do not offer a precise template here—it is helpful to anticipate the specific challenges to implementing rights that are commonly encountered in the contemporary environment. For example, defining only narrow, security-based exceptions to the right to speak and making clear that criticism of the government is constitutionally allowed can help to head off some attacks. Under conditions of democratic erosion, the exception is likely to prove the rule, and finding ways to ensure that those exceptions do not swallow the norm of robust discourse will hence be especially important. It is also difficult to think sensibly about free speech without acknowledging background asymmetries in political power and the concomitant ability to monopolize voters' attention. Regulations that limit journalists from airing information critical of the government, however, is not the same as regulations that hedge the risk that well-heeled voices will crowd out socially or economically marginal voices. A constitutional law regime that mechanically extends to all forms of "political" speech will not be a sturdy brake on erosion, and will not obviously foster the wide participation that is the predicate condition of meaningful democratic practice. Instead, formalism in the construction of election-related speech and association rights, like formalism in the consideration of the separation of powers, is an invitation to dismaying dynamics of democratic failure.

Constitutional protection of the public sphere is not exhausted by the creation of rights. Many countries also have media commissions to help ensure fair use of the media, as well as to assign rights to the broadcast spectrum. While these obviously work as two-edged swords insofar as they can be deployed by erosion's advocates to control information, they can play a particularly important role when it comes to preventing erosion: ensuring adequate competition among media outlets, so that no single source gains monopoly power over the news. Whether or not this will serve to enlighten the public in our post-truth era, it at least ensures that oligarchs who own media companies are in competition with each other. It hence increases the probability that dissenting voices will be available.

Cultivating Political Competition

The final mechanism of democratic erosion involves attacks on electoral competition, either directly by assailing political foes with brute force or using the coercive powers of the state, or indirectly by rigging the system to ensure one-party rule. Once again, we caution that our analysis focuses on the topline question of constitutional design. Since bad election administration can take many forms—not all of which can or should be regulated by constitutional law—our suggested reforms are necessarily only part of the project of ensuring free and fair elections.[80] Our suggestions here are instead general in form, and would need to be fleshed out, given national particularities and the pathologies of election administration observed on the ground.

We have previously noted that many new constitutions establish a nonpartisan electoral commission as a safeguard against partisan capture of the electoral machinery. We estimate that some 45% of constitutions currently in force have such a body. In a sign of the central importance of a robust electoral rule-of-law, this body is often the only administrative entity to be elevated to formally entrenched status in the constitutional text. But in other national contexts, it is but one of several such entities. In either case, formally entrenching this body in the constitution sends an explicit and powerful signal that election administration should be free of partisan interference. It also offers a platform for fashioning such independence from partisan forces through concrete design measures. The same effect can be achieved by statute, albeit more weakly. Democracies that lack a constitutionally mandated election commission generally create one on par with other important administrative entities.[81] Although the US Constitution assigns the design of electoral machinery to political actors, as we discuss in the next chapter, the possibility of nonpartisan election administration has not entirely vanished in the domestic context. Instead, thirteen American states currently use such commissions for state electoral districts. Scholars have shown that the political systems of these states are more politically responsive than those in states where districts are drawn by the partisan legislatures.[82]

Independent election bodies that assume all aspects of election governance, including the resolution of election-related disputes, have been particularly important in Latin America. The modal approach there, initially adopted in Uruguay in 1924 and then diffused across the continent, has been to create a special branch of the judiciary with jurisdiction limited to election-related matters. These tribunals manage elections from the voter registration process to the certification of results and have been crucial in resistance to erosion. In Mexico, for example, the interventions of the Mexican Supreme Electoral Tribunal were "critical" in loosening the one-party rule of the Partido Revolucionario Institucional (PRI).[83] Tellingly, an important element of this body's success has been its nationalization of disputes over gubernatorial elections that had previously been resolved on a provincial level. Changing the forum for the resolution of political disputes in this fashion diminishes the power of parochial, entrenched interests to shape outcomes.

Establishing effective supervision of electoral processes and guarding against corruption of various sorts are not the only ways of using auxiliary institutions to safeguard against democratic erosion. Recalling the parallel tracks of partisan degradation and charismatic populism, it might also seem worthwhile to consider whether the regulatory structure for political parties ought also to be altered to slow these processes. Here, however, the efficacy of likely reform is less clear. For instance, taking inspiration from militant democracy's practices, a constitution might require a certain level of intraparty democracy before allowing a political party to compete in national polls. But alternatively, and not necessarily consistently, a constitution might impose a candidate-selection mechanism that prevented charismatic populists from seizing a nomination and steering a nationally important party in a direction that imperils democracy, say by guaranteeing a controlling role to party insiders.[84] Whether one or the other of these safeguards is truly warranted is a difficult question that cannot be answered outside specific national contexts. The second idea, for example, implies a large degree of state control over the otherwise autonomous operation of even opposition political parties. Moreover, it is hardly clear that party insiders will always make wise choices—most notoriously, the fall of the Weimar regime shows how political elites can fail. In short, we remain unconvinced that there is any general "best practice" when it comes to the constitutional treatment of intraparty democracy or candidate-selection measures.

A Note on Emergencies

We conclude by drawing attention to one final area in which constitutional design has seen large, generally well-warranted changes, while the US Constitution has lagged. This is the question of emergency powers, where the relevant risk is one of collapse rather than erosion. Although we think there is commonly only a small risk that emergency powers will be directly misused to dismantle democracy, that possibility is sufficiently worrisome in the context of new constitutions that such powers warrant a brief discussion here. In the face of that concern, there are relatively promising models of how an effective system of emergency powers might be crafted to minimize the risk of democratic backsliding.

A first lesson from other countries is that, contra the American experience, key design decisions can and should be specifically identified and resolved in the constitution's text. Consider, as a recent example of how this can be done, the newly fashioned Constitution of Nepal of 2015. Its text mentions "emergency" fifty-seven times. It provides in detail for how an emergency is declared, under what conditions it persists, and what effect it has in practice. In rough paraphrase, the nation's president may declare a state of emergency under conditions of war, revolt, economic breakdown, natural calamity, or epidemic outbreak. Such a declaration must be approved by a two-thirds majority of the legislature, a threshold designed to prevent abuse by a majority party acting in bad faith. Like the famous Roman model of dictatorship, the new substantive powers to respond to a crisis have a fixed expiration date: Legislative approval endures for only a three-month period. Regular meetings of the legislature are required as a way to prevent the displacement of elected government seen in Germany in the 1930s. Moreover, although the president is empowered to issue orders to deal with emergencies, these too lapse when the state of emergency ends and, as a categorical matter, they cannot impinge on rights of equality, access to fair trial, and freedom from torture, among others. One especially innovative element of the Nepalese scheme is that salaries of judges and bureaucrats, while generally protected from diminution, can be reduced in the event of an economic emergency but not other kinds of crises.

More generally, it is worth giving serious consideration to proposals such as Bruce Ackerman's suggestion of a legislative "supermajoritarian escalator" provision for the authorization of emergency powers when it comes to a new constitutional text.[85] Pursuant to Ackerman's proposal, which was inspired by the current South African Constitution, a presidentially declared state of emergency would be temporally limited and could be extended only by legislative majorities that increased in size with each successive vote. This design choice would minimize the chance of a permanent state of emergency, while formalizing and channeling the deployment of emergency powers into carefully defined periods. While Ackerman's design is by no means foolproof, it is an excellent example of how our modern-day Madison would leverage comparative constitutional experience for more general lessons.

Contrary to the dire predictions of executive-power mavens, then, there is no evidence that such carefully calibrated powers will be self-defeating in practice. To the contrary, the best available evidence is that emergency declarations are now generally employed without precipitating either dissolutions of constitutional order or catastrophic policy outcomes.[86] Fears of a Schmittian unraveling in the face of a violent crisis seem more like hypothetical phantoms than real concerns, given this comparative experience.

Reinventing Democracy?

Many of the institutional solutions that we have surveyed are drawn from existing constitutions. Our recommendations are thus addressed mainly to a hypothetical designer of a new constitution. Yet because the challenges to liberal constitutional democracy are occurring in many parts of the world, we would be naive to suggest that there is an ideal design that can immunize a polity completely from the threat of erosion. We would also go astray if we were read to suggest that the risk of democratic erosion was confined to new regimes. To the contrary, just as we have stressed that current concern about democratic erosion cannot be confined to emerging and adolescent democracies, so we should not limit our proposals to the moment of constitutional creation.

As a general matter, we are currently suffering in part from what David Van Reybrouck calls "democratic fatigue syndrome": the configuration of low voter turnout, declining support for political parties, and chronic electoral campaigning, among other things, that exhausts public support for democracy as a system.[87] Even if these concerns are cyclical, as we suggested in chapter 1, this does not make them any less powerful. Van Reybrouck's diagnosis relies on a reduction of democracy to its representative form and a further reduction of representation to elections. But, as he notes, the standard technologies of facilitating democratic participation, which to many form the core of liberal constitutional democracy, are hopelessly outdated. How many inventions of the late eighteenth century, he pointedly asks, are still of much use in the present day in the same form?

Van Reybrouck's remedies are manifold. They involve a reinvigoration of direct modes of political participation, including deliberative polling, citizen assemblies, and random selection of legislators, using the full tool-kit of modern technologies and learning. Deliberative polling involves asking citizens about their views both before and after exposure to information and discussion with fellow citizens; citizen assemblies allow ordinary people to discuss policy issues together. Random selection of officials, which is also known as sortition, traces back to the ancient Greeks. These forms of political participation have been the subject of much recent experimentation around the world, particularly at the subnational level. Some well-known examples include the idea of participatory budgeting developed in the Brazilian city of Porto Allegre, in which citizens come together to select projects for funding under limited budget constraints; the innovative British Columbia revision of its electoral law in 2004 by a randomly selected set of 160 citizens; and the Icelandic process of drafting a citizens' constitution in 2011–12 in the wake of a destabilizing financial crisis. More generally, we take Van Reybrouck's lesson to be that there is no reason to accept as given the specific channels of democratic voice. There is instead every reason to look widely for innovative means through which meaningful, informed citizen participation can be cultivated.

For our purposes, it is worth lingering on the last of his examples. Iceland's experiment in democratic constitution-making was, in many ways, the first serious attempt to design a constitution in the social media era, with its immanent possibilities of round-the-clock transparency and engagement. While many countries have had Twitter revolutions, and the social media have been used to monitor and mobilize support for constitution-making, Iceland's constitution-making process involved unprecedented mechanisms of ongoing, direct public involvement. One thousand randomly selected citizens came together to generate ideas for the constitution; twenty-five citizens were elected to a drafting commission, with the only requirement being that they not be sitting politicians. The process included the release of several drafts to the general public for online input.

While the draft was not ultimately adopted as Iceland's constitution—it required the formal vote of the existing parliament, which declined to pass it in a marvelous example of the outdated vetoing the innovative—the process that yielded it has nonetheless inspired several other efforts to incorporate participation in constitution-making. In 2016, in a similar vein, Chile's government facilitated small-group discussions that involved two hundred thousand citizens in deliberation about the directions of constitutional reform. Finally, Mexico City drafted a new organic document in 2016 using an assembly of one hundred people, made up of randomly selected citizens and a minority of political actors and civil society representatives. Mongolia held a deliberative poll on constitutional design in 2017. Closer to home in the United

States, California candidate for governor John Cox has proposed a "neighbor-hood legislature" in which there would be many more legislative districts that would in turn select a smaller group of lawmakers. Other proposals are more theoretical, such as that developed by former Vermont legislator Terrill Bou-ricious of an elaborate system of interlocking bodies, some of which would be filled by sortition. Bouricious has also proposed a scheme in which different legislative tasks are assigned to different bodies, some selected for fixed terms and others temporary, all linked by complex interactions.[88]

At the same time, we have no evidence yet that mechanisms of sortition or citizen-led deliberation can work on the scale of a large country like the United States. In particular, we simply do not know what liberal constitutional de-mocracy at the national level might look like without political parties or other intermediating institutions. In the absence of comparative evidence to the contrary, we ought to remain agnostic as to the possibilities for transposing these innovations into the context of a large nation-state. Experimentation, not a blind rush to one particular solution, is required until we know more. In any event, our focus is not on improving constitutional democracy so much as maintaining it in the face of potential erosion. The proponents of reinvent-ing democracy not only have the burden of showing that new mechanisms can scale up to the level of a complex and geographically extended polity, but also that they are less truly responsive to the risk of democratic erosion. It is an experiment in which we hope some polity will soon engage.

Constitutional Hedges against Erosion

The world of constitutional design, we hope you see, is richer and more strange than anyone bounded within the walls of their own national tradition might perceive. That institutional diversity can be exploited to general gain. All these experiments in constitutional design remind us that our existing institutional vocabulary does not exhaust the possibilities of liberal consti-tutional democracy. We are supportive of such experiments. We think they have some promise for reviving democratic participation through innovative institutional design. With these general lessons in mind, we now turn to our own, quite local, context, and ask whether and how the US Constitution can be improved by new hedges against the risk of democratic erosion.

7

Saving Democracy, American Style

Everyone thinks of changing the world, but no one thinks of changing himself.
LEO TOLSTOY

What do Al Sharpton, Rand Paul, retired Supreme Court Justice John Paul Stevens, and Fox news commentator Marty Levin all have in common? They are among the prominent public figures in recent years to call for a new Constitutional Convention akin to that held it Philadelphia in 1787. Most Americans are unaware that Article V of the US Constitution contains, in addition to the mechanism that has been used to adopt the first twenty-six amendments, a provision under which two-thirds of the states' legislatures can call on Congress to create a new Constitutional Convention. Such a convention is no longer a purely theoretical possibility. When Michigan's legislature voted in 2014 to ask for a Constitutional Convention to adopt a balanced budget amendment, it became the thirty-fourth state to have issued a call of some kind for a convention. Because several other states had withdrawn their requests, and because uncertainty still exists on whether a convention, if approved by Congress, would be limited in scope or general, we think that it is unlikely that a convention will actually materialize under current conditions. But conditions change. And the mere possibility raises the interesting threshold question of whether those concerned about the possibility of erosion ought to pursue a convention. This is a good place, moreover, to begin our discussion of what erosion-proofing reform in the United States might look like, were a political window to open in which some might be achieved.

Written some 230 years ago, and thereafter nearly impossible to amend by conventional means, the US Constitution is the world's oldest operative, organic document. It is a technology adopted a century before the light bulb. It predates the telegram by fifty-one years. And it is roughly contemporaneous with James Watt's first steam engines. Unlike the engine that resides under the hood of your automobile, however, the text has not been upgraded with new technology, and is largely bereft of learning from other constitutions and subsequent political developments. It is, in other words, a quill in a world of smartphone styluses. Stylish, elegant, yet not eminently practicable. Perhaps the greatest difficulty in thinking about how the US Constitution might best be updated is knowing where to start, were one to update it: Many of the constitutional designs discussed in the previous chapter might be adopted, including a constitutional court, a set of accountability institutions, and majoritarian institutions like eliminating the Electoral College. More conventionally, proposals to constitutionalize a balanced budget or to overturn the *Citizens United* decision that allows for unlimited corporate spending in the electoral process could be adopted as part of a grand bargain.[1]

All this is not to say that a constitutional convention would be a wise idea. While we would endorse any amendments that enhance liberal constitutional democracy as we have defined it, a constitutional convention is too risky a strategy for an established democracy such as the United States, *especially* if it is facing a clear and present risk of erosion through partisan degradation and charismatic populism. There would, most importantly, be no way to insulate against the risk that a convention would be captured by antidemocratic forces. These forces could easily stoke and exploit disgust with established politics. Such disaffection has been assiduously cultivated by cynical politicians who seek national power by railing (without discernible irony) against Washington insiders in order to become Washington insiders. There would also be no way to hold at bay the resurgence of open hostility to members of the polity whose racial, religious, or sexual identity offended a silent majority. Experience with constitutional conventions in Ecuador, Bolivia, and Venezuela—to say nothing of the original effort to amend the US Articles of Confederation in 1787—suggests that we should not rely on formal, legal limits on the power of a constitutional convention. In any case, the Constitution itself does not provide guidelines for the convention's operation, and it is not clear, as a legal matter, whether statutory or other softer norms would be lawful, let alone effective in practice. In other words, it is possible that all that would restrict a new constitutional convention in the United States would be the fragile and malleable political norms of civility and respect then in effect. Under these circumstances, it is plain to see that constitution-making can easily and quickly go off the rails.[2] After all, the 1787 Constitutional Convention itself was called to adopt a limited set of amendments to the Articles of Confederation, but ended up overstepping its boundaries to produce the document we revere today. Just because all ended well in 1787, though, is no reason to think that all would end well today.

In any case, there is ample reason, as we have already seen, to think that the US Constitution was not optimal or ideal. Rather, Americans have muddled through and, by the third quarter of the twentieth century, had made democracy a going concern for most, regardless of race or gender. They accomplished as much *despite* the institutional limitations of the Constitution—most importantly its sheltering and nurturing of the peculiar institutions of slavery and racial hierarchy—and not necessarily *because of* the wisdom distilled in its text. In this regard, it is worth recalling that the regime of electoral authoritarianism that characterized the American South for much of its history was perceived as (and probably was in fact) faithful to the founding promise in ways that multiracial, pluralist democracy was not.

There is a flip side to this point: The systemic problems of American democracy today—most profoundly its declining responsiveness to all but elite opinion, its corresponding malign neglect of the interests of the socially and economically marginalized, and its institutional gridlock that precludes and increases partisan polarization—do not follow inexorably from the Constitution's design, any more than a commitment to racial segregation does. Rather, they flow from more contingent policy choices and shifts in political economy.[3] Subconstitutional fixes for the problems of political inequality and partisan polarization are imaginable. But all such fixes require political will of a kind that currently seems in notably short supply. If we do not have the necessary determination to attack these problems in a time of ordinary politics, there is no reason to expect that we will spontaneously act in a moment of extraordinary constitutional politics.

In short, we think that a constitutional convention would be far more likely to damage the quality of democracy at this moment than to improve it. Instead, this chapter focuses on subconstitutional steps that can be taken to avoid backsliding in the United States. As chapter 5 has explored, existing constitutional law not only fails to prevent erosion, but in many cases can facilitate it. This means that many of the solutions do not require the grand heights of constitutional amendment, but they would require some sort of formal change. An implication of our analysis so far is that many of the safeguards that do obtain now in the US system against democratic erosion are subconstitutional in character. They take the form of unwritten political norms or constitutional conventions—that is, expectations about official conduct that reflect established practice and are enforced through public criticism and condemnation rather than through formal sanctions. Our emphasis throughout is on formal constitutional rules that might mitigate erosion risk, however, and not on interventions to strengthen norms and conventions of political life through some other means. We acknowledge that such norms are critically important. Imagine, for example, a Twitter campaign akin to the one that was triggered by the Harvey Weinstein sexual abuse scandal, but this time concerning excessive partisanship or extreme pandering to the wealthy at the cost of the modal American. Such efforts might well be wise and worth supporting, but they fall outside our bailiwick here. Stated otherwise, we ask what *law*—in particular, constitutional law—can do to support and sustain the three key structures of liberal constitutional democracy: competitive elections, core rights to freedom of association and speech, and the bureaucratic rule of law.

It is also important to concede at the outset that this may not seem a propitious moment in American history for good-government-type reforms. Should the risks already inherent in our constitutional design materialize, attempts at institutional recalibration will likely come too late. We thus readily acknowledge that some of the following proposals are unlikely to be incentive-compatible with the interests of national leaders already lodged in place. Any significant reform today is further impeded by the socioeconomic and cultural forces that have contaminated, soured, and divided American politics. Nevertheless, the risk of erosion today presents an opportunity for rethinking first principles. Further, in the event of a swing of the political pendulum, perhaps analogous to the reforming moment that emerged in the wake of the Nixon presidency, the presently available evidence of American vulnerability to democratic erosion may have an upside: It may elicit a generally shared public desire for enhancing our machinery of democratic accountability. We should not exclude the experience of alternative political systems. Instead, we should think expansively, in the same spirit of optimistic experimentation that animated the Constitution's original designers.

Maintaining Electoral Integrity

We begin with elections as a basic building block of democratic practice. We have already seen that the American system of managing elections is deeply flawed. There is no consistent professional management of elections. At the state level, secretaries of state, often elected in partisan races and committed openly or covertly to partisan ends, are too often in charge of printing ballots, managing voter registration, and organizing polling. They can and do misuse these authorities to tip the scales in favor of one candidate or another. As the 2016 election demonstrated, moreover, the integrity of election administration is under threat from outside the country. The consensus view of the US intelligence community is that Russian intelligence or its proxies attempted to hack election-related networks. Whether or not these efforts made a difference to the national result is impossible to know, and in any event is not as relevant as a more general diagnosis of the threat. Web-based attacks targeting voter registration data and possibly even the enumeration of votes seem likely to continue. Now that Russia has demonstrated their potency, we should expect other nondemocratic competitors to the United States to deploy them too. In the short term, therefore, the prospects for administrative rule-of-law in respect to election management in the United States are dimming.

Shoddy administration and a hostile geopolitical environment do not exhaust the deep well of challenges confronting efforts to maintain democratic competition at the state or national level. Part of the reason for the current state of public disaffection in the United States that has led to partisan degradation and created the space for charismatic populism is the larger phenomenon of partisan polarization among legislative elites, which drives congressional deadlock and creates a wide space of discretion for the executive branch to act.[4] Polarization, which arises to varying degrees among legislators, national political elites, and the general public, is a complex problem. Its causes, dynamics, and effects at the popular and political elite levels vary in complex ways. Among other important factors are a nationwide geography of residential sorting, a growing rural/urban divide, and changes in election law on primaries and redistricting.[5] We think that polarization is an important problem to be addressed on its own terms, potentially through a mix of legal design and rhetorical strategies.[6] It is relevant here insofar as the American electoral structure is undermined by a lack of faith, driven by perceptions of gridlock or irreconcilable differences across the partisan aisle. To the extent that polarization creates an incentive for parties to engage in winner-takes-all strategies of entrenchment, it encourages erosion, reducing the meaningful possibility of democratic rotation further down the road.

The Constitution works as a significant barrier to meaningful professionalization of election administration at the national level. It also impedes efforts to tamp down the effects of partisan polarization. Article I, section 4, commits election administration to state legislatures, although the Supreme Court has wisely declined so far to disallow states from delegating certain election-related tasks to neutral, expert bodies. This decentralization means that reform of election administration must, to a large extent, proceed on a state-by-state basis. It is hence vulnerable to state-by-state efforts at capture by interest groups committed to ensuring that their preferred candidate wins at whatever cost. Perhaps the likelihood that foreign governments will continue to attack election infrastructure, engaging in increasingly aggressive efforts to shape American political outcomes might, in the medium–term, prompt a shift to greater national control, standardization, and professionalization.

If so, what should be done? Even if it would be impossible to constitutionalize a nonpartisan electoral commission for national elections in the United States of the kind observed in other constitutions, some steps can be taken to improve electoral responsiveness. Most obviously, those states that have not yet adopted independent electoral commissions to draw boundaries for legislative districts could do so. Even if the federal government cannot assume control of election administration, it can provide the tools to improve states' policies. In this vein, Congress might create a nonpartisan center for excellence in poll management, capable of identifying and disseminating best practices; providing careful empirical studies of barriers to voting (and discrediting fallacious claims of voter fraud aimed at suppressing voter turnout for political opponents and, in some instances, racial and ethnic minorities); and developing regulation in response to systemic threats to election administration at the national level—say, of the kind posed by Russian interference in the 2016 national polls. This kind of professional, nonpartisan, and democracy-oriented body would in many respects be the antithesis of the highly partisan voter fraud task force established briefly by the White House in 2017.

But even if that proposal seems unlikely to materialize, the federal courts are not powerless to improve election management. The Supreme Court could develop a more rigorous doctrine on redistricting; indeed, as we write, it is considering whether there is a judicial remedy available for excessively partisan gerrymanders. Although the courts have been reluctant to intervene because of the absence of a "workable standard" for rejecting or accepting partisan districting, they possess formidable equitable powers. Judges, for example, could appoint a special master to evaluate the proposals for conformity with the principles of neutrality and fairness (or, were our earlier proposal to be enacted, lean on the empirical expertise of a national election administration body), consistent with what is already done in racial gerrymandering cases. In any event, the concern expressed by some justices about the existence of "workable standards" for judging partisan gerrymanders rings hollow when set in historical context. A generation ago, the Court was willing to reject racially motivated malapportionment in the line of cases beginning with *Baker v. Carr*, even though it had no alternative "workable standard" immediately to hand.[7] More recently, the Court has been perfectly willing to operationalize inchoate ideas such as "the separation of powers" and "federalism" in specific cases, even though the Constitution mentions neither phrase—let alone draws "workable standards" for their adjudication. Today, the Court could follow that legacy or at least recognize that a decision to stay its hand is just as likely to be perceived as "political" as an affirmative intervention. Better, the Court can and should take account of excessively partisan malapportionment as a *constitutional* problem and provide a judicial backstop against extreme forms of partisan entrenchment.

Interbranch Checks against Democratic Erosion

What, though, of the bodies that are elected at the national level? We have seen that the dynamic of legislative-executive relations is an important predicate of democratic erosion. Our cautious endorsement of parliamentary over presidential systems in the previous chapter carries little weight for the United States, where such a transition is not plausible without wholesale constitutional revision, and where such a change would almost certainly generate unpredictable consequences of its own. Nevertheless, we think there is a substantial reform agenda in terms of altering relations between Congress and the executive with both short-term and long-term fixes. We begin, however, by sketching one leading diagnosis and proposed remedy, explaining why we would resist it, and then turn to an affirmative agenda comprising three items.

A common starting point for thinking about institutional reform is the disaffection with contemporary politics that many Americans feel. That discontent is commonly linked to concerns about the perceived inability of the country's leaders to come together to solve widely acknowledged problems and is no doubt a source of the erosion of faith in democracy. Some of the gridlock is hardwired into the original Madisonian constitutional design, which was intended to prevent tyranny by forestalling rapid government action. But there is also a sense that increasing partisan polarization has rendered the Madisonian scheme unworkable.

Reasoning in this vein, William Howell and Terry Moe have recently argued that the original design of Congress did not create a body capable of playing its intended role.[8] They argue that Congress is by design an aggregate of varied and shifting interests, and a hotbed of localism, even though it is the body constitutionally responsible both for making national policy and for ensuring accountability for singular national decisions. Among their other ideas, Howell and Moe propose that fast-track authority, now used in international trade agreements, be extended more generally to legislation. In a fast-tracking system, the president would be able to send legislation to Congress for an up-or-down vote, without amendment. This system has worked tolerably well in the United States for trade. Congress, knowing that it will not be able to resist pressures to amend trade agreements, intentionally ties its own hands and promises to vote up or down. Lending support to their proposal is the fact that a substantially similar arrangement exists in Brazil, where the president has the ability to cut off legislative debate and demand a vote on the proposal as it then stands.

Howell and Moe's idea has many important merits. Vesting the president with greater control over the legislative agenda would facilitate policymaking.

It would reduce gridlock and the concomitant discontent with government sclerosis. But we are not persuaded that it is either an effective response to public discontent with national politics, or a wise move in a context of democratic erosion risk. To begin with, we are not persuaded that public discontent with Congress is a simple result of legislative deadlock. Rather, skepticism of government has been deliberately cultivated by politicians casting themselves as outsiders to Washington politics, often in a populist vein. The same politicians generate deliberative deadlock to stoke those concerns.[9] Once such tactics are used, they are unlikely to be abandoned unilaterally, and to merely make policymaking easier would not resolve the underlying problem of corrosive strategic action by politicians. Public dissatisfaction with Congress, furthermore, may reflect political polarization of a kind that would be intensified rather than ameliorated by fast-tracking all legislation. It is easy to imagine, that is, a situation in which fast-tracking precipitates violent discontent, as one side of the polarized, partisan divide rushes to entrench a policy agenda in the face of deeply held disagreements.[10]

Worse, Howell and Moe's proposal is likely to exacerbate the risks of democratic erosion, because a strong executive is the principal (although not the only) locus of such risk. Under their system, a charismatic president may be able to make national policy without significant legislative debate. Given sufficient partisan degradation, indeed, it is possible that fast-tracking would accelerate the ongoing systemic drift to a wholly presidentialist form of government, one that had a far higher risk of charismatic populism than current arrangements. Finally, and more subtly, fast-tracking communicates to the public the idea that collective deliberation in which local differences are hashed out is somehow illegitimate: It implies instead the existence of a single, supervening national good. In this way, it stands in tension with a key background assumption of pluralist democracy—the existence of extensive reasonable disagreement that must be negotiated but never suppressed.

How then might the current separation-of-powers arrangements be improved in ways that reduce the risk of democratic erosion without sacrificing performance or responsiveness? We offer here three ideas: opposition rights; presidential discipline; and congressional cabinet members.

Our first idea harks back to our notion of formal opposition powers observed in the German and British contexts. We think that the United States could benefit from these other countries' experiments with the creation of legal powers for the legislative opposition. In these countries, we explained, the opposition party in the legislature has some power in the form of committee chairmanships. These positions carry with them investigative tools and even agenda-setting jurisdiction over new legislation. Such arrangements need not be memorialized in a constitution. In some cases, such as that of the United Kingdom, they currently result from laws or even unwritten conventions. Minority powers to demand information, either in documentary or testimonial form, provide a way to challenge the factual justifications for decisions and claims made by a presidential administration. Hearings, although not quite analogous to prime ministerial question time, can supply a focal point for opposition to an administration policy to emerge. They also work as a platform for legislators to draw public attention to elements of erosion that might otherwise escape public notice. Moreover, there is no reason to think that such minority powers would exacerbate gridlock, since they need not necessarily be part of the process of crafting new legislation. Rather, they provide the minority party with a way to ventilate issues of concern without gumming up potentially important legislation.

Congress already has at hand a mechanism for fashioning instruments for loyal opposition: each house's Article I power to establish "rules of Procedure" for itself, which is the source of its authority to create committees and structure legislative debate.[11] How might this power to employed to fashion minority rights? Imagine that during a period of unified government, the minority party in each house demanded a new set of minority rights to committee chairs and related investigative powers to convene hearings, demand testimony, and subpoena documents. Currently, these broad investigative powers are controlled by committee chairs, who are members of the majority party. A party in power often struggles to secure major substantive legislation because of internal divisions. There may be instances in which it is willing to trade the immediate gain of a policy win for the uncertain future loss of granting opposition procedural rights. Indeed, to the extent that investigative rights do not infringe on a specific, near-term policy agenda of the dominant party—and may even benefit the dominant party if it were to return to the minority—the quid pro quo would be relatively costless. If that party is worried that the future majority might renege by altering each house's rules, there is also historical precedent for Congress enacting legislation that imposes certain rules by law—hence rendering them harder to change.[12] Ideally, such a law would require that subpoenaed executive-branch officials offer live testimony and documentary production at the behest of minority committee chairs.

Indeed, an important function of these legislative opposition rights is epistemic. They enable the elected legislative opposition to extract, and hence publicize, information from the executive that might compromise or contradict pubic justifications for policies. We think this is generally a healthy feature of democracy, even in the absence of any risk of democratic erosion. But the efficacy of such mechanisms is not simply a matter legislators' motivations alone.

There are ways for Congress to strengthen its capacity to obtain and use information about the executive branch, even holding constant legislators' motives. In particular, Congress can recalibrate its oversight by organizing its committees to have greater or lesser degrees of overlap, or by assigning more or less professional, nonpartisan support to such bodies.[13] To demand such congressional action is not wholly wishful thinking. As a historical matter, Congress has at some moments demonstrated its willingness to expend scarce political resources on measures such as the 1946 Legislative Reorganization Act. This streamlined and strengthened oversight committees in response to the growth of executive power during World War II.[14] In contrast, the last eighty years have seen few new efforts to recalibrate legislative authorities in light of the still-evolving state of the executive branch beyond the intelligence oversight context. There has been no effort, for example, to strengthen Congress's ability to assert its legal and constitutional interests—say, by creating an in-house counsel to maintain an institutional memory of how Congress interprets Article I and to be able to bring suit to defend those institutional prerogatives.

Courts also have a role to play in ensuring interbranch accountability. As a result, opposition rights should be crafted with the possibility of judicial intervention in mind. The White House and executive agencies have often stonewalled or slow-walked congressional requests for information. Although Congress has its own powers of contempt and even imprisonment that could be used to elicit compliance, we think that under current conditions the use of those powers would be simultaneously inflammatory and ineffective. Enlarging Congress's capacity for direct coercion, moreover, would likely affect how it interacts with ordinary citizens. We thus think that it is implausible to suggest that Congress should use contempt and imprisonment to elicit information from executive branch officials or anyone else. That leaves the courts. But when legislators have turned to the federal courts for injunctions requiring disclosure, judges have too often been unwilling to act, especially when they do not think it is the whole of one or the other House seeking the information.[15] Instead, judges explicitly prefer to allow the elected branches to reach a negotiated solution. This is regrettable. In the ensuing negotiations, the executive has tended to have the upper hand, since it has the advantage of favoring the status quo. Executive branch lawyers can also string out litigation until the next legislative election cycle, when a new set of potentially more sympathetic or less experienced representatives may be installed. Judicial neutrality, in other words, is really a way of placing a thumb on the scales in favor of the executive. An important part of the institutional design of opposition rights, therefore, should be an explicit statutory right to a judicial order of disclosure—although one stronger than the slow and incomplete remedies now available under the Freedom of Information Act—and a mandate for rapid judicial relief, including expedited appeals in case a district court denies a legislative request.

Our second idea starts from the observation that the Constitution contains very few devices for disciplining presidents who overtly violate the law or violate what we have called the administrative rule of law by using prosecutorial and bureaucratic resources for personal or partisan ends. Even if legislators' incentives may fluctuate between periods of unified and divided government, Congress has a role to play. At a minimum, informal norms about presidential disclosure of assets, liabilities, and tax returns in respect to both domestic and foreign holdings, which had been observed for several presidencies until the election of Donald Trump, should be codified into law. This way, the public will be able to determine which policy directives stand to benefit the president himself, so as to be able to assess whether they also serve the public interest.

Another way to ensure presidential accountability might be to revive the impeachment power as a device for removing from office presidents and other officials who deploy prosecutorial or regulatory discretion to target their political enemies or to shield their friends. At present, the requirement of a "high crime" or "misdemeanor" as a predicate for impeachment is generally viewed as imposing a relatively high bar. Impeachment, therefore, is treated as a nuclear option, "the most powerful weapon in the political armory, short of civil war."[16] But constitutional history does not command this reading. "High crimes and misdemeanors" was a vague phrase of uncertain meaning even at the time of the Constitutional Convention. The original proposal was to limit impeachment only to cases of treason or bribery, but George Mason of Virginia worried that those bases would not cover a president who was inclined toward tyranny. He thus proposed adding "maladministration" as a basis for impeachment and removal from office. When Madison objected that maladministration was a vague term, Mason proposed the term "high crimes and misdemeanors," which had a long history in English law and parliamentary practice.

In England, impeachment had long been used to remove the king's ministers, and it provided a central power of parliamentary accountability but was not limited to serious crimes. As a congressional report issued during the Nixon impeachment recounts, the phrase "High Crimes and Misdemeanors" had been first used in 1386 during a procedure to remove the Earl of Suffolk for failing to follow parliamentary instructions about improving the king's estate and for failing to deliver a ransom for the town of Ghent. These seem less like what we call a crime and more akin to dereliction of official duty. In addition, even as the debates about the Constitution were roiling the United States, Edmund Burke was spearheading an effort to impeach Warren Hastings, the first Governor-General of India, for high crimes and misdemeanors in the form of gross maladministration. Viewed in historical context, therefore, the impeachment power is plausibly understood as *not* contiguous with the criminal process, and therefore not predicated on the identification of a federal felony contained in the statute books. As the Nixon-era congressional report concludes in assessing the perspective of the framers, "It is apparent that the scope of impeachment was not viewed narrowly."[17]

Moreover, the phrase "high crimes and misdemeanors" is akin to "cruel and unusual punishment" (in the Eighth Amendment) or "right to bear arms" (in the Second Amendment) in its essential ambiguity when viewed out of context. Just as the Eighth Amendment is not limited to drawing and quartering, and the Second Amendment is not limited to flintlocks and muskets, so too "high crimes and misdemeanors" should not be limited to the specific enumeration of such offenses in 1787. Rather, the phrase should (like the Second and Eighth Amendments) be understood in terms of its function within the larger constitutional scheme.[18] That function is simple: Impeachment is a historically important pathway for punishing high-level officials aligned with the president. It is important in part because it is not limited to criminal offenses. And its significance further derives from the fact that the president has a broad-ranging and unreviewable power to pardon. Especially given the evidence that voters do not always evaluate incumbents on the basis of their policy performance, but on the basis of other considerations, the wise use of impeachment to police the democratic bargain is of great importance.[19] Impeachments might thus be more common and should focus not only on disloyalty to the nation ("treason") or improper pecuniary motives ("bribery"), but also on improper self-dealing that undermines principles of democratic rotation and choice.

We should add that changing the scope of impeachment does not mean it will necessarily be used more often. It is just as possible that the prospect of impeachment for derelictions of official duty will induce more diligent efforts to take care that laws are duly enforced. The logic of deterrence, that is, does not stop at the White House lawn. Moreover, whereas Article I requires a majority of the House to impeach, conviction requires a two-thirds supermajority of the Senate, a threshold that will often be difficult to obtain even under conditions of divided government. For impeachment of the president, the process presently leaves the vice-president in charge, which reduces the possibility of partisan abuse of the power to remove. We nevertheless think that it would be useful for Congress and the public to affirm that the Impeachment Power does extend beyond crimes, and that it focuses on presidential efforts to subvert the democratic elements of the Constitution. A clear and public decoupling of impeachment and the criminal process, moreover, has the healthy effect of clarifying that the two are not substitutes: There are many instances in which criminal investigation and prosecution (including, perhaps, of the president) might be warranted without regard to whether impeachment is appropriate or legally available.

While we think impeachment ought to be used to prevent erosion, we are skeptical, absent (unlikely) alterations in the constitutional text, that impeachment should function akin to the vote of no confidence in a parliamentary system, as a means of relieving chief executives who lack legislative support. Given the different electoral bases of the president and the Congress, as well the frequency of divided government, we do not think transposition of that element of parliamentary government would work well in the US system.

Our third suggestion is concededly counterintuitive. It involves increasing the extent of coordination between executive and legislative branches. Some commentators have argued for a repeal of Article I, section 6, paragraph 2 of the Constitution in order to allow members of Congress to serve in the president's cabinet.[20] That clause prohibits members of either house from being appointed to a "civil Office under the Authority of the United States" and hence disallows officers from also serving as members of Congress. We think that a targeted repeal of this provision does not present the risks of a constitutional convention, although we concede that, like all constitutional amendments, it would be exceedingly difficult to achieve. Rather, it might be understood as a relatively technical and minor amendment that would not trigger a new round of the Culture Wars—particular if cross-branch appointments were subject to a "partisan balancing" rule to the effect that each copartisan appointment had to be matched with an appointment from the other party.

Licensing members of the cabinet to serve in Congress would allow the president to align her administration more closely with Congress so as to facilitate her legislative agenda. Increased coordination between the two political branches might ease the present difficulty of passing new legislation, as information could be easily shared across institutional lines, and effective coalitions could be more quickly formed. But in achieving this benefit, presidents would have to reach across the partisan divide in ways that at least had a possibility of mitigating some of the partisan polarization that characterizes our era. Doing so would introduce real diversity into the cabinet: Administrative agencies with partisan balance requirements are these days staffed with truly diverse leaders as a result of the balance rule.[21] Although we recognize a risk that a charismatic populist might seek to co-opt or bribe representatives of the other party, we think that this risk is outweighed by the benefit of giving a public platform to those members of the opposition party to act as whistle-blowers or internal dissenters. We also think that there is considerable symbolic value in a constitutional repudiation of a charismatic populist's claim that his (or her) vision of America is the only valid one: A partisan balance rule for the cabinet appointments from the legislative branch is inconsistent with that sort of exclusionary vision.

This seemingly minor fix would not compromise the separation of powers. The two branches would still need to cooperate to enact laws and treaties, to spend money, and to accomplish other essential government functions. But these separated powers would be conjoined by one bridging institution that is barely mentioned in the Constitution, despite its paramount contemporary importance—the Cabinet. This would strengthen the Executive in ways that enhance political responsiveness.

What Good Are Federal Courts? (And What Good Can They Be?)

The process for selecting federal judges is hard-wired in Article II of the Constitution, and it is telling that few other countries have processes that are so thoroughly political. Nomination by the president, followed by approval after public confirmation hearings in the Senate, means that the formal process is dominated by active politicians. Short of constitutional amendment, the room for institutional fixes is quite small, notwithstanding the scheme's glaring weaknesses. Nevertheless, we think that improvements to both the selection and the performance of federal judges are possible to imagine.

Clearly, American judges serve too long. In most other countries, judges who nominally serve for life are subject to mandatory retirement age, but not in the United States. Of course, life expectancy was lower in the eighteenth century than it is today, so judges would not expect to stay in office for many decades. Countries with constitutional courts typically provide them with terms ranging from nine to fifteen years, long enough to insulate judges from partisan pressures but not so long as to lock in particular positions for long periods.

The effect of lifetime tenure on judicial polarization is indirect. As a result of the high stakes of lifetime appointments, the selection of federal judges has become increasingly partisan rather than bipartisan in character, with widespread stalling of nominations; the elimination of the Senate filibuster, first for lower-court and later for Supreme Court nominees; and finally the allegedly wholesale assignment of selection power to an ideologically motivated outside group under President Trump. The search for ever-younger candidates who can stay in office for many decades means that judges have less experience than they might have in a system of fixed terms, with appointments later in life. This also means that the judges have less detailed public records. As a result, the public has less information on which to base a prediction of future behavior. In addition, the nomination process has become increasingly an arena for heated interest-group activity, which further prompts judges to adopt a partisan perspective once they have been elevated to the bench. Creation of a politically aligned bench may advance immediate ideological goals, but it also undermines the likelihood that the judiciary will resist erosion measures pursued by copartisans. Judges committed to a specific ideology (say, of deregulation and smaller government) may well be inclined to indulge the antidemocratic initiatives of a president who pursues that ideological program. Like legislators, that is, judges may be willing to allow a president to dismantle democratic governance so long as their own policy preferences are furthered.

Worse, the current federal judiciary is asymmetrically biased toward those least likely to carefully scrutinize exercises of state power. Former prosecutors outnumber former public defenders three to one. Whereas four members of the Supreme Court (as of 2018) formerly had prosecutorial experience, the last one to have significant defense-side experience was Thurgood Marshall. (Others, such as Ruth Bader Ginsburg, have significant litigation experience of a different sort). A majority of the current Court also formerly worked in the executive branch; only one worked for Congress. As of 2016, fewer than 4% of federal judges had worked in public-interest organizations (a fact that is especially striking, given the number of exceedingly gifted law students we have seen take that route).[22] Given the concentration of prosecutors and executive-branch officials on the federal bench, it should be no surprise that remedies for violations of the Constitution by prosecutors and executive-branch officials are in a state of general disrepair.[23] And the absence of meaningful remedies for individuals whose constitutional rights are violated by the coercive arms of the state (for example, police, prosecutors, officers of the Department of Homeland Security, and the military) should dispel any claims that former prosecutors are more diligent in policing their former peers than others would be. To the contrary, the current federal judiciary is extraordinarily state-oriented, and has produced a body of doctrine that makes state power very easy to misuse.

What might be done to secure a less ideological and partisan system of federal courts? Although the Constitution speaks to the roles of the president and a Senate majority in nominating and confirming judges, it does not stipulate that these be exclusive. From the mid-1950s until the presidency of George W. Bush, the American Bar Association (ABA) would provide a recommendation about the suitability of all nominees as part of the process. The use of Senate supermajorities was an important institutional guarantee of moderation in appointments, the loss of which of which is deeply regrettable. The filibuster should be restored for all federal judges, but with the understanding from both parties that each can generally make appointments when it is in power.

Moreover, the Senate Judiciary Committee should examine nominations, and in particular slates of nominations, for their effects on professional and ideological diversity. A target of balance among prosecutors, state supreme court judges, trial judges, and defense lawyers would give the federal judiciary far more diversity than it has today. By Senate rule, nominations that increase the judiciary's professional uniformity would be returned to the president's desk. We suspect that a charge to maintain professional diversity of this kind would have beneficial ramifications in regard to other forms of diversity. More ambitiously, we think that professional organizations such as the American Bar Association, or ABA, could once again play a larger role in crafting pools of nominees and in vetting not just the qualifications of particular nominees, but in evaluating the effect of their appointment on the bench as a whole. The ABA is well positioned to play this role: it has generally assessed the nominees of both parties to be well qualified over the past few decades (though in the first year of the Trump administration, its nominees have been found to be "unqualified" at a record rate.)

Second, a Congress concerned with installing a check on erosion could enact jurisdictional statutes that enlist the courts to help in preventing certain discrete elements of such a process. The current judiciary, in our opinion, is excessively disposed to privilege its authority and prestige over its role in the vindication of constitutional rights. But judges might be nudged toward greater protection of democratic institutions. Hence, statutes might assign courts a larger role not only in congressional-executive disputes over information, but also in disputes that implicate the administrative rule of law. At present, court-made doctrine limits litigants' ability to allege partisan (or other forms of) bias among administrators or prosecutors.[24] Congress could direct federal judges to allow controlled discovery and careful exposition of allegations of bias, either in the operation of federal criminal law or regulation. Moreover, the courts could play a larger role in protecting the civil service. In the 1940s, the Court invoked the Bill of Attainder Clause to protect civil servants against ideologically motivated penalties.[25] It could revive and expand that jurisprudence as a basis for a larger degree of civil service protection from congressional measures such as the Holman Rule, the targeted exercise of which would threaten the institutional quality of bureaucratic autonomy and professionalism.

When it comes to ideologically motivated job decisions within the executive branch, however, the Court has moved in the other direction. In a series of cases interpreting the Free Speech Clause of the First Amendment, the Court has expanded the authority of public-sector institutions to punish employees for their speech.[26] We disagree with these decisions. Rather than pressing for their reversal, though, we think it easier for Congress to step into the breach and supply statutory remedies for ideologically motivated personnel decisions. Federal whistle-blower statutes are a good start, but are hardly adequate today.[27] They should be supplemented with more robust statutory protections of job tenure and penalties for officials who misuse bureaucratic resources for partisan ends.

As federal coercive capacity expands in some areas (especially immigration), corresponding checks are becoming more important. But at present there is no federal statute that provides for a damages remedy when a federal official violates a person's constitutional rights. (There is an analogous statute, enacted in 1871, that applies when a state official violates a constitutional right, although the justices have invented several lines of case law that gut this remedy of its potential to check unlawful and abusive state action). The Supreme Court relies on this absence, incorrectly in our view, to dismiss requests for relief from plaintiffs who have suffered gross and substantial physical harms at the hands of federal officers.[28] There are many reasons to fill this shameful gap in federal law, but one of them is the role that a remedy for constitutional torts would play in restraining the kinds of coercion and censorship witnessed in other cases of democratic erosion. Damages remedies are no panacea, especially for a class of noncitizens who are not in a financial or a practical position to sue in many instances. Still, they do provide one mechanism for bringing to light objectionable government behavior and for obtaining legal rulings to the effect that such behavior is unlawful.

One specific area in which a new judicial remedy is warranted concerns government speech. Today, when an official acting in a formal capacity slanders a private citizen—say, by suggesting that he engaged in treasonous activities—there is no remedy. Such accusations, sometimes paired with libel suits against the victims, have contributed to erosion in Turkey and elsewhere. By contrast, if the *New York Times*, *Washington Post*, CNN, Fox News, Breitbart, or even a private citizen campaigning for office utters a slander, the courts stand open. Certainly, remedies are not unlimited. Worried about potentially chilling effects on press, the Supreme Court has rightly erected high hurdles to defamation damages in landmark Free Speech cases such as *New York Times v. Sullivan* and *Gertz v. Robert Welch*.[29] The Constitution itself does not extend any protection from reputational harms, and the relevant federal statutes that do allow for government liability have an exception for intentional torts, such as libel and slander. This omission, however, was never intended to be permanent. Testifying about government tort liability in 1940 before the House of Representatives, Attorney General Alexander Holtzoff accepted the need for such liability, but suggested that Congress should move by increments. Of course, seventy years later, it hasn't taken the first step. A remedy against government defamation, in fact, would be relatively easy to install. Congress should enact a judicial remedy for any person defamed by an official of the federal government speaking or writing to the public. To foreclose the need for burdensome discovery or depositions, liability could turn on whether a reasonable person in the official's position would have known the statement was false. This standard is similar to the "actual malice" used in *Sullivan*; however, it would not hinge on what the official in fact knew, but on what they could have found out.[30]

Finally, Congress has established specialized courts tasked with overseeing different areas of law. For instance, the Federal Circuit Court of Appeals, which sits in the nation's capital, has a prominent role with respect to patent law. Creating a specialized court is a way to nudge the incentives of jurists toward a specific substantive aim. For example, if judges are presently too cautious about vindicating constitutional rights, why not create a special bench expressly tasked with that responsibility and staffed with judges who have prior career experience in the vindication of constitutional rights? This might include not only public defenders but also advocates for specific issues (think again of Thurgood Marshall and Ruth Bader Ginsburg), as well as former officials within the Department of Justice's Civil Rights division. This court would be empowered and oriented toward the vindication of constitutional rights and the protection of democracy. Although some measure of Supreme Court supervision is probably constitutionally required, we note that in other domains, Congress has narrowed Supreme Court supervision to what might be the constitutional minimum, and we think that the same might be done here.[31] The key, though, is to have judges who are specifically tasked with enforcing rights—for example, through the use of professional qualifications geared to a disposition to vindicate the interests of those harmed by the government.

Checking Presidential Administration

Written well before the advent of the modern administrative state, Article II of the Constitution is vague and unrevealing about the structure and functioning of the government today. It contains none of the institutional innovations discussed in earlier chapters. This is a deficiency—evidence once more of the Constitution's age and its corresponding inability to incorporate new learning. Ironically, the minimalist quality of Article II's text has left space for a good deal of creative thinking by constitutional scholars about how the Constitution speaks to executive power. Much of this scholarship, which is avowedly "originalist" in bent, ignores the revolutionary context in which the colonists repudiated royal rule. Instead, it focuses on the first decades of the Republic—after the Constitution's adoption—which marked a period of nation-building and correspondingly ambitious claims about executive power.[32] Political actors, however, are likely to behave quite differently in the run-up to a constitution's adoption and in the first period after that adoption. Because of this, it is relatively easy to cherry-pick the historical record for quite different accounts of the presidency, depending on the felt needs of the historical moment. (The possibility of selection of this sort is but one of the many perils of "originalism" as a method of constitutional interpretation, and one of the reasons we eschew it). Accounts of particular historical debates, moreover, do not advance our understanding of how best to respond to the contemporary challenge of democratic erosion. History furnishes evidence. It doesn't dictate solutions.

More recently, scholars on the left and right have praised what Elena Kagan, before she joined the Supreme Court, called "presidential administration." This involves the White House making the regulatory activity of the executive branch agencies an extension of the president's own policy and political agenda. According to Kagan's influential account, the explicit centralization and politicization of the bureaucracy is justified because it promotes both transparency by "enabling the public to comprehend more accurately the sources and nature of bureaucratic power," and accountability, because "presidential leadership establishes an electoral link between the public and the bureaucracy."[33] Kagan's approach is consistent with a centralizing tendency in the Supreme Court's jurisprudence on executive-branch appointments and removals, as well as with political science literature that emphasizes public assignment of blame and credit to the president, regardless of the actual responsibility.[34] Along with pro-executive readings of the eighteenth-century history, it yields the main intellectual support for judicial acquiescence and support for broad presidential control of the bureaucracy.

When presidential administration provides the dominant framework for viewing executive power, it undermines the idea of independent horizontal protections against erosion. So, unsurprisingly, we are skeptical of its merit. We are not convinced that the democratic legitimacy and transparency gains to be had from presidential administration fully offset the costs it creates through its centralizing and politicizing tendencies. Even if presidential administration might look attractive when a sympathetic president is in the White House, it cannot be evaluated without thinking about the worst-case state of the world—in which a reckless president stands at the helm and seeks to take over the entire system.

Indeed, we think the project of presidential centralization can be abandoned without much harm to the values it seeks to promote.

To be more specific, it is not at all clear that public attributions of responsibility are influenced by the internal organization of the executive branch, and Kagan's work does not identify evidence to suggest as much. We think it is more likely that the public attributes responsibility for new policies to a sitting president without regard to the extent of centralization within the executive. That is, we would predict that the public applies the same notion of accountability to an immigration-related executive order from the White House and a financial directive that emerges from notice-and-comment rule-making within an independent regulatory agency. Even if there was a difference in public perceptions of accountability, we are skeptical that this would make much practical difference. Presidents are responsible for many different policy domains. A small number are consequential and will elicit attributions of presidential responsibility, regardless of policymaking form. Immigration is an especially good example of this during the Obama-Trump era. The overwhelming number of policy decisions, though, simply have no effect on public approval of the president.

On the other side of the ledger, we think that an independent, professional bureaucracy oriented toward advancing policies defined by statute is both inherently valuable and especially important to checking democratic erosion. It is a fallacy to think that merely because administrators are not elected, their presence and their fidelity to professional and institutional norms are somehow antithetical to government. Quite the contrary is true. However beneficial it might be when a president is well-intentioned, presidential administration presents clear risks of partisan policy distortion and politicization of the bureaucracy in ways that are inconsistent with a robust administrative rule of law. This is not lost on the agencies themselves, which take precautions to insulate themselves where possible from presidential control.[35]

Liberals and conservatives alike have been captivated by the prospect of a decisive president capable of slicing through the Gordian knot of partisan disagreement to achieve great things for the people. Whether it is the audacity of hope or the backward-looking call to "Make America great again" that has been invoked, presidents of both parties have claimed that they wanted to improve the performance of the system. Although we agree that deadlock is undesirable—and, indeed, have already suggested some solutions—we do not think that giving up on bureaucratic autonomy is helpful for either party. The independence of the bureaucracy—as much as it is maligned in American political culture more generally—is a crucial component of the rule of law, and thereby an essential element of liberal constitutional democracy. A bureaucracy that is filled with members loyal to political factions—like the patronage-based systems of some developing countries and the early United States—undermines the power of the state to achieve democratically approved programs. Because it functions as the implementing arm of elected actors, the bureaucratic decision about whether to cooperate with a populist program of erosion determines whether such a program can succeed.[36] Increasing political controls over the bureaucracy hence creates considerable downside risks. Programs of erosion can become self-fulfilling: where bureaucrats think they are likely to succeed, they may rush to support the putative autocrat. In contrast, where bureaucrats believe that power will continue to alternate, they are likely to resist efforts to politicize their activities.

We think a number of measures can be taken to reduce the risk of erosion without compromising other structural goals. First, the legal protections of bureaucratic autonomy can be augmented. The United States already has statutory protections for the bureaucracy in terms of some merit-based appointment and statutory bodies, such as the Office of Personnel Management and the Merit Systems Protection Board. In addition, the Hatch Act prevents officials from using their positions to engage in political campaigns while in office.[37] Empirical work by political scientist David Lewis finds that these protections already underpin a bureaucracy that understands itself to be bound by "legal, moral, and professional norms," notwithstanding contrary presidential directives.[38] Ideally, these protections would be constitutionalized. We see little prospect for that now, to be sure. Nevertheless, they should, where possible, be strengthened and not rolled back. Measures such as the deceptively captioned Promote Accountability and Government Efficiency Act, introduced by an Indiana Republican, which would eliminate tenure protections and allow the reproduction of the nineteenth-century spoils system, would increase politicization, make fraud harder to detect, and corrode the quality of government services.[39] A better move would be to *expand* the number of nonpolitical, career positions; strengthen protections for whistle-blowing both internally inside the executive and externally to Congress and the media; and impose mandatory qualifications on political appointments related to the skills and knowledge necessary to the relevant agency's mission.[40] In addition to limiting White House control of personnel, the Holman Rule should also be abandoned as inconsistent with sound government under the rule of law.

Second, federal statutes create several governmental offices that play an ombudsman-like role of identifying fraud, abuse, or criminality and acting upon it. These include the Office of Government Ethics, the Government Accountability Office, and the several Inspectors General who sit in many government departments and agencies pursuant to a 1978 statutory reform.

Privacy offices in the Department of Homeland Security and the Department of State, among other agencies, are supposed to monitor the intrusiveness of their home agency's actions. Under President Obama, moreover, new offices of civil rights and civil liberties were installed in national security agencies such as the National Security Agency and the Department of Homeland Security.[41] These offices provide neutral assessments and investigations of corruption, mismanagement, rights violations, and ethical breaches. While these systems have fallen short at times—in particular on national security matters, where congressional and ad hoc investigations have taken up some of the slack—they nonetheless provide the kernel of an effective accountability system for all but the top echelons of the federal government.

Nevertheless, all of these institutional mechanisms of horizontal accountability could be considerably strengthened through increased powers, greater funding, and a measure of autonomy from political control. Because these institutions are diverse, we offer a series of illustrations, focused on the Office of Government Ethics and the Inspector General system as starting points for reform. The former head of the Office of Government Ethics, Walter Shaub, has argued that the office requires additional authority to obtain information from the White House, and further authority to communicate directly with Congress on budgetary and legislative matters. Having grappled with the Trump White House's reported tangle of ethical conflicts, Shaub persuasively contends that it is not only these new authorities that are needed now, but also additional laws imposing ethical rules on presidents respecting financial and familial conflicts of interest.[42]

The Inspector General system also has important gaps that could be addressed by statute. At present, numerous departmental heads, including the attorney general and the treasury secretary, have broad authority simply to shut down Inspector General investigations. Other departmental heads have broad authority to preclude investigations merely by citing a risk that information related to national security will be disclosed. These limitations are unwarranted. There is no reason, for example, why national security information cannot be appropriately handled by an internal investigation, and no reason that Inspector General reports cannot be published in redacted form without compromising matters that genuinely require secrecy. More generally, Inspector General investigations should be backed by greater formal powers to elicit information and, if necessary, to force the declassification of such information, in addition to a more robust and predictable stream of funding than is presently the case. Finally, privacy and civil liberties offices within agencies and departments could be placed on a firmer statutory footing, given formal investigation powers, and even permitted to seek relief in court on behalf of aggrieved persons both inside and outside the government. Many of the objections lodged when the victims of misfired counterterrorism sue would lose their force if these victims could claim an institutional sponsor when seeking relief from a court.

Third, these reforms do not address malfeasance or law-breaking at higher levels of office, including the Presidency. Such investigations are typically managed at the moment by the Department of Justice. It is headed by the attorney general, who is a direct appointee of the president. Where high-level malfeasance is suspected, federal regulations permit the attorney general, or a person acting in his stead, to appoint a "special prosecutor" or "special counsel" to pursue a criminal investigations and potentially issue indictments, when it is "warranted" and "in the public interest." The special counsel can only be fired by the attorney general and can only pursue criminal investigations within a mandate defined, again, by the attorney general. Once an investigation ends, the special counsel must file a confidential report with the attorney general, although it is at least arguable that the special counsel also has authority to make public her findings through a formal "presentment" to the grand jury. An indictment listing both those against whom charges have been filed and those who remain unindicted accomplices or coconspirators is also within the special counsel's powers.[43] Reasonable legal analysts disagree as to whether the special counsel has authority to indict a sitting president, given current legal rules. Deputy Attorney General Rod J. Rosenstein appointed former FBI director Robert Mueller in May 2017 to oversee an investigation, ongoing at this writing, into the Trump campaign's potential contacts with Russia.[44] However high the indictments reach, that investigation is an important check on law violations by powerful political actors.

Special counsels, however, have neither statutory nor constitutional protection from termination. The relevant regulations stipulate that the attorney general needs "good cause" to fire a special counsel. But this is a very elastic standard.[45] In practice, we think it is rather the anticipation of political costs that prevents a president from coaxing an attorney general into getting rid of a special counsel, either by firing that person or by repealing the relevant authorizing regulation (a move that would not require a showing, even notionally, of good cause). In this regard, they are quite unlike the "independent counsel" office created under Title VI of the 1978 Ethics in Government Act, which lapsed in 1999. The independent counsel had power to investigate and prosecute high-level misconduct, and was statutorily insulated from termination except for "good cause." It did so in more than fifteen cases. Despite a record of successful investigations, the idea of an independent counsel was heavily criticized, both on constitutional grounds, and also for enabling open-ended, and arguably politicized, investigations of sitting presidents, with Kenneth Starr's sprawling Whitewater investigation being the leading example. Congress, with Starr's express support, allowed the provision to lapse.

We think Congress erred. The constitutional criticism is based on a theory of the "unitary executive" that we reject. The politicization criticism, by contrast, conflates the pathological misuse of the Act (the Whitewater investigation) with its modal deployment. It assumes the fault is with the independent counsel's powers as opposed to the dubious choice of counsel made by the initial body of appointing judges in the Whitewater case, and the dubious exercise of prosecutorial discretion by one wayward official. As an early and important piece of scholarship by Ken Gormley demonstrated, there are numerous ways of narrowing or tweaking the Ethics in Government Act to deal with the problem of truly runaway prosecutors.[46] Indeed, as David Strauss has pointed out, merely "insisting that executive officials operate within, not outside, a bureaucracy" might be sufficient to create horizontal checks on abusive investigations to assuage earlier concerns.[47] What we have done is to repudiate the whole enterprise of independent investigations of high-level misconduct instead of reforming it, the proverbial tossing out of the baby with the bathwater. It is high time that a more robust statute enabling investigations into high-level wrongdoing be installed, so that if and when they are needed, the relevant mechanisms will be already in place.

Fourth, and finally, there is the problem of political influence over prosecutions and related investigative activities. Consider the case of criminal prosecutions. Federal statutes currently provide that "the conduct of litigation in which the United States is a party is reserved to officers of the Department of Justice, under the direction of the Attorney General," but leave the operationalizing of this command to elected actors and their delegates.[48] As a result, conventions and norms, not regulations or statutes, control the White House's communication with prosecutors in the Justice Department, to address the risk that specific criminal investigations or civil matters might become politicized. Hence, under a 2007 memo issued by then–Attorney General Michael Mukasey, communications between the White House and the Justice Department concerning ongoing cases, investigations, or adjudicative matters could take place only when necessary for the discharge of the president's constitutional duties and, if appropriate, from a law enforcement perspective.[49] This is all well and good. But political conventions and memos lack the force of law. As the first few months of the Trump Administration demonstrate, they can be flicked aside given sufficient disregard for the neutral administration of justice or the appearance thereof. The firing of FBI Director James Comey simply served as a graphic illustration of how presidential control over personnel—prized by both

the unitary executive theorists and by presidential administration advocates—
could be directly employed in an attempt to stymie lawful and proper criminal
investigations that touch on either the president or his close associates.[50]

In the first year of the Trump Administration, some commentators underscored the strength of professionalism and conventions of legality—often on
the basis of their own experience within the Justice Department. We do not
doubt the veracity of their observations, but we are skeptical that their confidence can be extended forward to periods of concerted democratic erosion.
Although as a matter of tradition, Justice Department lawyers have maintained
a sense of fidelity to the law over political direction, there is no structural reason that this norm could not be undermined through the appointment of an
aggressively partisan attorney general with personal loyalty to the president.
Indeed, to the extent that a president runs as a charismatic populist and rails
against existing elites, we think it is quite possible for him to target overtly the
conventions of Justice Department integrity and to make the politicizing capture of that department a central plank of his political agenda. We therefore
think statutory reform is needed to insulate the prosecutorial function from
White House communications and influence, except in the exceptional circumstances like those anticipated by the Mukasey memorandum. The Comey
firing merely underscores the importance of an independent structure in the
Justice Department to investigate high-level criminality, free of White House
interference. Of course, there would have to be mechanisms in place to prevent
this from institutionalizing witch-hunts, but as noted we think this is a distinctly second-order problem at present.

All this makes for a daunting reform agenda. But it is worth emphasizing
that our list of reforms here is not complete: we anticipate that future forms
of misconduct will reveal the need for additional safeguards. Moreover, none
of our suggestions will be foolproof. Most importantly, institutions of horizontal accountability can themselves become corrupted and politicized as a
result of sustained assault from corrupt officials. Indonesia's powerful counter-
corruption commission, for example, developed an early reputation as a highly
successful institution, prosecuting myriad cases in a context where corruption
had been endemic and unavoidable.[51] In 2012, though, the commission's standing was badly damaged when its own chairman was found to have been taking
bribes. This sort of self-inflicted wound can happen in any system, and indeed,
some might view the Whitewater investigation as an example. Nevertheless,
the lesson of recent constitutional design innovations is that dispersing power
minimizes the probability of significant harm, because other institutions can
guard the guardians. There is no guarantee that any individual institution will
be immune from capture—just the possibility that a plurality of several such

institutions will be harder to subdue than a single one. This is the major insight of Madison for the twenty-first century.

The American Public Sphere

A classic view of democracy is of political parties competing in the public sphere for votes among an informed electorate. This idealized view of democracy does not describe the contemporary United States. Liberals and conservatives are increasingly divided in values and beliefs—with the exception of their shared fear and distrust of each other. The common ground of shared, publicly agreed-upon facts is under threat across several fronts. One relates to the trustworthiness of news sources. Candidate and President Trump has fiercely and consistently attacked the integrity and veracity of news sources such as the *New York Times*, *Washington Post*, and CNN that report critically on him, while he has embraced websites such as Breitbart and Infowars that have a consistent track record of false reporting.[52] Trump's view of "mainstream" news sources as full of "fake news" is now shared by almost two-thirds of the public.[53] It is no coincidence that this position has been pushed by news sources that are seeking to compete with the traditional media, often by offering false stories that appeal by pandering to prejudices and paranoias.

It is easy to see how these beliefs can facilitate democratic erosion. Imagine, for instance, that the government starts a program of investigating and prosecuting political enemies, or installs a policy restricting the movement of people based on their religion, race, or ethnicity. Even if facts about such a policy were known, would the truth or falsity of purported explanations for such policies be widely disseminated and credited? A world in which established media are distrusted is a world in which coercion and democratic erosion are far easier to achieve.

To put our cards on the table, our view is that media such as the *New York Times*, the *Wall Street Journal*, and CNN, while far from perfect, do try to follow a code of journalistic ethics that prioritizes factual accuracy and the suppression of bias. We think that Breitbart and its ilk do not. Any outlet that self-consciously characterizes its enterprise as "war" is by definition not aspiring to journalistic integrity. When President Trump attacks the media in an undifferentiated way in the service of partisan advantage, he is trashing the possibility of shared epistemic premises for democracy. Those who attack the mainstream sources as "fake" typically can identify only minor errors of fact, which are later subject to correction by the sources themselves. The attackers' main concern seems to be to try to shift the mainstream news in their partisan direction, an attempt to "work the referee" of democracy, like a complaining coach in a college sports game.

While many eroding democracies have witnessed the aggressive use of libel laws or NGO regulation, the United States has not to date seen either of these forms of suppression, or more overt forms of censorship and suppression. The First Amendment, as interpreted by the courts now, seems to take these tools off the table. The country still has a vigorous press and a lively associational life that generally seems inclined to stand up to direct attacks by the state. Nevertheless, we think that one of the most serious threats to constitutional democracy in the United States derives from a steady degradation of its public sphere, and in particular the disappearance of a shared universe of facts about which policy debate can occur. To be clear, this erosion of the shared epistemic premises of democracy is partially due to the behavior of political figures such as President Trump, who find misrepresentation or outright lies quick to the tongue, and who exhibit varying degrees of contempt for the news media. Nevertheless, we think the fragility of democracy's epistemic premises runs deeper and relates to the larger trends of partisan polarization and residential sorting by ideological beliefs that the United States has been experiencing for some years now.

In contrast, we are fortunate in the United States to have a network of university-based researchers and private foundations that can support the gathering of facts. While there is surely a need for government to continue to produce a wide array of economic and scientific data, our research institutions have the capacity to supplement and in some cases substitute for official efforts. This may become especially important if government information becomes politicized by partisan agents of erosion. Of course, the vitality of the research infrastructure itself requires government investment, and hence is subject to some of the same pressures.

A related element of the factual foundation of the public sphere that has deteriorated is the diminished public standing of science as a source of trustworthy knowledge. Consider two recent findings from polling (which, we hasten to add, is as much an art as it is a science!). In 2016, a poll showed that a majority of self-described conservative Republicans believed that climate scientists' findings concerning global warming are motivated by their own political leanings, and a desire to advance their careers.[54] These respondents therefore do not really believe that science is a neutral enterprise devoted to truth-finding (and yet are happy to take medicines that have been subject to scientific testing, and to listen to doctors who employ the same scientific method). Lest you think that this disregard of basic science is a partisan phenomenon, consider that Democrats are almost twice as likely as Republicans to believe that the basic childhood vaccine for measles, mumps, and rubella is unsafe.[55] Liberals, no less than conservatives, have their convenient (and sometimes dumb) beliefs too.

To date, neither distrust of science nor reliance on junk science has seeped into the law—but even here there are worrying signs. For example, in upholding a controversial restriction on abortions, Justice Kennedy recently relied on a body of controversial (and, in our view, misleading) scientific studies about women's regret after terminating a pregnancy.[56] Proposals to allow administrative agencies to rely on political justifications rather than empirical data, by contrast, have yet to gain traction.[57] But the fracturing of democracy's epistemic ground presents a serious problem. Indeed, there is some evidence that once a false belief (say, in the connection between vaccines and autism) is assimilated, people respond to new falsifying information by switching from factual to normative grounds for their position.[58]

How might we start to go about responding to these deeply worrying trends? We concede up front that this is an enormous task of civic education, implicating the entire system of institutions of learning.[59] Our proposals focus on the top line of constitutional and institutional design, since we cannot flesh out a more general program here. But our suggestions are offered in the spirit of recognizing the need for such a larger program.

To begin with, we should rethink the role of the First Amendment. In a recent set of lectures criticizing the Supreme Court's campaign finance decision in *Citizens United v. Federal Elections Commission*, Robert Post develops the important point that First Amendment protections cannot be understood outside the context of the government institutions—such as legislatures, elections, and courts—that those rights are supposed to enable. In the institutional context of elections, Post observes, government necessarily has a large managerial role in relation to private speech, including decisions about who gets to appeal to voters by appearing on the ballot. In other contexts in which the state assumes a managerial role to achieve democratic ends—the legislature, the courtroom, and the schoolhouse, for example—the First Amendment plainly allows speech to be regulated with the aim of furthering the democratic function of the institution. Elections, he posits, are no different, and speech regulations must be understood as functions of the underlying aim of election integrity and management.[60] Although Post focuses on the regulation of campaign expenditures by corporate entities, his analytic framework extends to the issues that interest us. Elections require vigorous and adversarial speech, but are distorted by the absence of shared epistemic premises, just as they are distorted by speech that intimidates or that threatens violence.

In a world without political constraints, and where the federal government was already working well, we would counsel for an independent entity capable of promoting a shared epistemic basis for elections and of maintaining the channels of political contestation free of explicit and implicit violence. Such an institution would monitor and restrict candidates' and officials' attacks on the press, while working to promote a culture of journalistic integrity. That body might also focus on appropriate penalties for institutions that purposefully disseminate false news, perhaps in collaboration with a foreign government, intending to distort the electoral process.

At present, we see no prospect that such an institution could be adopted or would work free of political capture even if it were to be adopted. Hence, we do not recommend the creation of an independent body analogous to ones observed in other nations' constitutions to serve these ends. As a lesser ambition, we think that there may well a much greater role for informational intermediaries such as Facebook, Twitter, and Google to play in crafting platforms that limit, rather than enable, the dissemination of false news. Research into how they might do so without overbroad regulation remains in its infancy. And the impact of such policies on undemocratic regimes' efforts to suppress speech, such as those increasingly pursued by China, must also be carefully considered.[61] We should learn from the efforts of other states, such as Germany, which are more actively grappling with the problem, without assuming that solutions are either nonexistent or straightforward. The lesson of these tentative measures may be that the regulatory tools simply do not exist or that private forms of regulation work better. Assuming an answer to that hard problem in advance of a careful learning process, however, would be a mistake.

Second, we think there are potential solutions to the erosion of scientific authority. Consider, for example, a high-level commission, not directed at specific policies such as climate change, but focused on the *idea* of science and neutral and provisional methods of fact-finding as the basis of policymaking. (Call it "Make American Science Great Again"). This body, comprised of experts and political leaders from both sides of the aisle and tasked to explore the role that science already plays—in the technologies we adopt and the medicines we take—and to reaffirm the idea that both public policy and informed scientific progress are based on verifiable and transparent evidence and procedures, would have important consequences. This body would reaffirm what Karl Popper noted several decades ago—that the scientific method, based on provisional knowledge developed using open and transparent methodologies, has significant social and political value.[62]

A mind open to scientific progress is also one that is open to new political information. This attitude is liberal in its classical sense and is still embodied in the First Amendment's protection of speech. This constitutional provision is radical in its epistemic openness and its tolerance of the harms that speech can inflict, and it is a genuine mark of American exceptionalism. We recognize that such an effort would presently run up against powerful headwinds in the form of industrial interest groups that are specifically opposed to the dissemination of climate science. But we think that meeting this effort by embracing science and its self-correcting methods is far better than defeatism.

A related set of solutions emphasizes the defense of the values of civility and citizenship within the public sphere. The era of the twenty-four-hour news cycle, continuous political campaigning, and endless background noise seems to be incompatible with idealized notions of civic engagement by a politically informed electorate. Who can pay attention to the constant drumbeat of information? The demands of citizenship now are higher than ever, even as our attention to civics is declining. Incentivizing civic knowledge and civil debate is a task that can engage educational institutions, governments, foundations, and churches—a worthy national project for a divided society. There are some heinous and hateful views that have no place in a decent democratic society—and as such are worthy of neither respect or consideration—but we think that both sides of the political aisle have far to go in their efforts to understand the concerns and priorities of those on the other side of the partisan divide.

None of this will be easy, or even sufficient, in the absence of broader cultural change. The difficulty is hardwired into American constitutional culture. The First Amendment provides a powerful hook for the idea of the open society, even as it may contribute to the undermining of that very openness by facilitating a din of false and hateful views. Americans' support for the First Amendment remains strong (although it must be said that some 39% of Americans cannot name any of its freedoms).[63] While the First Amendment embodies the open society, it also stands for the idea that government cannot step in to prevent the development of a public culture in which the enemies of democracy and its epistemic predicates prevail. The institution-focused analysis offered by Post offers a way to reconcile these tensions. But it is not currently the law. Even if it were the law, it seems fair to say that the charismatic populists in the White House do not tend to have a great fondness for factual accuracy. As a result, the paradox of the First Amendment—which is also the paradox of liberal constitutional democracy more broadly—will continue to bedevil us.

The states, too, remain an important safeguard for American democracy, even if we are skeptical that, in the abstract, federalism is always a positive force. At a time when the public sphere and neutral forms of information have been subject to increasing politicization, states can serve as an important locus of data collection. Organizations such as the national associations of attorneys general, the governors' associations, and networks of state bureaucracy can speak out against efforts to overly politicize neutral administration. They deserve institutional protection and popular recognition of the fact that, in the face of any attempt to take over the system, a plurality of official sources of information can get us closer to the truth than any single source. Pluralism—of institutions, of information, and of ideas—is the heart of the American system of government, and will be what saves us if a threat materializes.

Possible Futures

Declines in the quality of liberal constitutional democracy are neither unidirectional nor permanent. The United States has suffered backsliding before. After the Civil War, a period of relative democratic openness in the South collapsed into a regional authoritarianism built upon explicit principles of racial hierarchy. This subnational regime lasted more than a half-century, but it too ultimately crumbled. Just as there is no reason to think that America cannot experience erosion again, so there is no reason to think that it lacks the tools to combat it. We have surveyed some of the tools available at the constitutional and legal design level. But instruments do not wield themselves. Political will and public mobilization behind democracy is also needed. The mobilization required to reverse the direction of change is costly, however, and especially challenging in an era of epistemic fractionalization. And it is as easy today to imagine sustained erosion as it is a more contested period of respectful give and take.

On Fighting Democratic Erosion

You may never know what results come of your actions, but if you do nothing, there will be no results.

MAHATMA GANDHI

The greatest danger the tyrant can inflict is to limit us to his range of options, not only for how to live, but also for how to exercise our options.

HISHAM MATAR

There is a story—probably apocryphal, but still enlightening—that Benjamin Franklin, upon leaving the Philadelphia Convention and being asked what it had done, explained its product as "a republic, if you can keep it."[1] This phrase is rather well worn, but not often fully explored or understood.[2] It has became a slogan rather than a piece of practical wisdom. Having investigated the institutional means through which liberal constitutional democracy is both attacked and defended, we turn in our conclusion to the puzzle concealed in Franklin's aphorism: What does it mean for the *participants in a democracy*—and notice that we avoid the loaded and hazardously totalizing term *the People*—to "keep" their political system intact? How, in practice, does one resist democratic erosion?

The problem is not a new one. Indeed, it has a Biblical precedent of sorts. In the Book of Samuel, the titular prophet, now aging and ailing, hands judicial authority to his two sons. Alas, they turn out to be ineffective and corrupt. The leaders of the people then approach Samuel, demanding a king to replace the judges that had ruled for centuries. Samuel warns them that this demand is short-sighted, in terms as resonant as Franklin's:

This is what the king who will reign over you will claim as his rights: He will take your sons and make them serve with his chariots and horses, and they will run in front of his chariots. Some he will assign to be commanders of thousands and commanders of fifties, and others to plow his ground and reap his harvest, and still others to make weapons of war and equipment for his chariots. He will take your daughters to be perfumers and cooks and bakers. He will take the best of your fields and vineyards and olive groves and give them to his attendants. He will take a tenth of your grain and of your vintage and give it to his officials and attendants. Your male and female servants and the best of your cattle and donkeys he will take for his own use. He will take a tenth of your flocks, and you yourselves will become his slaves. When that day comes, you will cry out for relief from the king you have chosen, but the LORD will not answer you in that day.[3]

This being a Biblical tale designed to instill good sense, the people of Israel choose to ignore the prophet's advice. Instead, they persist in demanding a strongman. "No!" they tell the dismayed leader, "We want a king over us. Then we will be like all the other nations, with a king to lead us and to go out before us and fight our battles."[4] In a tough world of powerful enemies, their leaders say, why should they have to be burdened by the special status that is their birthright? Frustrated by their short-sightedness, Samuel then asks God for advice and the Almighty tells him to listen to the people. Shortly thereafter, Samuel anoints Saul as the first king. The Jewish kingdom is initially successful under Saul and his successors, David and Solomon, but it then splits into two kingdoms. The remaining kings of the Jewish people are mostly mediocrities who have not been popular among the baby-naming set for the last few millennia. Their collective reign ends with the Babylonian invasion and sacking of Jerusalem in the sixth century BCE, when Samuel's prophecy ultimately comes to pass.

Franklin's and Samuel's warnings ought to be taken seriously. The risk to our republic is not in the particular ebb and flow of policy fights over abortion, national defense, or health policy. Nor are we concerned here with the particular hour-to-hour output of the president's Twitter feed. Instead, our concerns are more structural. We have argued that liberal constitutional democracy is a system that involves three discrete and mutually reinforcing elements, each of which must be safeguarded: electoral competition, associational and speech rights, and the rule of law, understood not so much as the supremacy of judges as the broader ideas of bureaucratic autonomy and rule-following. Our definition emphasizes the legal and institutional underpinnings of effective political competition. But it is also a "thin" definition compatible with a range of policy choices. We do not reject neoliberalism, socialism, or religious entanglements as inherently undemocratic, so long as the three core elements are utilized in determining the commitments of a polity.

The extent of the democratic decline in our current moment is open to much debate. We recognize that some concerns may seem overblown. In particular, in tracing two pathways away from democracy, we do not see much reason to fear the fast track of a military coup or a violent revolution in the United States, or any of the world's rich democracies for that matter.

At the same time, we see a real risk of what we have called democratic erosion, the slow and incremental path by which the core structures of democratic self-rule are eroded piecemeal. We observe, in several established democracies, attacks on associational freedoms and speech rights. Electoral participation is under threat, not just from indifference on the part of the population, but from sustained attempts by dominant political parties to disenfranchise. At the same time, populist forces demonize their opponents and both racial and religious minorities (especially Muslims and Jews), using rhetoric that harkens back to a much darker era. In the United States, this has been accompanied by a rhetorical attack from populist politicians against the very idea of government, even as those very leaders court interest groups that seek to manipulate state power for private gain.

The playbook for erosion has many chapters. It gives options rather than singular directives. There is no universal or ordained sequence of steps. In some countries, putative leaders start by consolidating media power in their hands even before they have been elected to office. In other contexts, they begin by launching an attack on independent courts and by rejiggering the machinery of electoral choice. Libel laws, calls for restrictions on assembly, and the bullying of journalists often play a role. Finding an enemy, preferably one that is swarthy or cosmopolitan, to demonize is useful as a distraction and a means of mobilization of the political base. Further, degrading the capacity of both the state and the society to generate independent information facilitates all the other steps.

While readers will note that all of these things have been proposed in the United States in recent months, our concern is not directly or solely focused upon President Trump. Rather, imagine a future leader who combines Trump's style of political communication with the ability of, say, a Lyndon Johnson to exploit skillfully the American machinery of government, and the long-term ambitions and tactical sophistication of a Vladimir Putin. Note too that many of the characters we have encountered in this book, including Putin, Viktor Orbán, and Polish leader Jarosław Kaczyński, have legal training, and benefit from cohorts of Ivy League–trained assistants. If such a person were to emerge in American politics in the coming decades, would our democracy survive?

We have argued that the United States Constitution, ordinarily venerated as a safeguard of our liberties, would do little in practice to protect us in such an event. Textually, the document lacks many of the features of modern constitutions, owing to its age and the circumstances of its adoption. Its structural rigidity—often characterized as the world's most difficult constitution to amend—has had the unforeseen consequence of empowering the Supreme Court to fill in some details and to try to keep the system up to date in some ways. But many of the doctrines the Court has developed have the effect of facilitating rather than inhibiting rights infringements. And the Court's record in keeping up with changing insights into effective democratic government, to say nothing of racial justice, has been at best spotty. Even the bright spots in constitutional doctrine—the First Amendment for example—may have perverse consequences in the hands of a sophisticated communicator, who can degrade the public sphere and wield hateful language that would be banned in many other democracies.

Democratic erosion is a distinct threat that poses particular challenges to our usual way of thinking about constitutional design. The emergency clauses are perhaps not as important as more structural provisions that limit executive overreach and the danger of takeover by an incumbent who refuses to leave. But while we have surveyed other possible designs and think that savvy institutional engineering is important, we also recognize that in the end, constitutions cannot save democracy: Only (small *d*) democrats can.

In the remainder of this conclusion, we aim to be a bit more helpful than Franklin and Samuel by pointing to ways in which social action and political mobilization can counter democratic erosion, especially in the United States. Again, we do not focus on collapse, because it is the less significant risk. We instead organize our discussion around three necessary elements of political action—the national political parties, the engaged and political public, and the courts.

We begin with the main political parties. The United States has two political parties that, by and large, remain committed to democratic politics, not simply to the permanent and entrenched capture of governmental power. Whether or not Karl Rove ever really harkened forward to a "permanent Republican majority," we do not think he meant the end of democratic competition. Rather, he hoped for a sustained political coalition that would endure through several election campaigns.

Still, as we have already discussed, there are reasons for concern. In some regards, the basis for worry is mutual: Both Republicans and Democrats now view their political opponents with both fear and anger. Both folded in populist movements in the last presidential election cycle. Both are responding to the way in which trust in government has been declining among Americans of all stripes, in increasingly partisan ways. In the eight years of George W. Bush's presidency, 47% of Republicans, on average, said they could trust the federal government just about always or most of the time. During Obama's presidency, however, average trust among Republicans fell to 13%, by far the lowest level of average trust among either party during any administration dating back to the 1960s.[5] The comparable figures among Democrats were 29% during Obama's presidency and 28% during George W. Bush's administration—a negligible partisan difference. But under Trump, Democrats are mimicking the partisan response of Republicans under Obama. A 2017 poll showed that, for the first time in decades, Republicans (28%) are now more likely than Democrats (15%) to trust the government.[6]

While both parties have exhibited antisystem impulses in recent decades, pressures for erosion have not been evenly distributed. It is the Republican Party that set itself the goal of defeating any and all of President Obama's policies in 2008, and in the course of endeavoring to do so turned the debt ceiling into a partisan free-for-all before engaging in an unprecedented refusal to even consider a nomination to the Supreme Court.[7] In addition, the Republican Party has also been running a sustained antigovernment campaign for many decades that has corroded confidence in the basic institutions of American government. President Trump's call for a shutdown of the very government he leads marked a new and distinctive interpretation of the presidential obligation to faithfully execute the laws. And in an August 2017 poll, more than half of Republican-leaning respondents said they would support efforts to postpone the 2020 election if Donald Trump said it was necessary to ensure that only eligible voters could participate.[8] The Republican Party, moreover, may be facing an increasingly hostile demographic reality in which younger cohorts do not respond to its appeal, and where increasingly racial diversity also limits its reach. Catastrophic alarmism as a means to preserve an eroding electoral base may well flow from these constraints. But it can hardly be embraced as good for democracy on the ground that it is instrumentally rational for one party at one moment in historical time.

We do not reject the possibility that the Republican Party could, as an institutional matter, defect from the historical consensus of support for the democratic system in favor of a process of partisan degradation covered by charismatic populism. The local Republican reaction to a gubernatorial defeat in 2016, recounted in chapter 5, illustrates how this might unfold. In response to Roy Cooper's narrow win in North Carolina, the Republican legislature attempted to redefine the governor's powers by removing the authority to appoint trustees of the state university, eliminating four-fifths of the office's staff, extending the term of the Republican director of the state elections board, and requiring cabinet appointments to be approved by the state Senate.[9] Some of these tactics were eventually rejected by the State Supreme Court, but this too has become a partisan battleground. Whether or not efforts at partisan degradation of the kind observed in North Carolina spread across the nation depends, in some measure, on the pressure placed on the party by a charismatic populist president, whether Trump or someone else (for there is no reason to think that charismatic populism, once demonstrably

CONCLUSION

successful, will pass silently into history), and on the response of party elites. In no small measure, therefore, it is quite possible that the maintenance of democracy could ultimately turn not only on structural factors or institutions, but also on the unpredictable decisions of a small number of elite political actors. Put otherwise, laws and institutions are tools. And the effects of tools depend on the motives and good-faith of those who wield them.

When partisan agendas overwhelm commitment to the institutional predicates of democratic competition—where, in effect, one party becomes an antisystem force—erosion becomes substantially more likely. Under what circumstances do political actors maintain fidelity to democratic politics, rather than seek to entrench themselves into permanent power? Norms of reciprocity are likely to do some work, but their persistence must also be explained. One possibility is that the political actors fear that they will be punished at the next elections should they violate the constitutional norms of democracy. Arguments of this kind about the robustness of constitutional protections ultimately fall back upon claims about the public at large.[10] They provide a theoretically robust basis for claiming that, without public acceptance and support, a democratic constitution is merely a piece of paper.

On this point, the evidence is mixed. As we have seen, public faith in democratic institutions has been damaged incalculably in recent years. But it is striking that when asked about specific government programs and policies, Americans' attitudes are much more positive. However much they dislike and distrust the government in the abstract, the actual operation of government seems to please them. The rising distrust in government is not only a result of sustained campaigns to discredit government by interest groups and politicians; it is also the fault of governments that have done far too little to "market" themselves to their customers. Yet another paradox of public opinion in the United States is that while constitutional veneration may be high, popular constitutional knowledge remains exceedingly poor.[11] In a recent poll, for example, only a quarter of Americans could name all three branches of government. A third could name none at all.[12] This is consistent with decades of findings on Americans' political knowledge generally: compared with citizens of other industrialized democracies, Americans rank near the bottom.[13]

Erosion presents a distinctive and difficult challenge under these circumstances. Even if popular knowledge of the Constitution were to be improved, popular constitutional enforcement requires the kind of mass agreement on violations that is difficult to obtain, especially under today's precarious and polarized political conditions. Given the availability of piecemeal, incrementalist pathways to weakened democratic structures, the public predictably lacks obvious threshold moments or focal points around which to mobilize.

This absence of legal safeguards, coupled with the difficulty of pro-democracy mobilization, suggests that seemingly excessive concern about erosion away from democratic practices is sensible at the current moment. Indeed, such concerns might help to facilitate the mobilization that is our democratic order's principal safeguard.

Here, there is some room for optimism. While Americans know little about the Constitution or their institutions, there are other ways in which we are remarkably politically engaged. The World Values Survey, for example, reports that more than 60% of Americans have signed a petition, as compared with 18% on average for all countries surveyed.[14] Only Australia, New Zealand, and Sweden score higher. Some 15% of Americans have joined a boycott; only those in Sweden and India score higher.[15] Other forms of political action are less popular, however: only 13.7% of Americans claim to have participated in a peaceful demonstration, just above the global average of 12.2%, and only 7.4% have participated in a strike, which is close to the global average of 7.7%. When asked about engaging in other forms of protest, Americans are more positive than any other people—fully 57.5% say they might do so, though only 5.6% actually have. In the event of serious threats of erosion, closing the gap between Americans' understanding of their abilities to engage in political action and their actual behavior will be critical.

Moreover, popular mobilization in defense of democratic values works. Important empirical work by Maria Stephan and Erica Chenoweth has demonstrated that organized, nonviolent protests, such as boycotts, strikes, protests, and organized noncooperation, can elicit concessions from otherwise unresponsive regimes. Equally insightful scholarship by Zeynep Tufekci has explored the way in which ad hoc movements enabled by social media have developed predictable strengths and weaknesses. She has drawn attention in particular to the way in which such movements can fail to develop resilient, collective decision-making capabilities that enable them to adapt to shifting circumstances.[16] But there are some cases in which particular protest movements have slowed erosive moves. In Poland, for example, the Justice and Development Party's proposed evisceration of judicial independence provoked massive street protests that in turn seem to have influenced the president's decision to veto some of those measures.[17] Political activism channeled into public protests, at least in that instance, worked for the moment.

This is not to say, though, that protest will always be the most effective means of responding to erosion. It may be in many instances that the best response to erosion is not a show of popular force but a conscious and careful effort to reach across a political divide to find common cause with those who might otherwise support a charismatic populist or a process of partisan degradation. In the United States, for example, imagine that campus activists angry at the policies of the Trump Administration eschewed violent protests targeting conservative speakers and instead organized a series of caravans to southern and Midwestern states where Trump gained a good deal of support. Such caravans would focus on reaching out to communities and individuals who perceive themselves as disrespected and disregarded by perceived coastal elites. It would aim to explore the common humanity of individuals, regardless of race or deeply held faith. A positive effort to reach out and engage fellow citizens, despite fear and anger, might do far more than yet another rally on a liberal college campus. Certainly, it would be more productive than self-defeating efforts at censoring legitimate policy debates.

Complementing Stephan and Chenoweth's findings, the political scientists Christian Welzel and Ronald Inglehart have demonstrated that beliefs that are diffused widely within a society, and that vary between national contexts, do influence both the emergence and survival of democracy. Their work underscores the role of "emancipatory orientations," which tap into aspirations for liberty, tolerance of nonconformity, trust in people, and self-esteem in predicting prodemocratic action and, in the long term, democratic survival.[18] Such orientations, and their public expression, are especially consequential when a populist leader or movement seeks to blame a racial or religious minority (be it Muslims, Jews, Kurds, or immigrants generally) for socioeconomic travails. At these moments, the public commitment to a very basic recognition of shared humanity across racial and religious barriers is being sorely tested. It is also sorely needed. There is some evidence today that norms of racial tolerance in particular are flagging, with an increasing share of voters being open to explicitly racist appeals by politicians.[19] As a result, there is a large question now of how prosocial and prodemocratic values can be cultivated or reinvigorated across the political aisle. This question is especially pressing at a moment when many Republicans and Democrats feel their prospects and values to be profoundly threatened, whether by gay marriage or by climate change, whether by affirmative action or by a rise of neo-Nazism. Again, we suspect that there is no complete substitute for the hard work of organizing, outreach, and coalition building. Electoral mobilization remains the primary and most important channel of public participation in the United States and other democracies. It is hard work—harder than litigating or invoking constitutional rights.[20]

We have focused in this book on constitutional and legal questions, in part because we think they are consequential yet poorly understood, and in part because we are legal scholars. Hence, it is appropriate here to say a word about how our concept of liberal constitutional democracy can inform courts' jurisprudence. American judges have an obsession with disclaiming their poli-cymaking role, and to some extent this may be appropriate. Dissembling about the true extent of judicial power might help judges to internalize some restraint and to diffuse some resistance to their rulings. We do not argue that judges should align with our particular policy preferences. But we do think that con-stitutional jurisprudence should better account for the very real threat of ero-sion and focus on the core features of partisan competition, electoral integrity, protection of bureaucratic rule-following, and core associational rights. The greatest threat to core individual rights in our moment is reflexive deference to government invocations of terrorism and its promises of security. By worrying excessively about the collapse of democracy through violent incursion by out-siders, courts may inadvertently be facilitating erosion.

At the same time, we emphatically do not want to be understood as suggest-ing that the maintenance of democratic rule is a manner of the right tweaks to legal institutions or a flick of the constitutional pen. This would be to grossly overstate the influence of lawyers and institutional designers. There is no de-mocracy without a decent measure of popular commitment to democracy. Maintaining that commitment depends on what people continue to want in terms of a government, in terms of a country for themselves and their children. It is a matter of beliefs and preferences, not incentives or stratagems, which are transmitted within families, schools, churches, mosques, synagogues, work-places, and social media networks. Without those beliefs, without a simple de-sire for democracy on the part of the many, the best institutional and constitu-tional design in the world will likely be for naught.

All this makes the case for American exceptionalism especially shaky. Even as they drew on Enlightenment ideals in their formation of the Constitution, the Founders of the American republic believed that time would inevitably bring corruption and decay. While they hoped that decay could be postponed through careful institutional design, they also knew that the handiwork of the Constitution would be imperfect, and subject over time to significant pressures. They viewed the United States as a great experiment, but one also subject to the universal laws of history, which include the inevitable decline of republics. They surely would have been skeptical of subsequent claims of American ex-ceptionalism. Today, surveying the risk of erosion, we think they would see no cause to revise any of these views. Nor would they abandon their trepidation about the ideal of a democratic future: indeed, they would say that a healthy skepticism about political actors is a powerful force for keeping those leaders honest and faithful to the moral and legal obligations of office. In this regard, if not in every other matter, we should heed their advice.

Notes

Introduction

1. Richard J. Evans, *The Pursuit of Power: Europe, 1815–1914* (London: Penguin Books, 2016), 166.

2. Ben Zimmer, "Did Stalin Really Coin 'American Exceptionalism'?," *Slate*, September 27, 2013; online at http://www.slate.com/blogs/lexicon_valley/2013/09/27/american_exceptionalism _neither_joseph_stalin_nor_alexis_de_tocqueville.html.

Chapter One

1. Javier Hernandez, "'We Have a Fake Election': China Disrupts Local Campaigns," *New York Times*, June 26, 2016, online at https://www.nytimes.com/2016/11/16/world/asia/beijing -china-local-elections.html; Minxin Pei, *China's Trapped Transition* (Cambridge, MA: Harvard University Press, 2016); "China Elections: Independent Candidates Fight for the Ballot," *BBC News*, November 17, 2016, online at http://www.bbc.com/news/world-asia-china-37997706; "China Holds Elections," *Economist*, November 10, 2016, online at http://www.economist.com/news /china/21709975-only-way-it-likes-them-china-holds-elections.

2. Cristina Cassidy, "Wisconsin Voter ID Law Proved Insurmountable for Many," *Milwaukee Journal Sentinel*, May 14, 2017; Nicholas Stephanopoulos and Eric McGhee, "Partisan Gerry-mandering and the Efficiency Gap," *University of Chicago Law Review* 82, no. 2 (2015): 831–900; Bill Whitford, "Why Wisconsin Is Not a Democracy," *Time*, June 23, 2017, online at http://time .com/4830145/supreme'-court-gerrymandering-wisconsin/.

3. The classical definition of institutions holds that they are "the rules of the game in a society or, more formally, are the humanly devised constraints that shape human interaction" (Douglass C. North, *Institutions, Institutional Change and Economic Performance* [New York: Cambridge University Press, 1990], 3).

4. W. B. Gallie, "Essentially Contested Concepts," *Proceedings of the Aristotelian Society* 56 (1956): 167–98; W. B. Gallie, "Art as an Essentially Contested Concept," *Philosophical Quarterly* 6, no. 23 (1956): 97–114.

5. Joseph Schumpeter, *Capitalism, Socialism and Democracy* (New York: Harper & Row, 1942), 269.

6. Josiah Ober, "The Original Meaning of 'Democracy': Capacity to Do Things, Not Majority Rule." *Constellations* 15, no. 1 (2008): 3–9.

7. Philippe C. Schmitter and Terry Lynn Karl, "What Democracy Is . . . and Is Not," *Journal of Democracy* 2, no. 3 (1991): 75–88; Larry Diamond, *Developing Democracy: Toward Consolidation* (Baltimore: Johns Hopkins Press, 1999), 10–12.

8. Freedom House, "Freedom in the World 2018: Democracy in Crisis," online at https://freedomhouse.org/report/freedom-world/freedom-world-2018.

9. Nancy L. Rosenblum, *On the Side of the Angels: An Appreciation of Parties and Partisanship* (Princeton, NJ: Princeton University Press, 2008), 356–57.

10. See Barry Weingast and Rui P. Figuieredo, "The Rationality of Fear: Political Opportunism and Ethnic Conflict," in *Civil Wars, Insecurity and Intervention, ed.* Jack Snyder and Barbara Walter (New York: Columbia University Press, 1999).

11. P. R. Cavill, "Parliamentarians at Law: Select Legal Proceedings of the Long Fifteenth Century Relating to Parliament–Edited by Hannes Kleineke," *Parliamentary History* 28, no. 3 (2009): 455–56.

12. For the political origins of the Fourth Amendment and the viability of a political Fourth Amendment today, see Aziz Z. Huq, "How the Fourth Amendment and the Separation of Powers Rise (and Fall) Together," *University of Chicago Law Review* 83, no. 557 (2016): 139–67; William Stuntz, "The Substantive Origins of Criminal Procedure," *Yale Law Journal* 105, no. 2 (1995): 393–447.

13. Lon L. Fuller, *The Morality of Law,* rev. ed. (New Haven, CT, Yale University Press, 1969), 33–94; Joseph A. Raz, "The Rule of Law and Its Virtue," in *The Authority of Law: Essays on Law and Morality* (Oxford: Clarendon Press, 1979), 211, 214.

14. Juan J. Linz and Alfred Stepan, "Toward Consolidated Democracies," *Journal of Democracy* 7, no. 2 (1996): 18.

15. Guillermo A. O'Donnell, "Why the Rule of Law Matters," *Journal of Democracy* 15, no. 4 (2004): 32–46.

16. O'Donnell, "Why the Rule of Law Matters," 32.

17. For a lucid and useful account of the "street-level . . . confusion" in the uses of the term *rule of law*, as well as its philosophical usages, see Jeremy Waldron, "Is the Rule of Law an Essentially Contested Concept (in Florida)?" *Law and Philosophy* 21, no. 2 (2002): 137–64.

18. Edward Aspinall, "The Surprising Democratic Behemoth: Indonesia in Comparative Asian Perspective," *Journal of Asian Studies* 74, no. 4 (2015): 889–902; Donald Horowitz, *Constitutional Change and Democracy in Indonesia* (New York: Cambridge University Press, 2013).

19. Jothie Rajah, *Authoritarian Rule of Law: Legislation, Discourse, and Legitimacy in Singapore* (New York: Cambridge University Press, 2012).

20. Mark Tushnet, "Authoritarian Constitutionalism," *Cornell Law Review* 100 (2014): 391–461.

21. Barry R. Weingast, "The Political Foundations of Democracy and the Rule of the Law," *American Political Science Review* 91, no. 2 (1997): 245–63; Tom Ginsburg, *Judicial Review in New Democracies* (New York: Cambridge University Press, 2003).

22. Robert Jervis, *System Effects: Complexity in Political and Social Life* (Princeton, NJ: Princeton University Press, 1998), 6 (discussing system-level effects); Adrian Vermeule, "System Effects and the Constitution," *Harvard Law Review* 123 (2009): 4, 6.

23. For a useful and accessible introduction to debate over these measures, see Seva Gunitsky, "How Do You Measure 'Democracy'?," *Washington Post,* June 23, 2015, online at https://

NOTES TO PAGES 15-19

www.washingtonpost.com/news/monkey-cage/wp/2015/06/23/how-do-you-measure-demo cracy/?utm_term=.2cb5edf51c17.

24. Max Weber, *The Methodology of the Social Sciences*, trans. and ed., Edward Shils and Henry Finch (Glencoe, IL: Free Press of Glencoe, 1997), online at https://archive.org/stream/max weberonmethod00webe/maxweberonmethod00webe_djvu.txt.

25. Dan Slater, "Democratic Careening," *World Politics* 65, no. 4 (2013): 729–63.

26. For recent historical work that stresses the Constitution's elitist slant, see Terry Bouton, *Taming Democracy: "The People," the Founders, and the Troubled Ending of the American Revolu- tion* (New York: Oxford University Press, 2007); and Woody Holton, *Unruly Americans and the Origins of the Constitution* (New York: Hill & Wang, 2008), 14.

27. Alexander Keyssar, *The Right to Vote: The Contested History of Democracy in the United States* (New York: Basic Books, 2009); Edward L. Gibson, *Boundary Control: Subnational Au- thoritarianism in Federal Democracies* (New York: Cambridge University Press, 2012).

28. Robert W. Mickey, "The Beginning of the End for Authoritarian Rule in America: *Smith v. Allwright* and the Abolition of the White Primary in the Deep South, 1944–1948," *Studies in American Political Development* 22, no. 2 (2008): 143–82; Robert W. Mickey, *Paths Out of Dixie: The Democratization of Authoritarian Enclaves in America's Deep South, 1944–1972* (Princeton, NJ: Princeton University Press, 2015).

29. See Zoltan Hajnal, Nazita Lajevardi, and Lindsay Nielson, "Voter Identification Laws and the Suppression of Minority Votes," *Journal of Politics* 79, no.1 (2017): 363–79 (presenting empirical evidence of effects of voter identification laws on partisan vote shares).

30. Daryl Levinson and Benjamin I. Sachs, "Political Entrenchment and Public Law," *Yale Law Journal* 125 (2015): 400, 408–26 (documenting the extensive range of formal and informal en- trenchment strategies).

31. Aziz Z. Huq, "Judicial Independence and the Rationing of Constitutional Remedies," *Duke Law Journal* 65, no. 1 (2015): 1–80.

32. Jennifer Nou, "Sub-Regulating Elections," *Supreme Court Review 2013* (2013): 135–82; Daniel P. Tokaji, "The Birth and Rebirth of Election Administration," *Election Law Journal* 6, no. 1 (2007): 118–31.

33. Stephen Skowronek, *Building a New American State: The Expansion of National Adminis- trative Capacities, 1877-1920* (New York: Cambridge University Press, 1982), 29.

34. Frederick G. Whelan, "Prologue: Democratic Theory and the Boundary Problem," *No- mos* 25 (1983): 13–47.

35. Robert E. Goodin, "Enfranchising All Affected Interests, and Its Alternatives," *Philoso- phy & Public Affairs* 35, no. 1 (2007): 40–68 (recognizing the case for "giving virtually everyone everywhere a vote on virtually everything decided anywhere"). We take no position on whether particular limits are justified here; we think the question is in fact a very difficult one.

36. Edmund Fawcett, *Liberalism: The Life of an Idea* (Princeton, NJ: Princeton University Press, 2015), xxi.

37. Jeff Manza and Fay Lomax Cook, "A Democratic Polity? Three Views of Policy Respon- siveness to Public Opinion in the United States," *American Politics Research* 30, no. 6 (2002): 630–67 (cataloging various metrics of responsiveness); Nicholas O. Stephanopoulos, "Elections and Alignment," *Columbia Law Review* 114, no. 1 (2014): 283 (criticizing conceptualization of re- sponsiveness measures).

38. Larry Diamond, *Developing Democracy: Toward Consolidation* (Baltimore: Johns Hop- kins Press, 1999), 8–15.

39. Fareed Zakaria, "The Rise of Illiberal Democracy," *Foreign Affairs 76, no. 6* (1997): 22–43.

40. Daniel Bell, David Brown, Kanishka Jayasuriya, and David Jones, *Towards Illiberal Democracy* (New York: Springer, 1995), vii.

41. Tushnet, "Authoritarian Constitutionalism."

42. Steven Levitsky and Lucan Way, "The Rise of Competitive Authoritarianism," *Journal of Democracy* 13, no. 2 (2002): 51–65.

43. Emilie M. Hafner-Burton, Susan D. Hyde, and Ryan S. Jablonski, "When Do Governments Resort to Election Violence?," *British Journal of Political Science* 44, no. 1 (2014): 149–79.

44. Human Rights Watch, "Cambodia's Democracy Faces Death: Diplomats and Donors Need to Act If Court Dissolves Opposition Party," November 15, 2017, online at https://www.hrw.org/news/2017/11/15/cambodia-democracy-faces-death.

45. Abbas Milani, "Iran's Paradoxical Regime," *Journal of Democracy* 26, no. 2 (2015): 52–60; Thomas Erdbrink, "Rouhani Wins Re-Election in Iran by a Wide Margin," *New York Times*, May 20, 2017.

46. These were once called "oligarchical" democracies; see Larry Diamond, "Thinking about Hybrid Regimes," *Journal of Democracy* 13, no. 2 (2002): 21–35.

47. Juan J. Linz, *Totalitarian and Authoritarian Regimes* (New York: Addison-Wesley, 1985). For similar approaches to authoritarianism, see Jason Brownlee, *Authoritarianism in an Age of Democratization* (New York: Cambridge University Press, 2007); Ozan O. Varol, "Stealth Authoritarianism," *Iowa Law Review* 100, no. 4 (2014): 1673–1742.

48. Ivan Krastev, "Paradoxes of the New Authoritarianism," *Journal of Democracy* 22, no. 2 (2011): 5–16.

49. Jason Brownlee, "Hereditary Succession in Modern Autocracies," *World Politics* 59, no. 4 (2007): 595–628.

50. Ran Hirschl, *Towards Juristocracy: The Origins and Consequences of the New Constitutionalism* (Cambridge, MA: Harvard University Press, 2004).

51. Tom Ginsburg and Alberto Simpser, eds., *Constitutions in Authoritarian Regimes* (Cambridge: Cambridge University Press, 2013); Carles Boix and Milan W. Svolik, "The Foundations of Limited Authoritarian Government: Institutions, Commitment, and Power-Sharing in Dictatorships," *Journal of Politics* 75, no. 2 (2013): 300–316.

52. Turkuler Isiksel, "Between Text and Context: Turkey's Tradition of Authoritarian Constitutionalism," *International Journal of Constitutional Law* 11, no. 3 (2013): 702–26.

53. Richard J. Evans, *The Third Reich in Power* (New York: Penguin Books, 2006), 12–14; Robert O. Paxton, *The Anatomy of Fascism* (New York: Vintage, 2004).

54. This draws on Waldron, "Rule of Law."

55. Larry Bartels, *Unequal Democracy: The Political Economy of the New Gilded Age* (Princeton, NJ: Princeton University Press, 2008).

56. Wolfgang Streeck, *Buying Time: The Delayed Crisis of Democratic Capitalism* (London: Verso Books, 2014); Wolfgang Streeck, "The Construction of a Moral Duty for the Greek People to Repay Their National Debt," *Socio-Economic Review* 11, no. 3 (2013): 614–25.

57. Streeck, *Buying Time*, 173–74.

58. Freedom House, "Freedom in the World 2018."

59. The overall "Democracy Index" score of the United States fell from 8.05 in 2015 to 7.98 in 2016. See Elena Holodnay, "The US has Been Downgraded to a 'Flawed Democracy,'" *Business Insider*, January 27, 2017, online at http://www.businessinsider.com/economist-intelligence-unit-downgrades-united-states-to-flawed-democracy-2017-1.

60. On the causes of authoritarian resilience, see Eva Bellin, "Reconsidering the Robustness of Authoritarianism in the Middle East: Lessons from the Arab Spring," *Politics* 44, no. 2 (2012): 127–49.

61. "What Hong Kong Can Teach China," *Economist*, July 1, 2017. Regulation of the internet is targeted not at isolated protest but at new vehicles of social mobilization that might challenge the Communist Party's hegemony. See Gary King, Jennifer Pan, and Margaret E. Roberts, "How Censorship in China Allows Government Criticism but Silences Collective Expression," *American Political Science Review* 107, no. 2 (2013): 326–43.

62. Daniel T. Rodgers, *Atlantic Crossings: Social Politics in a Progressive Age* (Cambridge, MA: Harvard University Press, 1998), 231, 496 (social welfare policies); Beth A. Simmons and Zachary Elkins, "The Globalization of Liberalization: Policy Diffusion in the International Political Economy," *American Political Science Review* 98, no. 1 (2004): 171–89 (diffusion of trade liberalization policy).

63. Jens Rydgren, "Is Extreme Right-Wing Populism Contagious? Explaining the Emergence of a New Party Family," *European Journal of Political Research* 44, no. 3 (2005): 413–37.

64. Esen Berk and Sebnem Gumuscu, "Rising Competitive Authoritarianism in Turkey," *Third World Quarterly* 37, no. 9 (2016): 1581–1606; Münevver Cebeci, "De-Europeanisation or Counter-Conduct? Turkey's Democratisation and the EU," *South European Society and Politics* 21, no. 1 (2016): 119–32; Isiksel, "Between Text and Context"; Murat Somer, "Understanding Turkey's Democratic Breakdown: Old vs. New and Indigenous vs. Global Authoritarianism," *Southeast European and Black Sea Studies* 16, no. 4 (2016): 481–503.

65. Suzy Hansen, "Inside Turkey's Purge," *New York Times*, April 13, 2017.

66. For an analysis of the Arab Spring that emphasizes the international relations dimension, see Marc Lynch, *The New Arab Wars: Uprisings and Anarchy in the Middle East* (New York: Public Affairs, 2016).

67. Patrick Heller, "Degrees of Democracy: Some Comparative Lessons from India," *World Politics* 52, no. 4 (2000): 484–519.

68. Aziz Z. Huq, "Uncertain Law in Uncertain Times: Emergency Powers and Lessons from South Asia," *Constellations* 13, no.1 (2006): 89–107.

69. Amrita Basu, "The Long March from Ayodhya: Democracy and Violence in India," in *Pluralism and Democracy in India: Debating the Hindu Right*, ed. Wendy Doniger, and Martha C. Nussbaum (New York: Oxford University Press, 2015): 152, 155.

70. Freedom House, "India: Freedom in the World 2017," online at https://freedomhouse .org/report/freedom-world/2017/india.

71. Subrata K. Mitra, "Encapsulation without Integration? Electoral Democracy and the Ambivalent Moderation of Hindu Nationalism in India," *Studies in Indian Politics* 4, no. 1 (2016): 90–101.

72. Sumit Ganguly, "The Risks Ahead," *Journal of Democracy* 25, no. 4 (2014): 56–60; Suhasini Raj and Elaine Barry, "Modi's Push for a Hindu Revival Imperils India's Meat Industry," *New York Times*, June 5, 2017; Ellen Barry, "Raids in India Target Founders of News Outlets Critical of Government," *New York Times*, June 5, 2017.

73. On the courts, see J. Art. D. Brion, "TROs and Judicial Corruption," *Manila Bulletin*, May 23, 2017, online at http://news.mb.com.ph/2017/05/23/tros-and-judicial-corruption/. On the human rights commission, see Mark R. Thompson, "Duterte's Illiberal Democracy," *East Asia Forum*, August 7, 2017, online at http://www.eastasiaforum.org/2017/08/07/80706/.

74. Freedom House, "Press Freedom in the Philippines, 2016," online at https://freedomhouse .org/report/freedom-press/2016/philippines.

75. Marc F. Plattner, "Is Democracy in Decline?" *Journal of Democracy* 26, no. 1 (2015): 5–10.

76. Thomas Carothers, "Democracy Aid at 25: Time to Choose." *Journal of Democracy* 26, no. 1 (2015): 59–73.

77. James Dawson and Seán Hanley, "The Fading Mirage of the Liberal Consensus," *Journal of Democracy* 27, no.1 (2016): 20–34, 30.

78. See Pippa Norris, "Is Western Democracy Backsliding? Diagnosing the Risks," and Eric Voeten, "Are People Really Turning Away from Democracy?" both in the *Journal of Democracy*, April 2017, online at http://journalofdemocracy.org/online-exchange-%E2%80%9C democratic-deconsolidation%E2%80%9D.

79. David Runciman, *The Confidence Trap: A History of Democracy in Crisis from World War I to the Present* (Princeton, NJ: Princeton University Press, 2015).

80. Runciman, *Confidence Trap*, 19–34.

81. Edmund Fawcett, *Liberalism: The Life of an Idea* (Princeton, NJ: Princeton University Press, 2015), 6.

82. Bryce is quoted in Robert Kagan, "The Weight of Geopolitics," *Journal of Democracy* 26, no, 1 (2015) 21–31; Runciman, *Confidence Trap*, 77–78.

83. Antony Beevor, *The Spanish Civil War* (London: Penguin Books, 2001), 340–41.

84. Robert O. Paxton, *The Anatomy of Fascism* (New York: Vintage, 2004), 198–99; Hiroshi Oda, *Japanese Law* (London: Butterworths, 1992), 19–20.

85. Tooze, *The Deluge* (London: Penguin Books), 239–40, 319; Eric D. Weitz, *Weimar Germany: Promise and Tragedy* (Princeton, NJ: Princeton University Press, 2013).

86. Apparently, he was speaking about the mass student movement of the 1960s, rather than the late eighteenth century.

Chapter Two

1. Anson Rabinbach, *Staging Antifascism: The Brown Book of the Reichstag Fire and Hitler Terror* (Durham, NC: Duke University Press, 2008).

2. This account draws on the work of several historians, including Richard J. Evans, *The Coming of the Third Reich* (London: Penguin Books, 2003), 328–37; Benjamin Carter Hett, *Burning the Reichstag: An Investigation into the Third Reich's Enduring Mystery* (New York: Oxford University Press, 2014), 1–15; Robert O. Paxton, *The Anatomy of Fascism* (New York: Vintage, 2004), 107; Anson Rabinbach, "Staging Antifascism: The Brown Book of the Reichstag Fire and Hitler Terror," *New German Critique* 35, no. 103 (2008): 97–126. Rabinbach supplies the first quotation attributed to Hitler. The details of Diels's recollections are supplied by Evans.

3. Evans, *Coming of the Third Reich*, 331–54; Paxton, *Anatomy of Fascism*, 109–10.

4. Paxton, *Anatomy of Fascism*, 67.

5. Sheri Berman, "Civil Society and the Collapse of the Weimar Republic," *World Politics* 49, no. 3 (1997): 401–29.

6. Paxton, *Anatomy of Fascism*, 128–31.

7. Eric Foner and Olivia Mahoney, *America's Reconstruction: People and Politics After the Civil War* (Baton Rouge: Louisiana State University Press, 1997), 97; C. Vann Woodward, *The Strange Career of Jim Crow* (New York: Oxford University Press, 1973), 44–59; Samuel Shapiro, "A Black Senator from Mississippi: Blanche K. Bruce (1841–1898)," *Review of Politics* 44, no. 1 (1982): 83–109.

8. Richard A. Primus, "The Riddle of Hiram Revels," *Harvard Law Review* 119 (2005): 1681–1734.

9. Eric Foner, *A Short History of Reconstruction* (New York: Harper Perennial, 1990), 242–47.

10. Woodward, *Strange Career of Jim Crow*, 89–90.

11. Foner, *Short History of Reconstruction*, 249–50; Michael J. Klarman, *From Jim Crow to Civil Rights: The Supreme Court and the Struggle for Racial Equality* (New York: Oxford University Press, 2004); J. Morgan Kousser, *Colorblind Injustice: Minority Voting Rights and the Undoing of the Second Reconstruction* (Chapel Hill: University of North Carolina Press, 2000), 12–20; Benno C. Schmidt, "Principle and Prejudice: The Supreme Court and Race in the Progressive Era. Part 3: Black Disfranchisement from the KKK to the Grandfather Clause," *Columbia Law Review* 82, no. 5 (1982): 835–905.

12. Robert W. Mickey, *Paths Out of Dixie: The Democratization of Authoritarian Enclaves in America's Deep South, 1944–1972* (Princeton, NJ: Princeton University Press, 2015). On the role of lynching as "a form of practical disenfranchisement," see David Garland, "Penal Excess and Surplus Meaning: Public Torture Lynchings in Twentieth-Century America," *Law & Society Review* 39, no. 4 (2005): 793–834, 823.

13. Hett, *Burning the Reichstag*, 317–22.

14. Hett, *Burning the Reichstag*, 19.

15. See Samuel P. Huntington, *The Third Wave: Democratization in the Late Twentieth Century* (Tulsa: University of Oklahoma Press, 1993), 11–13.

16. John Dunn, *Setting the People Free: The Story of Democracy* (New York: Atlantic, 2005), 11–13.

17. Kurt A. Raaflaub, Josiah Ober, and Robert Wallace, *Origins of Democracy in Ancient Greece* (Berkeley: University of California Press, 2007), 3–5.

18. The best survey of the considerable variety of forms of absolutism in Europe and beyond is Perry Anderson, *Lineages of the Absolutist State* (New York: Verso Books, 2013).

19. Myron Weiner, "The 1977 Parliamentary Elections in India," *Asian Survey* 17, no. 7 (1977): 619–26.

20. Tanel Demirel, "The Turkish Military's Decision to Intervene: 12 September 1980," *Armed Forces & Society* 29, no. 2 (2003): 253–80.

21. Gerassimos Karabelias, "The Evolution of Civil-Military Relations in Post-War Turkey, 1980–95," *Middle Eastern Studies* 35, no. 4 (1999): 130–51.

22. Steven Levitsky and James Loxton, "Populism and Competitive Authoritarianism in the Andes," *Democratization* 20, no. 1 (2013): 107–36, 121–22; Eduardo Ferrero Costa, "Peru's Presidential Coup," *Journal of Democracy* 4, no. 1 (1993): 28–40. On the relationship of the coup to popular reaction against neoliberal policies, see Kenneth M. Roberts, "Neoliberalism and the Transformation of Populism in Latin America: The Peruvian Case," *World Politics* 48, no. 1 (1995): 82–116.

23. Robert Barros, *Constitutionalism and Dictatorship: Pinochet, the Junta, and the 1980 Constitution* (New York: Cambridge University Press, 2002).

24. Dawn Brancati, "Democratic Authoritarianism: Origins and Effects," *Annual Review of Political Science* 17 (2014): 313–26; Daniela Donno, "Elections and Democratization in Authoritarian Regimes," *American Journal of Political Science* 57, no. 3 (2013): 703–16; Jennifer Gandhi and Ellen Lust-Okar, "Elections Under Authoritarianism," *Annual Review of Political Science* 12 (2009): 403–22; Joseph Wright, "Do Authoritarian Institutions Constrain? How Legislatures

Affect Economic Growth and Investment," *American Journal of Political Science* 52, no. 2 (2008): 322–43. For the Kazakh elections, see "Elections in Central Asia: No Choice," *Economist*, April 5, 2015, online at https://www.economist.com/news/asia/21647667-democracy-kazakhstan-and -uzbekistan-managed-affair-without-clear-rules-succession-no.

25. Ozan O. Varol, "The Democratic Coup d'Etat," *Harvard International Law Journal* 53, no. 2 (2012): 291–356.

26. Ozan O. Varol, *The Democratic Coup d'état* (New York: Oxford University Press, 2017), 38.

27. Frank Tachau and Metin Heper, "The State, Politics, and the Military in Turkey," *Comparative Politics* 16, no. 1 (1983): 17–33.

28. Graeme J. Gill and Roger D. Markwick, *Russia's Stillborn Democracy? From Gorbachev to Yeltsin* (New York: Oxford University Press, 2002), 295.

29. Liliia Fedorovna Shevtsova, "Russia's Hybrid Regime," *Journal of Democracy* 12, no. 4 (2001): 65–70; Archie Brown, "From Democratization to 'Guided Democracy,'" *Journal of Democracy* 12, no. 4 (2001): 35–41.

30. Andreas Schedler, "The Menu of Manipulation," *Journal of Democracy* 13, no. 2 (2002): 36–50.

31. Kim Lane Scheppele, "The Rule of Law and the Frankenstate: Why Governance Checklists Do Not Work," *Governance* 26, no. 4 (2013): 559–62.

32. The ancient Greeks knew this as the sorites paradox; see Terence Horgan, "Robust Vagueness and the Forced-March Sorites Paradox," *Philosophical Perspectives* 8 (1994): 159–88.

33. Levitsky and Loxton, "Populism and Competitive Authoritarianism," 123–24.

34. Levitsky and Loxton, "Populism and Competitive Authoritarianism," 123–24; Javier Corrales, "Autocratic Legalism in Venezuela," *Journal of Democracy* 26, no. 2 (2015): 37–51; Kirk A. Hawkins, "Chavismo, Liberal Democracy, and Radical Democracy," *Annual Review of Political Science* 19 (2016): 311–29; see also Aria Bendix, "Maduro Plans to Rewrite Venezuela's Constitution," *Atlantic*, May 24, 2017, online at https://www.theatlantic.com/news/archive/2017/05/maduro -plans-to-rewrite-venezuelas-constitution/528033/; Max Fisher and Amanda Taub, "How Venezuela Stumbled to the Brink of Collapse," *New York Times*, May 14, 2017.

35. Josh Keller, Iaryna Mykhyalyshyn, and Safak Timur, "The Scale of Turkey's Purge Is Nearly Unprecedented," *New York Times*, August 2, 2016.

36. Contrast Dexter Filkins, "The End of Democracy in Turkey," *New Yorker*, January 3, 2017 (online at http://www.newyorker.com/news/news-desk/the-end-of-democracy-in-turkey) with Christopher de Bellaigue, "Welcome to Demokrasi: How Erdoğan Got More Popular Than Ever," *Guardian*, August 30, 2016, online at https://www.theguardian.com/world/2016/aug/30/welcome -to-demokrasi-how-erdogan-got-more-popular-than-ever.

37. "Adiós to Venezuelan Democracy," *Economist*, July 1, 2017.

Chapter Three

1. Kate Hodal, "Thai Army Imposes Martial Law and Calls for Talks to Resolve Stalemate," *Guardian*, May 20, 2014, online at https://www.theguardian.com/world/2014/may/20/thailand -martial-law-talks-stalemate; "Thailand Military Seizes Power in Coup," *BBC News*, May 22, 1994, online at http://www.bbc.com/news/world-asia-27517591; International Crisis Group, "A Coup Ordained? Thailand's Prospects for Stability," December 16, 2014, online at https://www .crisisgroup.org/asia/south-east-asia/thailand/coup-ordained-thailand-s-prospects-stability (describing May 22, 2014 coup).

2. On the infringements of free association and speech around the process of constitutional reform in particular, see Duncan McCargo, Saowanee T. Alexander, and Petra Desatova, "Ordering Peace: Thailand's 2016 Constitutional Referendum," *Contemporary Southeast Asia: A Journal of International and Strategic Affairs* 39, no. 1 (2017): 65–95. On the lèse-majesté law, see David Streckfuss, *Truth on Trial in Thailand: Defamation, Treason, and Lèse-Majesté* (London: Routledge, 2010).

3. David Streckfuss, "In Thailand, A King's Coup?" *New York Times*, April 9, 2017. For discussion of the new constitution, see Nicholas Jenny, "Thailand's Undemocratic Constitution: 3 Takeaways," *Global Risk Insights*, March 2016, online at http://globalriskinsights.com/2016/03 /thailands-undemocratic-constitution-3-takeaways/; Chookiat Panaspornprasit, "Thailand: The Historical and Indefinite Transitions," *Southeast Asian Affairs* 2017, no. 1 (2017): 353–66; Saksith Saiyasombut, "Thailand's Next Post-Coup Constitution: The Dictatorship of the 'Good People'?," *Constitutionnet*, May 29, 2015, online at http://www.constitutionnet.org/news/thailands -next-post-coup-constitution-dictatorship-good-people.

4. Dan Slater, "Democratic Careening," *World Politics* 65, no. 4 (2013): 729–63.

5. On the history until 1990, see Chai-anan Samutwanit, "Educating Thai Democracy," *Journal of Democracy* 1, no. 4 (1990): 104–15. On later history, see Suchit Bunbongkan, "Thailand's Successful Reforms," *Journal of Democracy* 10, no. 4 (1999): 54–68; Duncan McCargo, "Democracy Under Stress in Thaksin's Thailand," *Journal of Democracy* 13, no. 4 (2002): 112–26. On the 1996 Constitution, see Michael Connors, "Framing the People's Constitution," in *Reforming Thai Politics*, ed. Duncan McCargo (Copenhagen: Nordic Institute of Asian Studies, 2002), 37–55.

6. "Thai Draft Constitution Approved," *BBC News*, July 6, 2007, online at http://news.bbc .co.uk/2/hi/asia-pacific/6276154.stm.

7. Taeko Hiroi and Sawa Omori, "Causes and Triggers of Coups d'état: An Event History Analysis," *Politics & Policy* 41, no. 1 (2013): 39–64, 52; Martin Gassebner, Jerg Gutmann, and Stefan Voigt, "When to Expect a Coup d'état? An Extreme Bounds Analysis of Coup Determinants," *Public Choice* 169, nos. 3–4 (2016): 293–313.

8. McCloud, "Democracy Under Stress in Thaksin's Thailand"; Paul Chambers and Napisa Waitoolkiat, "The Resilience of Monarchised Military in Thailand," *Journal of Contemporary Asia* 46, no. 3 (2016): 425–44. On Thaksin's history, see Ukrist Pathmanand, "The Thaksin Shinawatra Group: A Study of the Relationship between Money and Politics in Thailand," *Copenhagen Journal of Asian Studies* 13, no. 1 (1998): 60.

9. Phongpaichit Pasuk and Chris Baker, *Thaksin: The Business of Politics in Thailand* (Chiang Mai: Silkworm Books, 2004), 227–32.

10. McCloud, "Democracy Under Stress in Thaksin's Thailand"; Kate Hodal, "Thai Court Orders Yingluck Shinawatra to Step Down as PM," *Guardian*, May 7, 2014, online at https:// www.theguardian.com/world/2014/may/07/thai-court-orders-yingluck-shinawatra-resign.

11. Jonathan Powell, "Determinants of the Attempting and Outcomes of Coups d'état," *Journal of Conflict Resolution* 56, no. 6 (2011): 1017–40, 1118; Mark J. Ruhl, "Post-Coup Honduras: The Limits of Stabilization," *Security and Defense Studies Review* 13 (2012): 33–47.

12. Harold J. Gordon, *Hitler and the Beer Hall Putsch* (Princeton, NJ: Princeton University Press, 1972).

13. On the Philippine case, see Rolando V. Del Carmen, "Philippine Judicial System under the New Constitution and Martial Law," *Texas International Law Journal* 9, no. 2 (1974): 143–56.

14. On emergency powers in Latin America, see Brian Loveman, *The Constitution of Tyranny: Regimes of Exception in Spanish America* (Pittsburgh, PA: University of Pittsburgh Press,

1993); William C. Banks and Alejandro D. Carrio, "Presidential Systems in Stress: Emergency Powers in Argentina and the United States," *Michigan Journal of International Law* 15, no. 1 (1993): 1–76. On the reasons for the inclusion of emergency powers in Latin American constitutions, see Jorge Gonzalez-Jacome, "Emergency Powers and the Feeling of Backwardness in Latin American State Formation," *American University International Law Review* 26 (2010): 1073–1106. On coups in Latin America, see Aníbal Pérez-Liñán and John Polga-Hecimovich, "Explaining Military Coups and Impeachments in Latin America," *Democratization* 24, no. 5 (2017): 839–58; Francis Fukuyama, *Political Order and Political Decay: From the Industrial Revolution to the Globalization of Democracy* (New York: Farrar, Straus and Giroux, 2014), 281–83.

15. Loveman, *Constitution of Tyranny*, 9.

16. Arend Lijphart, "Emergency Powers and Emergency Regimes: A Commentary," *Asian Survey* 18, no. 4 (1978): 401–7, 403.

17. Gero Erdmann, "Decline of Democracy: Loss of Quality, Hybridisation and Breakdown of Democracy," in *Regression of Democracy?*, ed. Gero Erdmann and Marianne Kneuer (New York: Springer, 2011), 21–58.

18. Adam Przeworski, "Democracy as an Equilibrium," *Public Choice* 123, no. 3 (2005): 253–73, 263.

19. On the decline in the rate of collapses, see Dan Slater, "Democratic Careening," *World Politics* 65, no. 4 (2013): 729–63. On the declining rate of coups, see table 6.1 in Jonathan M. Powell and Clayton L. Thyne, "Global Instances of Coups from 1950 to 2010: A New Dataset," *Journal of Peace Research* 48, no. 2 (2011): 249–59.

20. Center for Systemic Peace, Data on Coups d'Etat, available online at http://www.system icpeace.org/inscrdata.html.

21. Andreas Schedler, "What Is Democratic Consolidation?," *Journal of Democracy* 9, no. 2 (1998): 91–107.

22. Erdmann, "Decline of Democracy," 34.

23. Jose Antonio Cheibub, Adam Przeworski, Limongi Neto, Fernando Papaterra, and Michael M. Alvarez, "What Makes Democracies Endure?" *Journal of Democracy* 7, no. 1 (1996): 39–55. Other empirical studies that find a correlation between economic well-being and democratic consolidation include Mark J. Gasiorowski and Timothy J. Power, "The Structural Determinants of Democratic Consolidation: Evidence from the Third World," *Comparative Political Studies* 31, no. 6 (1998): 740–71; Christian Houle, "Inequality and Democracy: Why Inequality Harms Consolidation but Does Not Affect Democratization," *World Politics* 61, no. 4 (2009): 589–622; and Milan Svolik, "Authoritarian Reversals and Democratic Consolidation," *American Political Science Review* 102, no. 2 (2008): 153–68.

24. For the affirmative argument, see Daron Acemoglu and James A. Robinson, *Economic Origins of Dictatorship and Democracy* (New York: Cambridge University Press, 2006). For the negative, see Dan Slater, Benjamin Smith, and Gautam Nair, "Economic Origins of Democratic Breakdown? The Redistributive Model and the Postcolonial State," *Perspectives on Politics* 12, no. 2 (2014): 353–74.

25. Edward Luttwak, *Coup d'Etat: A Practical Handbook* (London: Penguin Press, 1968), 15–16.

26. Daniel Treisman, "Income, Democracy, and Leader Turnover," *American Journal of Political Science* 59, no. 4 (2015): 927–42.

27. José Alemán and David D. Yang, "A Duration Analysis of Democratic Transitions and Authoritarian Backslides," *Comparative Political Studies* 44, no. 9 (2011): 1123–51; Ethan B.

Kapstein and Nathan Converse, "Why Democracies Fail," *Journal of Democracy* 19, no. 4 (2008): 57–68, 61; Adam Przeworski, *Democracy and Development: Political Institutions and Well-Being in the World, 1950–1990* (New York: Cambridge University Press, 2000), 50–51.

28. Svolik, "Authoritarian Reversals," 164.

29. Milan Svolik, "Which Democracies Will Last? Coups, Incumbent Takeovers and the Dynamic of Democratic Consolidation," *British Journal of Political Science* 45 (2015): 715–38.

30. Ethan B. Kapstein and Nathan Converse, *The Fate of Young Democracies* (New York: Cambridge University Press, 2008).

31. Christian Houle, "Ethnic Inequality and the Dismantling of Democracy: A Global Analysis," *World Politics* 67, no. 3 (2015): 469–505.

32. John Ferejohn and Pasquale Pasquino, "The Law of the Exception: A Typology of Emergency Powers," *I-CON* 2, no. 2 (2004) 210–39.

33. Niccolò Machiavelli, *Discourses on Livy*, trans. Harvey C. Mansfield and Nathan Tarcov (Chicago: University of Chicago Press, 1996), 74.

34. Data from the Comparative Constitutions Project, online at http://comparativeconstitu tionsproject.org/ (on file with authors).

35. Christian Bjørnskov and Stefan Voigt, "The Determinants of Emergency Constitutions," (2016), online at https://papers.ssrn.com/sol3/papers.cfm?abstract_id=2697144.

36. For particular examples, see Kim Lane Scheppele, "North American Emergencies: The Use of Emergency Powers in Canada and the United States," *International Journal of Constitutional Law* 4, no. 2 (2006): 213–43. On the pervasiveness of emergency powers in US law, see Jules Lobel, "Emergency Power and the Decline of Liberalism," *Yale Law Journal* 98, no. 7 (1989): 1385–1433.

37. Oren Gross, "Chaos and Rules: Should Responses to Violent Crises Always Be Constitutional?," *Yale Law Journal* 112 (2002): 1011–34.

38. Richard B. Lillich, "The Paris Minimum Standards of Human Rights Norms in a State of Emergency," *American Journal of International Law* 79, no. 4 (1985): 1072–81.

39. Robert M. Levine, *Father of the Poor? Vargas and His Era* (New York: Cambridge University Press, 1998), 46–47.

40. Rodrigo Uprimny, "The Constitutional Court and Control of Presidential Extraordinary Powers in Colombia," *Democratization* 10, no. 4 (2003): 46–69.

41. David F. Roth, "The Deterioration and Reconstitution of National Political Parameters: The Philippines during the 1970s," *Asian Survey* 13, no. 9 (1973): 812–25; Gretchen Casper, "*The Anti-Marcos Struggle: Personalistic Rule and Democratic Transition in the Philippines. By* Thompson, Mark R. New Haven, CT: Yale University Press, 1995. 258p. $32.50" (review), *American Political Science Review* 90, no. 4 (1996): 946–47.

42. Carl Schmitt, *Political Theology*, trans. George Schwab (Chicago: University of Chicago Press, 2005). For an excellent survey, see William E. Scheuerman, "Emergency Powers and the Rule of Law after 9/11," *Journal of Political Philosophy* 14, no. 1 (2006): 61–84.

43. Aziz Z. Huq, "Binding the Executive (by Law or by Politics)," *University of Chicago Law Review* 79, no. 2 (2012): 777–836.

44. Lijphart, "Emergency Powers and Emergency Regimes," 402–3; Clinton Rossiter, *Constitutional Dictatorship: Crisis Government in Modern Democracies* (Piscataway, NJ: Transaction, 1948).

45. Data from the Comparative Constitutions Project, online at http://comparativeconstitu tionsproject.org/ (on file with authors).

46. Peter L. Lindseth, "The Paradox of Parliamentary Supremacy: Delegation, Democracy, and Dictatorship in Germany and France, 1920s-1950s," *Yale Law Journal* 113, no. 7 (2004): 1341–1415; Gabriel L. Negretto, and José Antonio Aguilar Rivera, "Liberalism and Emergency Powers in Latin America: Reflections on Carl Schmitt and the Theory of Constitutional Dictatorship," *Cardozo Law Review* 21 (1999): 1797–1823. On the role of courts, see Karl Loewenstein, "Law in the Third Reich," *Yale Law Journal* 45, no. 5 (1936): 779–815. For a different view of the fall of Weimar, which emphasizes Article 48 more, see Kim Lane Scheppele, "Law in a Time of Emergency: States of Exception and the Temptations of 9/11," *University of Pennsylvania Journal of Constitutional Law* 6 (2003): 1001–82.

47. Eric A. Posner and Adrian Vermeule, *Terror in the Balance: Security, Liberty, and the Courts* (New York: Oxford University Press, 2007).

48. Aziz Z. Huq, "Structural Constitutionalism as Counterterrorism," 100 *California Law Review* 887 (2012): 897–98.

49. Hicham Bou Nassif, "Coups and Nascent Democracies: The Military and Egypt's Failed Consolidation," *Democratization* 24, no. 1 (2017): 157–74, 164.

50. Acemoglu and Robinson, *Economic Origins of Dictatorship and Democracy*.

51. Ahmed Mohamed, "Mauritania Army Stages Coup; Junta Takes Charge," *Associated Press*, August 12, 2008.

52. David Kuehn and Harold Trinkunas, "Conditions of Military Contestation in Populist Latin America," *Democratization* 24, no. 5 (2017): 859–80, 870–73.

53. Robert A. Scalapino, *Democracy and the Party Movement in Prewar Japan* (Berkeley: University of California Press, 1953); Harukata Takenaka, *Failed Democratization in Prewar Japan: Breakdown of a Hybrid Regime* (Stanford, CA: Stanford University Press, 2014).

54. Samuel P. Huntington, *The Soldier and the State: The Theory and Politics of Civil-Military Relations* (Cambridge, MA: Harvard University Press, 1957), 68–69, 83. The other leading work on professionalism as a solution to the problem of controlling the military is Morris Janowitz, *The Professional Soldier: A Social and Political Portrait* (Glencoe, IL: Free Press, 1960).

55. For a taxonomy of coup-proofing strategies, see Ulrich Pilster and Tobias Böhmelt, "Do Democracies Engage Less in Coup-Proofing? On the Relationship between Regime Type and Civil–Military Relations," *Foreign Policy Analysis* 8, no. 4 (2012): 355–72; Ulrich Pilster and Tobias Böhmelt, "Coup-Proofing and Military Effectiveness in Interstate Wars, 1967–99," *Conflict Management and Peace Science* 28, no. 4 (2011): 331–50.

56. Two recent large-*n* econometric studies find no effect on regime durability from coup-proofing. Holger Albrecht, "The Myth of Coup-Proofing: Risk and Instances of Military Coups d'Etat in the Middle East and North Africa, 1950–2013," *Armed Forces & Society* 41, no. 4 (2015): 659–87; Martin Gassebner, Jerg Gutmann, and Stefan Voigt, "When to Expect a Coup d'Etat? An Extreme Bounds Analysis of Coup Determinants," *Public Choice* 169, nos. 3–4 (2016): 293–313.

57. Svolik, "Authoritarian Reversals," 162.

58. Huntington, *Soldier and the State*, 190.

59. For a summary of the literature, see Peter D. Feaver, "Civil-Military Relations," *Annual Review of Political Science* 2, no. 1 (1999): 211–41, 226; Claude Emerson Welch, ed., *Civilian Control of the Military: Theory and Cases from Developing Countries* (Buffalo: SUNY Press, 1976).

60. For evidence that socialization on its own may not be sufficient and that institutional incentives matter too, see Risa Brooks, "Abandoned at the Palace: Why the Tunisian Military Defected from the Ben Ali Regime in January 2011," *Journal of Strategic Studies* 36, no. 2 (2013): 205–20.

61. Kristen A. Harkness, "Military Loyalty and the Failure of Democratization in Africa: How Ethnic Armies Shape the Capacity of Presidents to Defy Term Limits," *Democratization* 24, no. 5 (2017): 801–18.

62. Zoltan Barany, "The Role of the Military," *Journal of Democracy* 22, no. 4 (2011): 24–35; Erica Chenoweth and Maria J. Stephan, "Drop Your Weapons: When and Why Civil Resistance Works," *Foreign Affairs* 93, no. 4 (2014): 94.

63. Erica Chenoweth and Kathleen Gallagher Cunningham, "Understanding Nonviolent Resistance: An Introduction," *Journal of Peace Research* 50, no. 3 (2013): 271–76.

64. Barany, "Role of the Military," 25.

65. Eva Bellin, "Reconsidering the Robustness of Authoritarianism in the Middle East: Lessons from the Arab Spring," *Comparative Politics* 44, no. 2 (2012): 127–49; Brooks, "Abandoned at the Palace."

Chapter Four

1. Henry Kamm, "Hungarian Who Led '56 Revolt Is Buried as a Hero," *New York Times*, June 17, 1989.

2. Yigal Schleifer, "How Viktor Orbán is Slowly Destroying His Country's Democracy," *Slate*, October 3, 2014, online at http://www.slate.com/articles/news_and_politics/moment/2014/10 /viktor_orban_s_authoritarian_rule_the_hungarian_prime_minister_is_destroying.html.

3. Elisabeth Bakke, "Central and East European Party Systems Since 1989," in *Central and Southeast European Politics Since 1989*, ed. Sabrina P. Ramet (New York: Cambridge University Press, 2010); Jacques Rupnik, "How Things Went Wrong," *Journal of Democracy* 23, no. 3 (2012): 132–37. On the early history of Fidesz more generally, see Csilla Kiss, "From Liberalism to Conservatism: The Federation of Young Democrats in Post-Communist Hungary," *East European Politics and Societies* 16, no. 3 (2002): 739–63.

4. David Landau, "Abusive Constitutionalism," *University of California at Davis Law Review* 47 (2013): 189–260, 208–11; Miklós Bánkuti, Gábor Halmai, and Kim Lane Scheppele, "Disabling the Constitution," *Journal of Democracy* 23, no. 3 (2012): 138–46; see also Dan Bilefsky, "Socialists in Hungary Are Ousted in Elections," *New York Times*, April 25, 2010.

5. Schleifer, "Viktor Orbán." See also Judy Dempsey, "Hungary Waves Off Criticism over Media Laws," *New York Times*, December 25, 2010.

6. Cas Mudde, "The 2014 Hungarian Parliamentary Elections, or How to Craft a Constitutional Majority," *Washington Post*, April 14, 2014, online at https://www.washingtonpost.com /news/monkey-cage/wp/2014/04/14/the-2014-hungarian-parliamentary-elections-or-how-to -craft-a-constitutional-majority/?utm_term=.dc2e34b9d0cf.

7. "Viktor Orbán's speech at the XXV. Bálványos Free Summer University and Youth Camp, 26th July, 2014. Băile Tuşnad," *Budapest Beacon*, online at http://budapestbeacon.com/public-policy /full-text-of-viktor-orbans-speech-at-baile-tusnad-tusnadfurdo-of-26-july-2014/10592.

8. Mehmet Ali Birand, *"Toplum, derin bir "ohh" çekiyor,"* *Posta*, November 6, 2002 (translation Ilayda Gunes).

9. Patrick Kingsley, "Erdoğan Claims Vast Powers in Turkey After Narrow Victory in Referendum," *New York Times*, April 16, 2017,

10. Nancy Bermeo, "On Democratic Backsliding," *Journal of Democracy* 27, no. 1 (2016): 5–19.

11. "Turkey's 250-Mile Protest" (editorial), *New York Times*, July 4, 2017.

12. "Thousands Protest Over Threat to Soros University," *Guardian*, April 9, 2017.

13. Joshua Partlow and Rachelle Krygier, "How a New Kind of Protest Movement has Risen in Venezuela," *Washington Post*, June 3, 2017.

14. Tom Ginsburg, Jonathan S. Masur, and Richard H. McAdams, "Libertarian Paternalism, Path Dependence, and Temporary Law," *University of Chicago Law Review* 81, no. 1 (2014): 291–359; Katerina Linos, *The Democratic Foundations of Policy Diffusion: How Health, Family, and Employment Laws Spread Across Countries* (New York: Oxford University Press, 2013).

15. Larry Diamond and Leonardo Morlino, eds., *Assessing the Quality of Democracy* (Baltimore: Johns Hopkins Press, 2005); Gero Erdmann, "Decline of Democracy: Loss of Quality, Hybridisation and Breakdown of Democracy," in *Regression of Democracy?*, ed. Gero Erdmann and Marianne Kneuer (New York: Springer, 2011), 21–58; Steven Levitsky and Lucan Way, "The Myth of Democratic Recession," *Journal of Democracy* 26, no. 1 (2015): 45–58.

16. Erdmann used Freedom House categories, drawing on their ordinal scale. "Free" countries are those with a score of 1.0 to 2.5 on the index; "Partly Free" countries have scores from 3.0 to 5.0 and count as hybrid regimes; and "Not Free" autocracies have scores of 5.5 to 7.0.

17. Erdmann, "Decline of Democracy," 34–35; Ellen Lust and David Waldner, "Unwelcome Change: Understanding, Evaluating and Extending Theories of Democratic Backsliding" United States Agency for International Development, mimeo (June 2015), 5; online at http://pdf.usaid.gov/pdf_docs/PBAAD635.pdf.

18. Once a country is coded Partly Free, it is a bit more likely to collapse into the Unfree category ($n = 116$) than to revert to democracy ($n = 86$).

19. See www.comparativeconstitutionsproject.org/data for access to the file.

20. Bermeo, "On Democratic Backsliding," 6.

21. Thomas C. Schelling, *The Strategy of Conflict* (Cambridge, MA: Harvard University Press, 1980), 54–55; Barry R. Weingast, "The Political Foundations of Democracy and the Rule of the Law," *American Political Science Review* 91, no. 2 (1997): 245–63. On the function of constitutional texts as focal points, see John M. Carey, "Parchment, Equilibria, and Institutions," *Comparative Political Studies* 33, no. 6–7 (2000): 735–76.

22. Andreas Schedler, "What Is Democratic Consolidation?" *Journal of Democracy* 9, no. 2 (1998): 91–107, 95.

23. Kingsley, "Erdoğan Claims Vast Powers."

24. The idea of democratic muddling through is powerfully explored in David Runciman, *The Confidence Trap: A History of Democracy in Crisis from World War I to the Present* (Princeton, NJ: Princeton University Press, 2015).

25. Jan-Werner Müller, *What Is Populism?* (Philadelphia: University of Pennsylvania Press, 2016). For other treatments, see Margaret Canovan, *Populism* (New York: Houghton Mifflin, 1981).

26. Müller, *What Is Populism?*, 32, 69.

27. Christopher de Bellaigue, "Welcome to Demokrasi: How Erdoğan Got More Popular Than Ever," *Guardian*, August 30, 2016, online at https://www.theguardian.com/world/2016/aug/30/welcome-to-demokrasi-how-erdogan-got-more-popular-than-ever.

28. Bellaigue, "Welcome to Demokrasi"; Jan-Werner Müller, "Trump, Erdoğan, Farage: The Attractions of Populism for Politicians, the Dangers for Democracy," *Guardian*, September 2, 2016, online at https://www.theguardian.com/books/2016/sep/02/trump-erdogan-farage-the-attractions-of-populism-for-politicians-the-dangers-for-democracy; Ziya Öniş, "Turkey's Two Elections: The AKP Comes Back," *Journal of Democracy* 27, no. 2 (2016): 141–54.

29. Caroline Lancaster, "Ideology and Hegemonic Party Rule in South Africa, Hungary, and Turkey," *Politics, Religion & Ideology* 17, no. 4 (2016): 370–91.

30. The general phenomenon is described in Kurt Weyland, "The Threat from the Populist Left," *Journal of Democracy* 24, no. 3 (2013): 18–32; Carlos De la Torre, "Technocratic Populism in Ecuador," *Journal of Democracy* 24, no. 3 (2013): 33–46.

31. Margaret Canovan, "Populism for Political Theorists?," *Journal of Political Ideologies* 9, no. 3 (2004): 241–52.

32. Giovanni Capoccia, "Anti-system Parties: A Conceptual Reassessment," *Journal of Theoretical Politics* 14, no. 1 (2002): 9–35, 20–24.

33. Daniel Lansberg-Rodriguez, "When Nicholas Maduro Was Dictator for a Day," *Atlantic*, April 9, 2017, online at https://www.theatlantic.com/international/archive/2017/04/maduro-venezuela-supreme-court-chavez/522417/.

34. Ben Stanley, "The Thin Ideology of Populism," *Journal of Political Ideologies* 13, no. 1 (2008): 95–110; Müller, *What Is Populism?*

35. Dorottya Szikra, "Democracy and Welfare in Hard Times: The Social Policy of the Orbán Government in Hungary between 2010 and 2014," *Journal of European Social Policy* 24, no. 5 (2014): 486–500.

36. Müller, *What Is Populism?*, 47–48.

37. For details of the scandal, see Berivan Orucoglu, "Why Turkey's Mother of All Corruption Scandals Refuses to Go Away," *Foreign Policy*, January 5, 2015.

38. Jennifer McCoy, "Chávez and the End of 'Partyarchy' in Venezuela," *Journal of Democracy* 10, no. 3 (1999): 64–77; José Molina, "The Unraveling of Venezuela's Party System," in *The Unraveling of Representative Democracy in Venezuela*, ed. Jennifer McCoy (Baltimore: Johns Hopkins University Press, 2004), 152–79.

39. For a study of party realignment in the United States, see David R. Mayhew, "Electoral Realignments," *Annual Review of Political Science* 3, no. 1 (2000): 449–74; see also James L. Sundquist, *Dynamics of the Party System* (Washington, DC: Brookings Institute, 1983). For Europe, see Alessandro Chiaramonte and Vincenzo Emanuele, "Party System Volatility, Regeneration and De-Institutionalization in Western Europe (1945–2015)," *Party Politics* 23, no. 4 (2015): 376–88.

40. "How France Voted," *New York Times*, May 5, 2017; Alissa J. Rubin, Aurelien Bredeen, and Benoît Morenne, "Emmanuel Macron's Party and Allies Win Big in France," *New York Times*, June 18, 2017. On the UK see David Runciman, "The Choice Was Real," *London Review of Books*, June 29, 2017.

41. For a more formal explication of a similar model of democracy, see Adam Przeworski, "Democracy as an Equilibrium," *Public Choice* 123, no. 3 (2005): 253–73.

42. Weingast, "Political Foundations of Democracy." For the difference between narrow self-interest and common normative values as motivational premises in accounts of democracy, see John C. Harsanyi, "Rational-Choice Models of Political Behavior vs. Functionalist and Conformist Theories," *World Politics* 21, no. 4 (1969): 513–38.

43. James Melton and Tom Ginsburg, "Does De Jure Judicial Independence Really Matter? A Reevaluation of Explanations for Judicial Independence," *Journal of Law and Courts* 2, no. 2 (2014): 187–217.

44. Ellis S. Krauss and Robert J. Pekkanen, "The Rise and Fall of Japan's Liberal Democratic Party," *Journal of Asian Studies* 69, no. 1 (2010): 5–15; Ethan Scheiner, *Democracy without Competition in Japan: Opposition Failure in a One-Party Dominant State* (New York: Cambridge University Press, 2006).

45. David McNeill, "Nippon Kaigi and the Radical Conservative Project to Take Back Japan," *Asia-Pacific Journal* 13, no. 50 (2015): 4.

46. Defined as "social order" (社会秩序). Lawrence Repeta, "Japan at Risk—The LDP's Ten Most Dangerous Proposals for Constitutional Change," *Japan Focus*, July 14, 2013, online at http://apjjf.org/2013/11/28/Lawrence-Repeta/3969/article.html.

47. Mina Pollman, "Japan's Troubling State Secrets Law Takes Effect," *Diplomat*, December 18, 2014, online at http://thediplomat.com/2014/12/japans-troubling-state-secrets-law-takes-effect/; Office of the High Commission for Human Rights, "Japan: UN Rights Expert Warns of Serious Threats to the Independence of the Press," online at http://www.ohchr.org/EN/NewsEvents/Pages/DisplayNews.aspx?NewsID=19843.

48. "Japan Passes Controversial Anti-Terror Conspiracy Law," *BBC News*, June 15, 2017, online at http://www.bbc.com/news/world-asia-40283730.

49. See "Spying on Muslims in Tokyo and New York—'Necessary and Unavoidable'?," *Asia-Pacific Journal Report*, online at http://apjjf.org/2016/18/APJ.html (English).

50. "RSF Concerned about Declining Media Freedom in Japan," *Reporters without Borders*, April 11, 2016, online at https://rsf.org/en/news/rsf-concerned-about-declining-media-freedom-japan.

51. "Abe Seeks to Cut Question Time of Opposition Parties in Diet," Asahi Shimbun, October 28, 2017, online at http://www.asahi.com/ajw/articles/AJ201710280023.html.

52. We note that the Intelligence Unit downgraded Japan to a "flawed democracy" in 2015, albeit at the top end of the scale for that category; see Economist Intelligence Unit, "Democracy Index 2015: Democracy in an Age of Anxiety," online at http://www.eiu.com/public/thankyou_download.aspx?activity=download&campaignid=DemocracyIndex2015.

53. For a sample of contrasting views of Israeli democracy, see Michael Oren, "Israel's Resilient Democracy," *Foreign Policy*, April 5, 2012, online at http://foreignpolicy.com/2012/04/05/israels-resilient-democracy/; and Ilan Pappe, "No, Israel Is Not a Democracy," *Jacobin*, May 2017, online at https://www.jacobinmag.com/2017/05/israel-palestine-democracy-apartheid-discrimination-settler-colonialism. On the reliance on Arab parties to pass the Oslo Accords in the 1990s, see Rivka Weill, "Juxtaposing Constitution-Making and Constitutional Infringement Mechanisms in Israel and Canada: On the Interplay between Commonlaw Override and Sunset Override," *Israel Law Review* 49 (2016): 103.

54. Yair Ashkenazi, "Defunded for Politics, Israeli Arab Theater Reaches Deal with State," *Haaretz*, March 29, 2016, online at http://www.haaretz.com/israel-news/.premium-1.711620; Gregg Carlstrom, "The New Culture War in Israel," *Atlantic*, October 4, 2016, online at https://www.theatlantic.com/international/archive/2016/10/israel-culture-regev-netanyahu-palestine/501245/.

55. Gwen Ackerman, "Attack on Free Speech or Reality Check? Israel Debates Code," *Bloomberg*, June 26, 2017, online at https://www.bloomberg.com/news/articles/2017-06-25/attack-on-free-speech-or-reality-check-israel-code-fuels-debate; Judy Maltz, "U.S. Professors Who Fight Boycott of Israel Slam Plans to Gag Political Speech in Academia," *Haaretz*, June 28, 2017, online at http://www.haaretz.com/us-news/.premium-1.798242; "Ethics Code Section Shushing Campus Political Speech Scrapped—Report," *Times of Israel*, July 6, 2017, online at http://www.timesofisrael.com/liveblog_entry/ethics-code-section-shushing-campus-political-speech-scrapped-report.

56. Peter Beaumont, "Israel Passes Law to Force NGOs to Reveal Foreign Funding," *Guardian*, July 12, 2016, online at https://www.theguardian.com/world/2016/jul/12/israel-passes-law-to-force-ngos-to-reveal-foreign-funding; Jonathan Lis et al., "Israel's Nationalist 'Loyalty in Culture' Bill Passes Legal Test," *Haaretz*, February 26, 2016, online at http://www.haaretz.com

/israel-news/.premium-1.705312; Seymour D. Reich, "Israel's Assault on Democracy: Time to Speak Out," *Jewish Week*, April 26, 2016, online at http://jewishweek.timesofisrael.com/israels-assault-on-democracy-time-to-speak-out/; "The Economist Intelligence Unit's Democracy Index," online at https://infographics.economist.com/2017/DemocracyIndex/.

57. On the close relationship of party dynamics and the operation of constitutions, see Cindy Skach, "Political Parties and the Constitution," in *The Oxford Handbook of Comparative Constitutional Law, ed.* Michael Rosenfeld and András Sajo (New York: Oxford University Press, 2012).

58. Skach, "Political Parties," 884–87; Eduardo Alemán and Sebastian Saiegh, "Political Realignment and Democratic Breakdown in Argentina, 1916–1930," *Party Politics* 20, no. 6 (2014): 849–63.

59. For South Africa, Turkey, and Hungary, see Caroline Lancaster, "Ideology and Hegemonic Party Rule in South Africa, Hungary, and Turkey," *Politics, Religion & Ideology* 17, no. 4 (2016): 370–91. For Bolivia, see Jennifer Cyr, "Making or Breaking Politics: Social Conflicts and Party-System Change in Democratic Bolivia," *Studies in Comparative International Development* 50, no. 3 (2015): 283–303.

60. David M. Potter, *The Impending Crisis: America Before the Civil War, 1848–1861* (New York: Harper, 1978).

61. Ozan O. Varol, "Stealth Authoritarianism," *Iowa Law Review* 100, no. 4 (2014): 1673–1742

62. Landau, "Abusive Constitutionalism," 196.

63. Bánkuti, Halmai, and Scheppele, "Disabling the Constitution," 139; on Fidesz's reasons, see Rupnik, "How Things Went Wrong," 133.

64. Kim Lane Scheppele, "The Rule of Law and the Frankenstate: Why Governance Checklists Do Not Work," *Governance* 26, no. 4 (2013): 559–62.

65. R. Daniel Keleman, "Poland's Constitutional Crisis: How the Law and Justice Party Is Threatening Democracy," *Foreign Affairs*, August 25, 2016, online at https://www.foreignaffairs.com/articles/poland/2016-08-25/polands-constitutional-crisis.

66. Landau, "Abusive Constitutionalism." In addition, see Joel I. Colón-Ríos, "Carl Schmitt and Constituent Power in Latin American Courts: The Cases of Venezuela and Colombia," *Constellations* 18, no. 3 (2011): 65–388; David Landau, "Constitution Making Gone Wrong," *Alabama Law Review* 64 (2013): 923–73; Steven Levitsky and James Loxton, "Populism and Competitive Authoritarianism in the Andes," *Democratization* 20, no. 1 (2013): 107–36; for the measure of executive power, see Katja S. Newman, "Constitutional Coups: Advancing Executive Power in Latin American Democracies," paper presented at the 2011 meeting of the American Political Science Association (May 7, 2011), online at https://papers.ssrn.com/sol3/papers.cfm?abstract_id=1902006; for the 2007 referendum, see Enrique Krauze, "Hell of a Fiesta," *New York Review of Books*, March 8, 2018.

67. Weyland, "Threat from the Populist Left," 22.

68. Levitsky and Loxton, "Populism and Competitive Authoritarianism," 117; Landau, "Constitution Making Gone Wrong."

69. William Neuman, "President of Bolivia Claims Victory in Election," *New York Times*, October 12, 2014; "Bolivia's President Morales Can Seek Third Term," *BBC News*, April 30, 2013.

70. Jose Vivanco and Juan Pappier, "The Hypocrisy of Evo Morales," *New York Times*, November 20, 2017.

71. James Melton, Tom Ginsburg, and Zach Elkins, "On the Evasion of Executive Term Limits," *William and Mary Law Review* 52, no. 6 (2011): 1807–1872; Const. Sri Lanka (1978), 18th amendment; "Ecuador Legislature Lifts Presidential Re-Election Limit," *BBC News*, December 4, 2015, online at http://www.bbc.com/news/world-latin-america-35002846.

72. Edmund Fawcett, *Liberalism: The Life of an Idea* (Princeton, NJ: Princeton University Press, 2015), 44-45.

73. Hannah Arendt, "Rejoinder to Eric Voegelin's Review of *The Origins of Totalitarianism*," *Review of Politics* 15, no. 1 (1953): 76-85, 80.

74. For the idea of articulation as a feature of government, see Jeremy Waldron, *Political Political Theory* (Cambridge, MA: Harvard University Press, 2016). For a defense of unchecked executive power, see Eric A. Posner and Adrian Vermeule, *The Executive Unbound: After the Madisonian Republic* (New York: Oxford University Press, 2011).

75. Ian Kershaw, *To Hell and Back: Europe, 1914-1949* (London: Penguin, 2015). On the postwar tradition of European constitutionalism, see Jan-Werner Müller, *Contesting Democracy* (New Haven, CT: Yale University Press, 2011).

76. Daryl J. Levinson and Richard H. Pildes, "Separation of Parties, Not Powers," *Harvard Law Review* 119, no, 8. (2006): 2311-86.

77. For an excellent historical survey, see Eric Schickler, *Disjointed Pluralism: Institutional Innovation and the Development of the US Congress* (Princeton, NJ: Princeton University Press, 2001).

78. Samuel Issacharoff, *Fragile Democracies: Contested Power in the Era of Constitutional Courts* (New York: Cambridge University Press, 2015), 187-200.

79. Ceren Belge, "Friends of the Court: The Republican Alliance and Selective Activism of the Constitutional Court of Turkey," *Law & Society Review* 40, no. 3 (2006): 653-92.

80. Karl Loewenstein, "Law in the Third Reich," *Yale Law Journal* 45, no. 5 (1936): 779-815.

81. On the role of conflict in the political practice of liberalism, see Fawcett, *Liberalism*, 10-11. On the role of conflict in motivating constitutional design, see Tom Ginsburg and Aziz Z. Huq, "Introduction," in *Assessing Constitutional Performance*, ed. Tom Ginsburg and Aziz Z. Huq (New York: Cambridge University Press, 2016).

82. Waldron, *Political Political Theory*, 101. On the constitutional rights of opposition parties, see David Fontana, "Government in Opposition," *Yale Law Journal* 119, no. 3 (2009): 548-623.

83. Peter L. Lindseth, "The Paradox of Parliamentary Supremacy: Delegation, Democracy, and Dictatorship in Germany and France, 1920s-1950s," *Yale Law Journal* 119, no. 3 (2004): 1341-1415.

84. Issacharoff, *Fragile Democracies*, 201-2; Kim Lane Scheppele, "Constitutional Negotiations: Political Contexts of Judicial Activism in Post-Soviet Europe." *International Sociology* 18, no. 1 (2003): 219-38.

85. For the origins of PiS, see Ben Stanley, "Confrontation by Default and Confrontation by Design: Strategic and Institutional Responses to Poland's Populist Coalition Government," *Democratization* 23, no. 2 (2016): 263-82; Jean-Yves Camus and Nicolas Lebourg, *Far-Right Politics in Europe* (Cambridge, MA: Harvard University Press, 2017), 174-75. For the dynamics of the 2015 election, see Radoslaw Markowski, "The Polish Parliamentary Election of 2015: A Free and Fair Election That Results in Unfair Political Consequences," *West European Politics* 39, no. 6 (2016): 1311-22.

86. When the PiS parliament nominated five new judges, the court responded by ruling that it had power to fill only two vacancies. The PiS government retaliated by simply ignoring the court and swearing its new judges in anyway. To underscore the point, the Sejm then passed legislation that would have had the practical effect of disabling the court. The law required that all cases be decided by the plenary bench of the court, that decisions be taken by a two-thirds vote, and that thirteen out of fifteen judges be present to form a quorum. Since less than thirteen

judges had unambiguous appointment status, this meant that the tribunal would be unable to make any valid decisions.

87. Tamas Gyorfi, *Against the New Constitutionalism* (Cheltenham: Edward Elgar, 2016), 62–32.

88. Bojan Bugarič and Tom Ginsburg, "The Assault on Postcommunist Courts," *Journal of Democracy* 27, no. 3 (2016): 69–82; Joanna Fomina and Jacek Kucharczyk, "Populism and Protest in Poland," *Journal of Democracy* 27, no. 4 (2016): 58–68, 62–63; Lech Garlicki, "Die Ausschaltung des Verfassungsgerichtshofes in Polen?," in *Transformation of Law Systems in Central, Eastern and Southeastern Europe: Liber Amicorum Prof. Dr. Dres. H. C. Rainier Arnold,* ed. Andrzej Szmyt and Boguslaw Banaszak (Warsaw, Poland: Wydawnictwo Uniwersytetu Gdanskiego, 2016), 63, 65; see also Christian Davies, "Poland Is 'On Road to Autocracy,' Says Constitutional Court President," *Guardian,* December 18, 2016.

89. Marco Dani, "The 'Partisan Constitution' and the Erosion of European Constitutional Culture," in *The Partisan Constitution: The Fundamental Law of Hungary and European Constitutional Culture,* ed. Marco Dani and Roberto Toniatti (Oisterwijk, Netherlands: Wolf Legal Publishers, 2014).

90. The metric problem in the European Union context is discussed in Jan-Werner Müller, "Should the EU Protect Democracy and the Rule of Law Inside Member States?," *European Law Journal* 21, no. 2 (2015): 141–60.

91. Štěpán Drahokoupil, "The Introduction of a Semi-Presidential System," *Heinrich Böll Stiftung,* August 13, 2013, online at https://www.boell.de/en/2013/08/09/introduction-semi-presidential-system; Emily Tamkin, "Czech President Miloš Zeman to Run for Second Term," *Foreign Policy,* March 9, 2017, online at http://foreignpolicy.com/2017/03/09/czech-president-milos-zeman-to-run-for-second-term/; James Dawson, and Seán Hanley, "The Fading Mirage of the 'Liberal Consensus,'" *Journal of Democracy* 27, no. 1 (2016): 20–34.

92. Mariana Zuñiga and Nick Miroff, "Denounced as Dictator, Maduro Backs Down, Reverses Court's Ruling on Venezuela's Legislature's Powers," *Washington Post,* April 1, 2017.

93. Markowski, "Polish Parliamentary Election of 2015," 1313–14; James Traub, "The Party That Wants to Make Poland Great Again," *New York Times,* November 2, 2016.

94. Francis Fukuyama, *Political Order and Political Decay: From the Industrial Revolution to the Globalization of Democracy* (New York: Farrar, Straus and Giroux, 2014), 75.

95. On the British constitution, see Vernon Bogdanor, *The New British Constitution* (London: Bloomsbury, 2009). For the internal diversity of separation-of-powers systems, see Aziz Z. Huq and Jon D. Michaels. "The Cycles of Separation-of-Powers Jurisprudence," *Yale Law Journal* 126, no. 2 (2016): 346–437; M. Elizabeth Magill and Adrian Vermeule, "Allocating Power within Agencies," *Yale Law Journal* 120 (2011): 1032–83.

96. Henry S. Richardson, *Democratic Autonomy: Public Reasoning about the Ends of Policy* (New York: Oxford University Press, 2002), 3.

97. Thomas Christiano, "Democracy and Bureaucracy." *Philosophy and Phenomenological Research* 71, no. 1 (2005): 211–17. The problem of the role of the state in relation to democracy has received extensive attention in recent French political philosophy. See Wim Weymans, "Freedom Through Political Representation: Lefort, Gauchet and Rosanvallon on the Relationship between State and Society," *European Journal of Political Theory* 4, no. 3 (2005): 263–82.

98. Fukuyama, *Political Order and Political Decay,* 144, 148.

99. Francis Fukuyama, "Why Is Democracy Performing So Poorly?" *Journal of Democracy* 26, no. 1 (2015): 11–20.

100. Fukuyama, *Political Order and Political Decay*, 83–84.

101. There is disagreement among historians of early China as to how to characterize the extent of such constraint. Compare Karl August Wittfogel, *Oriental Despotism: A Comparative Study of Total Power* (New Haven, CT: Yale University Press: 1957) (emphasizing bureaucracy), with Mark Edward Lewis, *The Early Chinese Empires: Qin and Han* (Cambridge: Harvard University Press, 2009), 63 (emphasizing the influence of cliques around the emperor).

102. Magill and Vermeule, "Allocating Power within Agencies," 1035.

103. Dawn Brancati, "Democratic Authoritarianism: Origins and Effects," *Annual Review of Political Science* 17 (2014): 313–26, 317.

104. Fukuyama, *Political Order and Political Decay*, 86.

105. Norton E. Long, "Bureaucracy and Constitutionalism," *American Political Science Review* 46, no. 3 (1952): 808–18, 810; Ali Farazmand, "Bureaucracy and Democracy: A Theoretical Analysis," *Public Organization Review* 10, no. 3 (2010): 245–58.

106. Tiberiu Dragu and Mattias Polborn, "The Administrative Foundation of the Rule of Law," *Journal of Politics* 75, no. 4 (2013): 1038–50.

107. Zsolt Enyedi, "Populist Polarization and Party System Institutionalization: The Role of Party Politics in De-Democratization," *Problems of Post-Communism* 63, no. 4 (2016): 210–20, 214; Scheppele, "Rule of Law and the Frankenstate."

108. Yusuf Sarfati, "How Turkey's Slide to Authoritarianism Defies Modernization Theory," *Turkish Studies* 18, no. 3 (2017): 1–21, 9.

109. Ergun Özbudun, "AKP at the Crossroads: Erdoğan's Majoritarian Drift," *South European Society and Politics* 19, no. 2 (2014): 155–67. On the influence of the military on the judiciary prior to 2010, see Güneş Murat Tezcür, "Judicial Activism in Perilous Times: The Turkish Case," *Law & Society Review* 43, no. 2 (2009): 305–36.

110. Andrew S. Bowen, "How Putin Uses Money Laundering Charges to Control His Opponents," *Atlantic*, July 17, 2013), online at http://www.theatlantic.com/international/archive/2013/07/how-putin-uses-money-laundering-charges-to-control-his-opponents/277903/; Tina Burrett, *Television and Presidential Power in Putin's Russia* (London: Routledge, 2010), 43–44.

111. Nancy Fraser, "Rethinking the Public Sphere: A Contribution to the Critique of Actually Existing Democracy," *Social Text*, nos. 25/26 (1990): 56–80, 57; see also Jürgen Habermas, *The Structural Transformation of the Public Sphere: An Inquiry into a Category of Bourgeois Society*, trans. Thomas Burger with Frederick Lawrence (Cambridge, MA: MIT Press, 1989).

112. Nadia Urbinati, *Democracy Disfigured* (Cambridge, MA: Harvard University Press, 2014), 21.

113. "Liberal democratic vocabulary is often used propagandistically, in states whose practices fall too short of its ideals" (Jason Stanley, *How Propaganda Works* [Princeton, NJ: Princeton University Press, 2015], 50). Unlike Stanley, we do not think this problem has become so severe in the United States that the label *liberal democracy* no longer applies.

114. Joel B. Grossman, "The Japanese American Cases and the Vagaries of Constitutional Adjudication in Wartime: An Institutional Perspective," *University of Hawaii Law Review* 19 (1997): 649.

115. Corrales, "Autocratic Legalism," 40–41; Kirk A. Hawkins, "Chavismo, Liberal Democracy, and Radical Democracy," *Annual Review of Political Science* 19 (2016): 311–29.

116. "Media Freedom in Turkey: Sultanic Verses," *Economist*, August 6, 2016, online at http://www.economist.com/news/europe/21703375-turkish-governments-crackdown-extends-journalists-and-poets-sultanic-verses.

117. Sarfati, "Turkey's Slide to Authoritarianism," 8–13.

118. Fomina and Kucharczyk, "Populism and Protest in Poland,"63.

119. Freedom House, "Press Freedom in Sri Lanka," online at https://freedomhouse.org/re port/freedom-press/2015/sri-lanka.

120. Brancati, "Democratic Authoritarianism," 316. On the trend in media repression from Yeltsin to Putin, see Camille Jackson, "Legislation as an Indicator of Free Press in Russia: Patterns of Change from Yeltsin to Putin," *Problems of Post-Communism* 63, nos. 5–6 (2016): 354–66.

121. Tim Wu, "Is the First Amendment Obsolete?," *Knight First Amendment Institute at Columbia University*, September 2017, online at https://knightcolumbia.org/content/tim-wu-first -amendment-obsolete; Peter Pomerantsev, "The Menace of Unreality: How the Kremlin Weaponizes Information, Culture and Money," *Interpreter*, November 22, 2014, online at http://www .interpretermag.com/the-menace-of-unreality-how-the-kremlin-weaponizes-information -culture-and-money; Jill Dougherty, "How the Media Became One of Putin's Most Powerful Weapons," *Atlantic*, April 21, 2015, online at https://www.theatlantic.com/international/archive /2015/04/how-the-media-became-putins-most-powerful-weapon/391062/.

122. For an example, see "Russia's Fake Electronic Bomb," *Medium*, May 6, 2017, online at https://medium.com/dfrlab/russias-fake-electronic-bomb-4ce9dbbc57f8.

123. Zeynep Tufekci, *Twitter and Tear Gas: The Power and Fragility of Networked Protest* (New Haven, CT, Yale University Press: 2017), 265.

124. Sheri Berman, "Civil Society and the Collapse of the Weimar Republic," *World Politics* 49, no. 3 (1997): 401–29.

125. Clifford J. Levy, "At the Expense of All Others, Putin Picks a Church," *New York Times*, April 24, 2008.

126. For an analysis of the "flexible and durable" form of Iranian autocracy, see Abbas Milani, "Iran's Paradoxical Regime," *Journal of Democracy* 26, no. 2 (2015): 52–60.

127. Varol, "Stealth Authoritarianism," 1696. For the text of the 2012 law, see Thomas M. Callahan, "The Right to Reputation and the Case for Boris Nemtsov," *Fordham International Law Journal* 39 (2015): 1289, 1315. For examples, see *Porubova v. Russia*, App. No. 8237/03, at 1, 4 (Eur. Ct. H.R. 2010) (appeal of eighteen-month criminal libel sentence levied on a journalist who published an article on corruption in a state railroad company).

128. Tim Arango, "In Scandal, Turkey's Leaders May Be Losing Their Tight Grip on News Media," *New York Times*, January 11, 2014.

129. "Indonesia Passes Law to Stop Criticism of Politicians" *Voice of America Online,* February 24, 2018, online at https://learningenglish.voanews.com/a/indonesia-law/4265678.html.

130. Lilia Shevtsova, "Forward to the Past in Russia," *Journal of Democracy* 26, no. 2 (2015): 22–36, 30.

131. Darin Christensen and Jeremy M. Weinstein, "Defunding Dissent: Restrictions on Aid to NGOs," *Journal of Democracy* 24, no. 2 (2013): 77–91; Chip Pitts and Anastasia Ovsuannikova, "Russia's New Treason Statute, Anti-NGO and Other Repressive Laws: Sovereign Democracy or Renewed Autocracy," *Houston Journal of International Law* 37, no. 1 (2015): 83; "Russian NGOs Refuse to Abide by Kremlin Law Ordering Some to Declare Themselves 'Foreign Agents,'" *CBS News*, September 28, 2012, online at http://www.cbsnews.com/news/russian-ngos-refuse-to-abide-by-kremlin-law-ordering -some-to-declare-themselves-foreign-agents; "Russian NGOs Undergoing Unprecedented Kremlin Sweeps," *Bellona*, April 2, 2013, online at http://bellona.org/news/russian-human-rights-issues /russian-ngo-law/2013-04-russianngos-undergoing-unprecedented-kremlin-sweeps.

132. "NGO Laws," website of former UN Special Rapporteur Maina Kiai, online at http://freeassembly.net/tag/ngo-law/; see also Thomas Carothers and Saskia Brechenmacher, *Closing Space: Democracy and Human Rights Support Under Fire* (Washington, DC: Carnegie Endowment for International Peace, 2014).

133. Corrales, "Autocratic Legalism in Venezuela," 42; Hawkins, "Chavismo, Liberal Democracy, and Radical Democracy," 314–15. On the 2017 elections, see Wil S. Hylton, "Can Venezuela be Saved?," *New York Times*, March 1, 2018, online at https://www.nytimes.com/2018/03/01/magazine/can-venezuela-be-saved.html. On the statistical evidence of fraud in the 2010 election, see Luis Pericchi and David Torres, "Quick Anomaly Detection by the Newcomb—Benford Law, with Applications to Electoral Processes Data from the USA, Puerto Rico and Venezuela," *Statistical Science* 26, no. 4 (2011): 502–16, 513–14.

134. "Sri Lanka's Opposition Alleges Electoral Fraud," *CBC News*, April 9, 2010, online at http://www.cbc.ca/news/world/sri-lankan-opposition-alleges-election-fraud-1.878438.

135. Ziya Öniş, "Turkey's Two Elections: The AKP Comes Back," *Journal of Democracy* 27, no. 2 (2016): 141–54; Sarfati, "Turkey's Slide to Authoritarianism," 9; Berk Esen and Sebnem Gumuscu, "Rising Competitive Authoritarianism in Turkey," *Third World Quarterly* 37, no. 9 (2016): 1581–1606, 1586–90.

136. Luke Harding, "Supreme Court Ban on Liberal Party Wipes Out Opposition to Putin," *Guardian*, March 24, 2007, online at https://perma.cc/9SRF-VWN3; Alexandr Litoy, "A Guide to Political Persecution in Russia," *Open Democracy*, March 13, 2015, online at https://perma.cc/VB7T-AQYE. On the Nemtsov killing, see "Uncontrolled Violence," *Economist*, March 7, 2015, online at http://www.economist.com/news/europe/21645838-assassination-boris-nemtsov-leaves-liberal-russians-fear-new-wave-violent.

137. Tamara Pearson, "Venezuelan President Designates New Caracas Head and Communications Minister," *Venezuela Analysis*, April 16, 2009, online at https://venezuelanalysis.com/news/4371; Daniel Lansberg-Rodriguez, "Maduro and His Imaginary Parliament," *Foreign Policy*, December 22, 2015, online at http://foreignpolicy.com/2015/12/22/president-maduro-and-his-imaginary-parliament-venezuela-elections/.

138. Michael Albertus and Victor Menaldo, "The Political Economy of Autocratic Constitutions," in *Constitutions in Authoritarian Regimes*, ed. Tom Ginsburg and Alberto Simpser (New York: Cambridge University Press, 2014), 53–82.

Chapter Five

1. Jan E. Leighley and Jonathan Nagler, *Who Votes Now? Demographics, Issues, Inequality, and Turnout in the United States* (Princeton, NJ: Princeton University Press, 2013), 20–21.

2. Christopher H. Achen and Larry M. Bartels, *Democracy for Realists: Why Elections Do Not Produce Responsive Government* (Princeton, NJ: Princeton University Press, 2016), 311.

3. For the campaign speech, see Jan-Werner Müller, *What Is Populism?* (Philadelphia: University of Pennsylvania Press, 2016), 22; for the acceptance speech, see "Donald Trump: 'I Alone Can Fix It,' RNC, Cleveland, OH, 7/21/16," Filmed (July 2016), YouTube video, October 12, 2016, online at https://www.youtube.com/watch?v=KGenVcak5nI. For the criminal threats, see Steven Levitsky and Daniel Ziblatt, "Is Donald Trump a Threat to Our Democracy?" *New York Times*, December 16, 2016, at SR5. For the threats to journalists, see Erik Wemple, "Megyn Kelly's Personal Horror Stories," *Washington Post*, November 13, 2016.

4. Jonathan T. Rothwell and Pablo Diego-Rosell, "Explaining Nationalist Political Views: The Case of Donald Trump," Working Paper, November 2, 2016, online at https://ssrn.com /abstract=2822059.

5. Stephen Wolf, "Republicans Now Dominate State Governments, with 32 State Legislatures, and 33 Governors," *Daily Kos*, November 16, 2016.

6. On the Supreme Court, see Burgess Everett and Glenn Thrush, "McConnell Throws Down the Gauntlet: No Scalia Replacement under Obama," *Politico*, February 13, 2016; Daniel S. Cohen, "Do Your Duty (!)(?) The Distribution of Power in the Appointments Clause," *Virginia Law Review* 103 (2017): 673. On the debt ceiling, see Christopher Langner, "Dagong Downgrades US to A- from A," *Reuters*, October 17, 2013, online at https://www.reuters.com/article /idUSL3N0I71YW20131017.

7. On the effects of voter-identification laws, see Zoltan Hajnal, Nazita Lajevardi, and Lindsay Nielson, "Voter Identification Laws and the Suppression of Minority Votes," *Journal of Politics* 79, no. 2 (2017): 363–79; Benjamin Highton, "Voter Identification Laws and Turnout in the United States," *Annual Review of Political Science* 20 (2017): 149–67. On gerrymanders, see Nicholas Stephanopoulos and Eric McGhee, "Partisan Gerrymandering and the Efficiency Gap," *University of Chicago Law Review* 82, no. 2 (2015): 831–900.

8. Christopher Hare and Keith T. Poole, "The Polarization of Contemporary American Politics," *Polity* 46, no. 3 (2014): 411–29; Gary C. Jacobson, "Partisan Polarization in American Politics: A Background Paper," *Presidential Studies Quarterly* 43, no. 4 (2013): 688–708.

9. Publius Decius Mus, "The Flight 93 Election," *Claremont Review of Books*, September 5, 2016. The author, Michael Anton, later became a senior aide in the Trump White House. Polling data: Pew Research Center, "Partisanship and Political Animosity I, 2016," June 2016, online at http://www.people-press.org/2016/06/22/partisanship-and-political-animosity-in-2016/.

10. Bruce Ackerman, *We the People: Transformations, vol. 2* (Cambridge, MA: Harvard University Press, 1998).

11. Glenn Thrush and Julie Hirschfield Davis, "Trump, in Poland, Asks If West Has 'Will to Survive,'" *New York Times*, July 6, 2017. For other attacks on the New Deal, see Richard A. Epstein, *The Classical Liberal Constitution* (Cambridge, MA: Harvard University Press, 2014), 45–71; Philip Hamburger, *Is Administrative Law Unlawful?* (Chicago: University of Chicago Press, 2014).

12. Ira Katznelson, *Fear Itself: The New Deal and the Origins of Our Times* (New York: Liveright, 2013), 12, 56–57; John P. Diggins, "Flirtation with Fascism: American Pragmatic Liberals and Mussolini's Italy," *American Historical Review* 71, no. 2 (1966): 487–506.

13. Katznelson, *Fear Itself*; Peter H. Irons, *The New Deal Lawyers* (Princeton, NJ: Princeton University Press, 1993).

14. William E. Leuchtenburg, *The Supreme Court Reborn: The Constitutional Revolution in the Age of Roosevelt* (New York: Oxford University Press, 1996). For the best evidence that the Court-packing plan influenced the crucial swing vote of Justice Owen Roberts, see Daniel E. Ho and Kevin M. Quinn, "Did a Switch in Time Save Nine?" *Journal of Legal Analysis* 2, no. 1 (2010): 69–113.

15. Michael J. Korzi, "Theorizing Presidential Tenure: The Difficult Case of FDR's Fourth Term," *Congress & the Presidency: A Journal of Capital Studies* 35, no. 2 (2008): 39–64.

16. Cass R. Sunstein, "Constitutionalism After the New Deal," *Harvard Law Review* 101, no. 2 (1987): 421–510, 422.

17. James T. Sparrow, *Warfare State: World War II Americans and the Age of Big Government* (New York: Oxford University Press, 2011).

18. The leading revisionist account is supplied by Barry Cushman, who has cast doubt on the efficacy of the Court-packing plan as a threat to the Court ("Rethinking the New Deal Court," *Virginia Law Review* 80, no. 1 [1994]: 201–61) and on the idea of a doctrinal rupture ("A Stream of Legal Consciousness: The Current of Commerce Doctrine from *Swift* to *Jones & Laughlin*," *Fordham Law Review* 61 [1992]: 105–60).

19. Katznelson, *Fear Itself*, 252–60.

20. On the dynamics of such entrenchment, see Paul Pierson, *Politics in Time: History, Institutions, and Social Analysis* (Princeton, NJ: Princeton University Press, 2004), 17–18.

21. Laura Weinrib, *The Taming of Free Speech* (Cambridge, MA: Harvard University Press, 2016).

22. Some also argue that the Act was also an effort to "hard-wire" New Deal policies into place against Republican backlash; see McNollgast, "The Political Origins of the Administrative Procedure Act," *Journal of Law, Economics, & Organization* 15, no. 1 (1999): 180–217. It may well have done both at the same time.

23. Friedrich Hayek, *The Road to Serfdom* (London: Routledge, 2014).

24. U.S. Const., Art. II, §2; David J. Barron and Martin S. Lederman, "The Commander in Chief at the Lowest Ebb: A Constitutional History," *Harvard Law Review* 121, no. 4 (2008): 941–1112.

25. Samuel P. Huntington, *The Soldier and the State: The Theory and Politics of Civil-Military Relations* (Cambridge, MA: Harvard University Press, 1957), 16–69, 177.

26. National Security Act of 1947, Pub. L. No. 80-253, 61 Stat. 495 (codified in scattered portions of the U.S. Code); Amy B. Zegart, *Flawed by Design: The Evolution of the CIA, JSC, and NSC* (Palo Alto, CA: Stanford University Press: 1999), 57–62.

27. Bruce Ackerman, *The Decline and Fall of the American Republic* (Cambridge, MA: Harvard University Press, 2010), 9–10, 24–36; Charles J. Dunlap Jr, "The Origins of the American Military Coup of 2012," *Parameters* 40 (Winter, 2011): 107.

28. On the extensive entanglement of military commanders in US regional centers in foreign policy matters, see Dana Priest, *The Mission: Waging War and Keeping Peace with America's Military* (New York: Vintage, 2004).

29. On the parallel function of the military in Turkey and Thailand, see Duncan McCargo and Ayşe Zarakol, "Turkey and Thailand: Unlikely Twins," *Journal of Democracy* 23, no. 3 (2012): 71–79.

30. John Ferejohn and Frances McCall Rosenbluth, *Forged Through Fire: War, Peace, and the Democratic Bargain* (New York: W. W. Norton, 2016).

31. Swati Srivastava, "Sovereignty under Contract: Tensions in American Security," manuscript, 3; adapted from Colonel Stephen J. Zamparelli, "Contractors on the Battlefield: What Have We Signed Up For?" *Air Force Journal of Logistics* 23, no. 3 (1999): 12; David Isenberg, *Shadow Force: Private Security Contractors in Iraq* (Westport, CT: Praeger Security International, 2008), 4.

32. Peter D. Feaver, "Civil-Military Relations," *Annual Review of Political Science* 2, no. 1 (1999): 211–41, 230.

33. See Zoltan Barany, "The Role of the Military," *Journal of Democracy* 22, no. 4 (2011): 24–35.

34. Thomas D. Beamish, Harvey Molotch, and Richard Flacks, "Who Supports the Troops? Vietnam, the Gulf War, and the Making of Collective Memory," *Social Problems* 42, no. 3 (1995): 344–60.

35. Rebecca U. Thorpe, *The American Warfare State: The Domestic Politics of Military Spending* (Chicago: University of Chicago Press, 2014).

36. Data from the Comparative Constitutions Project, online at http://comparativeconstitutionsproject.

37. Paul Halliday, *Habeas Corpus: From England to Empire* (Cambridge, MA: Harvard University Press, 2010); Aziz Z. Huq, "The President and the Detainees," *University of Pennsylvania Law Review* 164, no. 3 (2017): 449–593.

38. US Const. amend. XXV, §1. For the statutory succession rules, see Presidential Succession Act of 1947, 3 U.S.C. §19(d)(1).19(a)(1), (b), 19(d)(1). For criticisms, see Akhil Reed Amar and Vikram David Amar, "Is the Presidential Succession Law Constitutional?" *Stanford Law Review* 48, no. 1 (1995): 113–39; William F. Brown and Americo R. Cinquegrana, "The Realities of Presidential Succession: The Emperor Has No Clones," *Georgetown Law Journal* 75 (1986): 1389.

39. On the growth of emergency powers over the twentieth century, see Jules Lobel, "Emergency Power and the Decline of Liberalism," *Yale Law Journal* 98, no. 7 (1989): 1385–1433; Special Senate Committee on National Emergencies and Delegated Emergency Powers, 93d Cong., *A Brief History of Emergency Powers in the United States*, at v (Washington, DC: Senate, 1974). On gaps in rights, see David Cole, *Enemy Aliens: Double Standards and Constitutional Freedoms in the War on Terrorism* (New York: New Press, 2003). On the nonavailability of remedies, see Aziz Z. Huq, "Against National Security Exceptionalism," *Supreme Court Review* 2009, no. 1 (2009): 225–73.

40. The most important cases are in the Fourth Amendment context, where a government action (sometimes illegal) will prompt individuals to try to destroy evidence. See *Kentucky v. King*, 131 S. Ct. 1849, 1856–58 (2011).

41. *Holder v. Humanitarian Law Project*, 561 U.S. 1 (2010). For an analysis of the Court's treatment of material support laws, see Aziz Z. Huq, "Preserving Political Speech from Ourselves and Others," *Columbia Law Review Sidebar* 112 (January, 2012): 16–30.

42. Harry N. Scheiber and Jane S. Scheiber, *Bayonets in Paradise: Martial Law in Hawai'i during World War II* (Honolulu: University of Hawaii Press, 2016)

43. Abraham Diskin, Hanna Diskin, and Reuven Y. Hazan, "Why Democracies Collapse: The Reasons for Democratic Failure and Success," *International Political Science Review* 26, no. 3 (2005): 291–309.

44. Aziz Z. Huq, "The Function of Article V," *University of Pennsylvania Law Review* 162 (2013): 1165–1236; Michael Stokes Paulsen, "A General Theory of Article V: The Constitutional Lessons of the Twenty-Seventh Amendment," *Yale Law Journal* 103, no. 3 (1993): 677–789.

45. Tom Ginsburg, and James Melton, "Does the Constitutional Amendment Rule Matter at All? Amendment Cultures and the Challenges of Measuring Amendment Difficulty," *International Journal of Constitutional Law* 15 (2015): 686–713.

46. Zachary Elkins, Tom Ginsburg, and James Melton, *The Endurance of National Constitutions* (New York: Cambridge University Press, 2009), 101–40.

47. For a collection of criticism, see Huq, "Function of Article V."

48. For an excellent analysis, see Daniel Hemel and Eric Posner, "Presidential Obstruction of Justice," University of Chicago Law School, Public Law and Legal Theory Working Papers, 665 (July 2017).

49. Bar on independent redistricting commissions: *Arizona State Legislature v. Arizona Independent Redistricting Commission*, 576 U.S.___ (2015). Use of electorate rather than populations for districting: *Evenwel v. Abbott*, 578 U.S. ___ (2016).

50. For example, see S. J. Res. 180, 101st Cong., 1st sess. (1989 (flag burning).

51. Yaniv Roznai, "Unconstitutional Constitutional Amendments—The Migration and Success of a Constitutional Idea," *American Journal of Comparative Law* 61, no. 3 (2013): 657–720. For the Hungarian case, see Gábor Halmai, "Unconstitutional Constitutional Amendments: Constitutional Courts as Guardians of the Constitution?" *Constellations* 19, no. 2 (2012): 182–203.

52. For a comparison of the different species of congressional authority with this dichotomy in mind, see Aziz Z. Huq, "Tiers of Scrutiny in Enumerated Powers Jurisprudence," *University of Chicago Law Review* 80, no. 2 (2013): 575–656.

53. William N. Eskridge and John A. Ferejohn, *A Republic of Statutes: The New American Constitution* (New Haven, CT: Yale University Press, 2010).

54. On the general phenomenon, see David A. Strauss, "The Irrelevance of Constitutional Amendments," *Harvard Law Review* 114, no. 5 (2001): 1457–1505. The cases are: *District of Columbia v. Heller*, 554 U.S. 570 (2008); *Obergefell v. Hodges*, 576 U.S. ___ (2015); *National Federation of Independent Business v. Sebelius*, 567 U.S. 519 (2012); and *Citizens United v. Federal Election Commission*, 558 U.S. 310 (2010).

55. *Stuart v. Laird*, 5 U.S. (1 Cranch) 299 (1803).

56. U.S. Const., Arts I and II. For an excellent account of Congress's capabilities under Article I, see Josh Chafetz, "Congress's Constitution," *University of Pennsylvania Law Review* 160 (2011): 715–78.

57. James Madison, "Federalist No. 51," in *The Federalist Papers*, ed. Isaac Kramnick (New York: Penguin Books, 1987), 319–20; David Fontana and Aziz Z. Huq, "Institutional Loyalties in Constitutional Law," *University of Chicago Law Review* 85, no. 1 (2018): 1–84; Daryl J. Levinson and Richard H. Pildes, "Separation of Parties, Not Powers," *Harvard Law Review* 119, no. 8 (2006): 2311–86.

58. Grégoire Weber, "Loyal Opposition and the Political Constitution," *Oxford Journal of Legal Studies* 37, no. 2 (2017): 357–82.

59. On minority rights: David Fontana, "Government in Opposition," *Yale Law Journal* 119, no. 3 (2009): 548–623. On investigative powers of Congress: *U.S. House of Reps. v. Burwell*, 130 F.Supp.3d 53, 81 (D.D.C. 2015); *Committee on the Judiciary v. Miers*, 558 F. Supp. 2d 53, 89–90 (D.D.C. 2008).

60. Aziz Z. Huq and Jon D. Michaels, "The Cycles of Separation-of-Powers Jurisprudence," *Yale Law Journal* 126, no. 2 (2016): 346–437.

61. Steven Levitsky and James Loxton, "Populism and Competitive Authoritarianism in the Andes," *Democratization* 20, no. 1 (2013): 107–36.

62. Samuel Issacharoff, *Fragile Democracies: Contested Power in the Era of Constitutional Courts* (New York: Cambridge University Press, 2015), 168–86; Theunis Roux, *The Politics of Principle: The First South African Constitutional Court, 1995-2005* (Cambridge: Cambridge University Press, 2013).

63. Karl Loewenstein, "Law in the Third Reich," *Yale Law Journal* 45, no. 5 (1936): 779–815.

64. For a similar account, see Mark Tushnet, "Foreword: The New Constitutional Order and the Chastening of Constitutional Aspiration," *Harvard Law Review* 113, no. 1 (1999): 29.

65. Federal Judicial Center, Biographical Directory of Article III Federal Judges, 1789–Present, online at https://www.fjc.gov/history/judges/search/advanced-search.

66. Geoffrey R. Stone, *Perilous Times: Free Speech in Wartime from the Sedition Act of 1798 to the War on Terrorism* (New York: W. W. Norton, 2004), 16–20; James P. Martin, "When Repression Is Democratic and Constitutional: The Federalist Theory of Representation and the Sedition Act of 1798," *University of Chicago Law Review* 66, no. 1 (1999): 117–82.

67. On the development of the federal judiciary's institutional capacity, see Aziz Z. Huq, "Judicial Independence and the Rationing of Constitutional Remedies," *Duke Law Journal* 65, no. 1 (2015): 1–80; Justin Crowe, *Building the Judiciary: Law, Courts, and the Politics of Institutional Development* (Princeton, NJ: Princeton University Press, 2012). On *Brown*, see *Brown v. Board of Education*, 347 US 483 (1954); and Brad Snyder, "How the Conservatives Canonized *Brown v. Board of Education*," *Rutgers Law Review* 52 (1999): 383. On the Supreme Court's public support, see the discussion in Stephen P. Nicholson and Thomas G. Hansford, "Partisans in Robes: Party Cues and Public Acceptance of Supreme Court Decisions," *American Journal of Political Science* 58, no. 3 (2014): 620–36.

68. *United States v. Lee*, 106 U.S. 196 (1882); Huq, "Judicial Independence."

69. *Ashcroft v. al-Kidd*, 131 S. Ct. 2074, 2085 (2011). But see Joanna C. Schwarz, "How Qualified Immunity Fails" *Yale Law Journal* 127 (2017): 2–76.

70. Huq, "Judicial Independence"; Aziz Z. Huq and Genevieve Lakier, "Apparent Fault," *Harvard Law Review* 131 (forthcoming, 2018); James E. Pfander, *Constitutional Torts and the War on Terror* (New York: Oxford University Press, 2016).

71. See Matthew Hall, "The Semiconstrained Court: Public Opinion, the Separation of Powers, and the US Supreme Court's Fear of Nonimplementation," *American Journal of Political Science* 58, no. 2 (2014): 352–66.

72. Herbert Wechsler, "The Political Safeguards of Federalism: The Rôle of the States in the Composition and Selection of the National Government," *Columbia Law Review* 54, no. 4 (1954): 543–60.

73. Heather K. Gerken, "Second-Order Diversity," *Harvard Law Review* 118, no. 4 (2005): 1099–1196, 1102; Heather Gerken, "We're About to See States' Rights Used Defensively Against Trump," *Vox*, December 12, 2016. On nullification, see Kyle Scott, *Federalism: A Normative Theory and Its Political Relevance* (London: Bloomsbury, 2011), 94–115. On immigration law federalism, see Cristina Rodriguez, "Enforcement, Integration, and the Future of Immigration Federalism," *Journal on Migration and Human Security* 5, no. 2 (2017): 509–40.

74. Jacqueline Behrend and Laurence Whitehead, eds., *Illiberal Practices: Territorial Variance within Large Federal Democracies* (Baltimore: Johns Hopkins University Press, 2016).

75. Kristin N. Garrett and Joshua M. Jansa, "Interest Group Influence in Policy Diffusion Networks," *State Politics & Policy Quarterly* 15, no. 3 (2015): 387–417.

76. Guillermo A. O'Donnell, "Delegative Democracy," *Journal of Democracy* 5, no. 1 (1994): 55–69, 61; see also Guillermo A. O'Donnell, "Horizontal Accountability in New Democracies," *Journal of Democracy* 9, no. 3 (1998): 112–26.

77. *Lovett v. United States*, 66 F. Supp. 142 (1945), affirmed in *United States v. Lovett*, 328 U.S. 303 (1946).

78. Data from Comparative Constitutions Project, online at http://comparativeconstitutionsproject.

79. Stephen Skowronek, *Building a New American State: The Expansion of National Administrative Capacities, 1877–1920* (New York: Cambridge University Press, 1982).

80. Jerry L. Mashaw, "Recovering American Administrative Law: Federalist Foundations, 1787–1801," *Yale Law Journal* 115, no. 6 (2006): 1256; Jerry L. Mashaw, *Creating the Administrative Constitution: The Lost One Hundred Years of American Administrative Law* (New Haven, CT: Yale University Press, 2012).

81. Nicholas R. Parrillo, *Against the Profit Motive: The Salary Revolution in American Government, 1780–1940* (New Haven, CT: Yale University Press, 2013). On the Jacksonian system,

see Scott C. James, "Patronage Regimes and American Party Development from 'The Age of Jackson' to the Progressive Era," *British Journal of Political Science* 36, no. 1 (2006): 39–60.

82. Act of January 16, 1883, ch. 27, 22 Stat. 403; Skowronek, *New American State*, 64–80; Ronald N., Johnson and Gary D. Libecap, "Patronage to Merit and Control of the Federal Government Labor Force," *Explorations in Economic History* 31, no. 1 (1994): 91–119.

83. 1974 Act: 5 U.S.C. §§ 1201–1209, 2301–2305 (2000). Non-discrimination clauses in departmental hiring policies often disallow discrimination based on political affiliation as well. 28 CFR § 42.1(a). Supreme Court case law: *Rutan v. Republican Party of Illinois*, 497 U.S. 62, 74 (1990); see also *O'Hare Truck Serv. Inc. v. City of Northlake*, 518 U.S. 712, 720 (1996).

84. Adrian Vermeule, "Conventions of Agency Independence," *Columbia Law Review* 113, no. 5 (2013): 1163–1238.

85. William Sessions was fired by Bill Clinton for violating ethics rules, but only after Clinton sought a resignation.

86. Office of the Inspector General, Department of Justice, "An Investigation of Allegations of Politicized Hiring and Other Improper Personnel Actions in the Civil Rights Division" (July 2008), online at https://oig.justice.gov/special/s0901/final.pdf; Eric Lipton and Nicholas Fandos, "Departing Ethics Chief: U.S. Is 'Close to a Laughingstock,'" *New York Times*, July 17, 2017.

87. For appointments, see *NLRB v. Noel Canning*, 134 S. Ct. 2550, 2600-06 (2014). For removals, see *Free Enter. Fund v. PCAOB*, 561 U.S. 477 (2010). On the effects of such decisions, see Aziz Z. Huq, "Removal as a Political Question," *Stanford Law Review* 65, no. 1 (2013): 1–76.

88. Elena Kagan, "Presidential Administration," *Harvard Law Review* 114, no. 8 (2001): 2245–2385.

89. David J. Barron and Todd D. Rakoff, "In Defense of Big Waiver," *Columbia Law Review* 113, no. 2 (2013): 265–345.

90. See, for example, Daniel T. Deacon, "Administrative Forbearance," *Yale Law Journal* 125, no. 6 (2016): 1548–1614; Adam B. Cox and Cristina M. Rodríguez, "The President and Immigration Law," *Yale Law Journal* 119, no. 3 (2009): 458–547.

91. Originalist arguments: Steven G. Calabresi and Kevin H. Rhodes, "The Structural Constitution: Unitary Executive, Plural Judiciary," *Harvard Law Review* 105, no. 6 (1992): 1153–1216. Functional arguments: Adrian Vermeule, "Our Schmittian Administrative Law," *Harvard Law Review* 122, no. 4 (2008): 1095–1149; Eric A. Posner and Cass R. Sunstein, "*Chevron*izing Foreign Relations Law," *Yale Law Journal* 116, no. 6 (2007): 1170–1228.

92. Eric Posner, "Trump and the Paradox of Populist Government," January 3, 2017, online at https://papers.ssrn.com/sol3/papers.cfm?abstract_id=2893251.

93. Achen and Bartels, *Democracy for Realists*, 232–66.

94. The leading example is the socialist candidate for president, Eugene Debs, who ran for president five times and was repeatedly imprisoned for his political activity and speech.

95. *Keyishian v. Board of Regents*, 385 U.S. 589, 598 (1967).

96. *New York Times Co. v. Sullivan*, 376 U.S. 254 (1964) (public figures); *Gertz v. Robert Welch, Inc.*, 418 U.S. 323 (1974) (private figures); *Bose Corp. v. Consumers Union of United States, Inc.*, 466 U.S. 485 (1984) (appellate review).

97. *Snyder v. Phelps*, 562 U.S. 443, 453 (2011).

98. Respectively, these cases are *NAACP v. Alabama ex rel. Patterson*, 357 U.S. 449 (1958); *Communist Party of the United States v. Subversive Activities Control Board*, 367 U.S. 1 (1961); and *Holder v. Humanitarian Law Project*, 561 U.S. 1 (2010).

99. Lisa-Marie N. Neudert, "Computational Propaganda in Germany: A Cautionary Tale," 14–20 Working Paper No. 2017.7 (2017); Jeremy W. Peters, "Wielding Claims of 'Fake News,' Conservatives Take Aim at Mainstream Media," *New York Times*, December 26, 2016.

100. Laurens Cerulus, "Germany's Anti-Fake News Lab Yields Mixed Results," *Politico*, July 17, 2017.

101. *United States v. Alvarez*, 132 S. Ct. 2537, 2552 (2012); Alan K. Chen and Justin Marceau, "High Value Lies, Ugly Truths, and the First Amendment," *Vanderbilt Law Review* 68 (2015): 1435; Richard L. Hasen, "A Constitutional Right to Lie in Campaigns and Elections," *Montana Law Review* 74 (2013): 53.

102. Sampling cases: *Utah v. Evans*, 536 U.S. 452 (2002); *Department of Commerce v. U.S. House of Representatives*, 525 U.S. 316 (2000).

103. U.S. Const., Art. I, § 6, cl. 1.

104. Data from Comparative Constitutions Project; *Kaneko v. Japan (Hakata Station Film Case)* Sup.Ct. 1969.11.26 Keishu 23-11-l490 [Japan].

105. Mont. Const., Art. II, § 9; N.H. Const. pt. 1, Art. 8; Fla. Const. Art. I, § 24.

106. For an excellent cultural history of the idea of the right to know, see Michael Schudson, *The Rise of the Right to Know: Politics and the Culture of Transparency, 1945–1975* (Cambridge, MA: Harvard University Press, 2015), 1–27. On leaks and the First Amendment, see Mary-Rose Papandrea, "Leaker Traitor Whistleblower Spy: National Security Leaks and the First Amendment," *Boston University Law Review* 94, no. 2 (2014): 449–544; Geoffrey R. Stone, "Free Speech and National Security," *Indiana Law Journal* 84 (2009): 939–62.

107. On FOIA and its history: 5 U.S.C. § 552; Schudson, *The Rise of the Right to Know*, 280–63. On its use by journalists: James T. Hamilton, *Democracy's Detectives* (Cambridge, MA: Harvard University Press, 2016), 153–60. On criticisms: Margaret B. Kwoka, "FOIA, Inc.," *Duke Law Journal* 65 (2015): 1361–1437; David E. Pozen, "Freedom of Information beyond the Freedom of Information Act," *University of Pennsylvania Law Review* 165 (2016): 1097–1158.

108. On leaks: David E. Pozen, "The Leaky Leviathan: Why the Government Condemns and Condones Unlawful Disclosures of Information," *Harvard Law Review* 127, no. 2 (2013): 512–635. On overclassification, see House Committee on Government Reform, Subcommittee on National Security, Emerging Threats, and International Relations, *Too Many Secrets: Overclassification as a Barrier to Critical Information Sharing*, 108th Cong., 2nd sess, Aug. 24, 2005 (statement of John F. Tierney). On judges and the national security exemption, see Tom Ginsburg and Susan Nevelow Mart, "[Dis-]Informing the People's Discretion: Judicial Deference under the National Security Exemption of the Freedom of Information Act," *Administrative Law Review* 66, no. 4 (2014): 725–84.

109. Daryl J. Levinson, "Foreword: Looking for Power in Public Law," *Harvard Law Review* 130, no. 1 (2016): 31–143.

110. Keith G. Bentele and Erin E. O'Brien, "Jim Crow 2.0? Why States Consider and Adopt Restrictive Voter Access Policies," *Perspectives on Politics* 11, no. 4 (2013): 1088–1116.

111. Jack Ross, *The Socialist Party of America: A Complete History* (New York: Pantheon, 2015). The absence of a labor party in the United States is a more complex story related to the success of the New Deal Democrats' coalition building; see Barry Eidlin, "Why Is There No Labor Party in the United States? Political Articulation and the Canadian Comparison, 1932 to 1948," *American Sociological Review* 81, no. 3 (2016): 488–516.

112. Compare *North Carolina State Conference of NAACP v. McCrory*, 831 F.3d 204 (4th Cir. 2016), with *Crawford v. Marion County*, Election Bd., 553 U.S. 181 (2008).

113. *Compare Timmons v. Twin Cities Area New Party*, 520 U.S. 351 (1997) *with McConnell v. Fed. Election Comm'n*, 540 U.S. 93, 306 (2003) (Kennedy, J., concurring).

114. Michael Pal, "Electoral Management Bodies as a Fourth Branch of Government," *Review of Constitutional Studies* 21, no. 1 (2016): 85–113.

115. Jennifer Nou, "Sub-Regulating Elections," *Supreme Court Review* 2013, no. 1 (2014): 135–82; Daniel P. Tokaji, "The Birth and Rebirth of Election Administration," *Election Law Journal* 6, no. 1 (2007): 118–31. On the Federal Election Commission, see *Buckley v. Valeo*, 424 U.S. 1 (1976).

116. Colin Campbell, "Roy Cooper's Legal Battle Isn't Over Yet," *Citizen Times*, February 6, 2018; Mitch Smith, "North Carolina Judges Suspend Limits on Governor's Powers," *New York Times*, February 8, 2018; Jason Zengerle, "Is North Carolina the Future of American Politics?" *New York Times*, June 20, 2017; Richard Fausset, "North Carolina Governor Signs Law Limiting Successor's Power," *New York Times*, December 16, 2016.

117. John McKay, "Train Wreck at the Justice Department: An Eyewitness Account," *Seattle University Law Review* 31 (2007): 265–96. On the president's power to fire the FBI director, see Department of Justice, Office of Legal Counsel, "Constitutionality of Legislation Extending the Term of the FBI Director," June 20, 2011, online at https://www.justice.gov/file/18356/download.

118. *United States v. Armstrong*, 517 U.S. 456, 459 (1996); *Reno v. Am.-Arab Anti-Discrimination Comm.*, 525 U.S. 471 (1999).

Chapter Six

1. "Hardliner Wins Sri Lanka Election," *BBC News*, November 18, 2005. Hospital quotation: Walter Jayawardhana, "President Mahinda Rajapaksa Appeals to Unnamed Political Elements Not to Betray Motherland to Foreign Interests," *Asian Tribune*, August 13, 2007, online at http://www.asiantribune.com/index.php?q=node/6949.

2. Taylor Dibbert, "Sri Lanka's NGO Crackdown," *Foreign Policy*, July 25, 2014.

3. Indi Samarajiva, "Freedom of Expression in Sri Lanka, Circa 2011," *Sunday Leader*, January 30, 2011, online at http://www.thesundayleader.lk/2011/01/30/freedom-of-expression-in-sri-lanka-circa-2011/; International Crisis Group, "Sri Lanka's Compromised Judiciary: Politicized Courts, Compromised Rights, online at https://www.crisisgroup.org/asia/south-asia/sri-lanka/sri-lanka-s-judiciary-politicised-courts-compromised-rights, June 30, 2009; Asanga Welikala, "The Rajapaksa Regime and the Constitutionalisation of Populist Authoritarianism in Sri Lanka," *UCL: The Constitution Unit*, February 2, 2015, online at https://constitution-unit.com/2015/02/02/the-rajapaksa-regime-and-the-constitutionalisation-of-populist-authoritarianism-in-sri-lanka/.

4. Ellen Barry and Dharisha Bastians, "Sri Lankan President Concedes Defeat After Startling Upset," *New York Times*, January 8, 2015; "Sri Lanka's Rajapaksa Suffers Shock Election Defeat," *BBC News*, January 9, 2015, online at http://www.bbc.com/news/world-asia-30738671. On subsequent developments, see David Barstow, "Comeback Dims for Mahindra Rajapaksa, Sri Lanka's Ex President," *New York Times*, August 26, 2015.

5. On France, see Robert O. Paxton, *The Anatomy of Fascism* (New York: Vintage, 2004), 70–71. On Finland, see Marvin Rintala, *Three Generations: the Extreme Right Wing and Finnish Politics* (Bloomington: Indiana University Publications, 1962). On Denmark, see Agnes Cornell, Jørgen Møller, and Svend-Erik Skaaning, "The Real Lessons of the Interwar Years," *Journal of Democracy* 28, no. 3 (2017): 14–28.

6. Samuel P. Huntington, *The Third Wave: Democratization in the Late Twentieth Century* (Tulsa: University of Oklahoma Press, 1991), 266–67.

7. Sanford Levinson, *Constitutional Faith* (Princeton, NJ: Princeton University Press, 2008). For a different view, see Michael Klarman, *The Framers' Coup* (New York: Oxford University Press, 2017).

8. Alexander Hamilton, "Federalist, No. 1," in *The Federalist Papers*, ed. Isaac Kramnick (New York: Penguin Books, 1987), 87.

9. Letter from Thomas Jefferson to Samuel Kercheval, July 12, 1816, in *The Writings of Thomas Jefferson*, ed. Andrew Adgate Lipscomb and Albert Ellery Bergh, vol. 4 (Washington, DC: Thomas Jefferson Memorial Association, 1907), 40–41.

10. See respectively, Sanford Levinson, *Our Undemocratic Constitution: Where the Constitution Goes Wrong (and How We the People Can Correct It)* (New York: Oxford University Press, 2006); Larry J. Sabato, *A More Perfect Constitution: Why the Constitution Must Be Revised: Ideas to Inspire a New Generation* (New York: Macmillan, 2008); John Paul Stevens, *Six Amendments: How and Why We Should Change the Constitution* (New York: Little Brown, 2014).

11. Letter from Thomas Jefferson to Samuel Kercheval, July 12, 1816, 4:32, 40–41.

12. Karl Loewenstein, "Militant Democracy and Fundamental Rights, I," *American Political Science Review* 31, no. 3 (1937): 417–32; Karl Loewenstein, "Militant Democracy and Fundamental Rights, II," *American Political Science Review* 31, no. 4 (1937): 638–58; Gregory H. Fox and Georg Nolte, "Intolerant Democracies," *Harvard International Law Journal* 36, no. 1 (1995): 1–59. On party bans, see Angela K. Bourne, "Democratization and the Illegalization of Political Parties in Europe," *Democratization* 19, no. 6 (2012): 1065–85. The figure of twenty-one countries is from Comparative Constitutions Project data and includes all countries which constitutionally prohibit certain parties or types of parties and were classified as democracies (Polity > 6) during the year the constitution entered into force.

13. On demographics, see Doug Saunders, *The Myth of the Muslim Tide: Do Immigrants Threaten the West?* (New York: Vintage, 2012). On discrimination, see Claire L. Adida, David D. Laitin, and Marie-Anne Valfort, *Why Muslim Integration Fails in Christian-Heritage Societies* (Cambridge, MA: Harvard University Press, 2016). On European law, see Nehal Bhuta, "Two Concepts of Religious Freedom in the European Court of Human Rights," *South Atlantic Quarterly* 113, no. 1 (2014): 9–35. On counterterrorism, see Aziz Z. Huq, "The Uses of Religious Identity, Practice, and Dogma in 'Soft' and 'Hard' Counterterrorism," in *Security and Human Rights*, ed. Liora Lazarus and Benjamin Goold (London: Hart Publishing, 2018).

14. Hans-Georg Betz, and Susi Meret, "Revisiting Lepanto: The Political Mobilization against Islam in Contemporary Western Europe," *Patterns of Prejudice* 43, nos. 3–4 (2009): 313–34.

15. James Weinstein, "Hate Speech and Political Legitimacy," *Constitutional Commentary* 32 (2017): 557–58.

16. "Belgian Bishop Hauled Before Court for Church Teaching on Homosexuality Cleared of Charges," *Lifesite News* (June 6, 2008), online at http://www.tldm.org/news12/belgianbishop clearedofhatecrimecharges.htm.

17. "France Drops 'Hate Speech' Case Against Bob Dylan," *Wall Street Journal*, April 15, 2014, online at https://www.wsj.com/articles/france-drops-hate-speech-case-against-bob-dylan-1397592733.

18. For an alternative account of hate speech and its regulation, see Jeremy Waldron, *The Harm in Hate Speech* (Cambridge, MA: Harvard University Press, 2014).

19. Zachary Elkins, Tom Ginsburg, and James Melton, *The Endurance of National Constitutions* (New York: Cambridge University Press, 2009).

20. Indonesian Const., Art. 37, Ch. 16.

21. Ulrich K. Preuss, "The Implications of Eternity Clauses: The German Experience," *Israel Law Review* 44 (2011): 429.

22. Yaniv Roznai, "Unconstitutional Constitutional Amendments—The Migration and Success of a Constitutional Idea," *American Journal of Comparative Law* 61, no. 3 (2013): 657–720; Yaniv Roznai, *Unconstitutional Constitutional Amendments* (New York: Oxford, 2016).

23. Tom Ginsburg and James Melton, "Does the Constitutional Amendment Rule Matter at All?" *International Journal of Constitutional Law* 13 (2015): 686–713.

24. "Dutch Election: Wilders Defeat Celebrated by PM Rutte," *BBC News*, March 16, 2017.

25. Aurelien Bredeen and Benoît Morenne, "Emmanuel Macron's Party and Allies Win Big in France," *New York Times*, June 18, 2017.

26. Philip Oltermann, "Austrian Presidential Result Overturned and Must be Held Again," *Guardian*, July 1, 2016; Philip Oltermann, "Austria Rejects Far-right Candidate Norbert Hofer in Presidential Election," *Guardian*, December 4, 2016.

27. For an incisive critique, see Eric Maskin and Amartya Sen, "The Rules of the Game: A Better Electoral System," *New York Review of Books*, January 19, 2017.

28. Scott Mainwaring and Matthew Soberg Shugart, eds., *Presidentialism and Democracy in Latin America* (New York: Cambridge University Press, 1997). On the conflicts between kings and parliaments, see Adam Przeworski, Tamar Asadurian, and Anjali Bohlken, "The Origins of Parliamentary Responsibility," in *Comparative Constitutional Design,* ed. Tom Ginsburg (New York: Cambridge University Press, 2012), 101–38.

29. Elaine Thompson, "The 'Washminster' Mutation," *in Responsible Government in Australia,* ed. Patrick Weller and Dean Jaensch (Melbourne: Drummond, 1980).

30. Cindy Skach, *Borrowing Constitutional Designs: Constitutional Law in Weimar Germany and the French Fifth Republic* (Princeton, NJ: Princeton University Press, 2005), 2–11.

31. José Cheibub, *Presidentialism, Parliamentarism and Democracy* (New York: Cambridge University Press, 2006).

32. Jose Cheibub, Zachary Elkins, and Tom Ginsburg, "Beyond Presidentialism and Parliamentarism," *British Journal of Political Science* 44, no.3 (2014): 515–44.

33. Juan Linz, "The Perils of Presidentialism," *Journal of Democracy* 1, no. 1 (1990): 51–69; Juan J. Linz and Arturo Valenzuela, *The Failure of Presidential Democracy* (Baltimore: Johns Hopkins University Press, 1994); Arend Lijphart, ed. *Parliamentary Versus Presidential Government* (New York: Oxford University Press, 1992).

34. Milan Svolik, "Which Democracies Will Last? Coups, Incumbent Takeovers and the Dynamic of Democratic Consolidation," *British Journal of Political Science* 45 (2015): 715–38.

35. Seymour Martin Lipset, *American Exceptionalism: A Double-Edged Sword* (New York: W. W. Norton, 1996); David Mayhew, *Divided We Govern: Party Control, Lawmaking, and Investigations, 1946–1990* (New Haven, CT: Yale University Press, 1991). In a statistical examination of legislation passage rates in eras of divided and united government, Mayhew found no statistical difference between the two. But see Tyler Hughes and Deven Carlson, "Divided Government and Delay in the Legislative Process," *American Politics Research* 43, no. 5 (2015): 771–92, showing that the pace of legislative output declines.

36. Cheibub, *Presidentialism, Parliamentarism and Democracy.*

37. Cheibub, *Presidentialism, Parliamentarism and Democracy.*

38. For a study of presidential candidate systems, see Stephan Gardbaum and Richard Pildes, "Populism and Democratic Institutional Design: Methods of Selecting Candidates for Chief Executive in the United States and Other Democracies," *NYU Law Review__* (forthcoming, 2018).

39. Christopher de Bellaigue, "Welcome to Demokrasi: How Erdoğan Got More Popular Than Ever," *Guardian*, August 30, 2016, online at https://www.theguardian.com/world/2016/aug/30/welcome-to-demokrasi-how-erdogan-got-more-popular-than-ever.

40. Tom Ginsburg, Zachary Elkins, and James Melton, "On the Evasion of Executive Term Limits," *William and Mary Law Review* 52 (2011): 1807–72.

41. For empirical evidence of this trade-off, see George Tsebelis, "Decision Making in Political Systems: Veto Players in Presidentialism, Parliamentarism, Multicameralism and Multipartyism," *British Journal of Political Science* 25, no. 3 (1995): 289–325.

42. Walter Bagehot, *The English Constitution* (New York: Oxford University Press, 1992); originally published in 1867.

43. Woodrow Wilson, "Cabinet Government in the United States," *International Review* 7 (1879): 146–63.

44. Thomas E. Mann and Norman J. Ornstein, *It's Even Worse Than It Looks: How the American Constitutional System Collided with the New Politics of Extremism* (New York: Basic Books, 2016), 198.

45. For a useful study of how parliamentary question time can aid opposition, but also devolve, see Rob Salmond, "Grabbing Governments by the Throat: Question Time and Leadership in New Zealand's Parliamentary Opposition," *Political Science* 56, no. 2 (2004): 75–90.

46. Jeremy Waldron, *Political Theory* (Cambridge, MA: Harvard University Press, 2016), 101; David Fontana, "Government in Opposition," *Yale Law Journal* 119, no. 3 (2009): 548–623.

47. Tom Ginsburg, "Economic Analysis and the Design of Constitutional Courts," *Theoretical Inquiries in Law* 3, no. 1 (2002): 49–85.

48. Anthony King and Ivor Crewe, *The Blunders of Our Governments* (London: Oneworld Publications, 2014), 1.

49. The Bangladeshi parliament is an instance of interparty conflict leading to paralysis; see Nizam Ahmed, "From Monopoly to Competition: Party Politics in the Bangladesh Parliament (1973–2001)," *Pacific Affairs* 76, no. 1 (2003): 55–77.

50. On the ambivalent responses of conservative parties to the presence of the far right in a national legislature, see William M. Downs, "Pariahs in Their Midst: Belgian and Norwegian Parties React to Extremist Threats," *West European Politics* 24, no. 3 (2001): 23–42.

51. On the strategic mistakes made by democratic parties, particularly the Social Democrats, in Weimar Germany, see Heinrich August Winkler, "Choosing the Lesser Evil: The German Social Democrats and the Fall of the Weimar Republic," *Journal of Contemporary History* 25, no. 2 (1990): 205–27.

52. Rick Lyman, "Poland's President Vetoes 2 Proposed Laws Limiting Court's Independence," *New York Times*, July 24, 2017.

53. Ozan O. Varol, *The Democratic Coup d'état* (New York: Oxford University Press, 2017).

54. Ginsburg, Elkins and Melton, "Evasion of Executive Term Limits."

55. Data from the Comparative Constitutions Project on file with authors.

56. Samuel Issacharoff, *Fragile Democracies* (New York: Cambridge University Press, 2015).

57. Tom Ginsburg and Zachary Elkins, "Ancillary Powers of Constitutional Courts," *Texas Law Review* 87, no. 7 (2009): 1432–61; Samuel Issacharoff, *Fragile Democracies: Contested Power in the Era of Constitutional Courts* (New York: Cambridge University Press, 2015).

58. Manuel José Cepeda Espinosa and David Landau, *Colombian Constitutional Law* (New York: Oxford University Press, 2017).

59. Rosalind Dixon and David Landau, "Transnational Constitutionalism and a Limited Doctrine of Unconstitutional Amendment," *I-CON* 15, no. 3 (2015): 606–38.

60. Dixon and Landau, "Transnational Constitutionalism," 617.

61. This section draws on Tom Ginsburg, *Judicial Review in New Democracies* (New York: Cambridge University Press, 2003); James Melton and Tom Ginsburg, "Does De Jure Judicial Independence Really Matter? A Reevaluation of Explanations for Judicial Independence," *Journal of Law and Courts* 2 (Fall 2014): 187–217; and Nuno Garoupa and Tom Ginsburg, *Judicial Reputation* (Chicago: University of Chicago Press, 2015).

62. Vargas is quoted in Guillermo A. O'Donnell, "Why the Rule of Law Matters," *Journal of Democracy* 15, no. 4 (2004): 32–46. Brad Epperly discusses the function of judges in *Political Competition and Judicial Independence in Dictatorship and Democracy*, manuscript.

63. Garoupa and Ginsburg, *Judicial Reputation*.

64. Melton and Ginsburg, "Does De Jure Judicial Independence Really Matter?"

65. Guillermo A. O'Donnell, "Delegative Democracy," *Journal of Democracy* 5, no. 1 (1994): 55–69, 61.

66. John Gerring and Strom Thacker, "Political Institutions and Corruption: The Role of Unitarism and Parliamentarism," *British Journal of Political Science* 34, no. 2 (2004): 295–330; Jana Kunicova and Susan Rose-Ackerman, "Electoral Constraints and Constitutional Structures as Constraints on Corruption," *British Journal of Political Science* 35 (2005): 573–606.

67. Adrian Vermeule, "Our Schmittian Administrative Law," *Harvard Law Review* 122, no. 4 (2008): 1095–1149.

68. Eric A. Posner and Adrian Vermeule, *Terror in the Balance: Security, Liberty, and the Courts* (New York: Oxford University Press, 2007); Eric A. Posner and Adrian Vermeule, *The Executive Unbound: After the Madisonian Republic* (New York: Oxford University Press, 2011).

69. See, for example, Saikrishna Bangalore Prakash, *Imperial from the Beginning: The Constitution of the Original Executive* (New Haven, CT: Yale University Press, 2015).

70. For criticism of Posner and Vermeule's logic and empirics, see Aziz Z. Huq, "Binding the Executive (by Law or by Politics)," *University of Chicago Law Review* 79, no. 2 (2012): 777–826.

71. For a summary of the mixed evidence of retrospective voting, see Andrew Healy and Neil Malhotra, "Retrospective Voting Reconsidered," *Annual Review of Political Science* 16 (2013): 285–306. For a more skeptical view, see Christopher H. Achen and Larry M. Bartels, *Democracy for Realists: Why Elections Do Not Produce Responsive Government* (Princeton, NJ: Princeton University Press, 2016), 311.

72. For useful and careful studies of this question, see Jennifer L. Hochschild and Katherine Levine Einstein. "Do Facts Matter? Information and Misinformation in American Politics," *Political Science Quarterly* 130, no. 4 (2015): 585–624; Michael X. Delli Carpini and Scott Keeter, *What Americans Know about Politics and Why It Matters* (New Haven, CT: Yale University Press, 1996).

73. Bruce Ackerman, "The New Separation of Powers," *Harvard Law Review* 113 (2000): 633–725.

74. Ulf Lundvik, "Sweden," *in International Handbook of the Ombudsman*, ed. Gerald Caiden (Norwich, CT: Greenwood Press, 1983), 179.

75. Const. South Africa, Sec. 182.

76. Illinois, Louisiana, Massachusetts, Michigan, New Jersey, New York, and Pennsylvania all have bodies specifically designated as Civil Service Commissions.

77. The relationship between constitutional design and corruption is more complex than a focus on anti-corruption bodies alone would suggest. See Jana Kunicova and Susan Rose-Ackerman, "Electoral Rules and Constitutional Structures as Constraints on Corruption," *British Journal of Political Science* 35, no. 4 (2005): 573–606.

78. Civicus, *Civil Society Watch Report*, June 2016, online at http://www.civicus.org/images /CSW_Report.pdf.

79. United Nations Human Rights Office of the High Commissioner, "UN Expert Raises Alarm at Global Trend of Restricting Civil Society Space on Pretext of National Security and Counter-Terrorism," October 26, 2015, online at http://www.ohchr.org/EN/NewsEvents/Pages /DisplayNews.aspx?NewsID=16653&LangID=E.

80. On the complexities of election maladministration, see Sarah Birch, *Electoral Malpractice* (New York: Oxford University Press, 2011), 12–13.

81. Michael Pal, "Electoral Management Bodies as a Fourth Branch of Government," *Review of Constitutional Studies* 21, no. 1 (2016): 85–113.

82. Nicholas Stephanopoulos, "Our Electoral Exceptionalism," *University of Chicago Law Review* 80, no. 2 (2103): 769–858.

83. Issacharoff, *Fragile Democracies*, 206–7; Susana Berruecos, "Electoral Justice in Mexico: The Role of the Electoral Tribunal under New Federalism," *Journal of Latin American Studies* 35, no. 4 (2003): 801–25.

84. See Gardbaum and Pildes, "Populism and Democratic Institutional Design."

85. Bruce Ackerman, *Before the Next Attack: Preserving Civil Liberties in an Age of Terrorism* (New Haven, CT: Yale University Press, 2006).

86. For data on the use of emergency constitutions, see Christian Bjørnskov and Stefan Voigt, "The Determinants of Emergency Constitutions" (2016), online at https://papers.ssrn .com/sol3/papers.cfm?abstract_id=2697144. For the skeptical view, see Adrian Vermeule, "Self-Defeating Proposals: Ackerman on Emergency Powers," *Fordham Law Review* 75 (2006): 631.

87. David Van Reybrouck, *Against Elections: The Case for Democracy*, trans. Liz Waters (London: Bodley Head, 2016).

88. Terrill G. Bouricious, "Democracy Through Multi-Body Sortition: Athenian Lessons for the Modern Day," *Journal of Public Deliberation* 9, no. 1 (2013): article 11, online at http://www .publicdeliberation.net/jpd/vol9/iss1/art11.

Chapter Seven

1. *Citizens United v. Federal Electoral Commission*, 558 U.S. 310 (2010).

2. David Landau, "Constitution-Making Gone Wrong," *Alabama Law Review* 64 (2013): 923–81.

3. Larry M. Bartels, *Unequal Democracy: The Political Economy of the New Gilded Age* (Princeton, NJ: Princeton University Press, 2016); Richard H. Pildes, "Why the Center Does Not Hold: The Causes of Hyperpolarized Democracy in America," *California Law Review* 99, no. 2 (2011): 273–333.

4. On the relationship between polarization and deadlock, see Stephen Ansolabehere, Maxwell Palmer, and Benjamin Schneer, "What Has Congress Done?" in *Governing in a Polarized Age: Elections, Parties, and Political Representation in America*, ed. Alan Gerber and Eric Schickler (New York: Cambridge University Press, 2016), 243; Gary C. Jacobson, "Polarization,

Gridlock, and Presidential Campaign Politics in 2016," *ANNALS of the American Academy of Political and Social Science* 667, no. 1 (2016): 226-46.

5. Michael Barber and Nolan McCarty, "Causes and Consequences of Polarization," in *Political Negotiation: A Handbook*, ed. Jane Mansbridge and Cathie Jo Martin (Washington, DC: Brookings Institute Press, 2015), 37.

6. Nathaniel Persily, ed., *Solutions to Political Polarization in America* (New York: Cambridge University Press, 2015).

7. 369 U.S. 186 (1962).

8. William Howell and Terry G. Moe, *Relic: How Our Constitution Undermines Representative Government and Why We Need a More Powerful Presidency* (New York, Basic Books, 2016).

9. Thomas E. Mann and Norm Ornstein, "How the Republicans Broke Congress," *New York Times*, December 2, 2017.

10. On the relationship between polarization and deadlock, see Ansolabehere, Palmer, and Schneer, "What Has Congress Done?"; Jacobson, "Polarization, Gridlock, and Presidential Campaign Politics."

11. U.S. Const. art. I, § 5, cl. 2.

12. Some have argued that such rules cannot be binding, consistent with Article I, but this argument has never prevailed in court or persuaded Congress. See Aaron-Andrew P. Bruhl, "Using Statues to Set Legislative Rules: Entrenchment, Separation of Powers, and the Rules of the Proceedings Clause," *Journal of Law and Politics* 19 (2003): 345-415.

13. Brian Feinstein, "Congress in the Administrative State," *Washington University Law Review* 95 (2018): 1189-249.

14. On committee structures, see Anne Joseph O'Connell, "The Architecture of Smart Intelligence: Structuring and Overseeing Agencies in the Post-9/11 World," *California Law Review* 94, no. 6 (2006): 1655-1744. On the development of internal legislative capacity, see Eric Schickler, *Disjointed Pluralism: Institutional Innovation and the Development of the US Congress* (Princeton, NJ: Princeton University Press, 2001).

15. An excellent statement and careful application of current law is Judges Bates's opinion in Committee on Judiciary, *U.S. House of Representatives v. Miers*, 558 F. Supp. 2d 53 (D.D.C. 2008).

16. T. F. T. Plucknett, "Presidential Address," *Transactions of the Royal Historical Society* 3 (1953): 145-58. The leading treatments include Charles L. Black, *Impeachment: A Handbook* (New Haven, CT: Yale University Press, 1974), and Laurence H. Tribe, "Defining High Crimes and Misdemeanors: Basic Principles," *George Washington Law Review* 67 (1998): 712.

17. *Constitutional Grounds for Presidential Impeachment*, H. Comm. Rep. 28-959, 93rd Congress, 1974, at 5; Jack N. Rakove, "Statement on the Background and History of Impeachment," *George Washington Law Review* 67 (1998): 682. For an excellent treatment of the Hastings trial that situates it in the context of colonial debates, see Mithi Mukherjee, "Justice, War, and the Imperium: India and Britain in Edmund Burke's Prosecutorial Speeches in the Impeachment Trial of Warren Hastings," *Law and History Review* 23, no. 3 (2005): 589-630.

18. The seminal source for this style of interpretation is, as luck would have it, by the leading commentator on impeachment; see Charles Black, *Structure and Relationship in Constitutional Law* (Baton Rouge: Louisiana State University Press, 1969).

19. Cass Sunstein, *Impeachment: A Citizens' Guide* (Cambridge, MA: Harvard University Press, 2018).

20. Paul Manuel and Anne Cammisa, *Checks and Balances? How a Parliamentary System Could Change American Politics* (Boulder, CO: Westview Press, 1999).

21. Brian Feinstein and Daniel Hemel, "Partisan Balance with Bite," *Columbia Law Review* 118, no. 1 (2017): 1–68.

22. Alliance for Justice, "Broadening the Bench: Professional Diversity and Judicial Nominations," March 2016, online at www.afj.org/reports/professional-diversity-report.

23. Aziz Z. Huq, "Judicial Independence and the Rationing of Constitutional Remedies," *Duke Law Journal* 65, no. 1 (2015): 1–80.

24. *United States v. Armstrong*, 517 U.S. 456, 459 (1996); *Reno v. Am.-Arab Anti-Discrimination Comm.*, 525 U.S. 471 (1999). See Aziz Huq, "Judging Discriminatory Intent," *Cornell Law Review* 103 (forthcoming, 2018).

25. *Lovett v. United States*, 66 F. Supp. 142 (1945), affirmed in *United States v. Lovett*, 328 U.S. 303 (1946).

26. *Garcetti v. Ceballos*, 547 U.S. 410 (2006). Employee rights under the Petition Clause of the First Amendment have also been narrowed; see *Borough of Duryea v. Guarnieri*, 564 U.S. 379 (2011).

27. See Consolidated Appropriations Act of 2010, 123 Stat. 3034 (2010); Whistle-blower Protection Act of 1989, 5 U.S.C. § 1213 et seq.

28. *Ziglar v. Abbasi*, 137 S. Ct. 1843 (2017). The reliance on the absence of an express remedy is incorrect, because Congress has developed a more general scheme for remedies for official torts that expressly recognizes and accounts for the presence of judicially created remedies for constitutional torts. See James E. Pfander and David Baltmanis, "Rethinking Bivens: Legitimacy and Constitutional Adjudication," *Georgetown Law Journal* 98, no. 1 (2009): 117.

29. *New York Times Co. v. Sullivan*, 376 U.S. 254 (1964); *Gertz v. Robert Welch, Inc.*, 418 U.S. 323 (1974). For a comprehensive account of the law, see Robert D. Sack, *Sack on Defamation* (New York: Practicing Law Institute, 2010).

30. Aziz Huq, "When Government Defames," *New York Times*, August 10, 2017.

31. *Felker v. Turpin*, 518 U.S. 651 (1996).

32. For a scholarly example of this genre, see Saikrishna Bangalore Prakash, *Imperial from the Beginning: The Constitution of the Original Executive* (New Haven, CT: Yale University Press, 2015).

33. Elena Kagan, "Presidential Administration," *Harvard Law Review* 114 (2001): 2245–2385. For a discussion of more recent literature in a similar vein, see Kathryn A. Watts, "Controlling Presidential Control," *Michigan Law Review* 114 (2015): 683.

34. *NLRB v. Noel Canning*, 134 S. Ct. 2550, 2600-06 (2014); *Free Enterprise Fund v. PCAOB*, 561 U.S. 477 (2010). On presidential accountability, see Jide Nzelibe and John Yoo, "Rational War and Constitutional Design," *Yale Law Journal* 115 (2006): 2512–41; Howell and Moe, *Relic*.

35. Jennifer Nou, "Agency Self-Insulation Under Presidential Review," *Harvard Law Review* 126, no. 7 (2013): 1755–1837.

36. Tiberiu Dragu and Mattias Polborn, "The Administrative Foundation of the Rule of Law," *Journal of Politics* 75, no. 4 (2013): 1038–50.

37. See Pub. L. No. 76-252, 53 Stat. 1147 (1939). On the role of the civil service in the American constitutional order, see Jon D. Michaels, "An Enduring, Evolving Separation of Powers," *Columbia Law Review* 115, no. 3 (2015): 515–97.

38. David E. Lewis, *The Politics of Presidential Appointments* 30 (Princeton, NJ: Princeton University Press, 2008); Robert Maranto and B. Douglas Skelley, "Neutrality: An Enduring Principle of the Federal Service," *American Review of Public Administration* 22, no. 3 (1992): 173–87.

39. H.R. 6278, Promote Accountability and Government Efficiency Act, online at https://www.congress.gov/bill/114th-congress/house-bill/6278/text?format=txt.

40. These ideas are developed at length in two excellent recent volumes: Paul Verkuil, *Valuing Bureaucracy* (New York: Cambridge University Press, 2017); and Jon Michaels, *Constitutional Coup: Privatization's Threat to the American Republic* (Cambridge, MA: Harvard University Press, 2017).

41. Paul C. Light, *Monitoring Government: Inspectors General and the Search for Accountability* (Washington, DC: Brookings Institution Press, 2011); Mark Moore and Margaret Jane Gates, *Inspectors-General: Junkyard Dogs or Man's Best Friend?* (New York: Russell Sage Foundation, 1986); Kenneth A. Bamberger and Deirdre K. Mulligan, "Privacy Decision-making in Administrative Agencies," *University of Chicago Law Review* 75, no. 1 (2008): 75–107; Margo Schlanger, "Offices of Goodness: Influence without Authority in Federal Agencies," *Cardozo Law Review* 36, no. 1 (2014): 53–118.

42. Walter Shaub, "How to Restore Government Ethics in the Trump Era," *New York Times*, July 18, 2017; Betty B. Vega, "Inspectors General: Evaluating Independence and Increasing Capacity," *Government, Law and Policy Journal* 13, no. 2 (2011): 48–54.

43. Such reports are presently found at 28 C.F.R. § 600.1.

44. Rebecca R. Ruiz and Mark Landler, "Robert Mueller, Former F.B.I. Director, Is Named Special Counsel for Russia Investigation," *New York Times*, May 17, 2017.

45. See John F. Manning, "The Independent Counsel Statute: Reading Good Cause in Light of Article II," *Minnesota Law Review* 83 (1998): 1285.

46. For a history of the statute and its early uses, as well as a penetrating analysis of potential reforms, see Ken Gormley, "An Original Model of the Independent Counsel Statute," *Michigan Law Review* 97, no. 3 (1998): 601–95. For a rehearsal of criticisms, see Julie O'Sullivan, "Independent Counsel Statute: Bad Law, Bad Policy," *American Criminal Law Review* 33 (1995): 463; Cass R. Sunstein, "Bad Incentives and Bad Institutions." *Georgetown Law Journal* 86 (1997): 2267–85.

47. David A. Strauss, "The Independent Counsel Statute: What Went Wrong," *Administrative Law Review* 51, no. 2 (1999): 651–56.

48. 28 U.S.C § 516.

49. Michael B. Mukasey, *Communications with the White House*, Memorandum for Heads of Department Components and U.S. Attorneys, December 19, 2007, online at https://assets.documentcloud.org/documents/3371650/Mukasey-12-19-07.pdf. For an excellent overview of the issues, see United to Protect Democracy, "White House Communications with the DOJ and FBI," March 8, 2017, online at https://unitedtoprotectdemocracy.org/agencycontacts/#footnote-11.

50. For example, see Massimo Calabresi, "The FBI Talked to the White House about Its Russia Probe. That Was Probably Against the Rules," *Time*, February 25, 2017; Isaac Arnsdorf, "Priebus Request to FBI Violated Norms, If Not Rules; Longstanding White House and DOJ Policy Prohibits Contact without Clearance from Lawyers," *Politico*, February 24, 2017.

51. Simon Butt, *Corruption and Law in Indonesia* (London: Routledge, 2011).

52. On the dissemination of false news by social media in the 2016 election, see Hunt Allcoot and Matthew Gentzkow, "Social Media and Fake News in the 2016 Election," *NBER Working Paper*, January 2017, online at http://www.nber.org.proxy.uchicago.edu/papers/w23089/.

53. Tom Porter, "Over Two-Thirds of Americans Think Media Publishes Fake News," *Newsweek*, May 24, 2017.

54. Cary Funk and Brian Kennedy, "The Politics of Climate," *Pew Center*, October 4, 2016, online at http://www.pewinternet.org/2016/10/04/the-politics-of-climate/.

55. "83% Say Measles Vaccine Safe for Children," *Pew Research Center*, February 09, 2015, online at http://www.people-press.org/2015/02/09/83-percent-say-measles-vaccine-is-safe-for-healthy-children/.

56. The deliberate dissemination of pseudoscience on this point is well described in Reva B. Siegel, "The Right's Reasons: Constitutional Conflict and the Spread of Woman-Protective Antiabortion Argument," *Duke Law Journal* 57, no. 6 (2008): 1641–92.

57. Kathryn A. Watts, "Proposing a Place for Politics in Arbitrary and Capricious Review," *Yale Law Journal* 119, no. 1 (2009): 2–85. To be clear, we think that Watts is a serious scholar with nonpartisan reasons for her proposal.

58. Justin P. Friesen, Troy H. Campbell, and Aaron C. Kay, "The Psychological Advantage of Unfalsifiability: The Appeal of Untestable Religious and Political Ideologies," *Journal of Personality and Social Psychology* 108, no. 3 (2015): 515.

59. For a recent study of civil education as it pertains to democracy maintenance, see Arthur Lupia, *Uninformed: Why People Know So Little about Politics and What We Can Do about It* (New York: Oxford University Press, 2015).

60. Robert C. Post, *Citizens Divided: Campaign Finance Reform and the Constitution* (Cambridge, MA: Harvard University Press, 2014). Post is not the first to make this point, as he fairly acknowledges. See Frederick Schauer, "Principles, Institutions, and the First Amendment," *Harvard Law Review* 112, no. 1 (1998): 84.

61. For a useful survey of the issue, see Nicco Mele, David Lazer, Matthew Baum, et al., "Combating Fake News: An Agenda for Research and Action," May 2017, online at https://shorensteincenter.org/combating-fake-news-agenda-for-research/.

62. Karl Popper, *The Open Society and Its Enemies* (1945; repr., Princeton, NJ: Princeton University Press, 2002).

63. Roger Yu, "Survey: Americans' Support for First Amendment Strong," *USA Today*, June 30, 2016, online at https://www.usatoday.com/story/news/2016/06/30/survey-americans-support-1st-amendment-strong/86564972/.

Conclusion

1. "Papers of Dr. James McHenry on the Federal Convention of 1787," *American Historical Review* 11, no. 3 (1906): 595–624, 611.

2. One of us reports with embarrassment that he ended another book on constitutional law with the same quotation some ten years ago; see Frederick A. O. Schwarz Jr. and Aziz Z. Huq, *Unchecked and Unbalanced: Presidential Power in a Time of Terror* (New York: New Press, 2007), 200. It was true then too. Cass Sunstein, in a recent volume on impeachment, also starts with Franklin's dictum; see Cass R. Sunstein, *Impeachment: A Citizen's Guide* (Cambridge, MA: Harvard University Press, 2017).

3. 1 Samuel 8:11–18

4. 1 Samuel 8:19–20.

5. Carroll Doherty, Jocelyn Kiley, Alec Tyson, and Bridget Jameson, "Beyond Distrust: How Americans View Their Government," *Pew Research Center*, November 23, 2015, online at http://www.people-press.org/2015/11/23/1-trust-in-government-1958-2015/.

6. Carroll Doherty, Jocelyn Kiley, and Bridget Johnson, "Public Trust in Government Remains Near Historic Lows as Partisan Attitudes Shift," *Pew Research Center*, May 3, 2017, online at http://www.people-press.org/2017/05/03/public-trust-in-government-remains-near-historic-lows-as-partisan-attitudes-shift/.

7. For a detailed examination of the unprecedented nature of the refusal to consider the Garland nomination, see Robin Bradley Kar and Jason Mazzone, "The Garland Affair: What

History and the Constitution Really Say about President Obama's Powers to Appoint a Replacement for Justice Scalia," *NYU Law Review Online* 91 (2016): 53–114.

8. Ariel Malka and Yphtach Lelkes, "In a New Poll, Half of Republicans Say They Would Support Postponing the 2020 Election If Trump Proposed It," *Washington Post*, August 10, 2017, online at https://www.washingtonpost.com/news/monkey-cage/wp/2017/08/10/in-a-new -poll-half-of-republicans-say-they-would-support-postponing-the-2020-election-if-trump-pro posed-it/?undefined=&utm_term=.a93d19654fef&wpisrc=nl_most&wpmm=1.

9. Richard Fauset, "North Carolina Governor Signs Law Limiting Successor's Power," *New York Times*, December 16, 2016.

10. Larry Kramer, *The People Themselves: Popular Constitutionalism and Judicial Review* (New York: Oxford University Press, 2006).

11. Mila Versteeg and Nicholas Stephanopoulos, "The Contours of Constitutional Approval," *Washington University Law Review* 94 (2015): 113–90.

12. Annenberg Public Policy Center, "Americans' Knowledge of the Constitution Is Declining," September 13, 2016, online at http://historynewsnetwork.org/article/163845.

13. A classic source is Michael X. Delli Carpini and Scott Keeter, *What Americans Know about Politics and Why It Matters* (New Haven, CT: Yale University Press, 1996). See also Vincent Hutchings and Spencer Piston, "Knowledge, Sophistication, and Issue Publics," in *The Oxford Handbook of American Public Opinion and the Media*, ed. Lawrence R. Jacobs and Robert Y. Shapiro (New York: Oxford University Press, 2011), 572.

14. World Values Survey, "Wave 6 2010–2014 Official Aggregate v.20150418," *World Values Survey Association* (2016): 181.

15. World Values Survey, "Wave 6 2010–2014 Official Aggregate v.20150418," *World Values Survey Association* (2016): 183.

16. Maria J. Stephan and Erica Chenoweth, "Why Civil Resistance Works: The Strategic Logic of Nonviolent Conflict," *International Security* 33, no. 1 (2008): 7–44; Zeynep Tufekci, *Twitter and Tear Gas: The Power and Fragility of Networked Protest* (New Haven, CT: Yale University Press: 2017), 268–70.

17. Rick Lyman, "Poland's President Vetoes 2 Proposed Laws Limiting Court's Independence," *New York Times*, July 24, 2017.

18. Christian Welzel and Ronald Inglehart, "Mass Beliefs and Democratic Institutions," in *The Oxford Handbook of Comparative Politics*, ed. Carles Boix and Susan C. Strokes (New York: Oxford University Press, 2007), 297–316.

19. Nicholas A. Valentino, Fabian G. Neuner, and L. Matthew Vandenbroek, "The Changing Norms of Racial Political Rhetoric and the End of Racial Priming," *Journal of Politics 80, no. 3* (2017): n.p.

20. Ruth Gavison, "Some Concluding Comments: What Is the State of Democracy? How to Defend It?" *International Journal of Constitutional Law Blog*, August 26, 2017, online at http:// www.iconnectblog.com/2017/08/some-concluding-comments-what-is-the-state-of-democracy -how-to-defend-it/.

Index